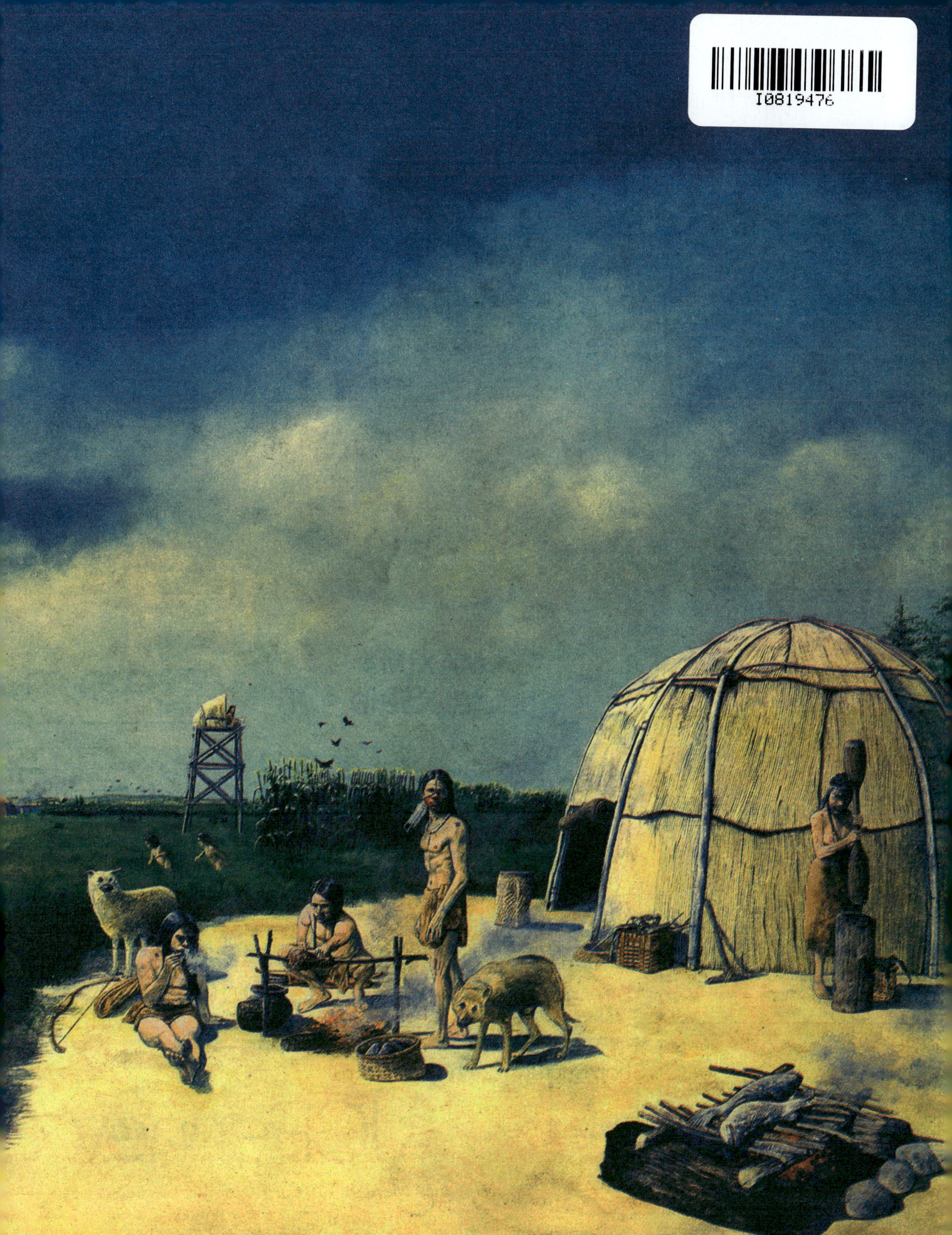
I0819476

Indian Basketry of the Northeastern Woodlands

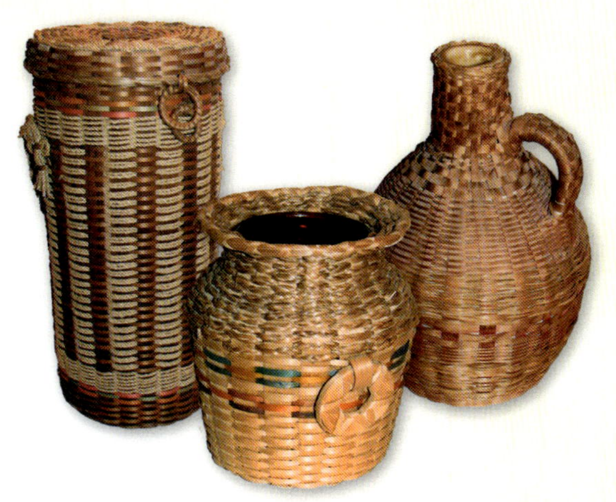

Indian Basketry of the Northeastern Woodlands

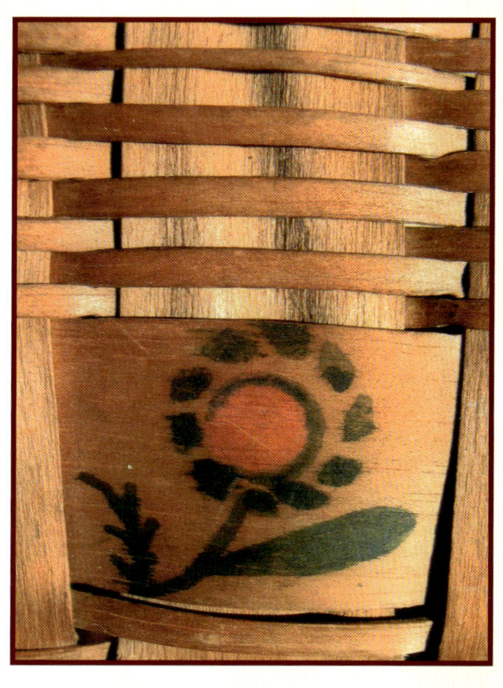

SARAH PEABODY TURNBAUGH
AND
WILLIAM A. TURNBAUGH

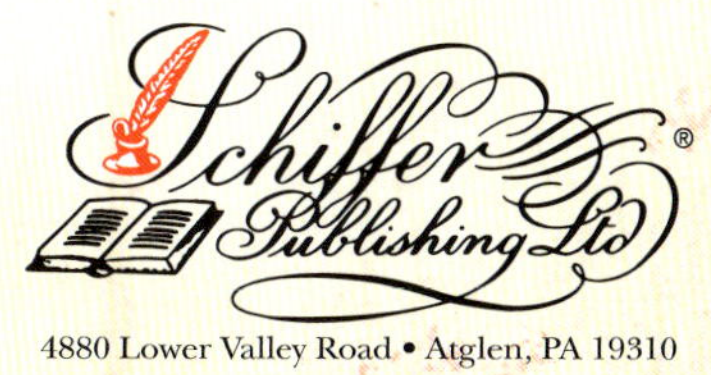

4880 Lower Valley Road • Atglen, PA 19310

Library of Congress Control Number: 2014948472

Library of Congress Cataloging-in-Publication Data

Indian Basketry of the Northeastern Woodlands/
Sarah Peabody Turnbaugh ; William A. Turnbaugh.
176 p. ; cm.
Includes bibliographical references and index.
1. Indian baskets – North America – History. 2. Basket making – North America. 3. Indians of North America – Crafts. 4. Indian baskets – Collectors and Collecting. I. Turnbaugh. Sarah Peabody. II. Turnbaugh, William A., joint author. III. Title.

Interior designed by Matt Goodman
Type set in Papyrus, Lithos & Adobe Caslon Pro

ISBN: 978-0-7643-4729-0
Printed in China

Published by Schiffer Publishing, Ltd.
4880 Lower Valley Road
Atglen, PA 19310
Phone: (610) 593-1777; Fax: (610) 593-2002
E-mail: Info@schifferbooks.com

CONTENTS

SECTION TWO:
GLOOSKAP'S GALLERY . . . 87

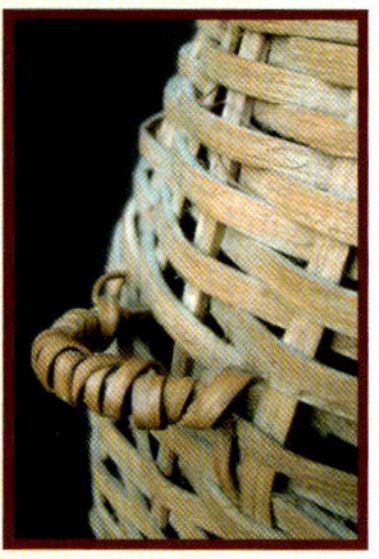

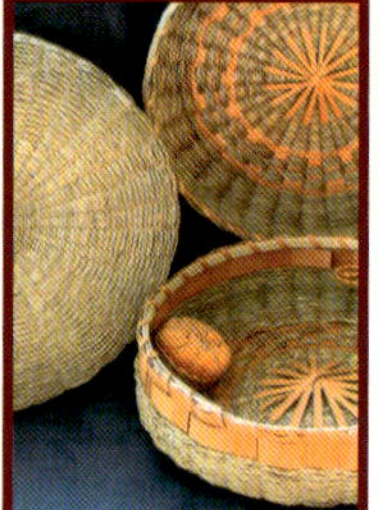

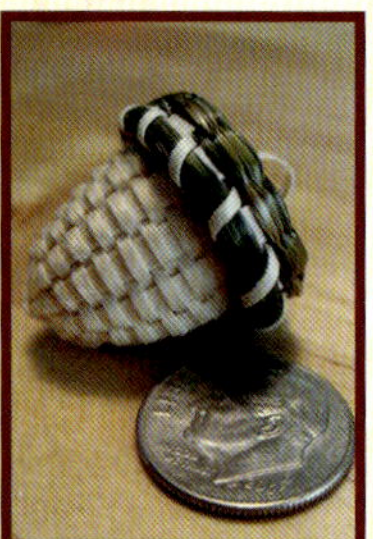

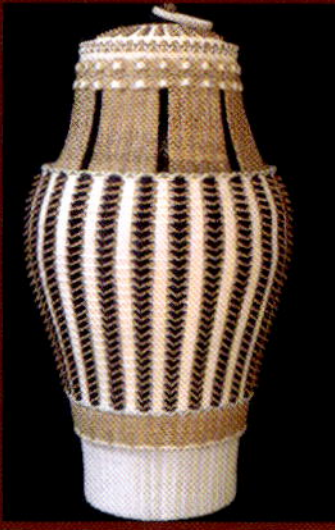

SECTION THREE:
RESOURCES . . . 163

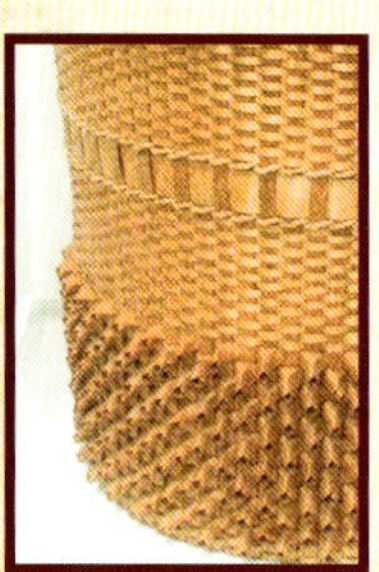

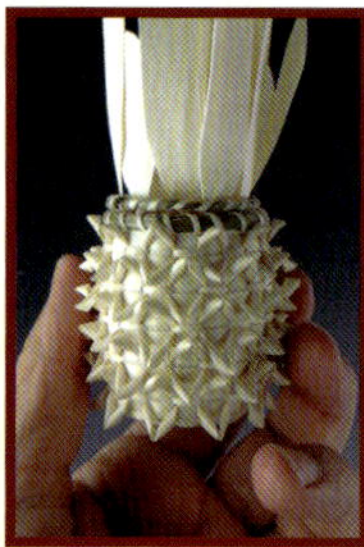

INTRODUCTION

WHY THIS TOPIC MATTERS

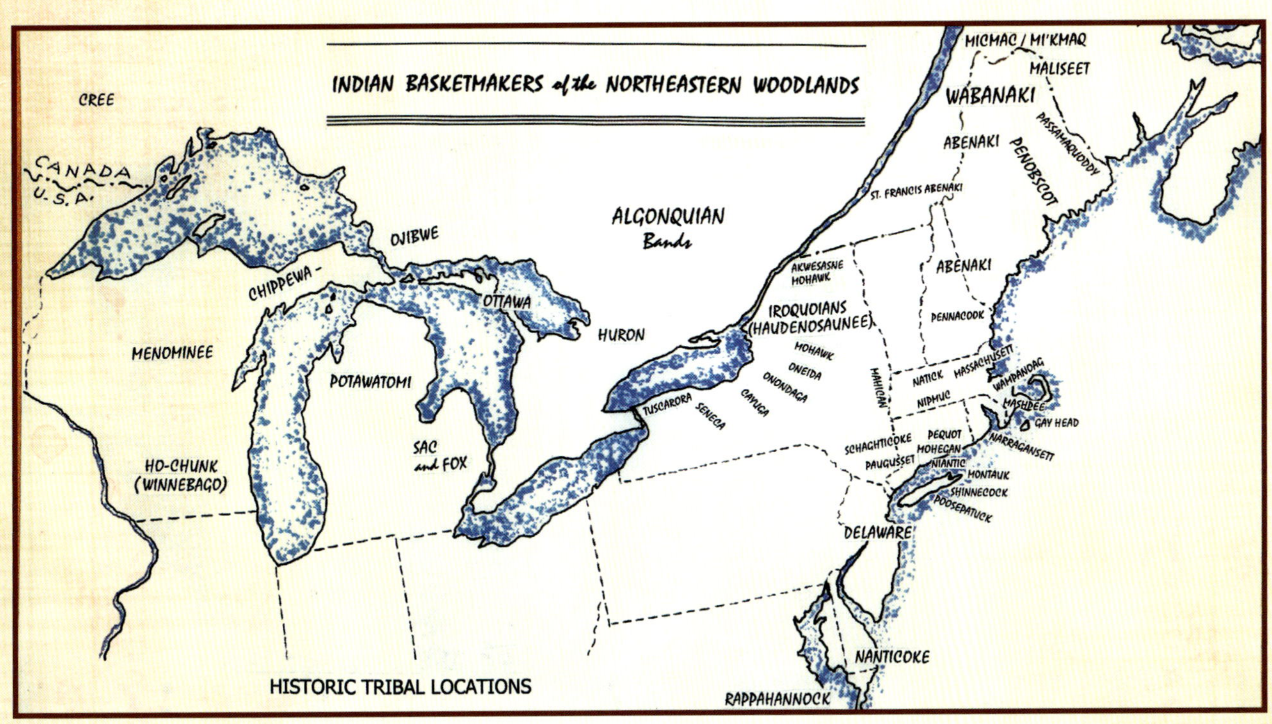

We have written *Indian Basketry of the Northeastern Woodlands* to highlight a relatively neglected topic within the field of Native American arts. Too long regarded merely as Indian-made utility goods or souvenir trinkets, the Native basketry of the northeastern United States and Canada was generally dismissed by connoisseurs. Compared to those from most other North American regions, Indian baskets of the Northeast can still sometimes go unappreciated, or perhaps unrecognized, even by some modern-day collectors.

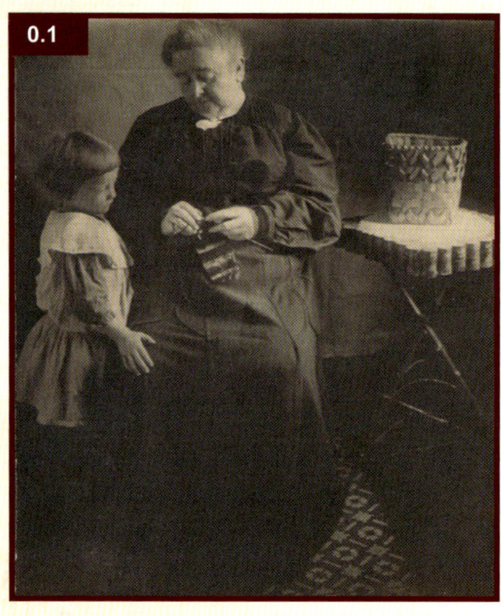

0.1. A little girl named Claire closely observes her grandmother knitting in a Worcester, Massachusetts, home, c. 1900. Note the Indian-made work basket on the Adirondack-style stand.

Native people in the Northeastern Woodlands fashioned a variety of baskets for their own use during the millennia prior to European contact. By the late 18th century, though, Indian basketmakers were routinely making wares specifically intended for daily use in colonial homes. In this period, simple and modestly adorned vessels were usually plaited of sturdy woodsplints to serve basic functions like carrying or storage. A century later, more delicate Indian baskets embellished with fragrant sweetgrass and other adornments were decorating Victorian homes.

Throughout the Northeast today, such baskets may yet be encountered in some of the households where they were long ago adopted, and where they have fulfilled various needs for decades or generations. These Native baskets have been passed along through families, together with quilts and linens, pots and pans, dishes and stemware. Along the way, "the Indian basket" has rested in cupboards and perched atop wardrobes. Nestled against sewing chairs, many have served as handiwork holders. Some have corralled combs and hair ribbons, scarves, keys, and flowers. Others have held hot rolls, sandwiches, pies, and beverage glasses. A few eventually retired onto mantles or bookshelves. But more have spent their later years in greater obscurity; for whenever the old baskets became less central to daily life, most were tucked away in attics, closets, trunks, chests, and sheds.

In time, many of these "Indian baskets" quietly morphed into "family baskets." By now they have become such familiar household belongings that current owners no longer can recall their precise origins. The Abenaki souvenir from a long-ago summer stay in the White Mountains is called simply "Grandma's old sewing basket." The Mohawk-made whimsey, carried home aboard a coal-burning train from a rustic trading post in the St. Lawrence lowlands, is by now considered just "Auntie's hankie box."

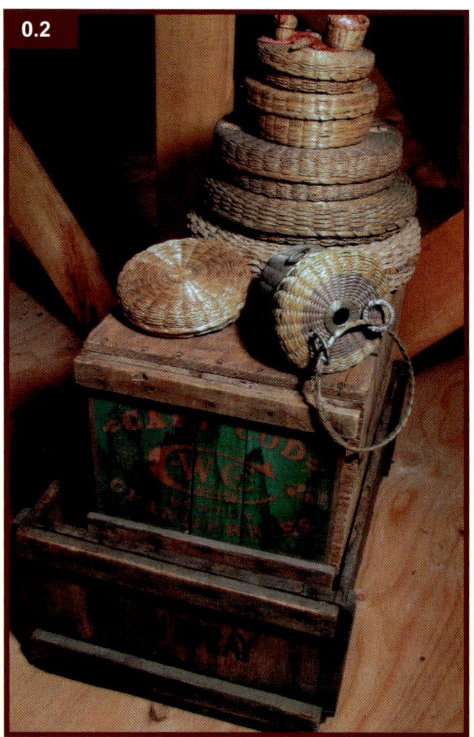

0.2. Generations of Yankee families acquired and used countless Northeastern Indian baskets. Some remain stowed away in the region's attics even today.

Some of these baskets have been so much a part of so many households for so many generations that they seem to be taken almost for granted. So familiar are they that, even in recent decades of enthusiastic Indian art collecting, many were routinely overlooked in favor of more highly prized baskets from the American Southwest or California. As collectors continue to seek out "real" Indian baskets today, some tend to bypass these humble products from the Northeast. The old baskets with their smoky patinas, richly aged splints, and colors washed by time may be ignored even when priced reasonably in antique shops, flea markets, local auctions, or tag sales. Yet, such baskets are a true hallmark of the Northeast.

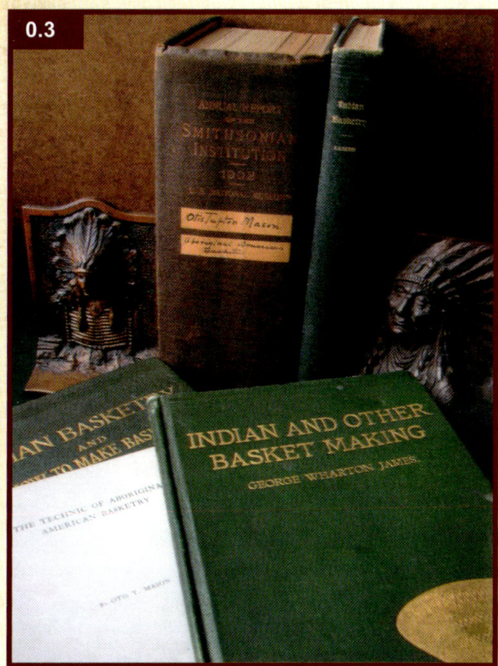

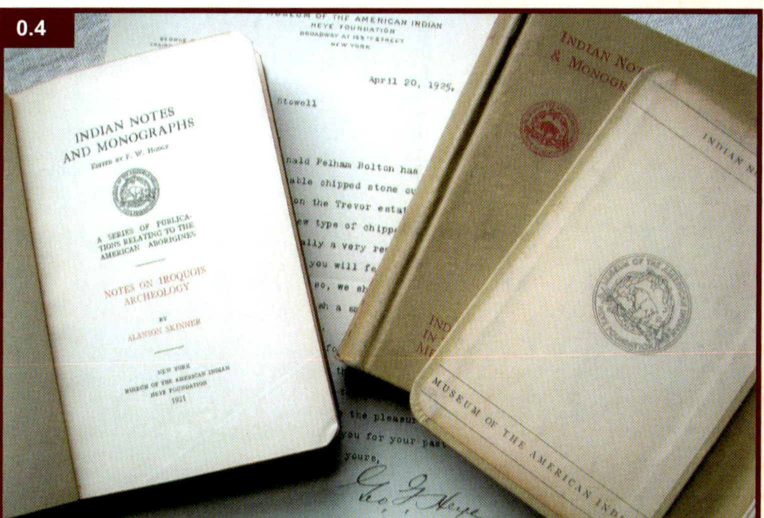

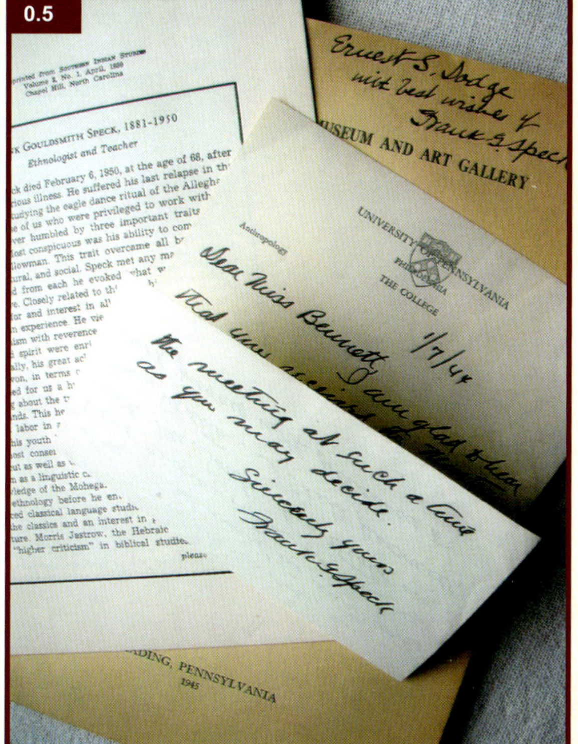

0.3. Even the primary Indian basketry studies of the early 20th century by Otis T. Mason and George Wharton James mostly overlooked Native baskets from the Northeast.

0.4. Most early 20th-century collectors bypassed them, but George G. Heye had the foresight to acquire Indian baskets from the Northeast for his private museum in New York City. His personal foundation also funded popular publications on Native American topics.

0.5. An energetic fieldworker and avid student of material culture, Frank G. Speck was the first professional anthropologist to focus on the region's Native basketry.

From the outset, most general publications on Native American basketry have likewise tended to avoid this field or to give the topic only minimal attention. Even Otis T. Mason's great opus had little to offer on Northeastern Indian baskets, and George Wharton James's several basketry books scarcely acknowledged them either.

To his credit, George G. Heye, a wealthy, early 20th-century oilman, was among the first (and few) collectors to systematically acquire Northeastern Indian baskets. The acquisitive Mr. Heye used his fortune to accumulate a massive assemblage of anthropological and archaeological materials representing the entire Western Hemisphere's original inhabitants. (Heye's comprehensive collection forms the core of today's National Museum of the American Indian in Washington, D.C.) When it came to Northeastern baskets, he faced little competition from rival collectors.

Heye relied on a network of contacts to augment his collection. Among them was Frank G. Speck, a University of Pennsylvania anthropologist. In 1912, Speck happened upon some early Indian baskets in Connecticut and became one of the rare scholars to directly address the subject during the first three-quarters of the 20th century. His brief but well-illustrated 1915 overview of Mohegan and Niantic basketry drew on Fidelia

Fielding and other Mohegan informants. Speck followed up some thirty years later with a more detailed study of Eastern Algonkian block-stamped basketry, this time informed by Gladys Tantaquidgeon, a Mohegan basketmaker and ethnologist, and presented in combination with background research by Eva L. Butler, an avid Connecticut historian. Speck's publications, though valuable in documenting the craft, were never widely disseminated.

A few researchers, led in more recent decades primarily by Ann McMullen, now at the Smithsonian Institution, have brought further attention to Northeastern Woodlands basketry through their insightful publications. At the same time, university-affiliated and independent museums—most notably the Hudson Museum at the University of Maine in Orono, and the Abbe Museum of Bar Harbor, Maine—began using collections and outreach programming to help forge and maintain links between the historical heritage of Native groups and the living Native basketmakers of the region. And, since 1993, the Maine Indian Basketmakers Alliance (MIBA), a Native guild, has actively fostered and promoted the craft and its practitioners.

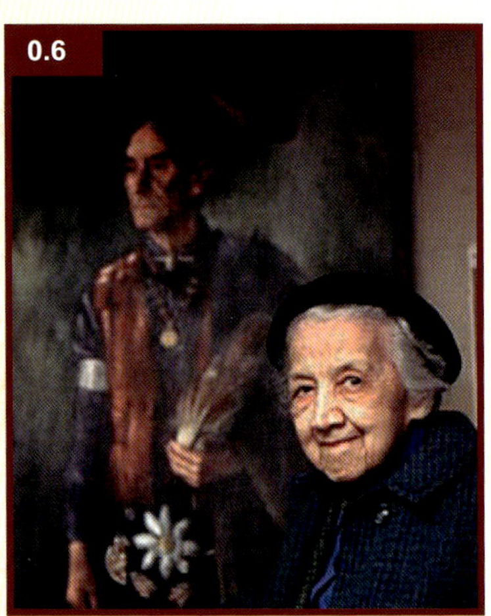

0.6. Gladys Tantaquidgeon, Mohegan anthropologist, folklorist, and authority on Native plant use and woodsplint basketry, assisted Speck with his research and studied with him at the University of Pennsylvania. She later worked for the Bureau of Indian Affairs and the Indian Arts and Crafts Board. Returning to Connecticut, Gladys ran the family museum, founded with her brother Harold (in portrait) and their father, for another half century before her death in 2005 at age 106.

Together, this three-pronged approach—academic, historical, and cultural—is helping to reinvigorate the Northeastern Woodlands basketmaking tradition as a living craft in Maine and elsewhere. This focus is also reinforcing Native pride in a number of communities.

This book features Native American basketry from the northeastern United States and Canada. A brief historical overview from pre-colonial times to the present day gives the reader an understanding of why the topic of Northeastern Woodlands basketry merits more interest and respect. Pointers in the second chapter aid in distinguishing Native baskets from four regions, including Southern New England and Long Island, Northern New England and Canadian Maritimes, Upper New York State, as well as the Great Lakes. A generous selection of photos that examine both "work" and "fancy" Indian baskets from these regions should prepare collectors to more confidently evaluate a potential purchase or assess a collection.

Scattered throughout the narrative and photo sections, interpretive sidebars include vignettes that provide cultural contexts and help bring the baskets back to life in their historical settings. A later segment of the book samples the vibrant products of contemporary Native basketmakers at work in the greater Northeast today. Some of these artisans fashion superb modern versions of long-familiar wares. Others adapt both customary and innovative forms, methods, designs, and materials as they reinterpret their craft and take it in exciting new directions.

The book's closing part offers a comprehensive bibliography of Northeastern Native basketry publications, audiovisuals, and websites, plus a guide to American public museums with collections of Native baskets from the Northeastern Woodlands. These accessible resources are intended to encourage and assist readers of *Indian Basketry of the Northeastern Woodlands* toward further exploration of the topic.

SECTION ONE

NORTHEASTERN BASKETRY BASICS

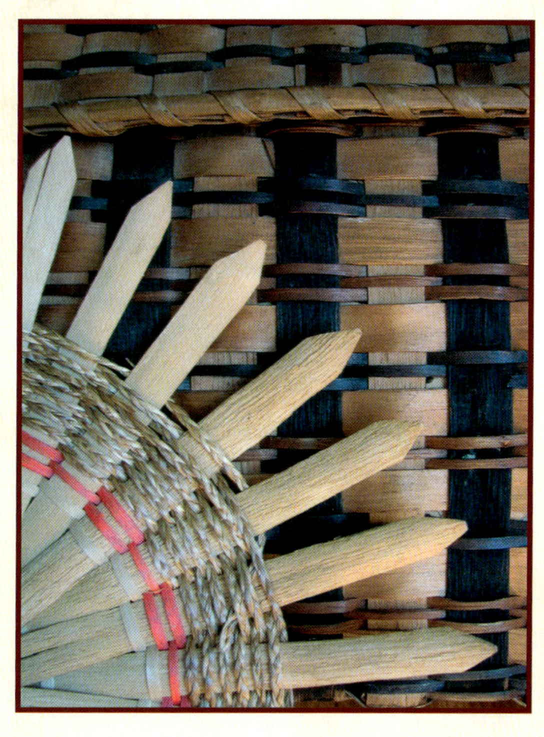

CHAPTER 1

WEAVING THE WOODS: A CHRONICLE OF NORTHEASTERN INDIAN BASKETRY

Digging for the Roots of an Ancient Craft

Basketry is a venerable craft. Because the need for containers is universal, we can clearly envision our ancestors everywhere routinely improvising receptacles from a variety of local materials. Using readily available animal hide, bark, large leaves, or plant fibers, many early societies in far-flung locations devised basically similar kinds of serviceable utensils.

In a few of these places, the interlacing of leaves or slender roots to make impromptu carriers seems to have evolved further into a more refined technique of true basketmaking. The earliest types of basketry so far recognized in several regions of the globe all appear to be made by the procedure of *twining*—essentially, wrapping horizontal weft elements, or weavers, around stationary warp elements, or standards.

SOME OF THEIR BASKETS ARE MADE OF RUSHES; SOME, OF BENTS; OTHERS, OF MAIZE HUSKS; OTHERS, OF A KIND OF SILK GRASS; OTHERS, OF A KIND OF WILD HEMP; AND SOME, OF BARKS OF TREES: MANY OF THEM, VERY NEAT AND ARTIFICIAL, WITH THE PORTRAITURES OF BIRDS, BEASTS, FISHES, AND FLOWERS, UPON THEM IN COLOURS. —*DANIEL GOOKIN, 1674*[2]

Archaeological sites in central Europe yield twined basketry textile fragments dating from as far back as the cave paintings, more than 25,000 years ago.[3] Of course, such fragile organic materials are preserved by chance and only rarely. But even those few scattered examples that survive do suggest that twined basketry may already have been in widespread use by this early period.

In North America, too, twined basketry has deep roots. Evidence from several parts of the continent reveals that twined textiles—most likely some form of basketry—were being made at least 9,000 years ago.

IN SUMMER THEY GATHER FLAGS [REEDS], OF WHICH THEY MAKE MATS FOR HOUSES, AND HEMP AND RUSHES, WITH DYEING STUFF OF WHICH THEY MAKE CURIOUS BASKETS WITH INTERMIXED COLORS AND PROTRACTURES OF ANTIC IMAGERY. THESE BASKETS BE OF ALL SIZES FROM A QUART TO A QUARTER [EIGHT BUSHELS], IN WHICH THEY CARRY THEIR LUGGAGE.

—*WILLIAM WOOD, 1634*[1]

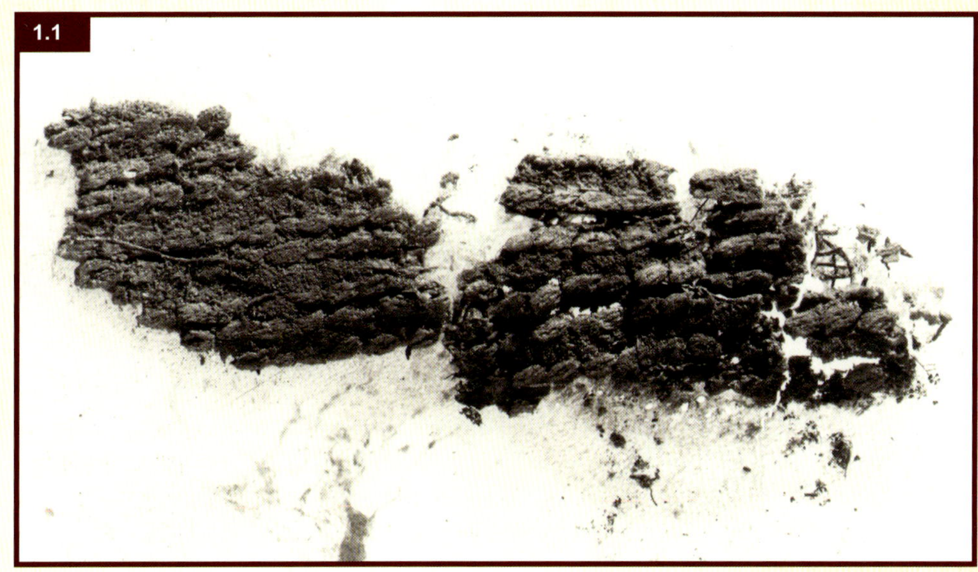

1.1. Archaeological fragments of an aboriginal twined basket excavated at Lake Cochituate, near Natick, Massachusetts, probably 1,500 to 2,000 years old, about 4" across.

1.2. Coastal Algonquians set up fish weirs in tidewater rivers and inlets all along the northeastern seaboard. This 1590 Theodore De Bry engraving depicts "Their manner of fishynge in Virginia." It was based on John White's original watercolor, painted several years earlier during an unsuccessful English colonization effort. The Boylston Street weir was probably of simpler construction than the trap shown at upper left.

Carbonized fragments of burned basketry, or sometimes just impressions of twined basketry or matting left on fire-hardened clay, occasionally survive on archaeological sites in the northeastern United States.[4] Though uncommon, these finds indicate that basketry in this region pre-dated pottery making by at least several millennia. In later times, imprints on ancient ceramic shards reveal that potters sometimes used discarded basket bottoms to support soft clay as they shaped a vessel's base.

SETTING:

The Boylston Street Fish Weir—A Super Basket?

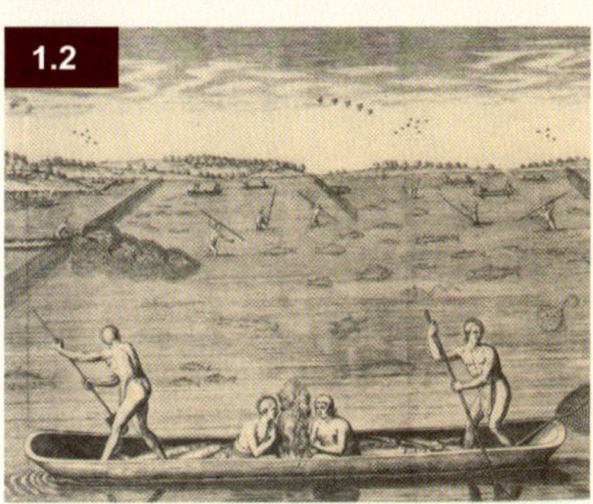

All around the globe, people along coastal rivers built obstructions to trap fish moving up or down stream with the daily tides or during seasonal migrations. Sometimes called weirs, these structures could be a dam-like arrangement of stacked stones or a fence-like series of wooden stakes. Their purpose was to channel fish into an enclosure where they could be speared or netted. Traps of this kind have been used for thousands of years.

Wooden weirs usually consisted of vertical support stakes driven deeply into the streambed and then interwoven with a lattice of brush, or wattle, that blocked the fish from returning downriver on the falling tide. The process of constructing a weir was, in essence, much like twining a basket on a very large scale.

The Boylston Street fish weir in Boston's Back Bay section was an especially impressive example. It first came to light a century ago during subway construction. Sealed more than thirty feet below the street level, under layers of tidal silt and as much as twenty feet of 19th-century fill, were tens of thousands of well-preserved wooden stakes. They had been driven into the muddy bottom across a two-acre section of the former Charles River tidal estuary.

Archaeologists now consider this site to be a jumbled overlay of many individual weirs, each 100 to 150 feet in length, that were set in the same general location over a period of perhaps fifteen centuries, beginning more than 5,000 years ago. Each spring, Algonquian families had labored to construct what were essentially oversized basketry sieves designed to intercept the herring as they ran in from the sea to spawn.

Persistent Technologies

As Europeans explored the western shores of the North Atlantic during the late 16th and early 17th centuries, they discovered that northeastern America was already occupied by hundreds of Native societies. For the most part, these communities comprised small family-centered bands who seasonally moved about within a local territory. Any number of kin-related bands living nearby might be loosely allied and so constitute what anthropologists consider a "tribe." Tribes living along the East coast, across lower Canada, and around the western Great Lakes spoke various Algonquian dialects. Unrelated tribes living further inland, along the upper St. Lawrence River, around the eastern Great Lakes, and through central New York, spoke Iroquoian languages.

1.3. A woman in the background works on a basket that is suspended upside down from a tree branch. This detail is part of a busy Iroquois village scene depicted in 1724 by Joseph-François Lafitau, a French Jesuit and early observer of American Indian culture.

Each of these peoples exploited their own local environments through some combination of hunting, gathering, and fishing. Some of them—particularly the Iroquoians—relied more heavily on cultivated agricultural products like maize, beans, and squash to supplement their wild diets. Everyone's daily routine required a variety of tools and utensils, including many forms of containers for carrying, gathering, storage, processing, cooking, ritual use, and other needs. Ceramic vessels did share some of these tasks, but pottery was both fragile and heavy, so the more mobile Algonquian groups used much less of it than did the more sedentary Iroquois village farmers. All made and used basketry.

Native Americans in the Northeast were employing several basketmaking techniques when the first European colonists arrived. In addition to twining bags and baskets with flexible materials, they also had been stitching bark vessels and plaiting rush mats.

Bark Containers

The products of ancient twining technology co-existed for a long time alongside practical containers of simpler types in the Northeast. For example, sheets of bark stripped from a tree, then folded and lashed together with lengths of vine or runner-roots, continued to serve as useful carriers or containers for berries, firewood, joints of meat, and other resources. One unusually well-preserved bark vessel of this type survived for many centuries in the dry interior of the prehistoric Sheep Rock Shelter site in southwestern Pennsylvania.

Their pails to fetch their water in, are made of birch barks, artificially doubled up, that it hath four corners and a handle in the midst. Some of these will hold two or three gallons; and they will make one of them in an hour's time.

—*Daniel Gookin, 1674*[5]

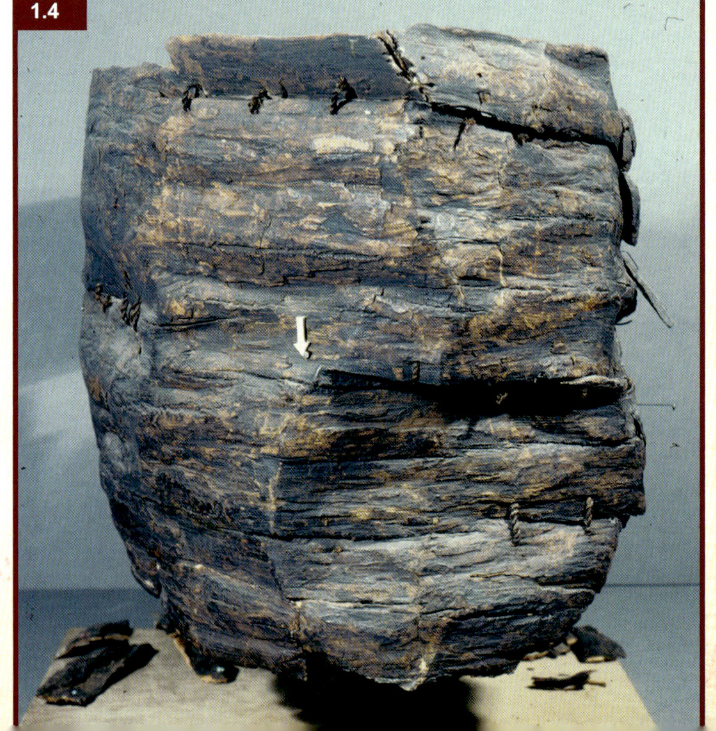

1.4. Practical bark containers, folded and lashed together with cordage or tough roots, were used throughout the Northeastern Woodlands. Many must have resembled this large prehistoric willow bark specimen recovered from central Pennsylvania's Sheep Rock Shelter archaeological site.

When we went farther inland we saw their [Narragansett] houses, which are circular in shape, about XIIII to XV paces across, made of bent saplings... covered with cleverly worked mats of straw which protect them from wind and rain....They move these houses from one place to another according to the richness of the site and the season. They need only carry the straw mats, and so they have new houses made in no time at all.
—*Giovanni da Verrazzano, 1524*[6]

Though the preservation of such a perishable artifact is highly unusual, bark receptacles of this type undoubtedly had long prevailed throughout the Northeastern Woodlands, where they were easily constructed from locally abundant material. In fact, bark products were still made and used throughout the last century, and some continue to be created (primarily for sale) even today.

Matting

In addition to fashioning various bark and twined basketry containers, Native Americans in the Northeast also regularly manipulated the tall, tough grasses, cattails, and rushes growing along their rivers and in their lakeside marshes and seashore wetlands to make useful matting.

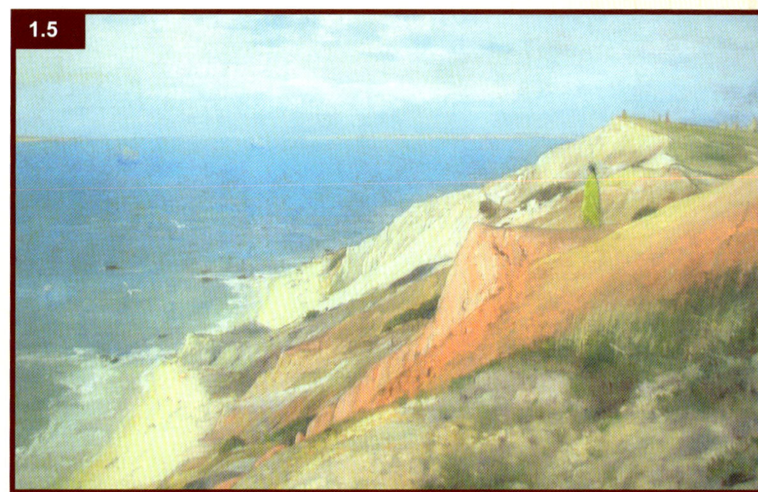

As he cruised along what is now the southern New England coast in the spring of 1524, the explorer Giovanni da Verrazzano became the first European to observe the Natives around Narragansett Bay as they utilized these resources. Some of their plaited mats covered the light wooden frames of their summer lodges and others served as sleeping pads. When the people moved from place to place with the seasons, their mats could be conveniently rolled up and carried along.

A century later, the Pilgrim settlers at Plymouth observed the same practices among their Massachusetts Bay neighbors, the Wampanoag.

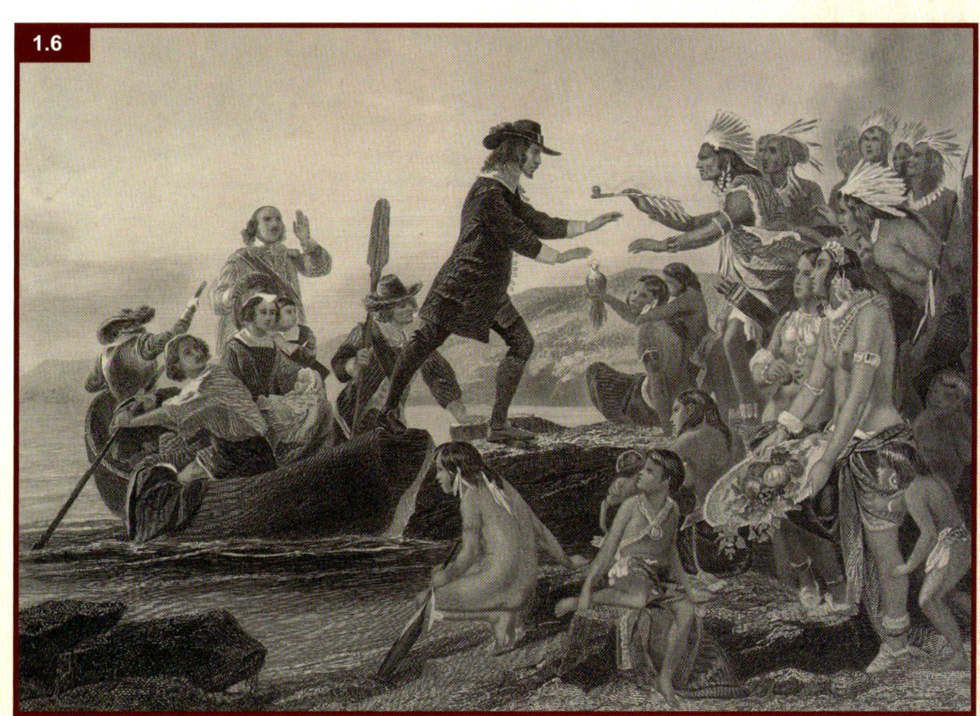

1.5. **In this view of the cliffs of Gay Head, painted by George Newell Bowers in 1874, a Wampanoag Indian observes the ships of Bartholomew Gosnold's 1602 expedition to Martha's Vineyard.**

1.6. ***The Landing of Roger Williams, 1636*, an engraving based on Alonzo Chappel's 1857 oil painting of Narragansett Indians welcoming the founder of Rhode Island.**

THE [WAMPANOAG] HOUSES WERE MADE WITH LONG YOUNG SAPLING TREES, BENDED AND BOTH ENDS STUCK INTO THE GROUND. THEY WERE MADE ROUND, LIKE UNTO AN ARBOR, AND COVERED DOWN TO THE GROUND WITH THICK AND WELL WROUGHT MATS, AND THE DOOR WAS NOT OVER A YARD HIGH, MADE OF A MAT TO OPEN. THE CHIMNEY WAS A WIDE OPEN HOLE IN THE TOP, FOR WHICH THEY HAD A MAT TO COVER IT CLOSE WHEN THEY PLEASED.... ROUND ABOUT THE FIRE THEY LAY ON MATS, WHICH ARE THEIR BEDS. THE HOUSES WERE DOUBLE MATTED, FOR AS THEY WERE MATTED WITHOUT, SO WERE THEY WITHIN, WITH NEWER AND FAIRER MATS.

—*MOURT'S RELATION, 1622*[7]

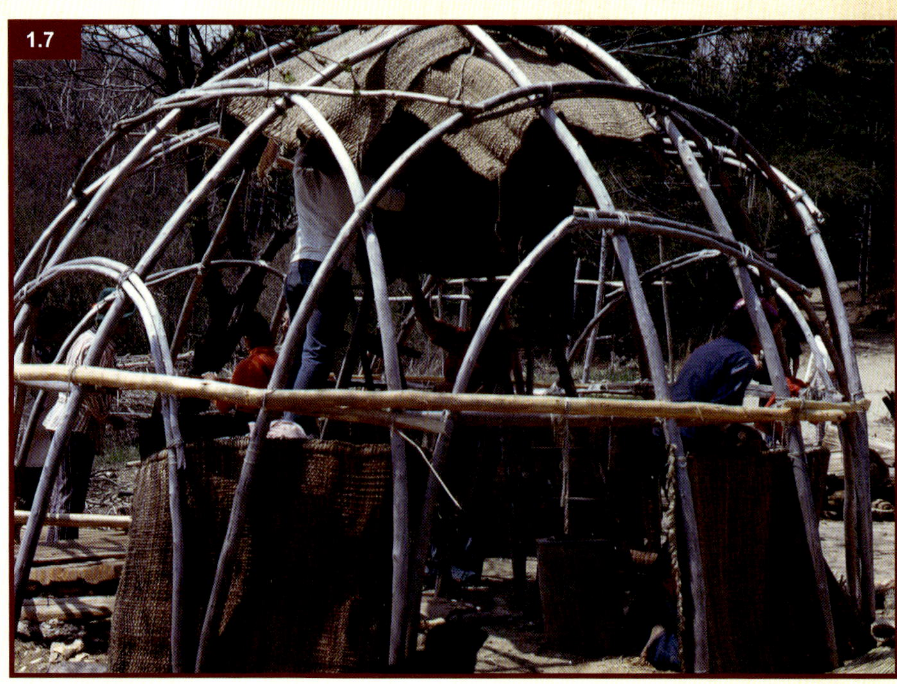

1.7

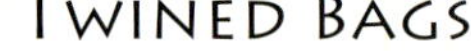

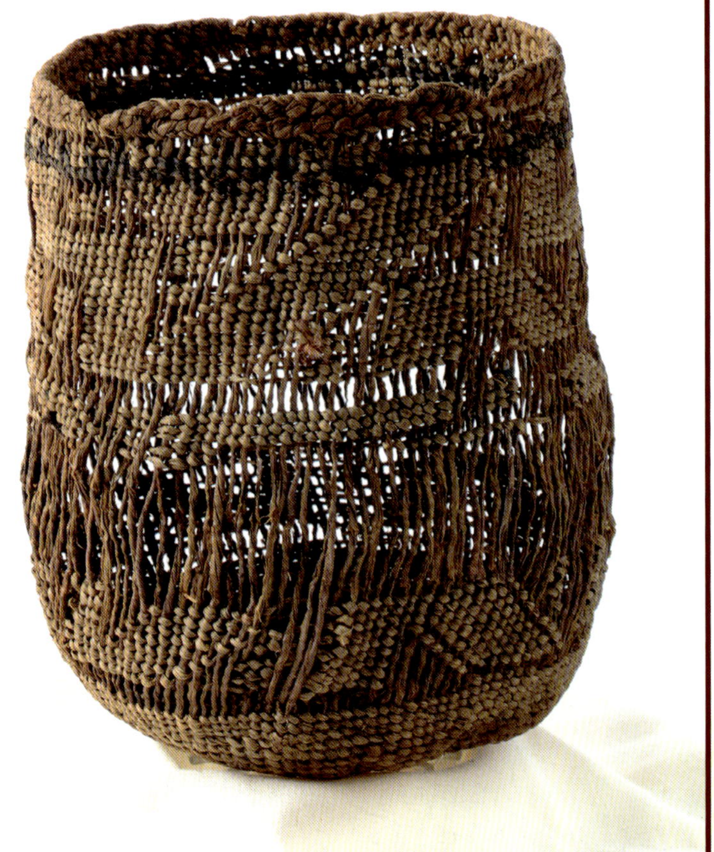

1.8

TWINED BAGS

The ancient technique of twining persisted for a time alongside other basketmaking procedures during the post-European contact period in the Northeast. Among the few remaining examples of 17th-century southern New England Indian basketry are several bags twined from flexible fibers of inner basswood bark (*Tilia* sp.) and dogbane or "Indian hemp" (*Apocynum cannabinum*), as well as introduced wool and cotton.

Algonquian travelers typically carried the smaller twined sacks as pouches for parched corn meal used in preparing their "jonny" (journey) cake. These surviving specimens were gifts from Narragansett and Mohegan makers to their European neighbors, who then carefully preserved them.

1.7. Narragansett Indians recreating a traditional Wampanoag summer house at Plimoth Plantation, Massachusetts, use twined reed mats to simultaneously cover and line the framework of bent saplings.

1.8. Dinah Fenner's Algonquian basket, c. 1675, twined of bark, wool, and cornhusk, is only 4.5" high.

FROM THE TREE WHERE THE BARK GROWS, THEY MAKE SEVERAL SORTS OF BASKETS, GREAT AND SMALL. SOME WILL HOLD FOUR BUSHELS, OR MORE; AND SO DOWNWARD, TO A PINT. IN THEIR BASKETS THEY PUT THEIR PROVISIONS.

—*DANIEL GOOKIN, 1674*[9]

MAKE WAY FOR WOODSPLINTS!

Eventually, twining lost favor altogether in this region. Twining gave way to another technique—

IN STEED OF SHELVES, THEY [THE NARRAGANSETT] HAVE SEVERALL BASKETS, WHEREIN THEY PUT ALL THEIR HOUSEHOLD STUFFE: THEY HAVE SOME GREAT BAGS OR SACKS OF HEMPE, WHICH WILL HOLD FIVE OR SIXE BUSHELLS. —*ROGER WILLIAMS, 1643*[8]

THIS...LITTLE BASKET, WAS GIVEN BY A SQUAW, A NATIVE OF THE FOREST, TO DINAH FENNER, WIFE OF MAJOR THOMAS FENNER.... THE SQUAW WENT INTO THE GARRISON; MRS. FENNER GAVE HER SOME MILK TO DRINK, SHE WENT OUT BY THE SIDE OF A RIVER, PEELED THE INNER BARK FROM THE WICKUP [BASSWOOD OR LINDEN] TREE, SAT DOWN, UNDER THE TREE, DREW THE SHREDS OUT OF HER BLANKET, MINGLED THEM WITH THE BARK, WROUGHT THIS LITTLE BASKET, TOOK IT TO THE GARRISON AND PRESENTED IT TO MRS. FENNER.

—*RHODE ISLAND HISTORICAL SOCIETY CATALOG ENTRY, 1842*[10]

AND IN THIS WAY HE [GLOOSKAP] MADE MAN: HE TOOK HIS BOW AND ARROWS AND SHOT AT TREES, THE BASKET-TREES, THE ASH. THEN INDIANS CAME OUT OF THE BARK OF THE ASH-TREES.

—*PASSAMAQUODDY LEGEND*[11]

plaited woodsplint work—which became the predominant basketmaking method, though bark work and matting persisted for a long time in some areas.

In plain plaiting, the warp and weft elements, often of equal size and flexibility, are interwoven at right angles to produce a basketry surface with a checkerboard appearance. Among Native groups throughout the Northeast, black ash (*Fraxinus nigra*, also called brown ash in Maine) was the preferred material, though white oak or hickory and other hardwoods could also be used.

By the later 18th century, Indians of this region generally employed woodsplint plaiting to produce baskets for their own use and also specifically for sale to their Euramerican neighbors.

THE PRINCIPAL OCCUPATION OF THE MEN IS TO HUNT AND FISH, BUT THAT OF THE WOMEN FOLK IS TO MAKE BASKETS OR SO CALLED TASSAR AS WELL AS RUGS AND OTHER SMALL THINGS OF WOODEN STRIPS.

—*ANDREAS HESSELIUS, 1712*[12]

Commerce in Native basketry was nothing new in New England. The Reverend John Eliot, an early missionary to the Natives of Massachusetts, wrote in 1647 that Indian women in the "praying town" of Natick spent the winter selling their brooms, staves, eelpots, baskets, and turkeys at market. Connecticut's first settlers were apparently engaging Indians living around Fort Saybrook, near the mouth of the Connecticut River, to make trays and mats for their use as early as the mid-1600s.[13]

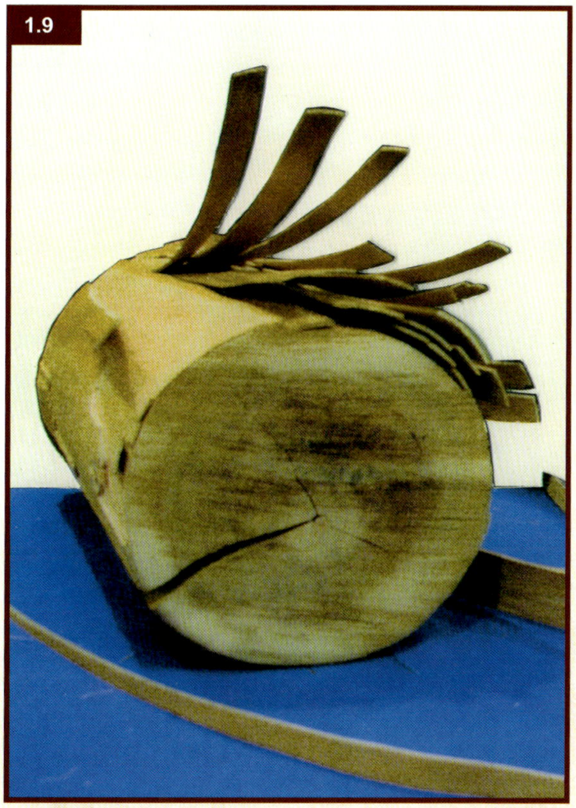

1.9

1.9. Repeated mallet blows have released annual growth rings along this section of black ash (*Fraxinus nigra*) log. The thin strips can now be pulled away then split and trimmed into pliable splints for basket weaving.

The heavy work of making woodsplints was usually, but not always, a man's task, while women generally fashioned the splints into baskets. A straight ash tree of about a foot in diameter and free from limbs along its lower portion was selected and felled. Its trunk was then cut into one or more six-foot sections and debarked. Steadily pounding the hardwood log up and down along its length and around its girth with a mallet or axe poll gradually loosened and separated the tree's annual growth rings, one by one.

Each layer peeled from the log would subsequently be split, trimmed, smoothed, and slit into ribbon-like strips of the desired width, length, and thickness (about 1/16 to 1/8 inch). The supple woodsplints were then ready to be plaited into sturdy baskets.

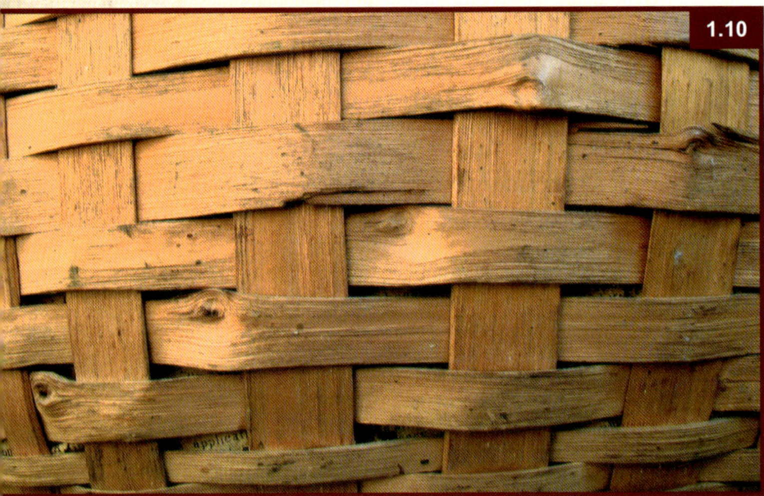

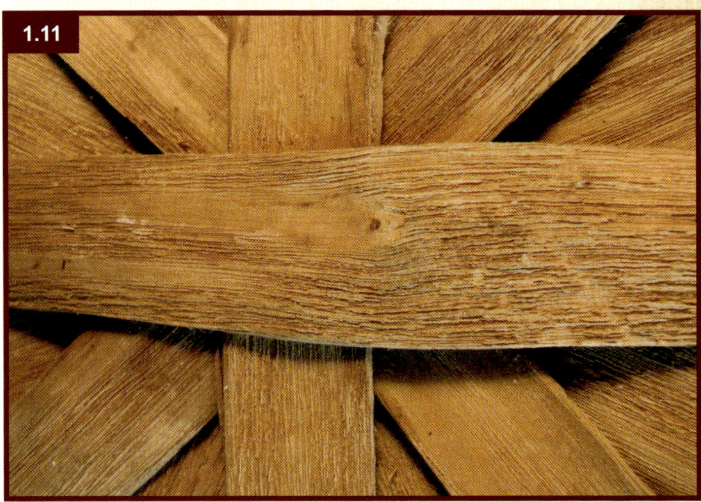

The origins of Northeastern woodsplint technology have not yet been clearly or fully determined. Some historians insist that Indians learned the craft from Europeans, while others maintain that the technique preceded the settlers and was deeply rooted in Native culture.

In 1975, anthropologist Ted Brasser argued that Native basketmakers of the Northeast first began making woodsplint baskets only after early 18th-century Swedish colonists brought the European craft into the Delaware River valley.[14] Still, not everyone agrees with the notion of an Old World origin. Penobscot researcher Jennifer Sapiel Neptune, for one, counters that the absence of pre-colonial splintwork specimens cannot be considered as proof that the process was unknown, especially since basketry of any type from this early period is so rarely preserved.[15]

For the moment, fragments of plaited corn sifters excavated from several mid-17th-century Seneca Iroquois sites in western New York state seem to offer the earliest known primary evidence for the antiquity of Native American splint products.[16] These artifacts do predate the Swedish homesteaders by a few decades, though Europeans of other nationalities had already been in contact with Northeastern tribes for some time. At present, no woodsplint work older than the era of European contact can be archaeologically documented in other parts of the Northeast.

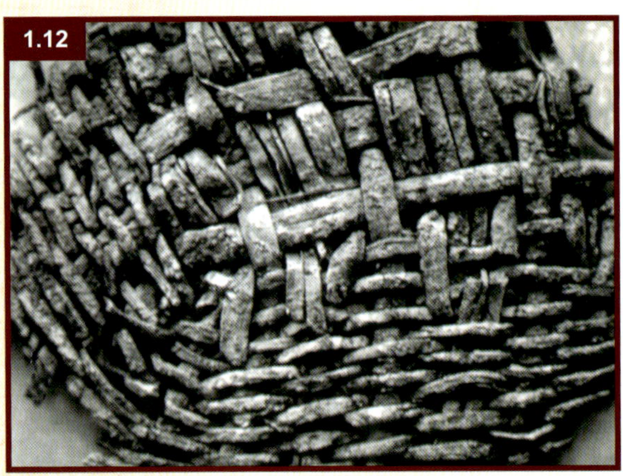

The tools routinely employed by Native Americans in the historic period for making their splint baskets—the metal "crooked knives," spokeshaves, gauges, and planes—significantly all appear to be of European form and origin. In fact, iron blades that might have made serviceable "crooked-knife" cutters were among the imported European trade goods placed as offerings in Narragansett Indian graves as early as the mid-1600s in southern Rhode Island.[17]

Regardless of origin, American Indian production of woodsplint baskets seems to have expanded both widely and quickly during the 18th century. The technique came

1.10. A close-up look at the side of an early 19th-century newspaper-lined woodsplint basket shows characteristics of older ash splintwork. Note variations in splint width and irregularities due to an occasional knot.

1.11. Closer inspection reveals the distinctive texture of wood grain on the "inner" side of splints that have been forcibly split from an adhering growth ring. A splint's "outer" surface feels and appears smoother.

1.12. This archaeological fragment, about 5" across, is one of the earliest preserved examples of plaited woodsplint basketry from the Northeast. Excavated from the Marsh Site (1650-1670), East Bloomfield, New York, it probably represents a bottom corner of a Seneca Iroquois corn sifter.

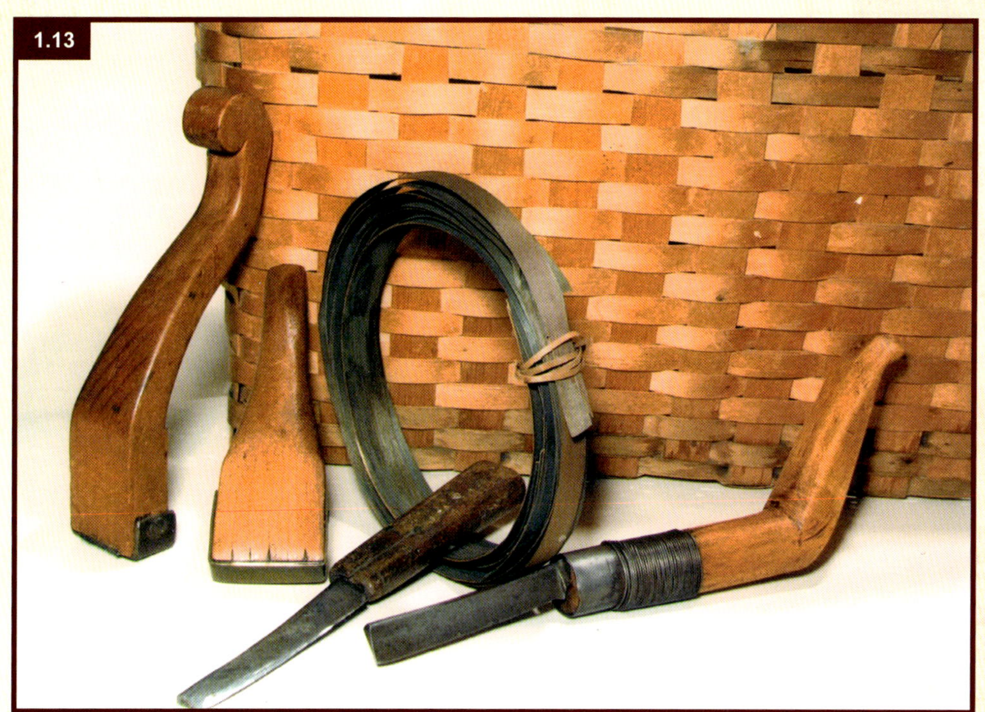

1.13. By the mid-19th century, woodsplints tended to be thinner and of consistent widths. The common use of the crooked knife (right), splint knife (center foreground), and especially the splint gauges (left) and splint splitters (not shown) produced lengths of uniformly thin, ribbon-like weaving material (center). The resulting baskets (background) are relatively lightweight and very evenly woven.

to dominate basketmaking throughout the Northeast by the late 1700s to early 1800s, eventually all but supplanting indigenous twined basketry and birchbark technology.

Whatever their lineage, some of those dour and unassuming Northeastern splint containers found today in many locations, from attics to exhibit cases, are among the very earliest Indian-crafted baskets that one can hope to encounter from anywhere in North America.

Woven for Work

Eighteenth- and 19th-century Native woodsplint baskets were made primarily for barter or sale. These products provided an essential source of income for their makers just as more traditional means of survival—hunting, fishing, farming—were in rapid decline. At the same time, basketmaking afforded Native people an opportunity to engage in the kinds of activities—considered "Indian Work"—that were most compatible with their customary lifeways and conventional skills.

With their tribes ravaged by warfare and disease, and dispossessed of most of their communal lands, many Northeastern Indians barely survived at the very margins of White society. But from this dire situation emerged a new role for their baskets. Native craftspersons—and by now more men had gotten involved in making basketry and matting as their other options disappeared—found Anglo-American customers willing to pay for their handiwork.

> YOU WON'T GO HUNGRY IF YOU CARRY A CROOKED KNIFE, BECAUSE THEN YOU CAN MAKE BASKETS.
> —*MICMAC ADVICE*[18]

Baskets of various kinds already had a place in New England households from the earliest period, as revealed by 17th- and 18th-century probate records of estate inventories. As we have seen, Northeastern Indians have had a history of providing at least some of those baskets to their Yankee neighbors, beginning more than three and a half centuries ago. From the start, Indian baskets have been readily accepted in places where their makers were not always welcomed. The brisk commerce in work baskets continued

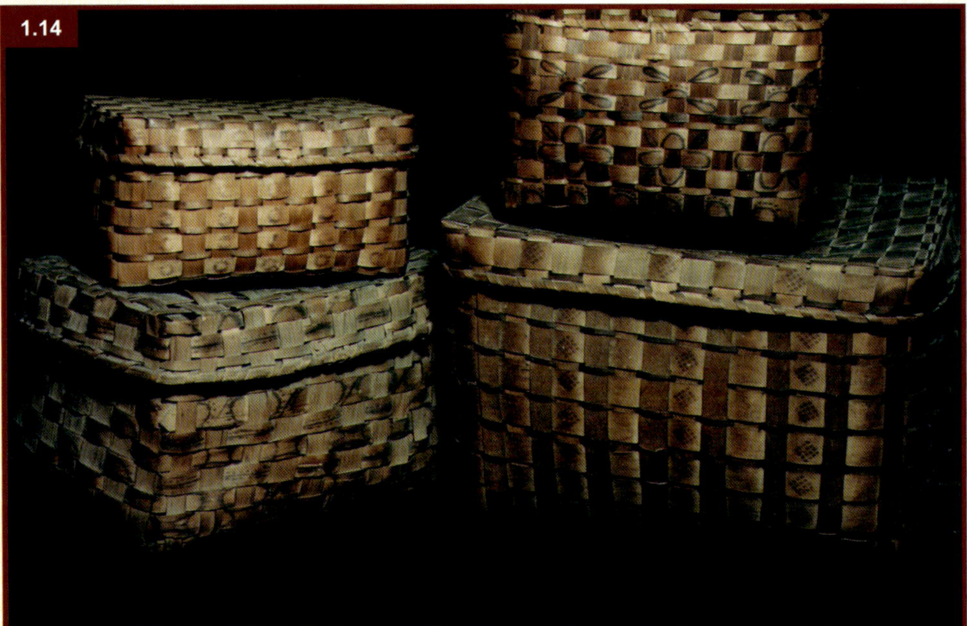

1.14. Four early 19th-century covered storage baskets (one without its lid) from southern New England. Though typically made for use in Yankee households, such containers proudly proclaimed their Indian heritage in both technique and decoration.

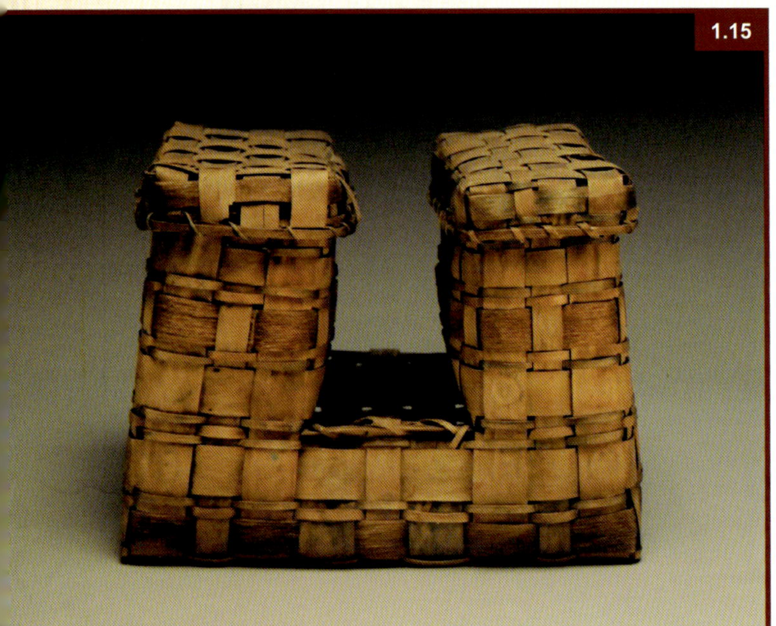

1.15. This southern New England splintwork basket with its open center and two high covered compartments is an unusual form that must have served some special purpose, early 19th century, 8.5" high.

1.16. John Thomas Stanton's watercolor *Going to Market* depicts Maliseet Indians peddling baskets, c. 1845.

in the wake of expanding colonial settlements all across the Northeast, where practical Indian basketry earned the approval of villagers and farmers alike.

These utilitarian products gave certain Native individuals and groups a portal through which they might engage with the newly prevailing society. At first, their wares adhered quite closely to basic and familiar functional forms—generally serviceable containers of various sizes and shapes, some of them hardly modified from Indian prototypes. Soon, though, variations appeared with the addition of handles, covers, and specialized contours that better suited Euramerican needs and preferences. Colonial town houses and farmsteads absorbed quantities of durable Algonquian-made splintwork storage boxes and laundry baskets, harvest baskets and egg carriers, covered feather and pie baskets, hat boxes and lunch baskets, as well as unique forms devised by the weavers.

SETTING:

A Northern New England Cabin

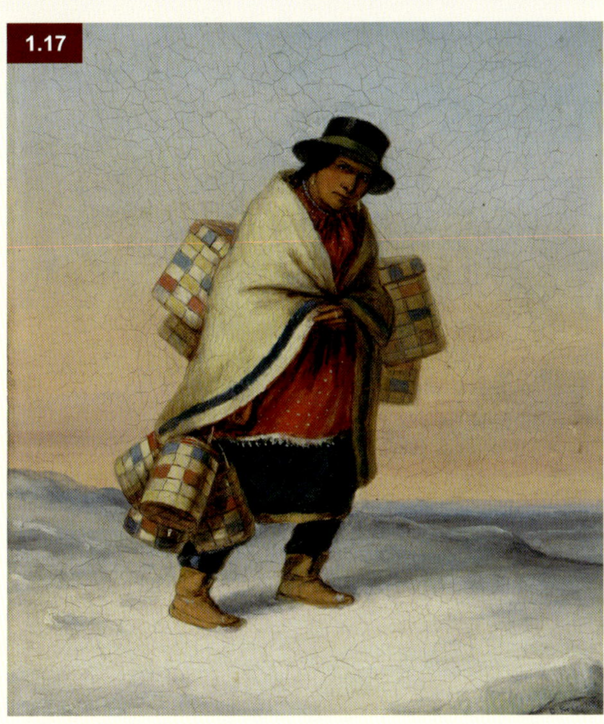

1.17. Cornelius Krieghoff painted *The Basket Seller*, c. 1850, as one of his studies of Canadian life and landscapes.

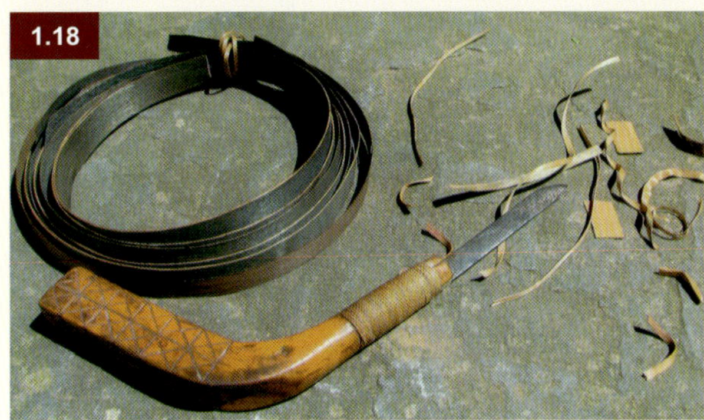

1.18. A splint-bound coil of dyed ash splint, accompanied by a splint knife with an incised maple handle.

Sam, the young Passamaquoddy boy, gazed from the front window of his family's small cabin. His eyes followed the solitary figure of his mother as she trudged down the dirt lane, away from their home, toward the distant village. The woman was bundled up in several layers of warm clothing and a tall black hat. She bent beneath the load of baskets and brooms on her back.

Despite her cumbersome burden, Sam's mother deftly dodged windrows of snow and half-frozen puddles along the lane. As a basket peddler, she likely would sleep in the hayloft of some farmer's barn tonight. Sam shivered. This damp, gray day felt more chilly than usual. At least, he thought, his mum had eaten well this morning before heading out on her journey. His mother was hoping to reach some kinfolk near Bangor, Maine, by eventide two days from now. But first, she would be selling her baskets at farms and villages along the way.

Sam hoped his mother would also trade some baskets for a sack of flour and a pound or two of butter. He really missed the butter his mother made, before the family cow's milk had dried up earlier this winter. Sam's mouth watered at the thought of hot buttered bread. He was tired of eating salt fish and the potatoes they had dug last fall.

The bulky figure of the woman shrank until it became a small speck in the distance. Only then did Sam turn from the window and cross the tiny room toward where his grandmother labored quietly beside the hard-working woodstove. She was sizing splints that Sam's father had pounded out of a brown ash log for basketmaking. As she pulled the wide strips of wood through her splint gauge, the rhythmic parting sound was followed by a "woosh" from narrower splint ribbons dropping to the floor.

Sam silently slipped into his little chair beside his grandmother. He hoped that when she was ready, she would tell him a story to pass the time. The boy picked up his crooked knife. He positioned a splint between the blade and his thigh. Wordlessly, Sam began. He pulled the splint upward against the blade, cleaning curly splinters from the edges of the length. Then he reached for the next splint.

The sized and smoothed ash splints were soon ready for basket weaving.

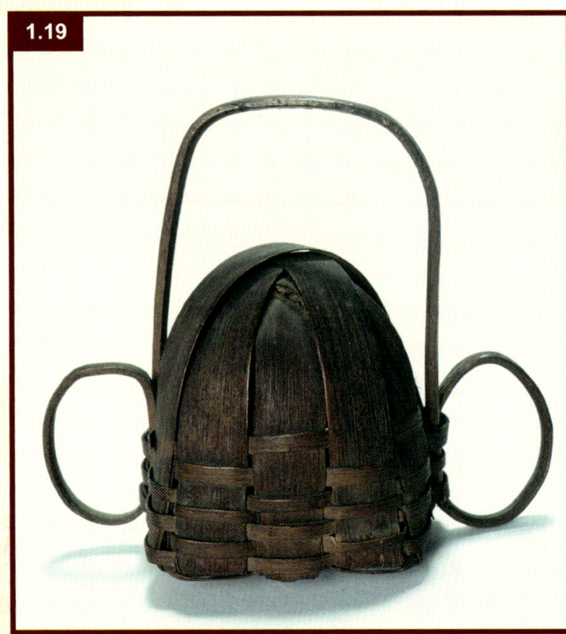

1.19. Stained by age, this early splint rattle, c. 1800, is attributed to the Paugusset basketmaker known as Molly Hatchett (1738-1829).

THERE ARE MANY PERSONS NOW LIVING WHO CAN WELL REMEMBER THAT THERE WERE A FEW REMNANTS OF SEVERAL TRIBES [MONTAUK, SHINNECOCK, POOSEPATUCK, MATINECOC] IN DIFFERENT PARTS OF THE ISLAND [LONG ISLAND], WHO FORMERLY TRAVELED ABOUT, WITH A HUGE BACK-LOAD OF BASKETS, WHICH THEY MADE AND FANCIFULLY ADORNED WITH VARIOUS COLORS: OR A LARGE BUNDLE OF HICKORY BROOMS AND SCRUB-BRUSHES, BY THE SALE OF WHICH THEY ASSISTED THEMSELVES TO BREAD AND CLOTHING. BUT SUCH A SIGHT IS NOW RARELY SEEN.

—*Nathaniel S. Prime, 1845*[19]

Bartering with Baskets

By at least the late 18th century, Native basketmakers throughout the region were making their rounds from town to town each year as they peddled the products of their winter labors. They exchanged baskets for currency or bartered them directly for staple supplies.

Others circulated from door to door, offering to repair splint- or rush-seated chairs and other worn out items.

Some of these itinerant Natives bargained with successive generations of customers, and their yearly arrival was anticipated as something of a homecoming.

The Paugusset basketmaker Molly Hatchett, of western Connecticut, was said to have "visited a hundred or more families twice a year, selling her little fancy stained baskets." And at the birth of a baby she would come by to present the child with a basket-rattle enclosing six kernels of corn.[22] Likewise, the early 19th-century Penobscot basketmaker Mary Nicola, better known by her nickname as "Molly Molasses," enjoyed legendary status in "Down East" Maine. Baskets identified with these and other recognized early makers remain especially prized today.

A story has long circulated in Connecticut about the plaited wares made by another well-known basketmaker, "Jim Pan" Harris, a later 19th-century Schaghticoke craftsman. He reputedly wagered the local miller that his woodsplint baskets could transport gallons of apple cider without leaking a drop. And Harris proved just that, though only after first quickly dipping his baskets into a stream and pulling them out to freeze during a cold late autumn night, thereby coating and sealing the closely interwoven splints!

THEY COME ROUND CONSTANTLY TO THE HOUSES, WITH BUNDLES OF MATERIALS ON THEIR BACKS—SUCH AS ASH FOR HOOPS, AND WILL SIT DOWN PATIENTLY FOR SEVERAL HOURS AND MEND UP ANY OLD BUCKETS OR TUBS THAT MAY BE BROUGHT TO THEM FOR REPAIR.

—*Rev. R. J. Uniacke, 1865*[20]

ANN WAMPY [PEQUOT BASKETMAKER, 1760—1836] USED TO MAKE AN ANNUAL TRIP IN THE EARLY SPRING PAST MY HOME UP THROUGH PRESTON CITY, GRISWOLD, AND JEWETT CITY, SELLING BASKETS SHE HAD MADE DURING THE PREVIOUS WINTER. WHEN SHE STARTED FROM HER HOME SHE CARRIED UPON HER SHOULDERS A BUNDLE OF BASKETS SO LARGE AS ALMOST TO HIDE HER FROM VIEW. IN THE BUNDLE WOULD BE BASKETS VARYING IN SIZE FROM A HALF-PINT UP TO FIVE OR SIX QUARTS, SOME MADE OF VERY FINE SPLINTS, SOME OF COARSE, AND MANY SKILLFULLY ORNAMENTED IN VARIOUS COLORS. HER BASKETS WERE SO GOOD THAT SHE WOULD FIND CUSTOMERS AT ALMOST EVERY HOUSE. AND AFTER TRAVELING A DOZEN OR TWENTY MILES AND SPENDING TWO OR THREE DAYS IN DOING IT, HER LOAD WOULD ALL BE GONE.

—*John Avery, 1901*[21]

Factory Baskets

By at least as early as the 1820s, individual Yankee farmers in a number of communities were making utility baskets on a part-time basis. Unlike most Indians, they generally preferred working with white oak splints, which they split, or rived, from wood billets using a mallet and froe. In due course, some of these basketmaking farmers became very adept at the craft and a few focused their efforts on larger-scale production and marketing.[24]

By the mid-19th century, Native-made woodsplint utility baskets had to compete with comparable wares being mass-produced in the specialized workshops that had sprung up in several New England locations. For example, the Gage Basket Manufactory began operations at a sawmill on the Connecticut River at Bellows Falls, Vermont, in 1842. Several years later, the Williams Manufacturing Company opened a rival basket business about fifty miles downriver, at Northampton, Massachusetts. Others soon followed.

The factory products were generally finished with nailed rims but were otherwise similar in form and overall appearance to the Indian handmade versions with splint-lashed rims. They were wholesaled through mail-order catalogs at a modest cost per dozen baskets. Finding competition impossible on the basis of volume or pricing, local Native makers saw the market for their own utility baskets all but disappear.

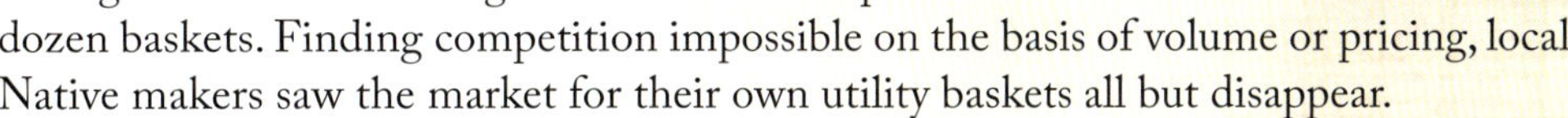

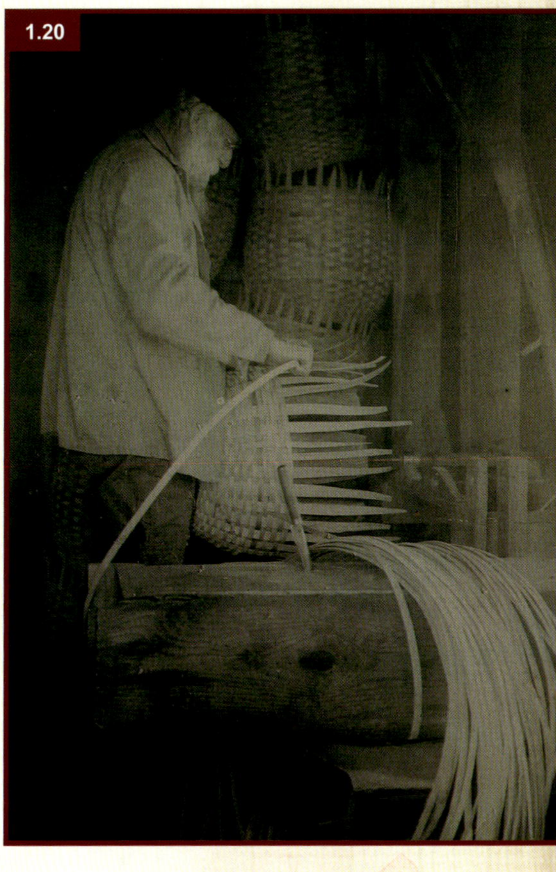

1.20

1.20. An unidentified Yankee basketmaker in his workshop quickly constructs another splint basket around a wooden form. Once finished, his stack of baskets will differ only in subtle ways from those made by the local Indians.

WE AIM TO PRODUCE THE BEST BASKETS THAT CAN BE MADE AND OUR PRICES ARE LOW.
—*Sidney Gage & Co., 1895*[23]

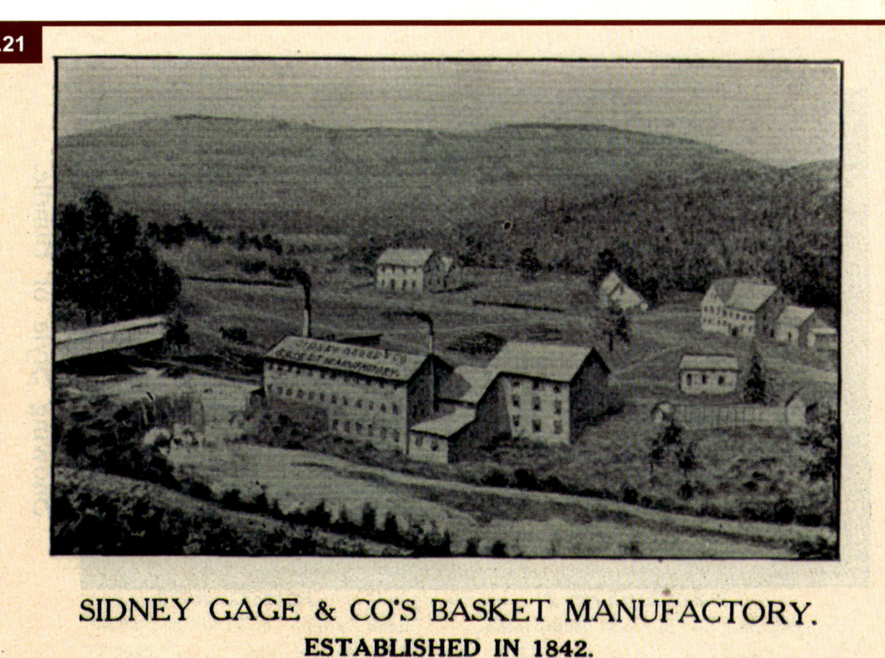

1.21

1.21. View of the Gage basket factory at Bellows Falls, Vermont, from an early catalog. Gage boasted of being the "Largest Manufacturers of Hand-Made Baskets in the United States." These baskets competed directly against Native-made splintwork.

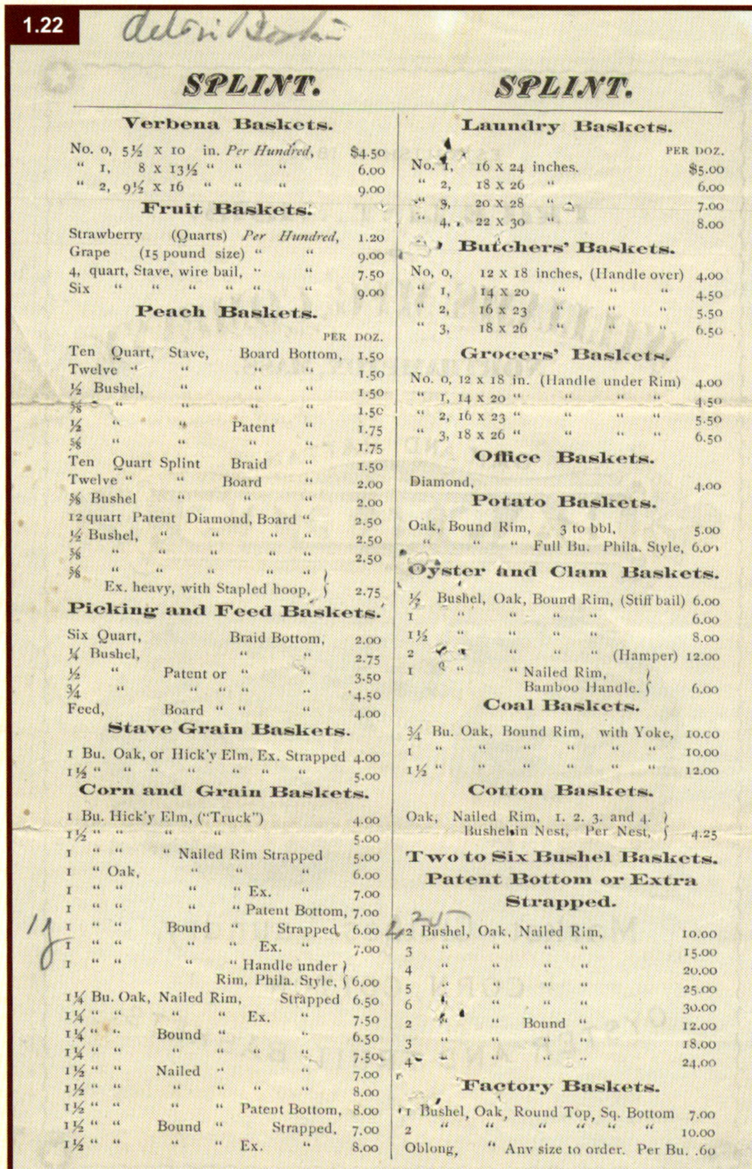

1.22

SPLINT.

Verbena Baskets.

No. 0, 5½ x 10 in. *Per Hundred*, $4.50
" 1, 8 x 13½ " " " 6.00
" 2, 9½ x 16 " " " 9.00

Fruit Baskets.

Strawberry (Quarts) *Per Hundred*, 1.20
Grape (15 pound size) " " 9.00
4, quart, Stave, wire bail, " " 7.50
Six " " " " " " 9.00

Peach Baskets.

PER DOZ.
Ten Quart, Stave, Board Bottom, 1.50
Twelve " " " " 1.50
½ Bushel, " " " 1.50
⅝ " " " " 1.50
½ " " Patent " 1.75
⅝ " " " " 1.75
Ten Quart Splint Braid " 1.50
Twelve " " Board " 2.00
⅝ Bushel " " " 2.00
12 quart Patent Diamond, Board " 2.50
½ Bushel, " " " " 2.50
⅝ " " " " " 2.50
⅝ " " " " " Ex. heavy, with Stapled hoop, 2.75

Picking and Feed Baskets.

Six Quart, Braid Bottom, 2.00
¼ Bushel, " " 2.75
½ " Patent or " " 3.50
¾ " " " " " 4.50
Feed, Board " " " 4.00

Stave Grain Baskets.

1 Bu. Oak, or Hick'y Elm, Ex. Strapped 4.00
1½ " " " " " " " 5.00

Corn and Grain Baskets.

1 Bu. Hick'y Elm, ("Truck") 4.00
1½ " " " " 5.00
1 " " " Nailed Rim Strapped 5.00
1 " Oak, " " " 6.00
1 " " " " Ex. " 7.00
1 " " " " Patent Bottom, 7.00
1 " " Bound " Strapped, 6.00
1 " " " " Ex. " 7.00
1 " " " " Handle under Rim, Phila. Style, 6.00
1¼ Bu. Oak, Nailed Rim, Strapped 6.50
1¼ " " " " Ex. " 7.50
1¼ " " Bound " " 6.50
1¼ " " " " " " 7.50
1½ " " Nailed " " 7.00
1½ " " " " " " 8.00
1½ " " " " Patent Bottom, 8.00
1½ " " Bound " Strapped, 7.00
1½ " " " " Ex. " 8.00

SPLINT.

Laundry Baskets.

PER DOZ.
No. 1, 16 x 24 inches. $5.00
" 2, 18 x 26 " 6.00
" 3, 20 x 28 " 7.00
" 4, 22 x 30 " 8.00

Butchers' Baskets.

No, 0, 12 x 18 inches, (Handle over) 4.00
" 1, 14 x 20 " " " 4.50
" 2, 16 x 23 " " " 5.50
" 3, 18 x 26 " " " 6.50

Grocers' Baskets.

No. 0, 12 x 18 in. (Handle under Rim) 4.00
" 1, 14 x 20 " " " " 4.50
" 2, 16 x 23 " " " " 5.50
" 3, 18 x 26 " " " " 6.50

Office Baskets.

Diamond, 4.00

Potato Baskets.

Oak, Bound Rim, 3 to bbl. 5.00
" " " Full Bu. Phila. Style, 6.00

Oyster and Clam Baskets.

½ Bushel, Oak, Bound Rim, (Stiff bail) 6.00
1 " " " " 6.00
1½ " " " " 8.00
2 " " " " (Hamper) 12.00
1 " " " Nailed Rim, Bamboo Handle. 6.00

Coal Baskets.

¾ Bu. Oak, Bound Rim, with Yoke, 10.00
1 " " " " " " 10.00
1½ " " " " " " 12.00

Cotton Baskets.

Oak, Nailed Rim, 1. 2. 3. and 4. Bushel in Nest, Per Nest, 4.25

Two to Six Bushel Baskets. Patent Bottom or Extra Strapped.

2 Bushel, Oak, Nailed Rim, 10.00
3 " " " " 15.00
4 " " " " 20.00
5 " " " " 25.00
6 " " " " 30.00
2 " " Bound " 12.00
3 " " " " 18.00
4 " " " " 24.00

Factory Baskets.

1 Bushel, Oak, Round Top, Sq. Bottom 7.00
2 " " " " " " 10.00
Oblong, " Any size to order. Per Bu. .60

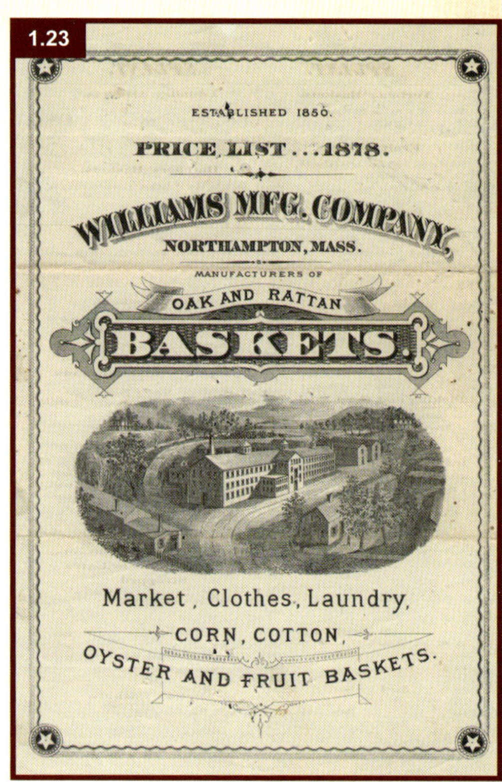

1.23

ESTABLISHED 1850.

PRICE LIST . . . 1878.

WILLIAMS MFG. COMPANY,

NORTHAMPTON, MASS.

MANUFACTURERS OF

OAK AND RATTAN

BASKETS.

Market, Clothes, Laundry,

CORN, COTTON,

OYSTER AND FRUIT BASKETS.

1.22, 1.23. An 1878 price list of the Williams basketmaking company of Northampton, Massachusetts, describes many categories of oak (*not* ash) splint baskets, some of which were offered with a choice of nailed or bound rims. Note the prices given are per one dozen baskets!

Fancy Baskets

The changeover to factory-made baskets was not the only setback to affect the Native peoples of the region. By the last quarter of the 19th century much of northern New England was over-logged, and the forest industries that had supported many Indian men were in rapid decline. Moreover, the scarcity of larger birch trees by the 1890s, followed by a general birch die-back across the Great North Woods in 1900, deprived Indian canoe and box makers of the essential material for their crafts.

Facing uncertain prospects for their very survival in a cash-dominated economy, many Indian families of Northern New England and the Canadian Maritimes were increasingly forced to seek new opportunities. Fortunately, they did not have far to look, for some "new opportunities" were literally coming to them!

Soldiers and travelers around the upper St. Lawrence valley and eastern Great Lakes had long provided a modest market for local Indian handiwork items. Eighteenth-century British and French officers and diplomats assigned to the American colonies often carried home lustrous glass-beaded bags and caps or moosehair-embroidered barkwork containers. By the 1840s, Iroquoian vendors were already greeting early visitors to Niagara Falls. Some industrious young Mohawks even traveled by train each winter in the late 1850s to market their wares as far away as St. Louis and New Orleans.[26]

At the time of the American Civil War, in the mid-19th century, railroad lines were advancing into even the most remote reaches of New England. New routes led into the interior mountains and extended northeastward along the seaboard. Astute developers followed the rails to create attractive new destinations for summer vacationers once peace was restored.

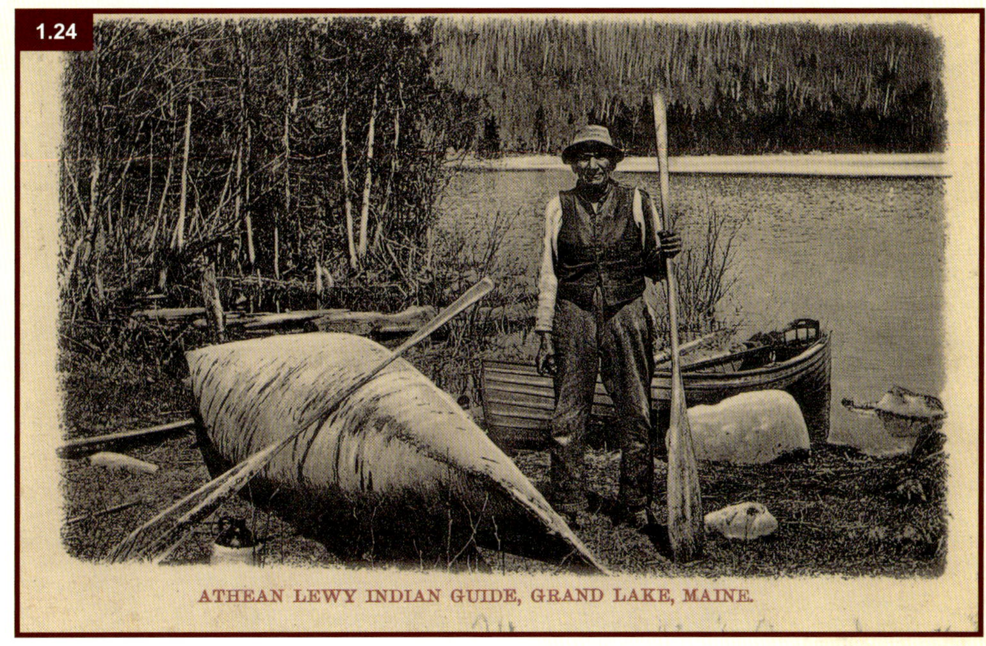

1.24. Birch trees large enough to make a full-sized bark canoe were no longer growing in his region by 1900, when Athean Lewy, a Penobscot Indian guide and tribal delegate to the Maine state legislature, posed for this postcard photo.

Grand hotels and other amenities were soon drawing visitors for extended stays in scenic locations that seemed far removed from bustling Philadelphia, New York, or Boston. Growing prosperity in the industrialized North supported an expanding middle class. More and more tourists and honeymooners made their way each year to favored resorts in the mountains of northern New England and upstate New York, or to Niagara Falls, Saratoga Springs, and Thousand Islands, as well as a host of seaside watering places from Newport to Bar Harbor.

To make the most of their own changing circumstances, many Indian artisans—especially those of the northern Wabanaki groups (Abenaki, Maliseet, Micmac/Mi'kmaq, Passamaquoddy, and Penobscot)—departed from turning out standard utilitarian wares by shifting increasingly to baskets that appealed to tourists and curio buyers. This enterprise catered directly to Victorian visitors and their impulse to acquire unique mementos that commemorated their travels. The specialized souvenir art created for and marketed to these outsiders generally either replicated stereotypical Native cultural objects (sometimes as models or miniatures) or else employed Native materials and techniques to make distinctive Indian versions of familiar Euramerican household items.[27]

A WOMAN MIGHT KEEP BUYING BASKETS FROM MY MOTHER YEAR AFTER YEAR, BECAUSE SHE LIKED MY MOTHER AND LIKED THE BASKETS. MY MOTHER WOULD ALWAYS GO AROUND AND SEE THE PEOPLE SHE HAD SOLD BASKETS TO BEFORE, SHE WOULD SEE THEM RIGHT AWAY, AFTER WE GOT TO A PLACE, AND SHE WOULD TRY TO GET THEM TO BUY MORE. SHE GOT TO BE FRIENDS WITH A LOT OF THESE PEOPLE, AND AFTER AWHILE THEY'D BUY BASKETS FROM HER IF ONLY BECAUSE OF THAT FRIENDSHIP.

—*MICMAC INFORMANT "SAMMY LOUIS" (PSEUDONYM), C. 1950*[25]

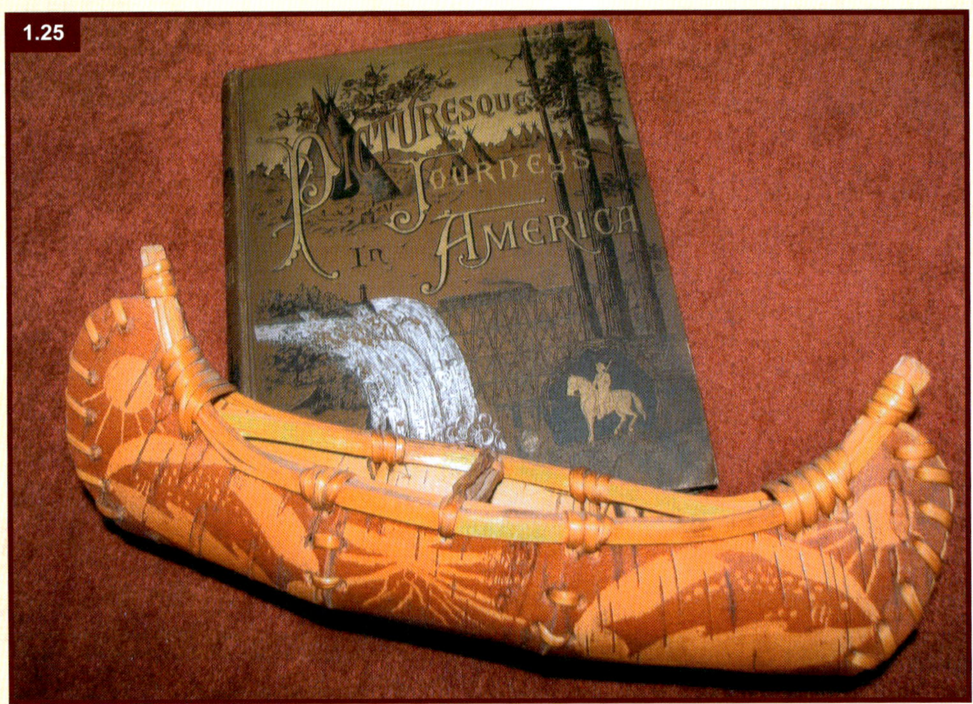

1.25. In addition to Indian baskets, tourists at many of the region's scenic attractions also carried home birchbark trinkets, including countless miniature canoes.

1.26. Three Abenaki or Micmac basketmakers work in the shade to convert a raft of unruly splints into an array of tidy baskets in this c. 1895-1915 photograph.

1.27. Margaret Sutermeister's image of a Native American couple, taken possibly in New Brunswick or Nova Scotia at the turn of the last century, illustrates the common division of Northeastern Indian basketmaking tasks. While women most generally did the weaving, men customarily pounded the ash logs to produce splints and also carved specialized components like shaped hardwood handles and rim hoops.

Known then and today as "fancy baskets," these goods were calculated to appeal to the seasonal influx of moneyed tourists as keepsakes or decorative housewares. Soon, profusions of whimsical sweetgrass and woodsplint handicrafts (as well as beadwork, barkwork, and other knick-knacks) began showing up each summer—along with the Indian families who made and sold them—at coastal, lake, and mountain resort communities throughout the region.

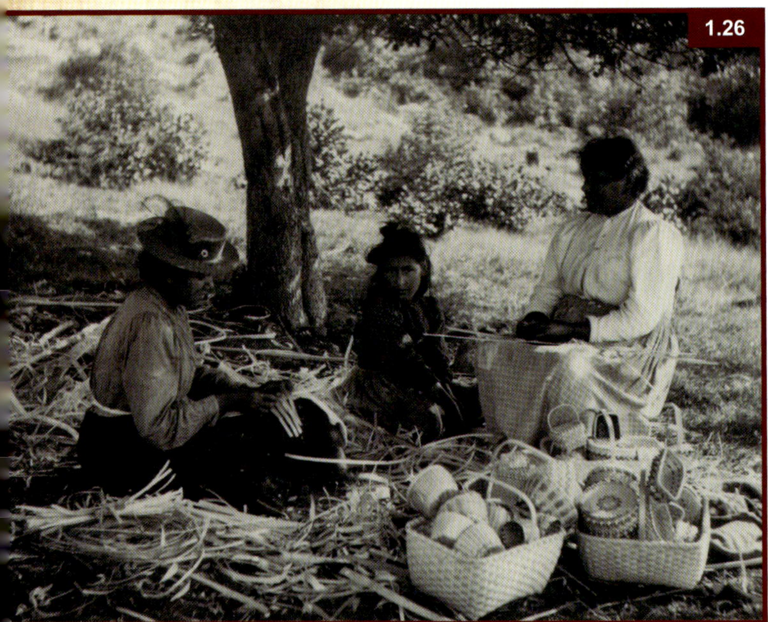

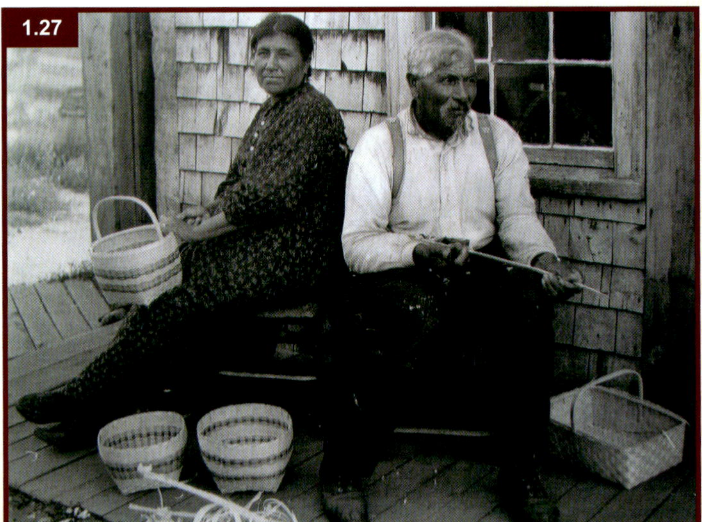

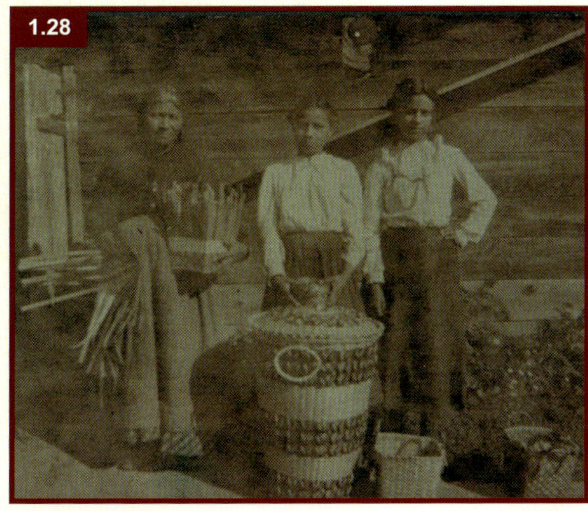

1.28. The women's pride in their decorated woodsplint baskets shows through this faded photograph.

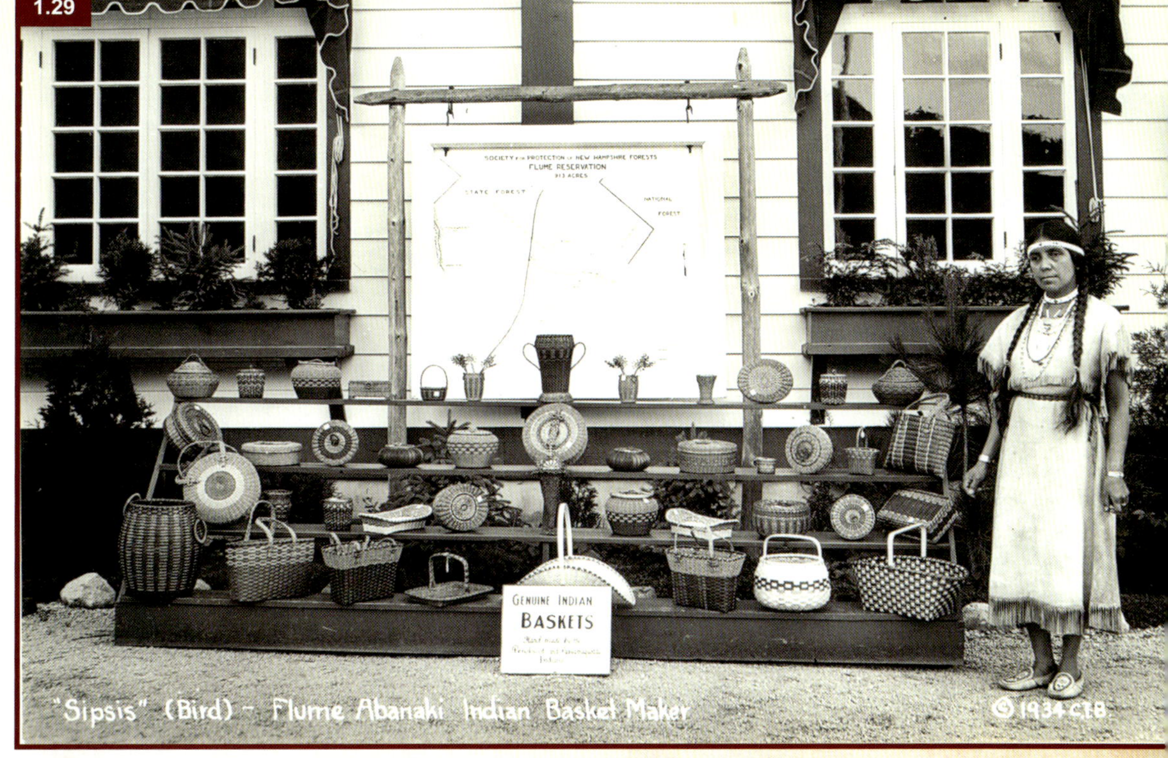

1.29. In 1934, Penobscot basketmaker Camilla Lyon Sockalexis, known also by her Indian name "Sipsis" (Bird), offered a wide array of basketry at the Flume Gorge, a popular attraction in New Hampshire's White Mountains.

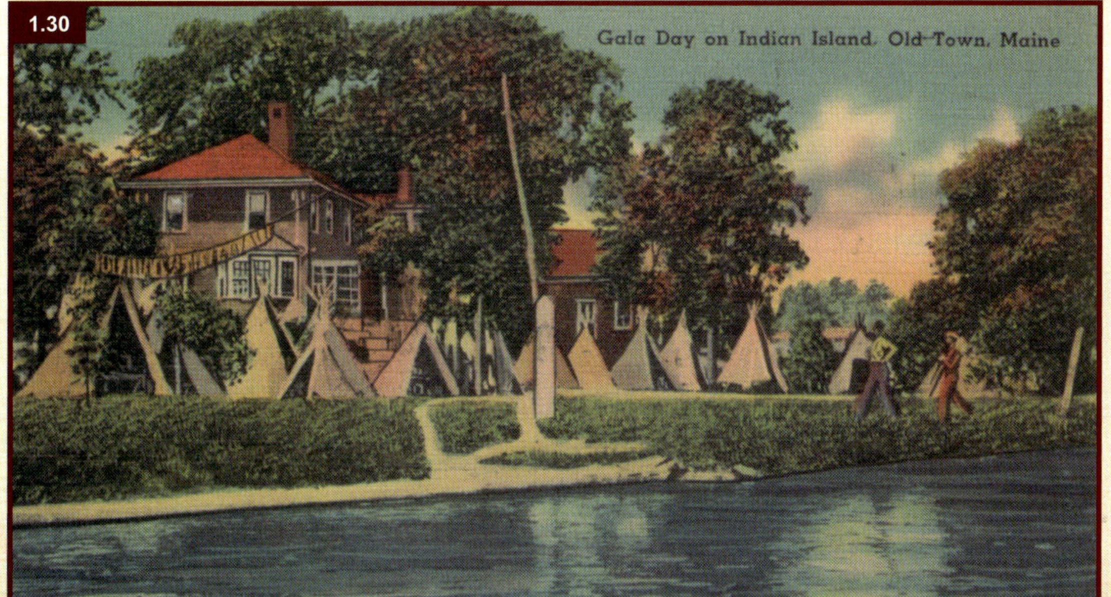

1.30. "Gala Day on Indian Island, Old Town, Maine" is the title of this c. 1900 postcard view. Visitors to the seasonal wigwam encampment purchased baskets and other Native-made souvenirs.

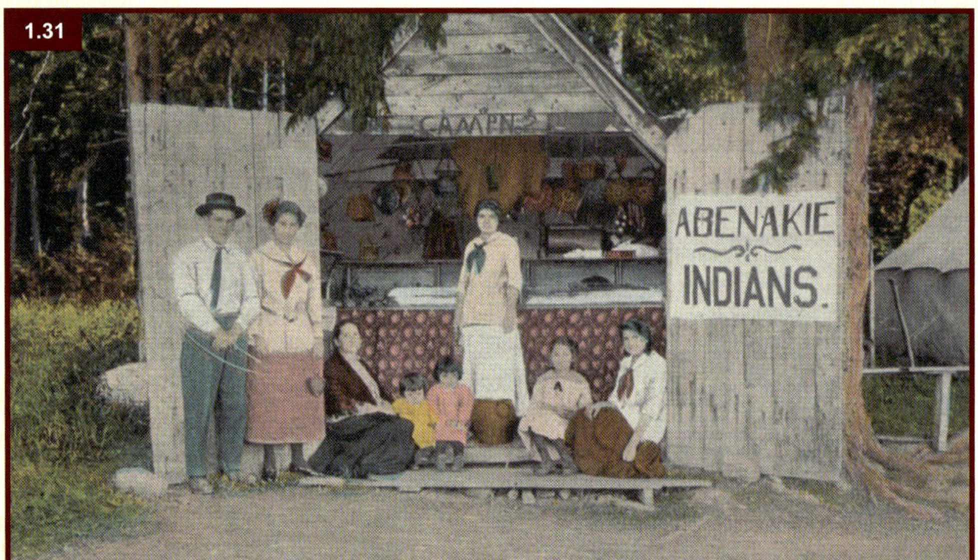

1.31. Semi-permanent structures offered convenience for vendors and visitors alike at the most popular summer resorts. Occupying the same rustic camps each season, Indian families like this one in the White Mountains greeted returning customers year after year.

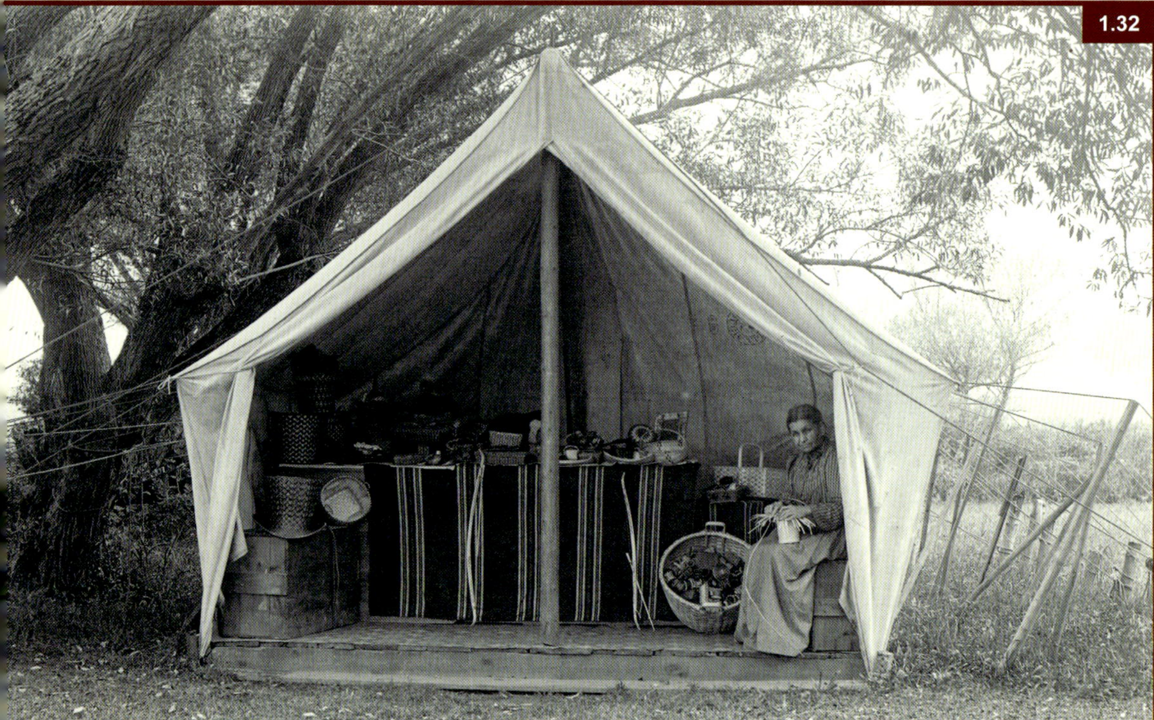

1.32. Sylvia Stanislaus sells her baskets near the Farragut Hotel at Rye Beach, New Hampshire, 1907. This basketmaker from the Penobscot community near Lincoln, Maine, demonstrated her craft in the Indian Village exhibit at the 1893 Columbian Exposition in Chicago.

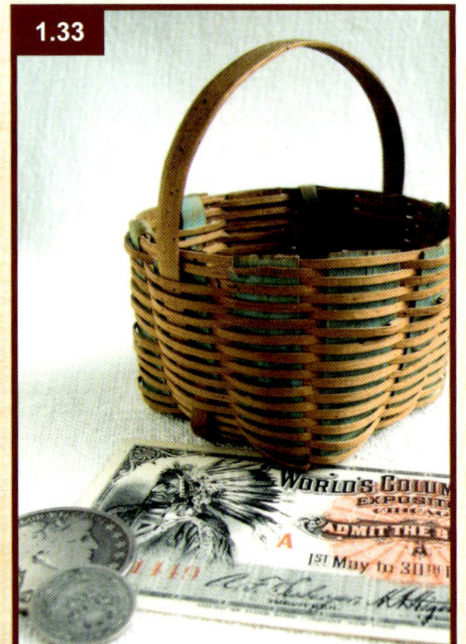

1.33. This typical "five-cents" basket has a simple rim and splint handle and was likely made and sold by an Indian child.

Entire families set up camp for the season at these popular tourist retreats, returning to the same venue year after year to display the baskets they had made during the winter months. Many also demonstrated their craft on-site, drawing tourists and enabling them to better appreciate the work involved in creating an attractive basket. Indian men pounded ash logs while the women generally wove. Endearing children learned to fashion and sell little "five-cents baskets" from their mother's splint scraps.

1.34. Sweetgrass (commonly *Hierochloe odorata*) was harvested in season, cleaned and straightened with a special wooden comb, then painstakingly twisted or braided into long coils that could be incorporated into baskets.

1.35. The Penobscot woman at left uses a special clamp to help her split ash splints for baskets, while the other braids sweetgrass. This photo was taken on Indian Island, Old Town, Maine, c. 1920.

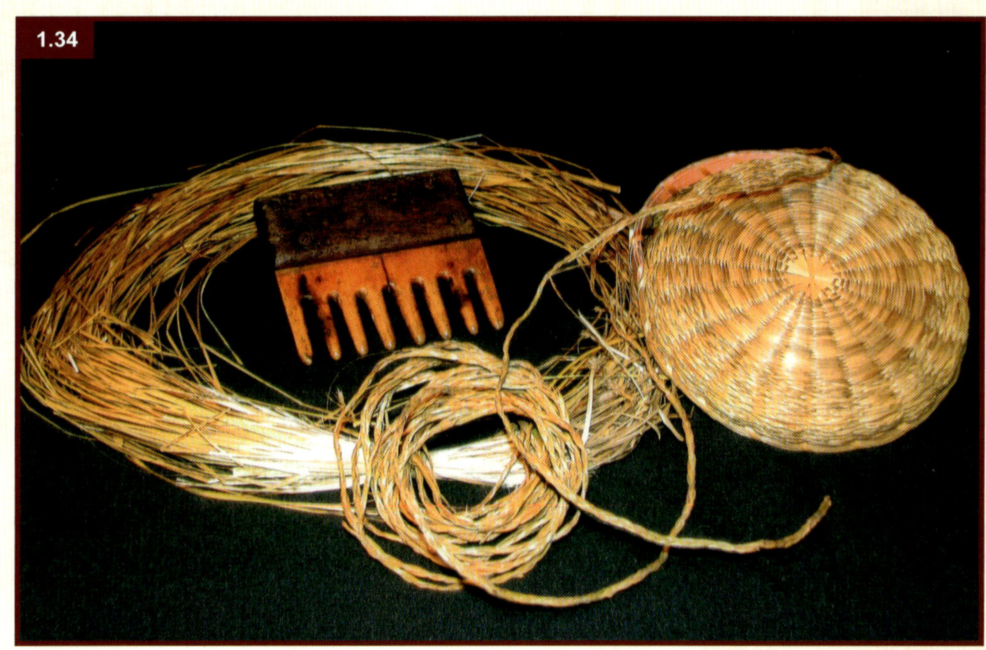

1.34

> BASKET MAKING BECAME THE PRIMARY SOURCE OF INCOME FOR MANY WABANAKI FAMILIES, AND BY THE TURN OF THE TWENTIETH CENTURY ALMOST EVERY PENOBSCOT AND PASSAMAQUODDY HOUSEHOLD WAS INVOLVED WITH IT. IT WAS TRULY A COMMUNITY EFFORT. MEN OFTEN TRAVELED TOGETHER TO THE WOODS TO HUNT FOR GOOD BASKET TREES.... SWEETGRASS THAT HAD BEEN PICKED ALONG THE COAST IN THE SUMMERTIME WAS BRAIDED INTO 100-YARD INCREMENTS TO BE WOVEN INTO BASKETS. WOMEN OFTEN HELD SWEETGRASS BRAIDING PARTIES TO KEEP EACH OTHER COMPANY DURING THIS LONG, TEDIOUS JOB.
>
> —*Jennifer Sapiel Neptune, Penobscot, 2008*[28]

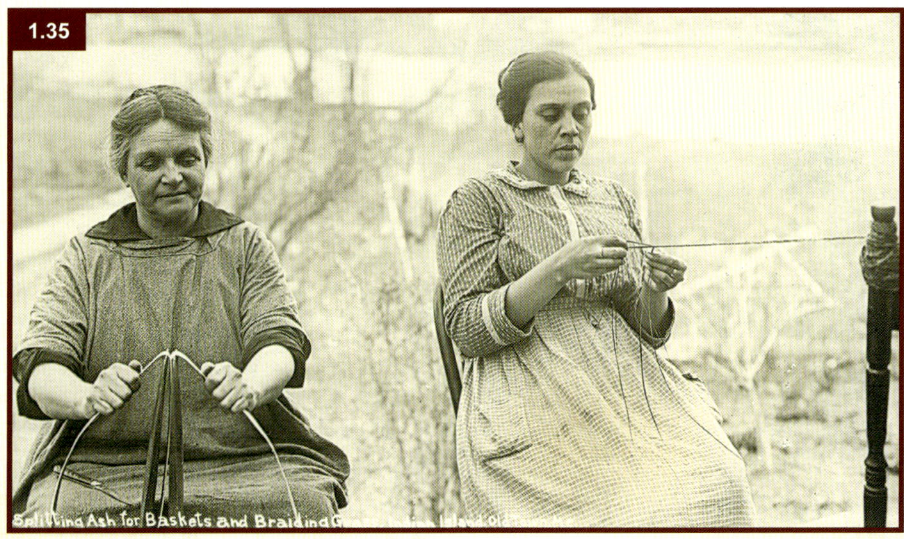

1.35

Indian handmade sewing and knitting baskets, glove and handkerchief boxes, pie baskets, wastepaper receptacles, shopper baskets, basketry-covered jars and vases, collar boxes, purses, trays, and other Victorian trifles, such as fans and bookmarks and doll cradles, were just a few of the many fancy basket items the vacationers carried home from Mount Desert, Poland Spring, or Old Orchard Beach in Maine, or from the White Mountains and Adirondacks, among many other locations.

Affluent visitors found the modest souvenirs hard to resist. Many of the products were actually useful to the Victorian homemaker, while at the same time serving as a reminder of a pleasant summer's getaway or a special gift for a friend.

Indian basketry became something of an industry for a while. Elsewhere across the country, too, Native basketmakers were responding to a developing "basket craze" associated with the American Arts & Crafts Movement at the opening of the 20th century. As attractive yet functional handcrafted products, Indian baskets perfectly complied with the principles espoused by the Movement's trend setters. Baskets came into vogue and were everywhere greatly admired and eagerly acquired.[29]

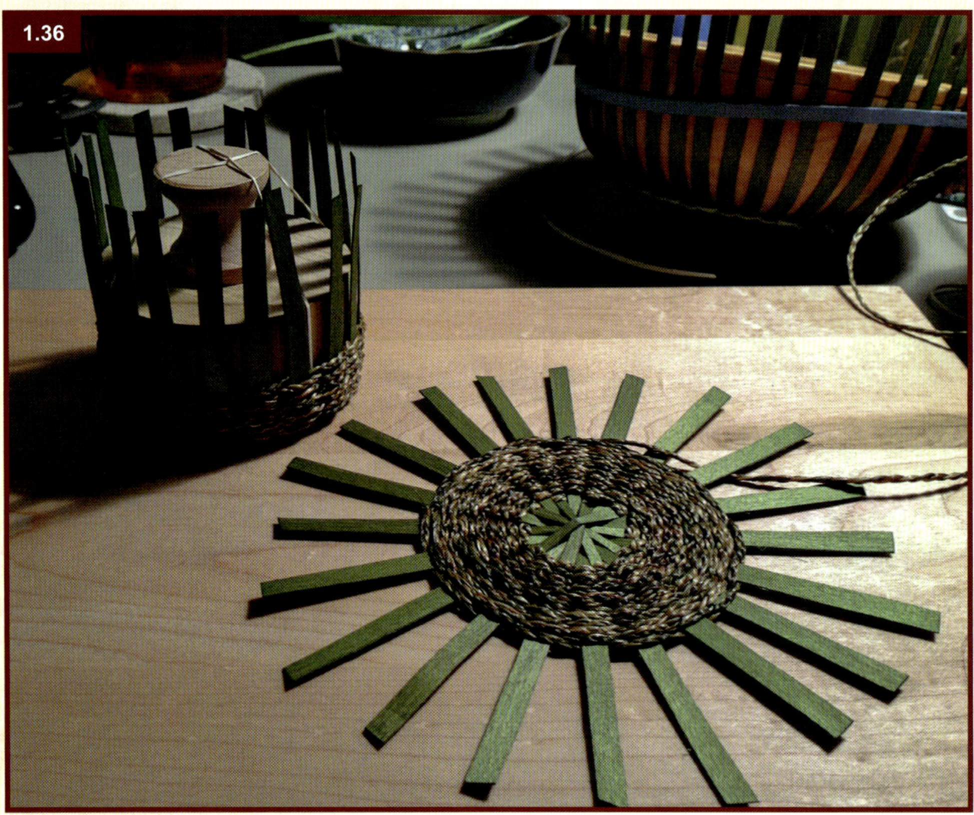

1.36. Penobscot basketmaker Jennifer Sapiel Neptune's work table holds several baskets-in-process. The green splints interlaced with braided sweetgrass (foreground) will become the cover for a basket taking shape around the wooden block at upper left.

1.37

Preparing Diamond Dyes to Produce New Fashionable Shades

There are 16 standard Diamond Dye colors as shown on the inside pages of this card.

From season to season a number of new shades are brought out by the textile manufacturers, some of which prove extremely popular, and all of which (in fact, ANY shade) can easily be produced by mixing two or more of the standard Diamond Dye colors.

If there is any shade you wish to match, not shown in our 16 standard colors, if you will send us a sample of the material to be dyed and a sample of the shade desired, we will tell you how to obtain the desired shade by combining our standard Diamond Dye colors.

AN IMPORTANT POINT IN DYEING IS TO DISCHARGE THE OLD COLOR—If the goods have been previously colored, better results will be obtained by removing the old dye completely as possible before redyeing. Boil the material from which the color is to be removed in clear water from ten to twenty minutes. If the water becomes discolored, drain it off and replace with clear water and repeat the boiling as long as color seems to be removed from the goods.

WELLS & RICHARDSON CO.
MANUFACTURERS OF DIAMOND PACKAGE DYES
BURLINGTON, VERMONT, U. S. A.

Customers' Diamond Dye Sample Card

Wells & Richardson Co.
Manufacturers of Diamond Package Dyes
Burlington, Vermont

USE DIAMOND DYE INK POWDERS

With the simple addition of water one 10-cent package makes a pint of excellent writing fluid.

Two Colors—
EOSINE FOR RED INK
SLATE FOR BLACK INK
FOR SALE BY YOUR DEALER

1.37, 1.38. Commercial aniline dyes gained popularity among Native basketmakers through the late 19th century. Their use sped up basket production, brightened the finished products, and appealed to customers. However, more than a century of exposure to light and air has by now muted or even completely faded the once-vivid colors on many vintage aniline-dyed baskets.

1.39

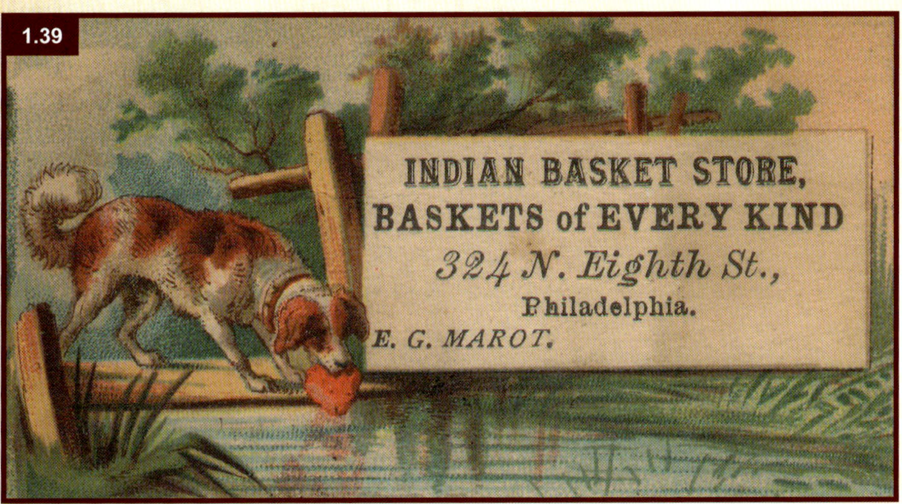

1.39. **Victorian lithographed trade card, c. 1880s, for the Indian Basket Store in Philadelphia advertises an early retail outlet. The shop's urban location, far from any Indian basketmaking center, is a measure of the craft's pervasive popularity.**

To streamline the production process as the basket business boomed in the Northeast, Native men designed wooden blocks that enabled their wives to weave baskets more quickly and uniformly around a standard form or "mold." Outside suppliers provided some of the busiest basketmakers with the prepared ash splints, lengths of braided sweetgrass, and commercial Diamond-brand dyes they needed to keep up with the demand for their finished products. White-operated craft shops soon opened their doors to profit from the fad, and wandering Gypsies at times appeared on the scene to compete for the trade by offering cheap imported knock-offs as their own handmade "Indian baskets."[30]

A 1902 report to the New York state assembly described the many small resort "parks" that were by then flourishing on the St. Lawrence River islands in Alexandria Bay: "At these places may be found a general store, meat market, and the ubiquitous dealer in Indian baskets or souvenirs of local interest."[31] As competition intensified, some northern New England Indians carried their baskets further afield, riding trains south and west

1.38

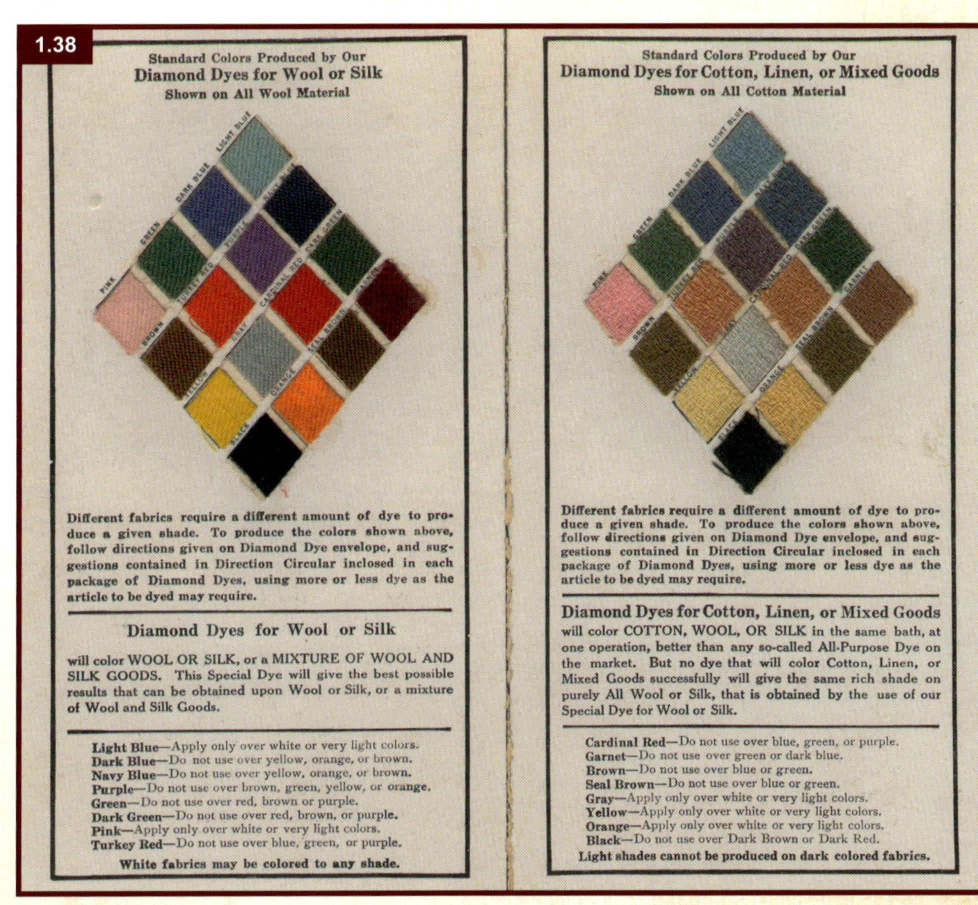

1.40

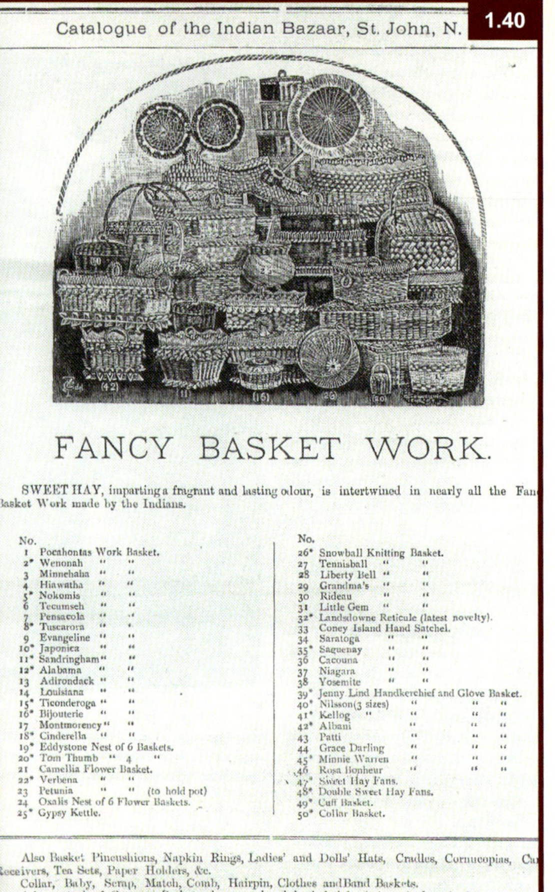

Catalogue of the Indian Bazaar, St. John, N.

FANCY BASKET WORK.

SWEET HAY, imparting a fragrant and lasting odour, is intertwined in nearly all the Fan Basket Work made by the Indians.

No.
1 Pocahontas Work Basket.
2* Wenonah " "
3 Minnehaha " "
4 Hiawatha " "
5* Nokomis " "
6 Tecumseh " "
7 Pensacola " "
8* Tuscarora " "
9 Evangeline " "
10* Japonica " "
11* Sandringham " "
12* Alabama " "
13 Adirondack " "
14 Louisiana " "
15* Ticonderoga " "
16* Bijouterie " "
17 Montmorency " "
18* Cinderella " "
19* Eddystone Nest of 6 Baskets.
20* Tom Thumb " 4 "
21 Camellia Flower Basket.
22* Verbena " "
23 Petunia " " (to hold pot)
24 Oxalis Nest of 6 Flower Baskets.
25* Gypsy Kettle.

No.
26* Snowball Knitting Basket.
27 Tennisball " "
28 Liberty Bell " "
29 Grandma's " "
30 Rideau " "
31 Little Gem " "
32* Landsdowne Reticule (latest novelty).
33 Coney Island Hand Satchel.
34 Saratoga " "
35* Saguenay " "
36 Cacouna " "
37 Niagara " "
38 Yosemite " "
39* Jenny Lind Handkerchief and Glove Basket.
40* Nilsson (3 sizes) " " "
41* Kellog " " " "
42* Albani " " "
43 Patti " " "
44 Grace Darling " " "
45* Minnie Warren " " "
46 Rosa Bonheur " " "
47* Sweet Hay Fans.
48* Double Sweet Hay Fans.
49* Cuff Basket.
50* Collar Basket.

Also Basket Pincushions, Napkin Rings, Ladies' and Dolls' Hats, Cradles, Cornucopias, Ca Receivers, Tea Sets, Paper Holders, &c.
Collar, Baby, Scrap, Match, Comb, Hairpin, Clothes and Band Baskets.
A large stock of Common Baskets always on hand, bushel, ½ bushel, peck, ½ peck, &c.
* Those marked with an asterisk are shown in above illustration.

1.41

You will find at....

"THE WIGWAM"

Sweet Grass and Splint Baskets, Bows and Arrows, Birch Bark Work, Canoes and Moccasins, the product of the Canadian and Oldtown Indian.

Birch Bark, Porcupine Quill Work.

Large line of local views in Platinums and water color. Birches, etc., framed and unframed.

Fine specimens of Moose and Deer Heads and Native Birds.

Burnt Leather Goods in great variety; burned or marked to order while you wait, without charge.

Russian novelties.

Painted Indian Hangers and Sofa Pillow Covers, Fir Balsam Pillows.

Rustic Wood Souvenirs.

Spruce Gum.

Maple Sugar.

Souvenir Books and China.

Souvenir Postal Cards in great variety, Albums, etc.

The Wigwam

AND

Indian Museum

The Most Original and Unique Store in the East. Devoted Entirely to

Souvenirs

Indian and Mexican Goods

D. E. GIBSON

North Conway, N. H.

Masonic Building, Main Street Opposite Kearsarge Hotel

Wholesale and Retail

into the major urban centers to offer their wares through general retail stores or even to peddle them along Atlantic City's famous Boardwalk.

Anyone, who for some reason may have missed the opportunities to buy directly from the seasonal basketmakers-in-residence, could purchase many of the same kinds of products by mail order. Supplied by the Abenaki and Penobscot, as well as Mohawk, Huron, and other northern Indian crafters, basketry and other novelty items were resold in volume by wholesale traders.

Doing business during the early 1900s, the St. Regis Indian Basketry Company was one of several such firms whose illustrated price lists offered many of the specialty baskets that are so well represented in today's collections. Operating out of Hogansburg, New York, the company capitalized on talented Mohawk basketmakers from the St. Regis (now Akwesasne) Reservation that straddles both sides of the St. Lawrence River along the international border shared with Canada.

1.42

Something New.

St. Regis Indian basket store. A grand display at No. 14 State street. Every one invited to see them: especially the ladies of Rochester. They include hampers waste baskets, fancy work of all kinds. Step in and see them; the prices are very low.

FEE BROS.

Other firms actively competed in this trade during the early decades of the 20th century. Among them were the Tanner Basket Company of New York City, Charles N. Saba of Toronto, and Phileas Launière, a Maliseet Indian operating out of Pierreville, Québec.[32] Each of these businesses employed some full-time basketmakers. They also made money by selling craft materials to independent artisans, most of whom had little choice but to offer their completed handiwork back to the jobbers at very low prices.

Unless marked, the commercial products of these Iroquoian and Northern Algonquian basketmakers are by now pretty much indistinguishable from one another. All were

1.40. This c. 1885 "Catalogue of the Indian Bazaar, St. John, N.B." displays and identifies 50 types of ash splint and sweetgrass basketry offered to consumers.

1.41. White-run shops in many resort communities, including The Wigwam in North Conway, New Hampshire, vied with Native sellers for whatever money tourists were willing to spend on Indian souvenirs.

1.42. The Fee brothers announced the opening of their St. Regis Indian basket store with a front-page notice in the Rochester, New York, *Democrat and Chronicle*, February 1, 1890.

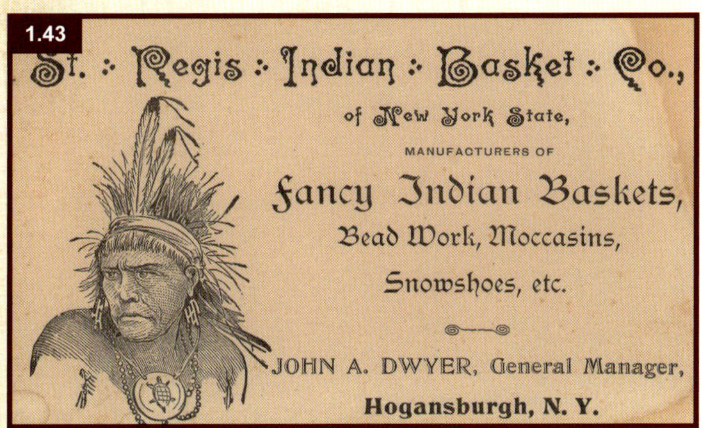

1.43. In later decades, the St. Regis Indian Basket Company, located close to the Akwesasne Mohawk reservation at Hogansburg, New York, became one of several major wholesale and mail-order businesses that supplied Indian baskets and related products to a nationwide market through the early 20th century. While a few Native basketmakers were employed in-house, many more worked at home, crafting baskets to company specifications.

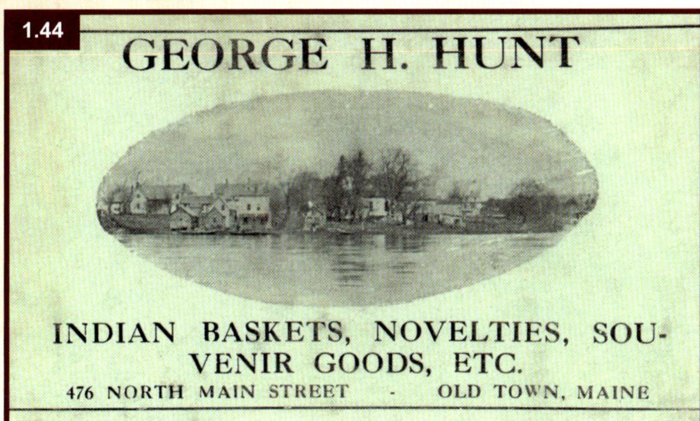

1.44. George H. Hunt was a merchant as well as the Penobscot Indian agent in Old Town, Maine. He marketed Penobscot-made novelties for several decades beginning in 1880. This business card dates to c. 1900 and features a view of the Penobscot village on Indian Island.

generally woven to the same specifications, resulting in a limited range of standardized items that could be effectively mass-marketed through widely-distributed catalogs.

In the meantime, some basketmaking families and individuals continued to offer their products independently wherever they could. A roadside tent sheltering a colorful array of fancy baskets was still likely to slow a passing automobile and maybe result in a sale. Other selling opportunities included state fairs and conventions that brought visitors to town. Special historical commemorative events or even major expositions, such as the 1893 Columbian Exposition in Chicago and the 1921 Pilgrim Tercentenary in Plymouth, Massachusetts, sometimes included space for an "Indian village" where Native families might encamp for up to weeks at a time as they made and sold their craft work.

1.45

Tanner Basket Company,
OFFICE AND SALESROOM:
467 BROADWAY. NEW YORK.
THE LARGEST HOUSE FOR INDIAN FANCY BASKETS 206868
BIRCH BOXES AND CANOES, SWEET GRASS ARTICLES, BOWS AND ARROWS, SNOW SHOES, MOCCASINS, SEAL SLIPPERS, INDIAN CLUBS, LA CROSSE STICKS.
RESIDENT BUYERS ON THESE RESERVATIONS: ST. REGIS. PENOBSCOT. CHIPPEWA. OTTOWA.
PRESENTED BY

1.45. Tanner Basket Company of New York City was another wholesaler, with warehouses in Hogansburg, New York, and Old Town, Maine. Tanner relied on "resident buyers" on several Indian reservations to acquire baskets and other articles for resale.

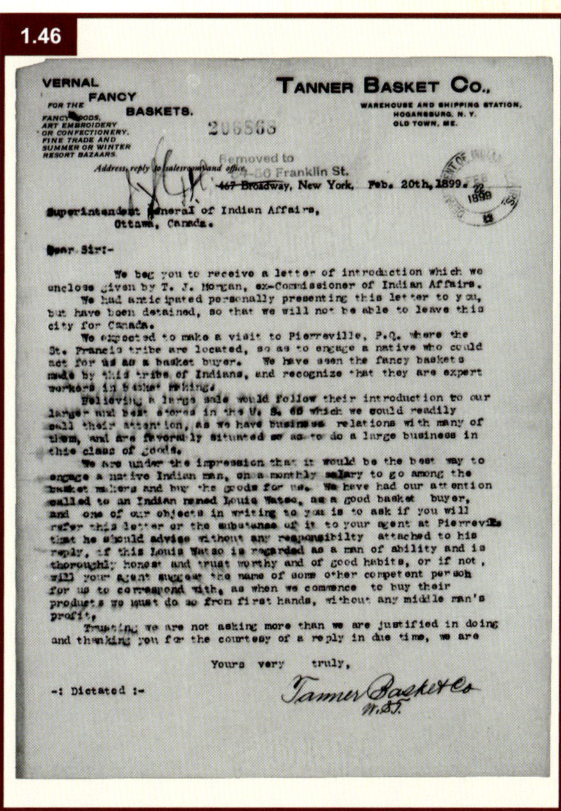

1.46

VERNAL FANCY BASKETS.
FOR THE FANCY GOODS, ART EMBROIDERY OR CONFECTIONERY, FINE TRADE AND SUMMER OR WINTER RESORT BAZAARS.

TANNER BASKET CO.,
WAREHOUSE AND SHIPPING STATION, HOGANSBURG, N. Y. OLD TOWN, ME.

206868

Address reply to salesroom and office,
Removed to 54-60 Franklin St.
~~467 Broadway~~, New York, Feb. 20th, 1899.

Superintendent General of Indian Affairs,
Ottawa, Canada.

Dear Sir:-

We beg you to receive a letter of introduction which we enclose given by T. J. Morgan, ex-Commissioner of Indian Affairs.

We had anticipated personally presenting this letter to you, but have been detained, so that we will not be able to leave this city for Canada.

We expected to make a visit to Pierreville, P.Q. where the St. Francis tribe are located, so as to engage a native who could act for us as a basket buyer. We have seen the fancy baskets made by this tribe of Indians, and recognize that they are expert workers in basket making.

Believing a large sale would follow their introduction to our larger and best stores in the U. S. 68 which we could readily call their attention, as we have business relations with many of them, and are favorably situated so as to do a large business in this class of goods.

We are under the impression that it would be the best way to engage a native Indian man, on a monthly salary to go among the basket makers and buy the goods for us. We have had our attention called to an Indian named Louis Watso, as a good basket buyer, and one of our objects in writing to you is to ask if you will refer this letter or the substance of it to your agent at Pierreville that he should advise without any responsibilty attached to his reply, if this Louis Watso is regarded as a man of ability and is thoroughly honest and trust worthy and of good habits, or if not, will your agent suggest the name of some other competent person for us to correspond with, as when we commence to buy their products we must do so from first hands, without any middle man's profit,

Trusting we are not asking more than we are justified in doing and thanking you for the courtesy of a reply in due time, we are

Yours very truly,

Tanner Basket Co
W.S.T.

-: Dictated :-

1.46. Writing to Canada's Superintendent General of Indian affairs in February 1899, Tanner Basket Company plans "to engage a native Indian man, on a monthly salary to go among the basket makers and buy the goods for us" at the St. Francis Abenaki reservation at Pierreville, Québec.

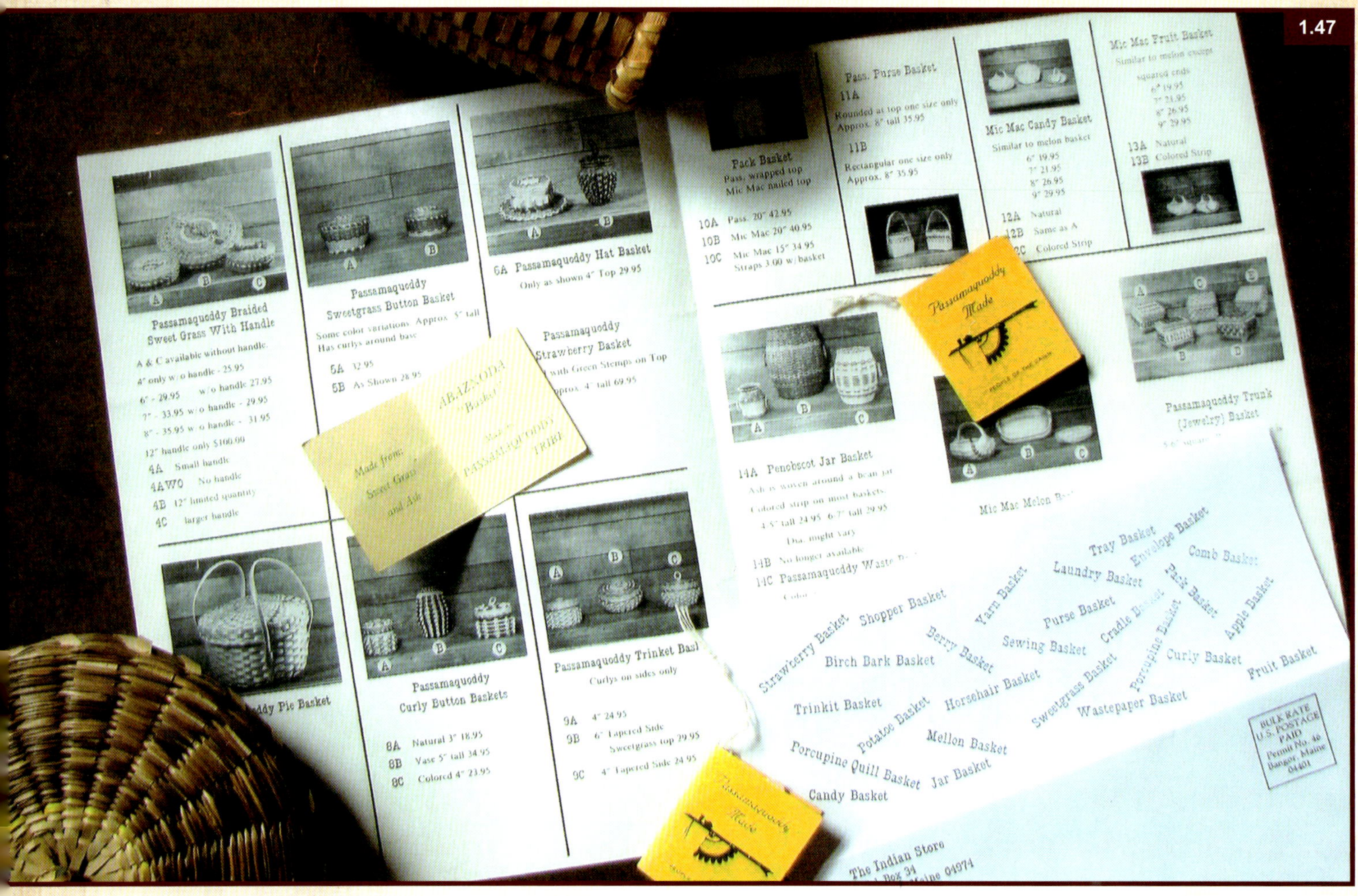

1.47

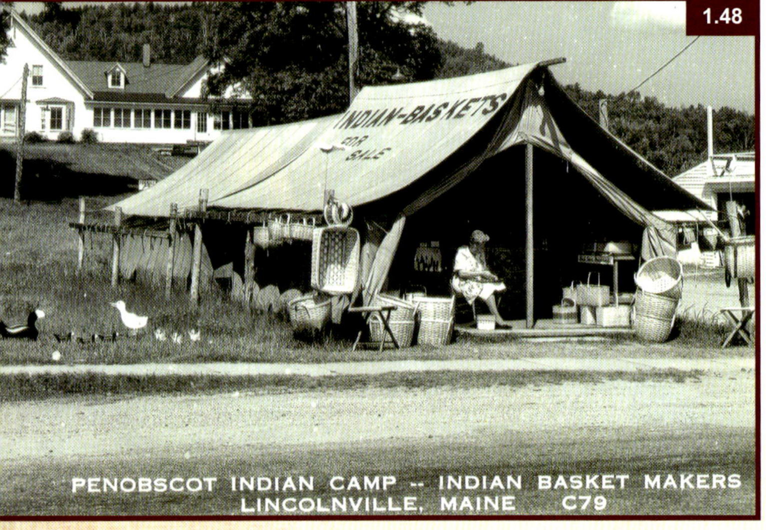

Although the Depression and war years saw interest greatly diminish, the popularity of these Indian curios has never abated completely. Northeastern Native basketmakers plied their craft throughout the 20th century, and some continue to produce similar basketry products even now.

For their part, the more useful Indian-made work or utility baskets also held on to their specialized markets well into the mid-20th century in the Northeast. Until mechanized harvesters finally eliminated demand for them, countless Micmac splint baskets dotted the potato fields of northern Maine, just as they had serviced the apple orchards of Prince Edward Island before cardboard boxes replaced them there, and the Down East fishing piers until plastic pails appeared.[33] A few of these sturdy splint baskets have continued to find their way out to a small and widely scattered clientele through L.L. Bean's famous catalog and other comparable outlets.

1.47. The mail-order Indian basket business continued into the 1970s, when The Indian Store in Searsport, Maine, sent this flyer to prospective customers. String tags attached to baskets from this era authenticated the items as Indian-made and sometimes identified the artists and materials.

1.48. A few roadside Indian basket stands like this one along the upper Penobscot River reappeared annually during summer tourist seasons right through the mid-20th century.

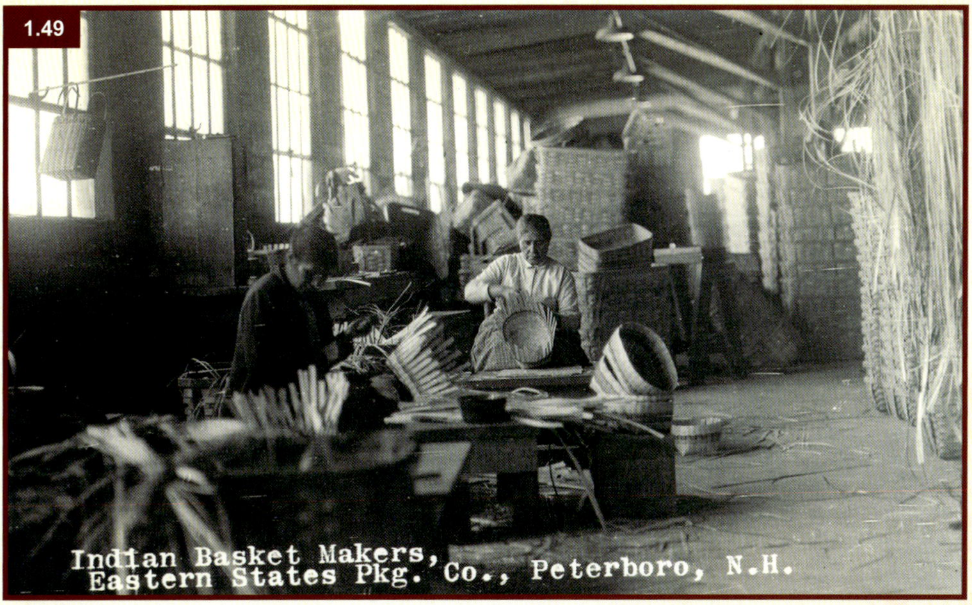

1.49. During the 20th century a few Native basketmakers earned a living from their craft as employees in commercial operations like the Eastern States Packaging Company. The modern Peterboro Basket Company traces its beginnings back to 1854 in this same southern New Hampshire town.

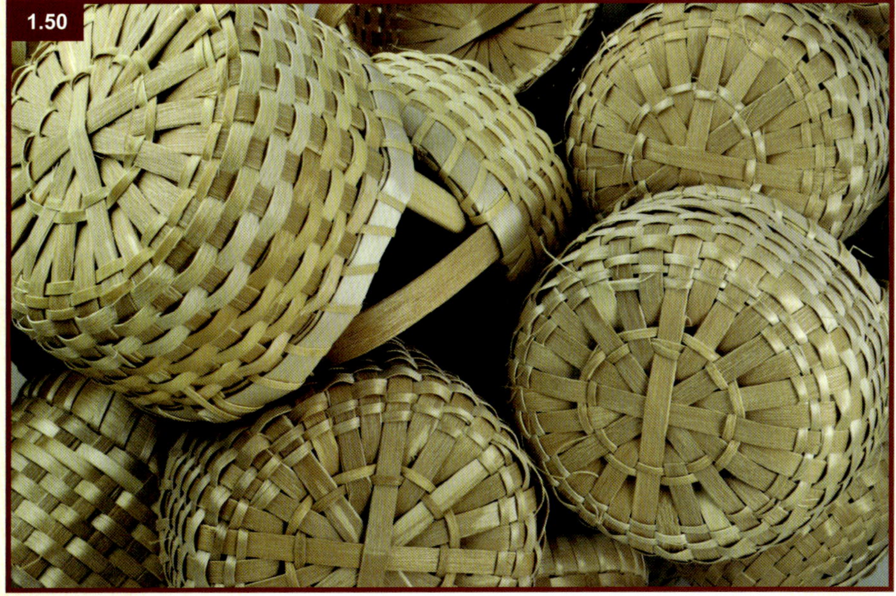

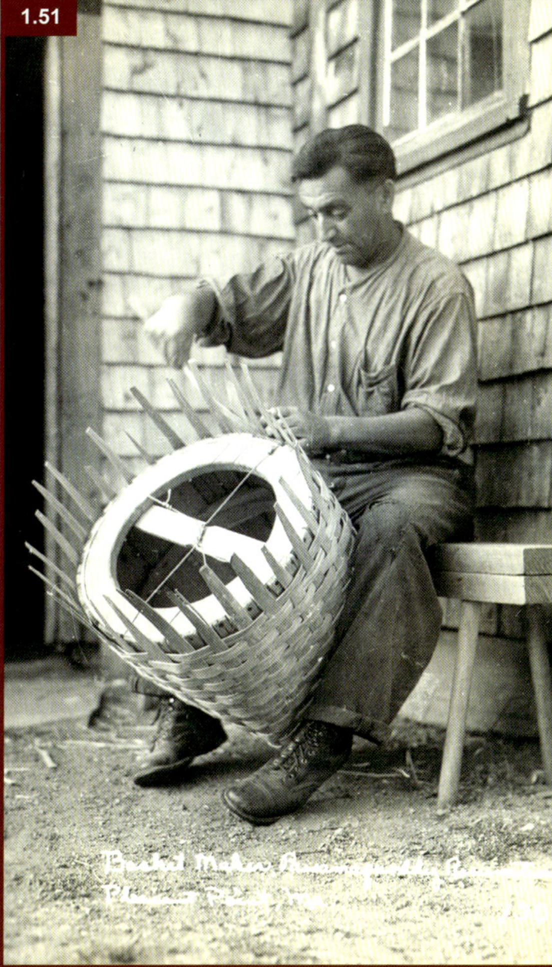

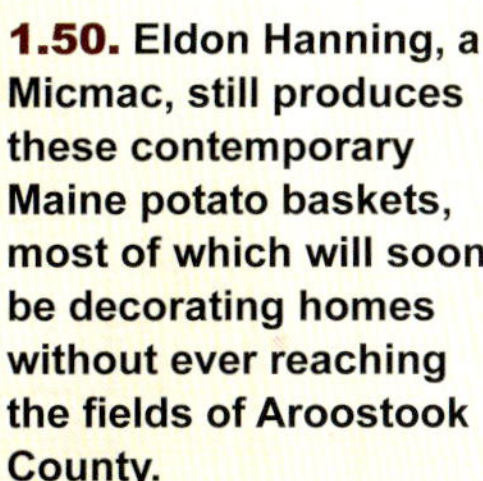

1.50. Eldon Hanning, a Micmac, still produces these contemporary Maine potato baskets, most of which will soon be decorating homes without ever reaching the fields of Aroostook County.

1.51. A Passamaquoddy basketmaker, identified as Peter Stanley, nears completion of a large work basket he has constructed around a wooden form, mid-20th century, Pleasant Point, Maine.

Most of the seasonal roadside camps set up at the tourist resorts closed forever, along with the grand hotels, during the sad years of the Great Depression. But after World War II, a few modern tourist shops and art galleries sited along northern New England's coastal thoroughfares once more catered to an increased flow of vacationers. And many of those travelers were looking for special souvenirs to take home from their trip. Colorful Indian baskets helped meet that need.

For several decades, popular tourist attractions like Chief Poolaw's Tepee at Old Town and Leslie and Christina Francis' Indian Store in Searsport, Maine, provided regional craftspersons with reliable access to the traveling public. Then, completion of Interstate 95 through Maine routed traffic away from these

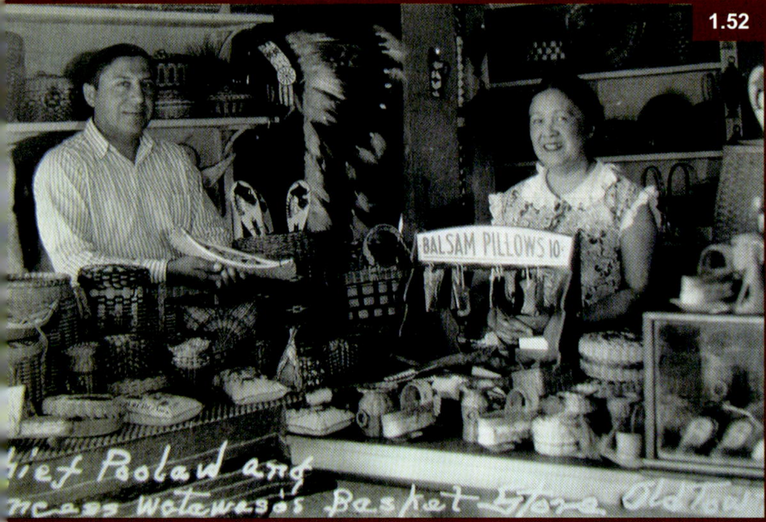

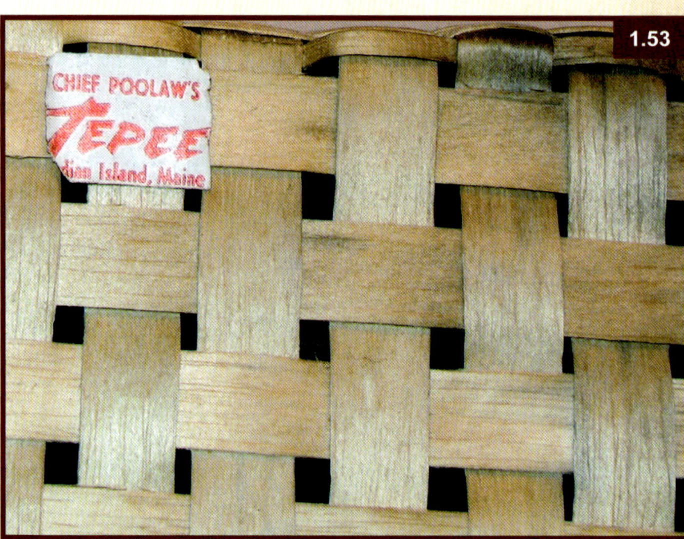

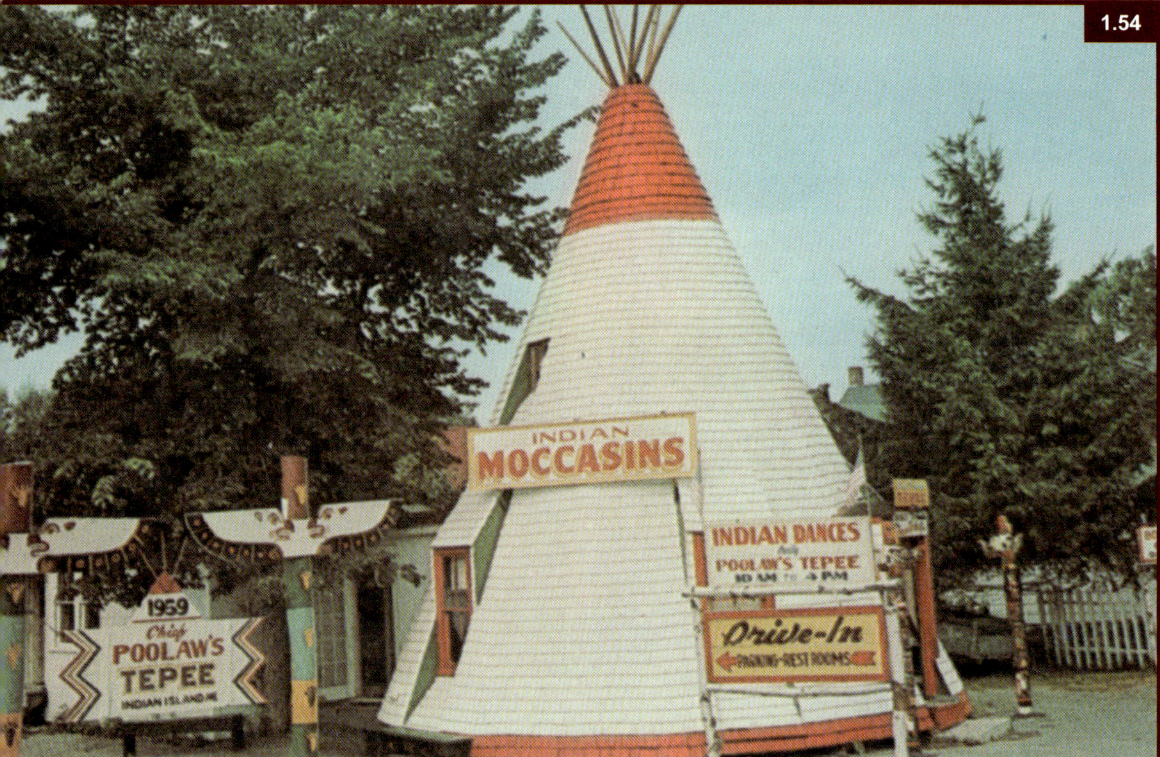

1.52. "Chief" Bruce Poolaw (a Kiowa from Oklahoma) and his wife "Princess Watawaso" (a Wabanaki born Lucy Nicolar) operated a popular tourist attraction on Indian Island, Maine, in the mid-20th century.

1.53. A splint basket base retains its original paper label.

1.54. Poolaw's signature Plains-style "tepee" building drew tourists inside to find a full range of Northeastern Indian basketry.

locations by the 1970s. As business declined, so once again did the ranks of the basketmakers.

Today, as it has since 1993, the Maine Indian Basketmakers' Alliance (MIBA) does much to nurture the craft and enlist new makers. Centered at Old Town, the Native artisans' cooperative actively supports and promotes both customary and innovative basketwork in the 21st century. A number of individual basketmakers affiliated with MIBA are winning national recognition and commanding high prices for their work. Unfortunately, the group's handsome retail outlet became victim to another economic downturn and tourism decline when it closed in late 2008.

The modern basketmakers face other new challenges, as well, including the recent arrival of the destructive emerald ash-borer beetle in the region and reduced access to

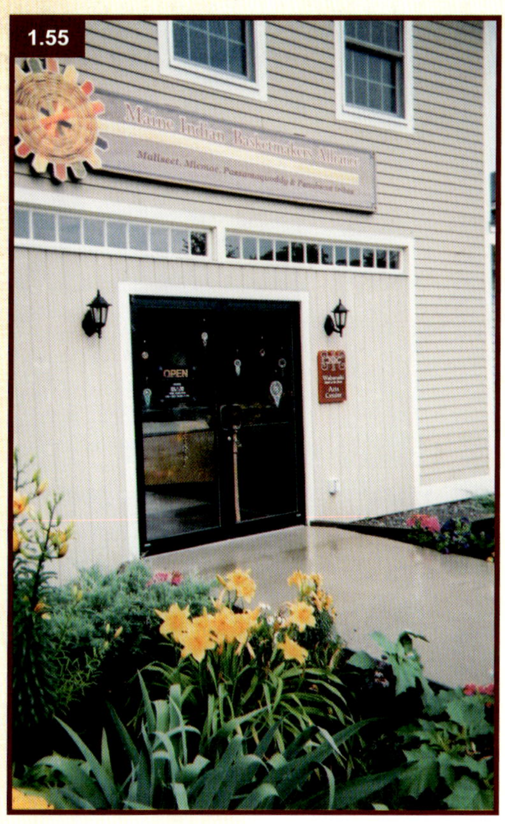

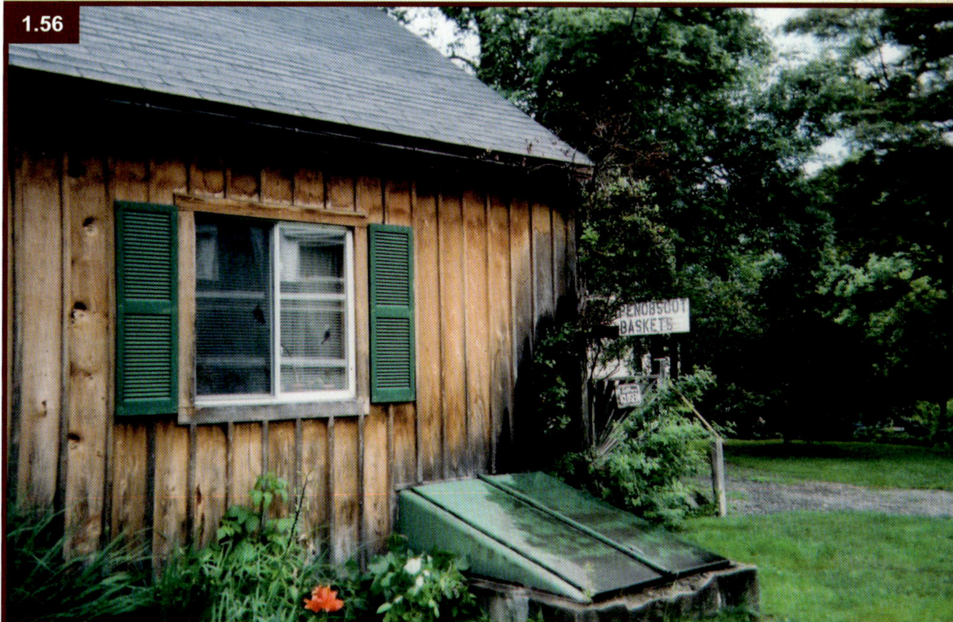

sweetgrass resources due to coastal development. Still, MIBA continues its mission through active workshops and regular public exhibitions, many held in association with the University of Maine's Hudson Museum.

1.55. The Maine Indian Basketmakers Alliance (MIBA) operated this gallery at Old Town, Maine, for several years before an economic downturn forced its closure in 2008.

1.56. Some Northeastern Indian basketmakers continue to craft and sell baskets through a variety of venues, including their private homes.

COLLECTING NORTHEASTERN INDIAN BASKETS TODAY

Some of the oldest Indian baskets in today's market originated in the Northeast two centuries ago or even earlier. Still, vintage Native baskets from this region remain among the most readily available and inexpensive. As we have noted, typical early forms include sturdy "work baskets" and lidded storage containers that saw service at both Native and non-Native homes and farms in the 18th and 19th centuries. Subsequently, by the mid- to late 1800s, the development of a regional tourist industry opened a new market for a very different range of distinctive souvenir goods, including Indian sweetgrass and woodsplint "fancy baskets," as well as birchbark trinkets, beadwork, and other curios.

> BASKETS HOLD OUR COMMUNITIES TOGETHER BY CONNECTING YOUNG TO OLD, AND WEAVERS TO APPRENTICES, ASH POUNDERS, BLOCK AND GAUGE MAKERS, SWEETGRASS GATHERERS AND BRAIDERS, AND OTHER WEAVERS AND FRIENDS IN OUR OWN TRIBES AND BEYOND. MORE THAN A MEANS OF SURVIVAL, BASKETS CONTINUE TO BE AN INSEPARABLE PART OF THE CULTURE AND TRADITIONS OF THE WABANAKI.
>
> —*JENNIFER SAPIEL NEPTUNE, PENOBSCOT, 2008*[34]

Some basket collectors have tended to more often overlook and less fully appreciate these kinds of products as they seek out more showy Apache trays or bright Hupa caps. Possibly they consider the highly-touted basketry of western tribes to be more "authentic" than the so-called "degenerate" products of Indian handiwork from the Northeast, where the Native basketry craft has for so long accommodated itself to Yankee practicality and varied marketing opportunities.

Many of these seemingly more humble baskets are of equal or greater vintage than their western counterparts. Furthermore, they document a significant chapter in Native American history. Sometimes unrecognized and often undervalued, they remain routine

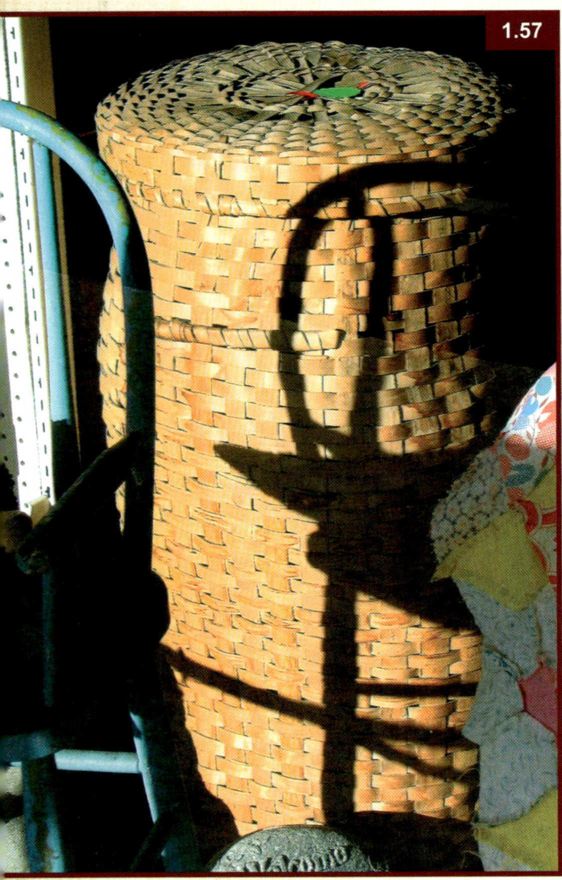

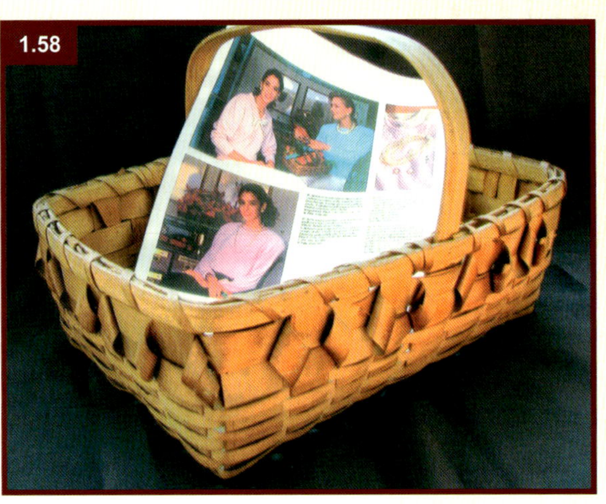

1.57. Older Indian baskets from the Northeast can sometimes be discovered "hidden in plain sight," especially in regions of the country where they are less common.

1.58. This vintage splint market basket enjoyed some attention when it was plucked from a collection and used as a prop in a 1989 Talbot's clothing catalog.

finds at yard sales, flea markets, and antique shops in many areas of the country.

Today, the contemporary basketry being created by an enduring people continues the region's Native basketmaking tradition into the current century. These "millennial baskets" afford new and exciting collecting opportunities for those who appreciate Northeastern Indian basketry.

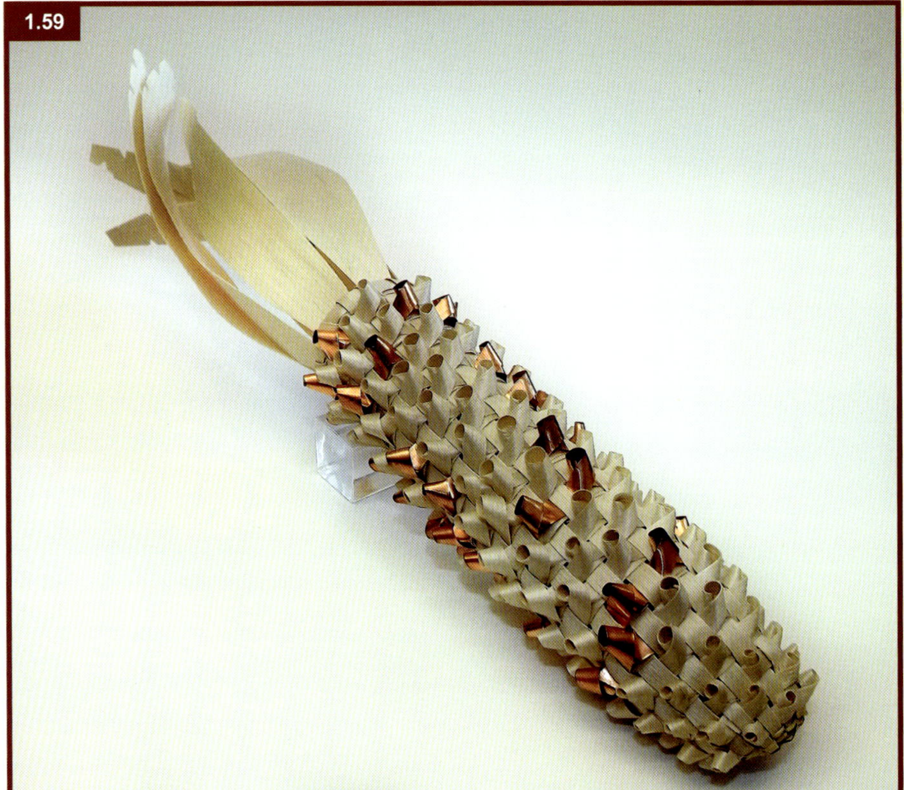

1.59. Kelly Church, a modern award-winning fifth-generation basketmaker of combined Irish-English and Ottawa-Ojibwe descent, has mixed ash splints and copper strips in her basketry interpretation of a bi-colored ear of maize, or "Indian corn."

CHAPTER ENDNOTES

1. Wood, William. 1977. *New England's Prospect* [1634], p. 114. Amherst, MA: University of Massachusetts Press.
2. Gookin, Daniel. 1970. *Historical Collections of the Indians in New England* [1674], p. 16. Boston, MA: Towtaid.
3. Adovasio, James M., Olga Soffer, and Bohuslav Kléma. 1996. "Upper Paleolithic Fibre Technology: Interlaced Woven Finds from Pavlov I, Czech Republic, c. 26,000 Years Ago." *Antiquity* 70: 526-534. Durham, UK: Department of Archaeology, University of Durham.
4. Petersen, James B., and Nathan D. Hamilton. 1984. "Early Woodland Ceramic and Perishable Fiber Industries from the Northeast: A Summary and Interpretation." *Annals of Carnegie Museum* 53: 413-445. Pittsburgh, PA: Carnegie Museum of Natural History.
5. Gookin 1970, p. 16.
6. Verrazzano, Giovanni da. 1524. *Letter to King Francis I of France, 8 July 1524.* In, Susan Tarrow (trans.), "Giovanni da Verrazzano Letter to King Francis I of France 8 July 1524 reporting on his voyage to the New World," p. 8. National Humanities Center. <http://nationalhumanitiescenter.org/pds/amerbegin/contact/text4>.
7. Heath, Dwight B. (ed.). 1963. *Mourt's Relation, a Journal of the Pilgrims at Plymouth* [1622], pp. 28-29. Bedford, MA: Applewood Books.
8. Williams, Roger. 1936. *A Key into the Language of America* [1643], pp. 36-37. Providence, RI: The Rhode Island and Providence Plantations Tercentenary Committee.
9. Gookin 1970, p. 16.
10. Catalog entry for c. 1675 Algonquian twined bag, 1842.2.1, Rhode Island Historical Society, Providence, RI. Quoted in Sarah Peabody Turnbaugh and William A. Turnbaugh, 1986, *Indian Baskets*, p. 121. Atglen, PA: Schiffer Publishing.
11. Leland, Charles G. 1884. *The Algonquin Legends of New England*, pp. 18-19. Boston, MA: Houghton Mifflin.
12. From 1712 journal entry of Swedish traveler Andreas Hesselius. Quoted in Ted J. Brasser, 1975, "A Basketful of Indian Culture Change," *National Museum of Man Mercury Series, Canadian Ethnology Service Paper* 22, p. 8. Ottawa, ON: National Museums of Canada.
13. See Reverend John Eliot's September 24, 1647, letter to "T.S." Quoted in "Tracts Relating to the Attempts to Convert to Christianity the Indians of New England," *Collections of the Massachusetts Historical Society*, ser. 3, vol. 4, p. 59. Boston, MA: Massachusetts Historical Society. See also the February 1652 letter from Lion Gardiner to John Winthrop, Jr., quoted in "The Winthrop Papers (Continued)," *Collections of the Massachusetts Historical Society*, ser. 4, vol. 7, p. 63. Boston, MA: Massachusetts Historical Society.
14. Brasser, Ted J. 1975. "A Basketful of Indian Culture Change." *National Museum of Man Mercury Series, Canadian Ethnology Service Paper* 22, p. 8. Ottawa, ON: National Museums of Canada.
15. Neptune, Jennifer Sapiel. 2008. *Spirit of the Basket Tree: Wabanaki Ash Splint Baskets from Maine.* Hanover, NH: Hood Museum of Art, Dartmouth College. See also Kathryn Bardwell, 1986, "The Case for an Aboriginal Origin of Northeast Indian Woodsplint Basketry," *Man in the Northeast* 31, pp. 49-67. Rindge, NH.
16. Handsman, Russell G., and Ann McMullen. 1978. "An Introduction to Woodsplint Basketry and Its Interpretation." In, Ann McMullen and Russell G. Handsman (eds.), *A Key Into the Language of Woodsplint Baskets*, pp. 16-35. Washington, CT: American Indian Archaeological Institute. See also Charles F. Wray, 1973, *Manual for Seneca Iroquois Archeology*, p. 24 and slides 1.6, 1.7. Rochester, NY: Cultures Primitive, Inc.

17. Simmons, William S. 1970. *Cautantowwit's House: An Indian Burial Ground on the Island of Conanicut in Narragansett Bay*, p. 109, fig. 74c, d. Providence, RI: Brown University Press.

18. DeBlois, Albert D. 1990. "Micmac Texts." *National Museum of Man Mercury Series, Canadian Ethnology Service Paper* 117, p. 49. Ottawa, ON: National Museums of Canada.

19. Prime, Nathaniel S. 1845. "A History of Long Island, New York." Quoted in Eva L. Butler, 1947, "Some Early Indian Basket Makers of Southern New England," p. 53. In, Frank G. Speck, *Eastern Algonkian Block-Stamp Decoration*, Addendum, pp. 35-54. Trenton, NJ: Archaeological Society of New Jersey.

20. Uniacke, Rev. R. J. 1958. *Sketches of Cape Breton and other Papers relating to Cape Breton Island* [1865], p. 108. Halifax, NS: Public Archives of Nova Scotia.

21. Avery, John L. 1901. "History of the Town of Ledyard, Connecticut." Quoted in Eva L. Butler, 1947, "Some Early Indian Basket Makers of Southern New England," p. 40. In, Frank G. Speck, *Eastern Algonkian Block-Stamp Decoration*, Addendum, pp. 35-54. Trenton, NJ: Archaeological Society of New Jersey.

22. Orcutt, Samuel, and Ambrose Beardsley. 1880. "History of Derby, Connecticut, 1642-1880." Quoted in Eva L. Butler, 1947, "Some Early Indian Basket Makers of Southern New England," pp. 48, 50. In, Frank G. Speck, *Eastern Algonkian Block-Stamp Decoration*, Addendum, pp. 35-54. Trenton, NJ: Archaeological Society of New Jersey.

23. Sidney Gage & Company. 1895. *Baskets* (catalog). Bellows Falls, VT: Privately published.

24. O'Brien, Gary. 1981. "The 19th-Century Basketmaker and His Trade." *Old Sturbridge Village Documents*. <http://resources.osv.org/explore_learn/document_viewer.php?DocID=1000>.

25. Sayres, William C. (ed.). 1956. *Sammy Louis: The Life History of a Young Micmac*, p. 7. New Haven, CT: Compass Publishing.

26. Phillips, Ruth B. 1998. *Trading Identities: The Souvenir in Native North American Art from the Northeast, 1700-1900*. Seattle, WA: University of Washington Press. See also Gerry Biron, 2006, *Made of Thunder, Made of Glass: American Indian Beadwork of the Northeast*, pp. 8-12. Saxtons River, VT: Author.

27. Phillips 1998.

28. Neptune 2008, p. 8.

29. Turnbaugh, William A., and Sarah Peabody Turnbaugh. 2013. *American Indian Baskets: Building and Caring for a Collection*, pp. 33-41. Atglen, PA: Schiffer Publishing.

30. McBride, Bunny. 1990. *Our Lives in Our Hands: Micmac Indian Basketmakers*, p. 18. Gardiner, ME: Tilbury House.

31. Strough, Arthur R. 1902. "The St. Lawrence Reservation or International Park." In, State of New York, *Seventh Report of the Forest, Fish, and Game Commission of the State of New York*, pp. 71-86. Albany, NY: J. B. Lyon.

32. Pelletier, Gaby. 1982. "Abenaki Basketry." *National Museum of Man Mercury Series, Canadian Ethnology Service Paper* 85. Ottawa, ON: National Museums of Canada.

33. Gordon, Jolene. 1990. "Micmac Indian Basketry," p. 36. In, Frank W. Porter, III (ed.), *The Art of Native American Basketry: A Living Legacy*, pp. 17-43. Westport, CT: Greenwood Press.

34. Neptune 2008, p. 11.

FOCUS:

Birchbark "Baskets"

Collectors and museum curators routinely count Northeastern birchbark vessels among the "baskets" in their collections. In many Native cultures across the more northerly expanses of the Northeastern Woodlands, folded and sewn bark containers have played more significant roles than have baskets. Simple bark forms have filled daily utility needs since archaeological times. Etched birchbark containers and porcupine quill- or moosehair-embellished items made in the post-contact era have enabled Native peoples to participate in a lucrative tourist market, easing their transition into a cash-based economy. Though bark containers are not truly "baskets" by definition, we include examples here.

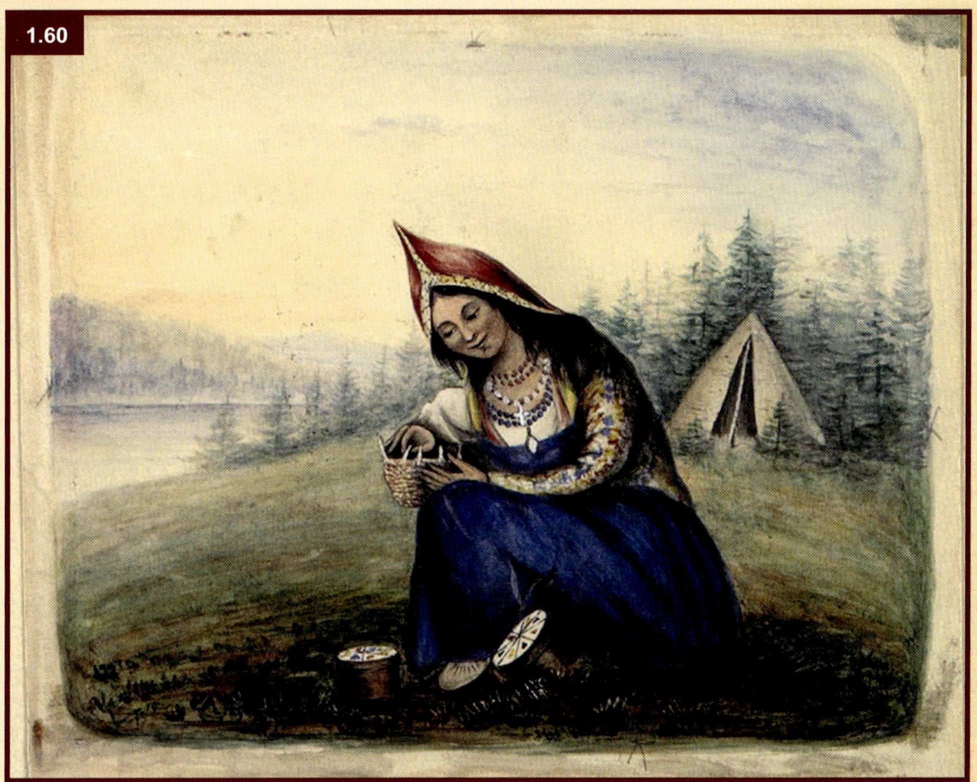

1.60. ***Mi'kmaq Woman Weaving Baskets [Nova Scotia]*****, c. 1845, watercolor by Mary R. McKie.**

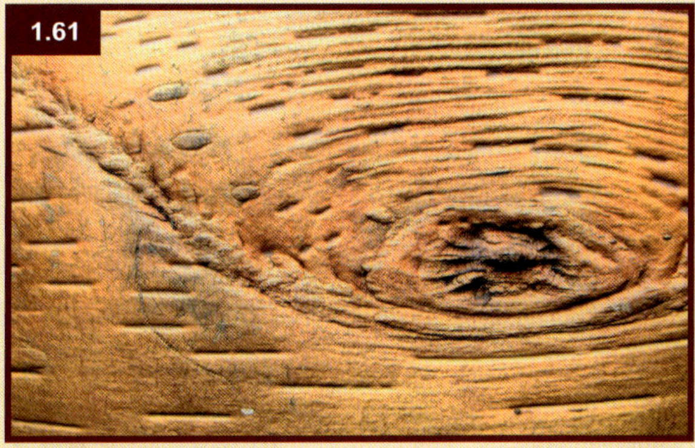

1.61. Close-up of prepared birchbark surface

FOCUS:

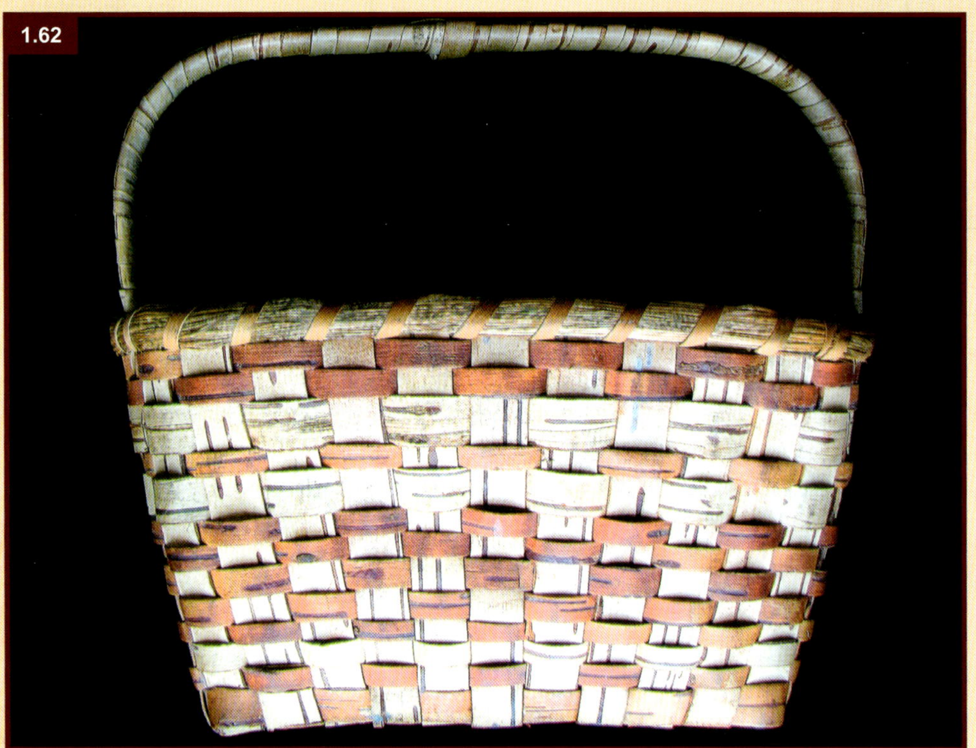

1.62. Plaited birchbark basket with sweetgrass edging, likely by Lola Sockabasin, Passamaquoddy, c. 1980s, 12" high. This recent birchbark container is unusual because it *is* a basket, having been plaited by substituting light and dark bark strips for more typical ash splints.

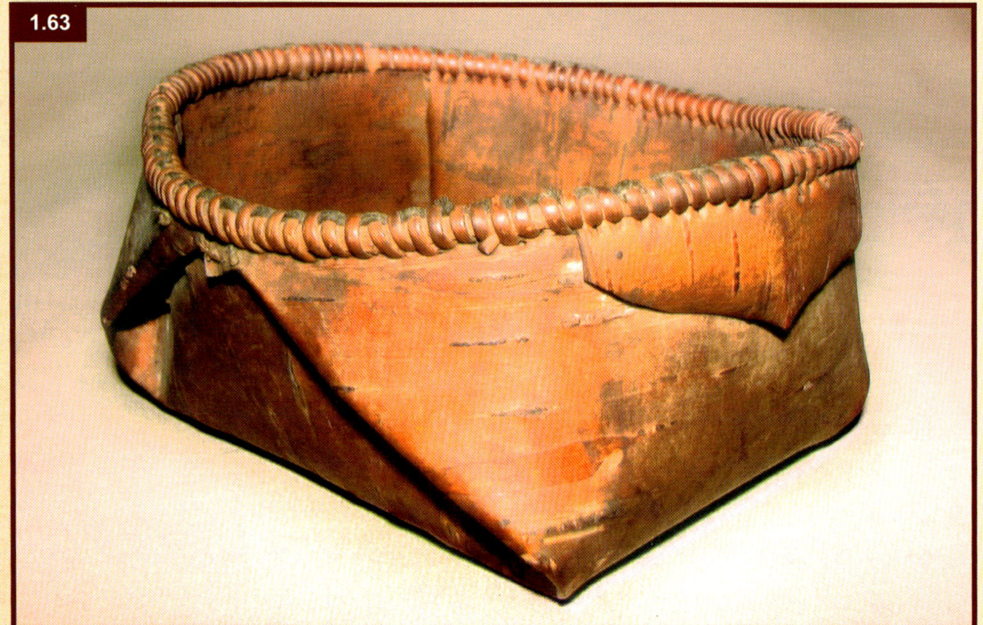

1.63. Folded and stitched birchbark vessels similar to this example have been made across the northern expanses of North America, including the northern portions of the Northeastern Woodlands, for generations, 6" diameter.

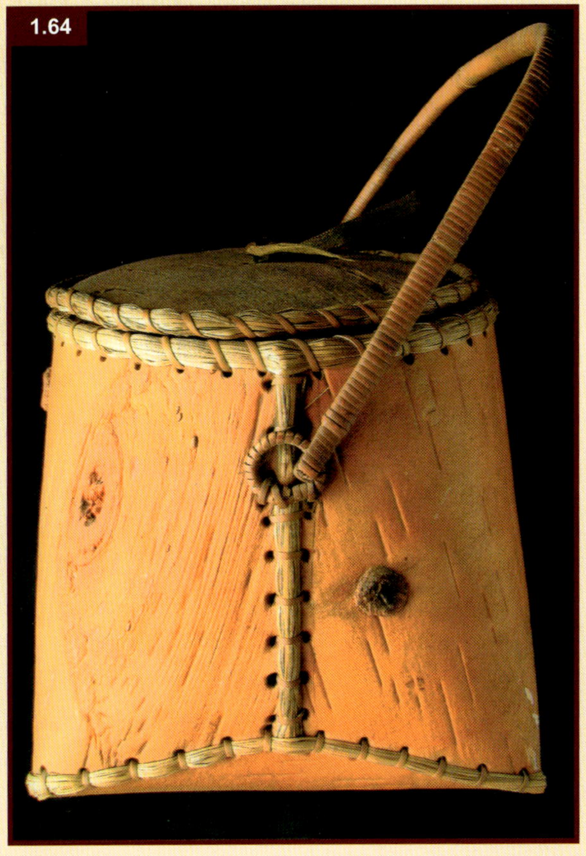

1.64. Small covered Northeastern birchbark *mokuk,* a folded and stitched container for gathering maple sap or berries or for storing maple sugar, has sweetgrass edging bound with spruce root lacing, c. 1880, 4.75" rim diameter.

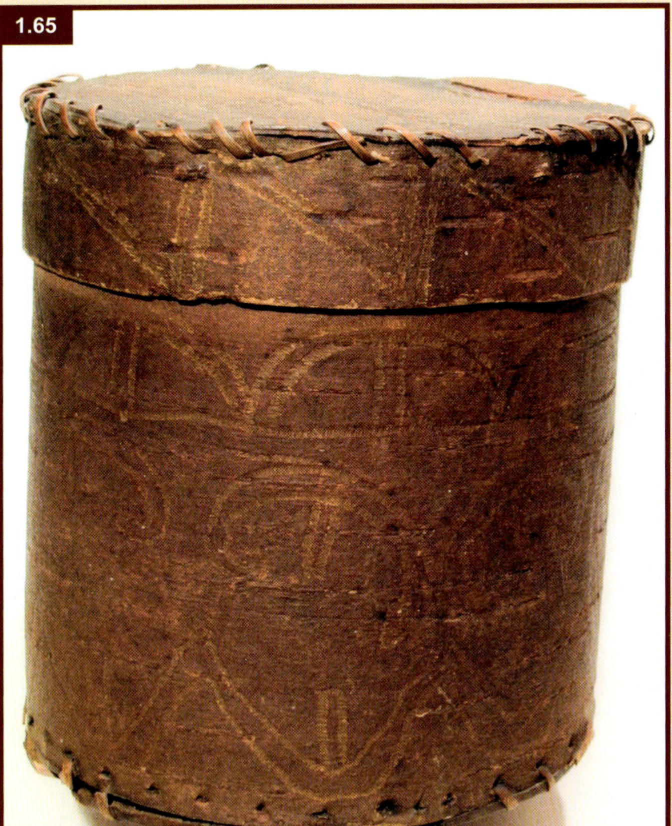

1.65. Birchbark box with negative-etched (light-on-dark) devices, northern Maine or Canadian Maritimes.

Focus:

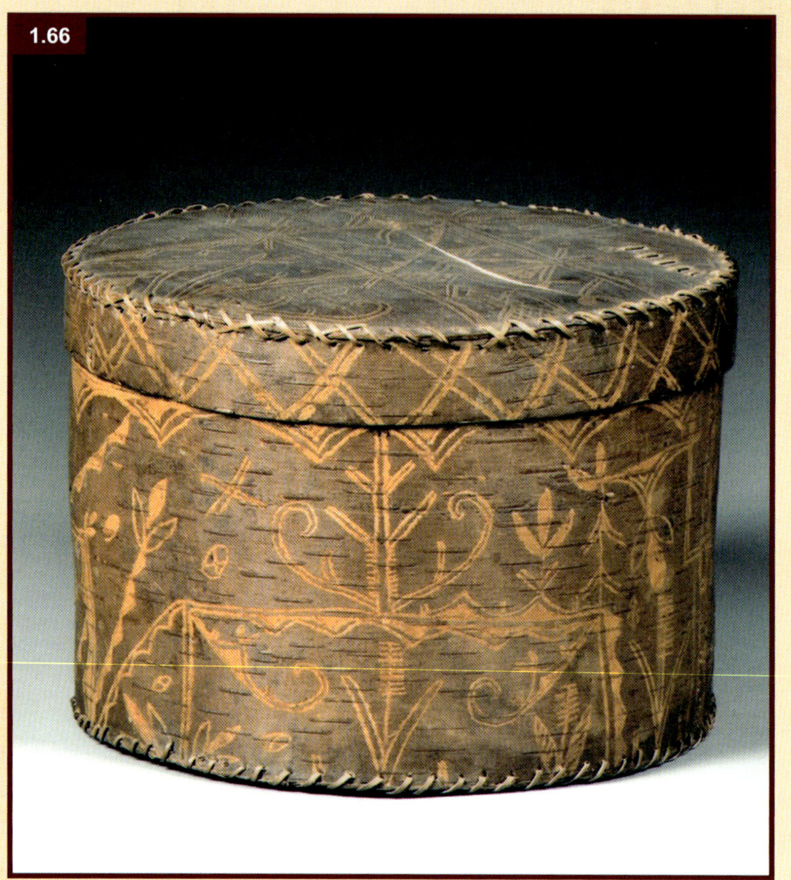

1.66. Penobscot birchbark box, negative-etched with traditional double-curve and foliate design elements, mid-1800s, 15.25" diameter.

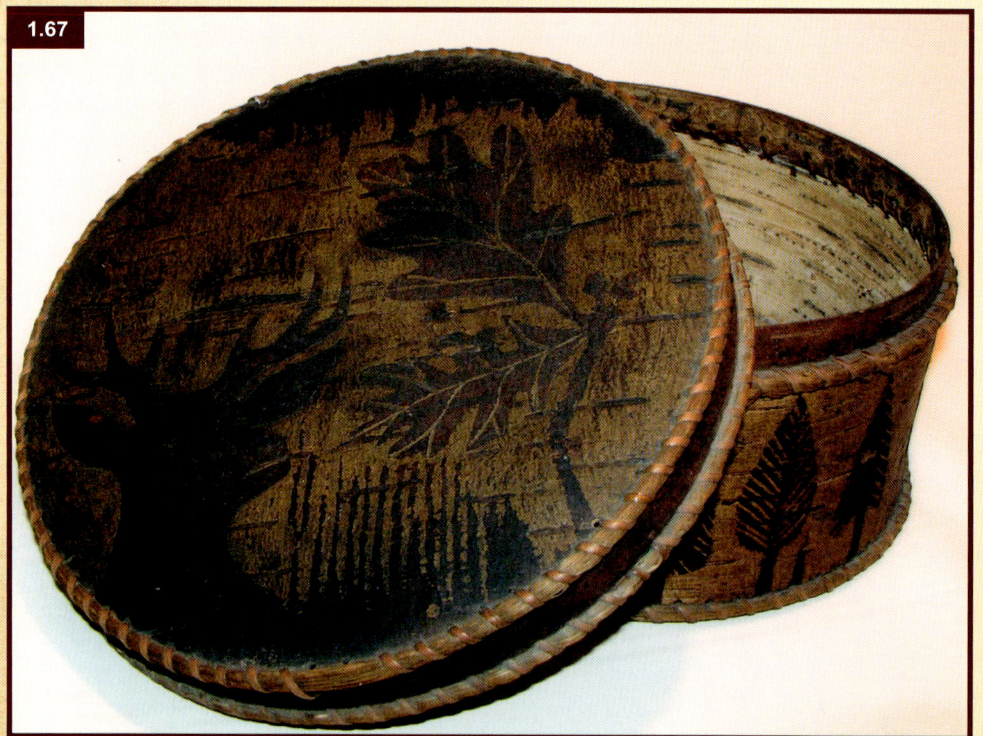

1.67. Covered birchbark box with positive (dark-on-light) etched representational design elements including a deer and oak leaves, likely Abenaki, c. 1910, 10" diameter.

1.68. Wastepaper basket of etched birchbark with picturesque motifs and the phrase "KOLELE MOOK" ("good luck"), worked by Sabattis Tomah, Passamaquoddy, of Peter Dana Point, Maine, 1933, 13.5" high.

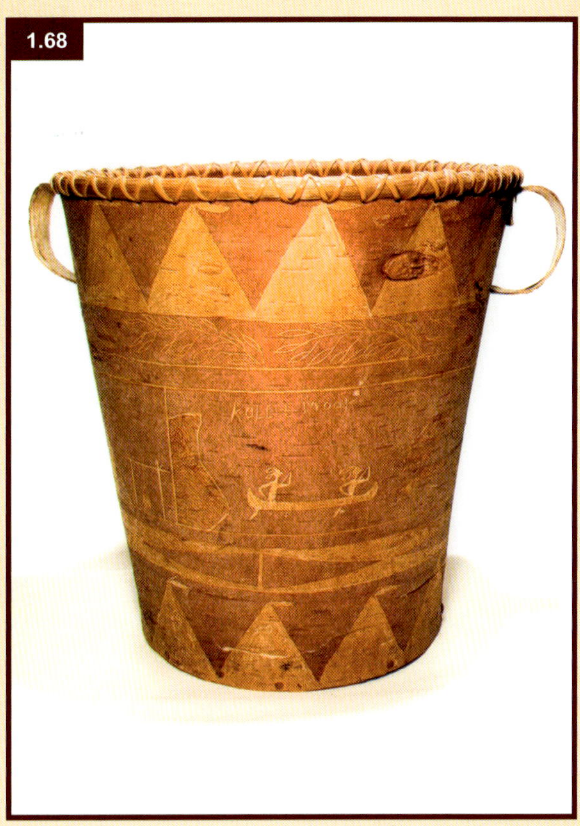

1.69. Birchbark *mokuk* with etched moose and floral devices intended to appeal to hunters and outdoorsmen, Cree, c. 1940s–1950s, about 9" wide.

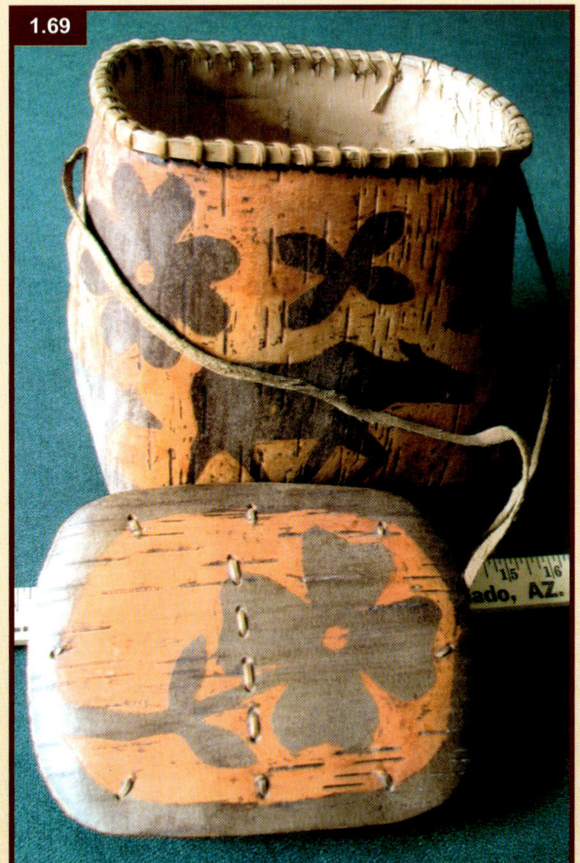

Focus:

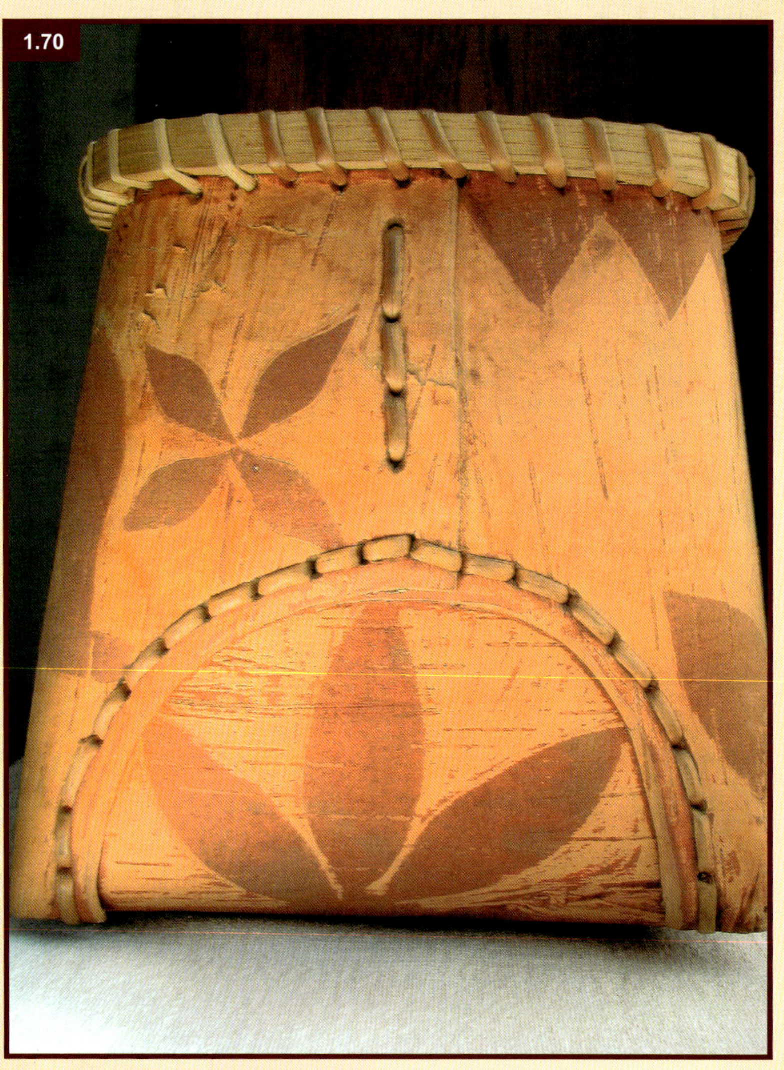

1.70. Detail of spruce root stitching on an etched birchbark *mokuk,* base signed "Max le Gros Huron," mid-1900s, about 5" high.

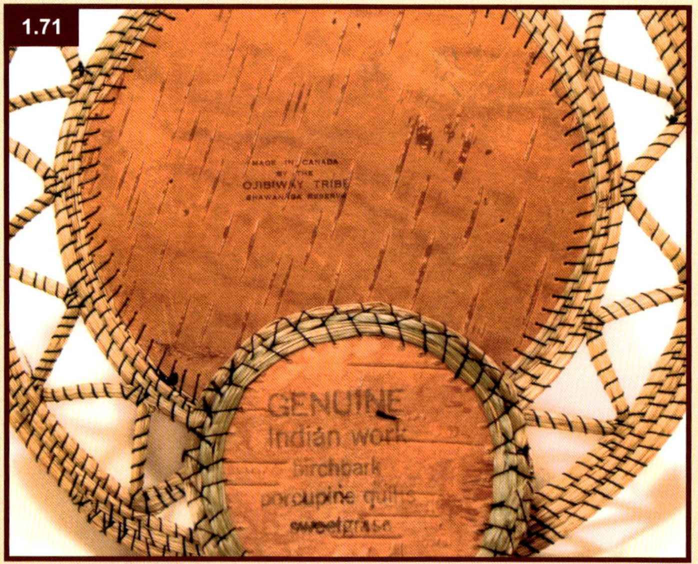

1.71. Birchbark novelties like these marked Ojibwe examples, often edged with sweetgrass and stitched with commercial black thread, sold readily in the Great Lakes region, mid-1900s.

Focus:

1.72. The practice of biting a paper-thin sheet of folded birchbark with one's incisors and canine teeth, then unfolding it to expose a symmetrical design, dates back to the 1600s or earlier. Among the Montagnais, the design sometimes became a pattern for silk embroidery or beadwork. Native peoples in the region's northern realms still create this art, Annabel Eyres, Canadian Cree, 1989, 5" by 7".

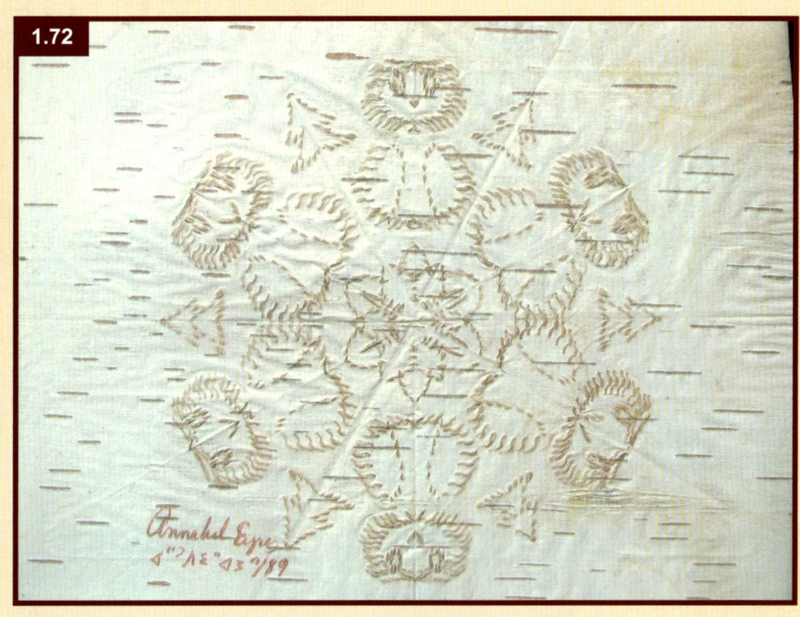

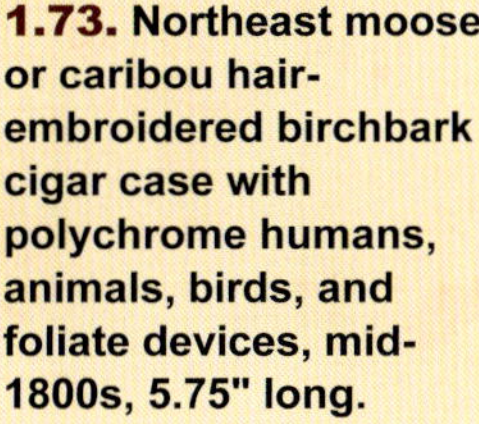

1.73. Northeast moose or caribou hair-embroidered birchbark cigar case with polychrome humans, animals, birds, and foliate devices, mid-1800s, 5.75" long.

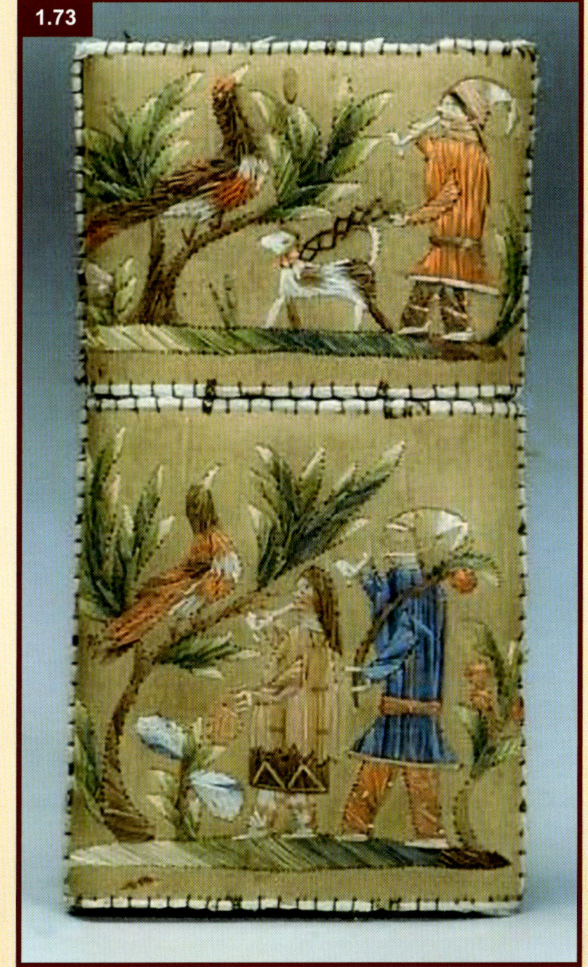

Focus:

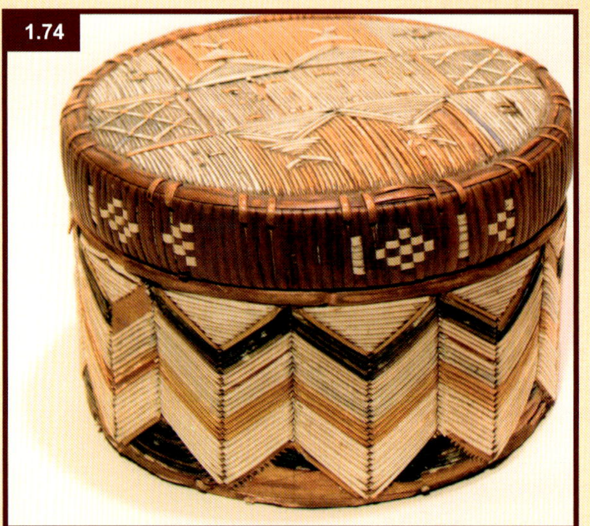

1.74. Round porcupine quill-decorated birchbark box, spruce root stitches and spruce root-wrapped lid ring with interwoven quills, quillwork body design of a fir tree-inspired chevron-zigzag element, Micmac, early to mid-1800s, 5" diameter.

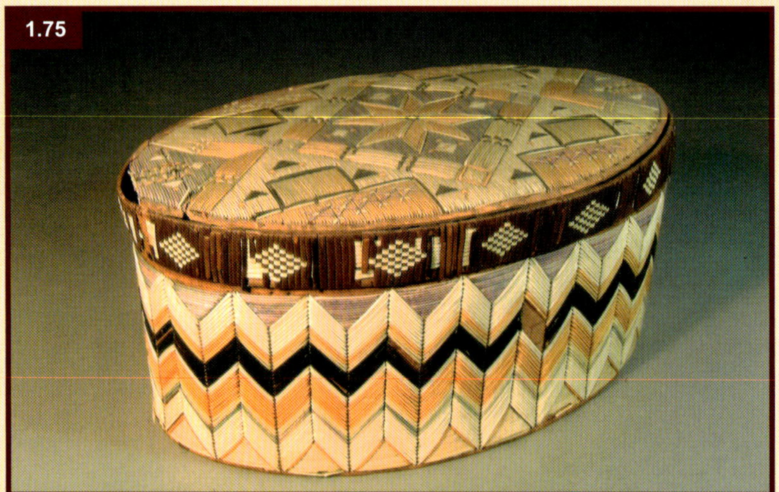

1.75. Oval birchbark box with cover, spruce root-wrapped lid ring with interwoven quills, quillwork body design of a chevron-zigzag element, and cover with a geometric pattern framing an eight-pointed star or sun, Micmac, c. 1850, 11" maximum diameter.

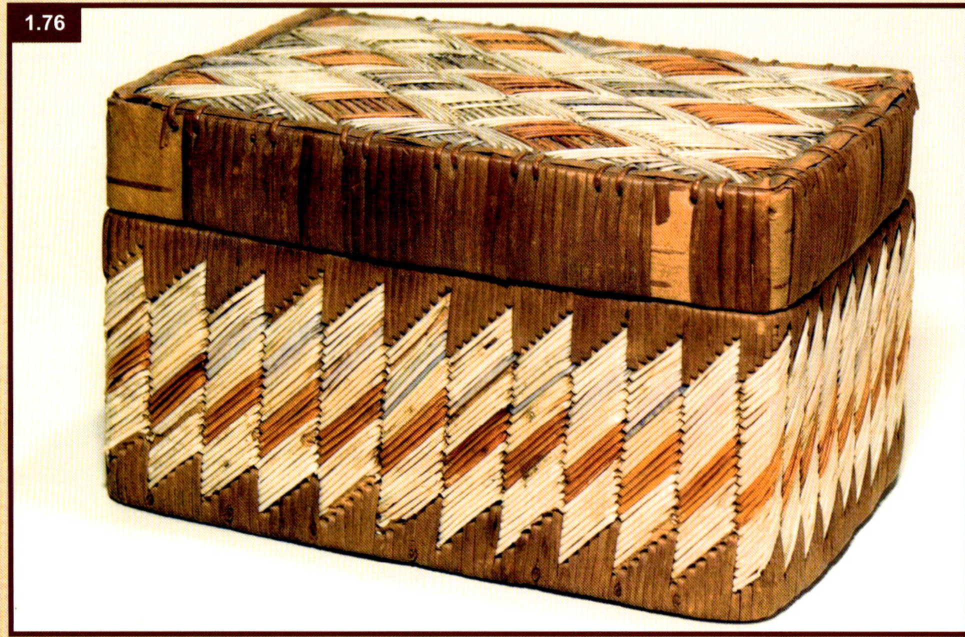

1.76. Rectangular porcupine quill-decorated birchbark box, spruce root stitches and spruce root-wrapped lid ring, half-chevron body pattern of quillwork, and repeating design on lid, Micmac, late 1800s, 6" long.

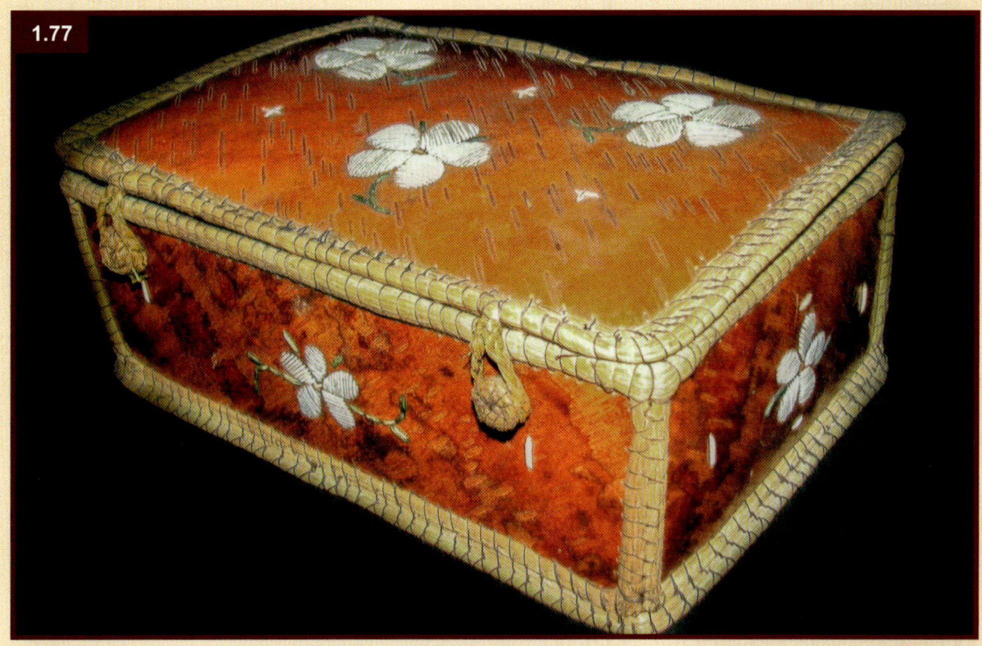

1.77. Covered rectangular birchbark box, with porcupine quill-embroidered floral elements plus sweetgrass closures and black thread-bound edging, a popular souvenir item in the Great Lakes region, 1930s–1940s, 9" long.

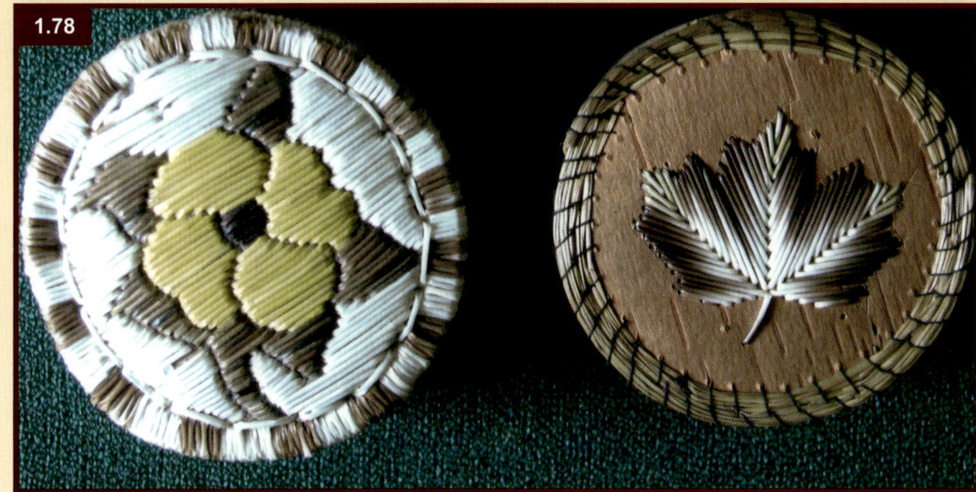

1.78. Small Great Lakes porcupine quill-decorated birchbark souvenirs: (left) covered box with all-over quillwork made by Yvonne Walker, Ottawa-Ojibwe, and (right) sweetgrass-edged box with central quilled maple leaf, Ojibwe, c. 1970, 3" diameter.

CHAPTER 2

RECOGNIZING NORTHEASTERN INDIAN BASKETS

Northeastern Indians have made baskets of many types. Twined bags, birchbark vessels, and the like have a long history in the region. But plaited woodsplint examples greatly outnumber other types of Native-made containers in most Northeastern Woodlands Indian collections today. These baskets are the primary focus of our attention in this volume.

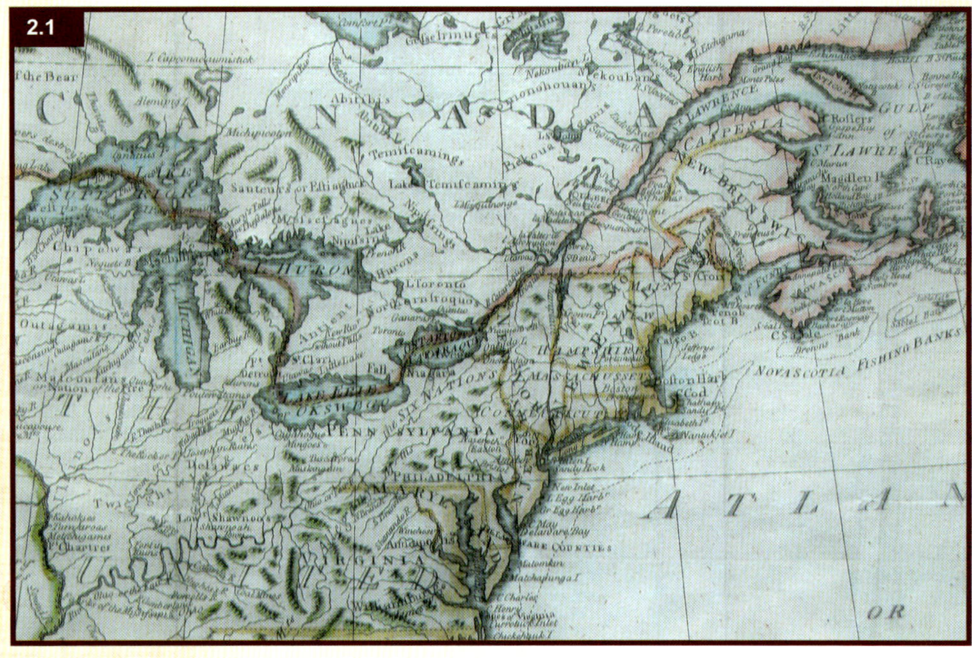

2.1. This detail from Thomas Bowen's 1784 map of northeastern North America at the end of the Revolutionary War shows eastern Canada and part of the newly formed United States.

Finding the "Indian" in Northeastern Baskets

To identify an otherwise undocumented woodsplint basket as a Northeastern American Indian basket, we have to start by determining that it is indeed Native-made, based on

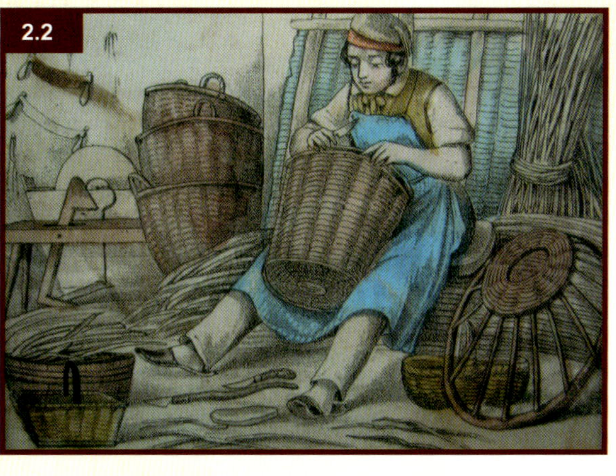

2.2. The European basket weaver in this mid-19th-century lithograph is using specialized tools and techniques to plait baskets that are sometimes confused with American Indian work.

its shape, construction, decoration, and materials. Only then may we try to attribute it to a certain region of the Northeast, or in rare cases perhaps even determine its particular tribal origin or individual maker.

This first step—confirming certain Northeast woodsplint baskets as Indian and distinguishing them from other Northeastern baskets made by non-Natives—is, quite frankly, not a simple task. After all, Euramericans too have shared in the long tradition of plaited woodsplint basketmaking. As we have seen, not everyone even agrees as to how splint basketmaking originated in the region. Nevertheless, large numbers of these Northeastern baskets are indeed Native-made, and the majority can be recognized and attributed as such.

For more than several centuries, various cultural factors have contributed to the blurring of woodsplint basket styles in the Northeast. Between 1620 and the late 1700s—from the time of European colonization to the decades following the Revolutionary War—almost two centuries of exposure to and interaction with immigrants and settlers and their associated diseases, settlements, and wars severely impacted indigenous Northeastern populations. By the late 1700s, with their tribal lands gone and their communities disrupted, Native families were fragmented and had been greatly reduced in number. Those still remaining had to adapt to survive.

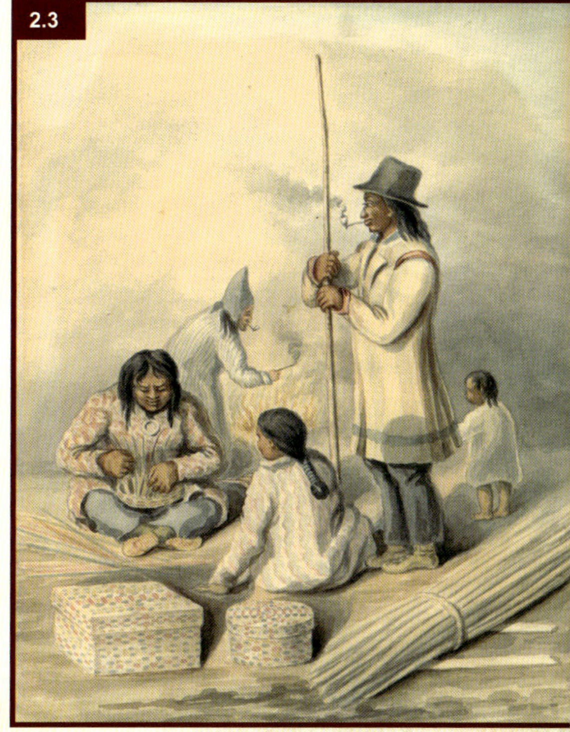

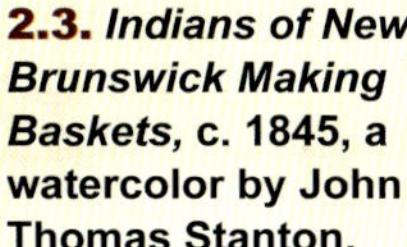

2.3. ***Indians of New Brunswick Making Baskets*****, c. 1845, a watercolor by John Thomas Stanton.**

With varying degrees of success, some Northeastern Indians assimilated into the newcomers' expanding communities through menial employment opportunities or other limited avenues, while quietly retaining many of their Native traditions. More often, remnant Native groups consisting of itinerant or unaffiliated individuals and families clustered at or beyond the edges of these newer settlements. As marginal as they were, these American Indian peoples were inevitably drawn into the new order's cash-based economy by the need to buy even the most basic necessities, like food and clothing. Some resorted to weaving baskets, mats, and related crafts, such as broom-making and chair-caning, for their non-Indian neighbors. Applying their Native skills to local natural and traded or commercial materials, they generated a modest but essential income.

Northeastern Indians from several displaced tribes also gathered into newly established reservations and "praying town" communities of Native converts to Christianity, like the Indian villages of Natick and Hassanamesit (later Grafton), Massachusetts. Similar communities were located elsewhere in central and western Massachusetts, New York state, and even further afield. Although the praying towns and reservation communities

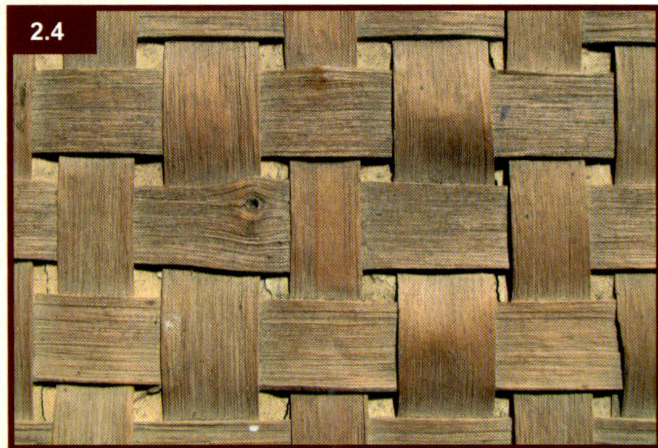

2.4. Plain plaiting

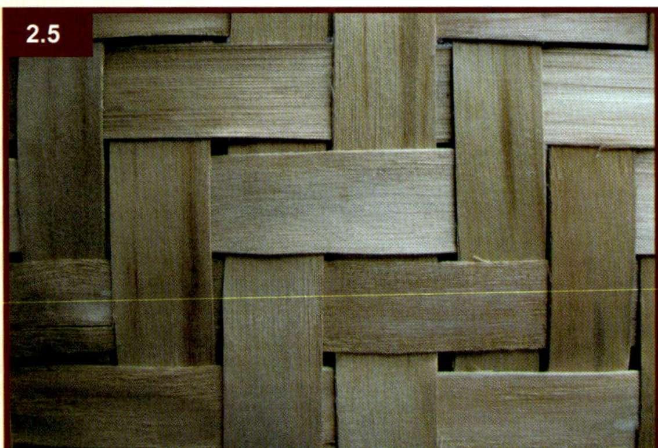

2.5. Twill plaiting

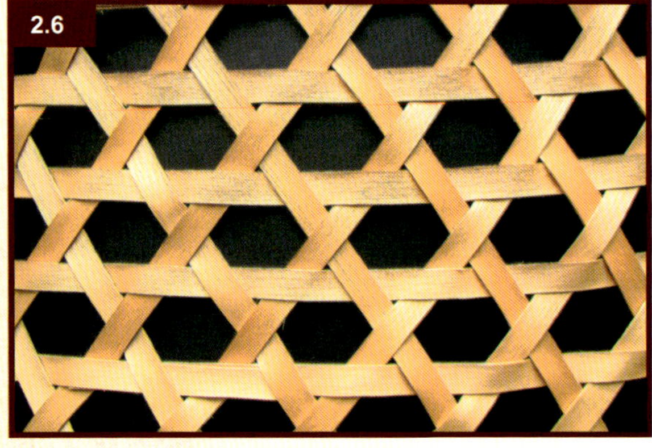

2.6. Hexagonal plaiting or "hex weave"

had defined boundaries, the populations that inhabited them tended to be more fluid. Individuals often came and went, traveling widely to visit kin and conduct business. Their social interactions, including intermarriages and itinerant Native missionary work, helped to disperse local customs and family news throughout the region.

One result was that a kaleidoscopic variety of widely shared basketmaking details drawn from different Northeastern cultural sources have contributed to the region's basketry heritage. Weaving techniques and decoration, as well as basketry forms and materials, became blended, resulting in any number of combinations.

At the outset we should state that, for these reasons, our ability to isolate a particular regional style, let alone a specific tribal style, from the mosaic of overlapping and intermixed basketmaking preferences, and to trace its likely origin, is limited. Further, determining the individual maker of a basket on the primary basis of its appearance is nearly impossible until at least the late 19th or early 20th century. After that time Native oral histories and specific family connections may offer some clues. Almost all Native Northeastern baskets made prior to the late 20th century are unsigned, and relatively few have been signed even in recent decades.

The earliest Northeastern Indian plaited woodsplint baskets found in collections today date from around 1780 to 1820, and they are quite scarce. Those baskets that can be confidently placed in this early period, on the basis of a combination of documentation, specific technical details, decoration, and materials, are mostly practical forms like covered storage baskets commonly used for holding clothing, bonnets, hats, or sundries. They also include a smaller number of market or gathering baskets with carved hardwood handles. These useful older basket forms tended to have been resistant to change, sometimes over more than a century. So, dating them with any precision can be a challenge without more direct corroborating evidence.

Northeastern Indian woodsplint baskets—especially when undecorated—may be virtually indistinguishable from similar products made by neighboring non-Indian people. For instance, the Shaker religious communities of New York state and New

2.7–2.11. Examples of early woodsplint baskets include: **(2.7)** a probable Wampanoag covered storage basket, c. 1820; **(2.8)** a covered storage basket made by Jacob Mauwee, Schaghticoke, c. 1815; **(2.9)** an eastern Connecticut (Mohegan or Pequot) work basket, 1810-1830; **(2.10)** a Mohegan or Pequot carrying basket, 1800-1810; and **(2.11)** an eastern Connecticut work basket, 1830.

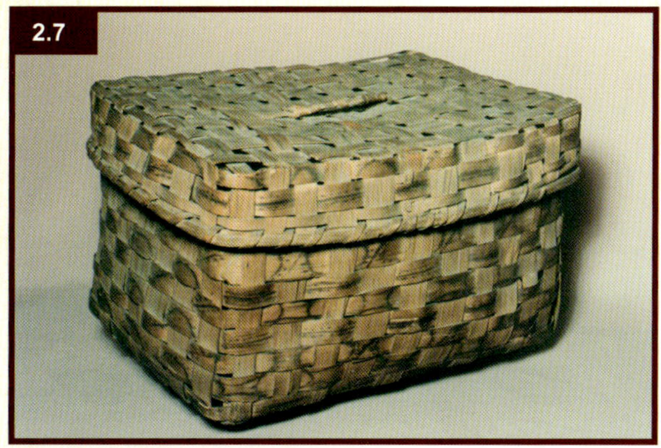
2.7

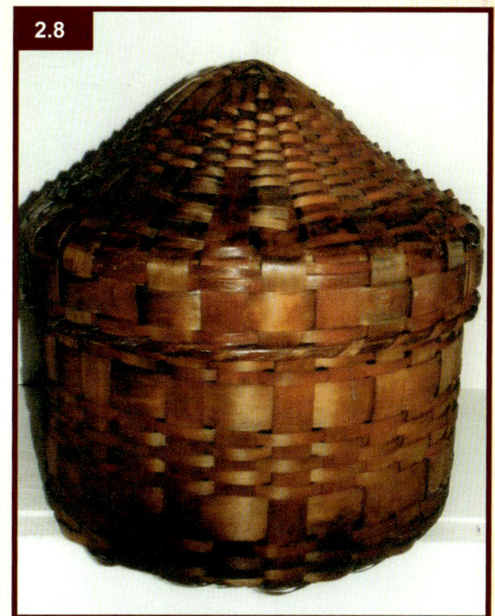
2.8

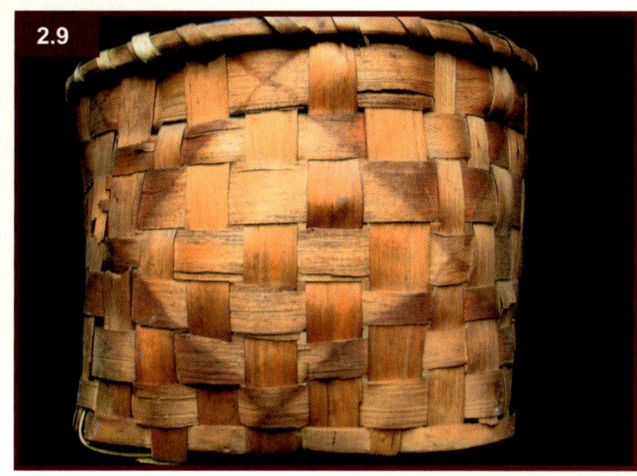
2.9

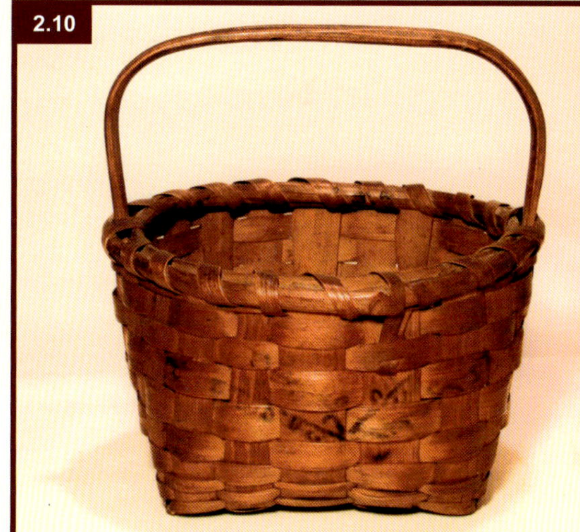
2.10

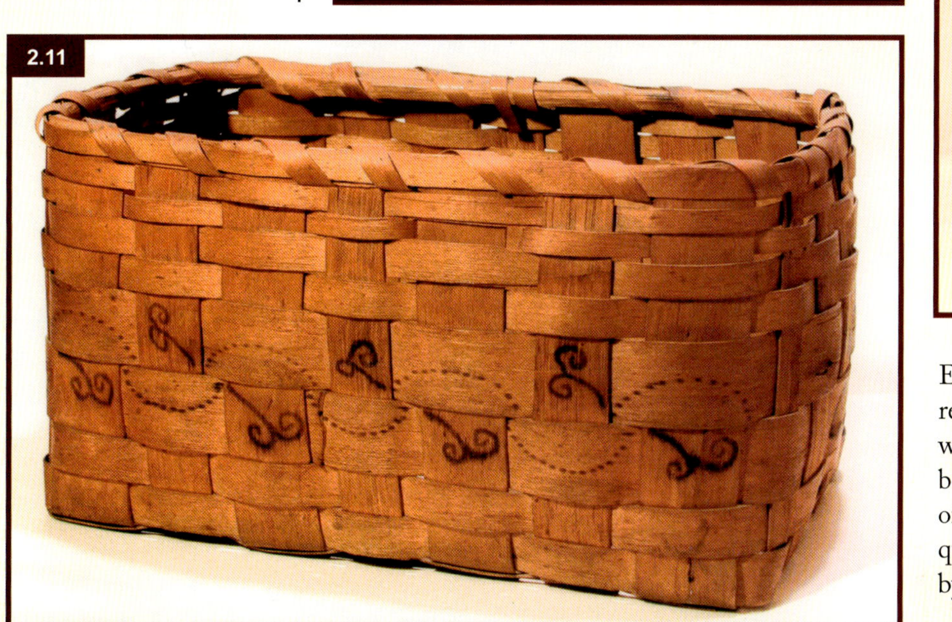
2.11

England became famous for their refined woodworking skills. Yet, while Shaker furniture and lidded boxes have no close parallels, many of their 19th-century splint baskets quite closely resemble those made by their Indian neighbors.

Likewise, Euramerican baskets produced by the so-called "Bushwhackers" in the Taconic area of western New England and upstate New York, as well as baskets from rural New Hampshire and even further afield in the Appalachians, also share many similarities with the Indian work.

Much of the 18th- and 19th-century basketry in the Northeast could be accurately described as "transcultural," in the sense that many diverse Native and non-Native groups were making baskets of the same common forms, using similar techniques and tools,

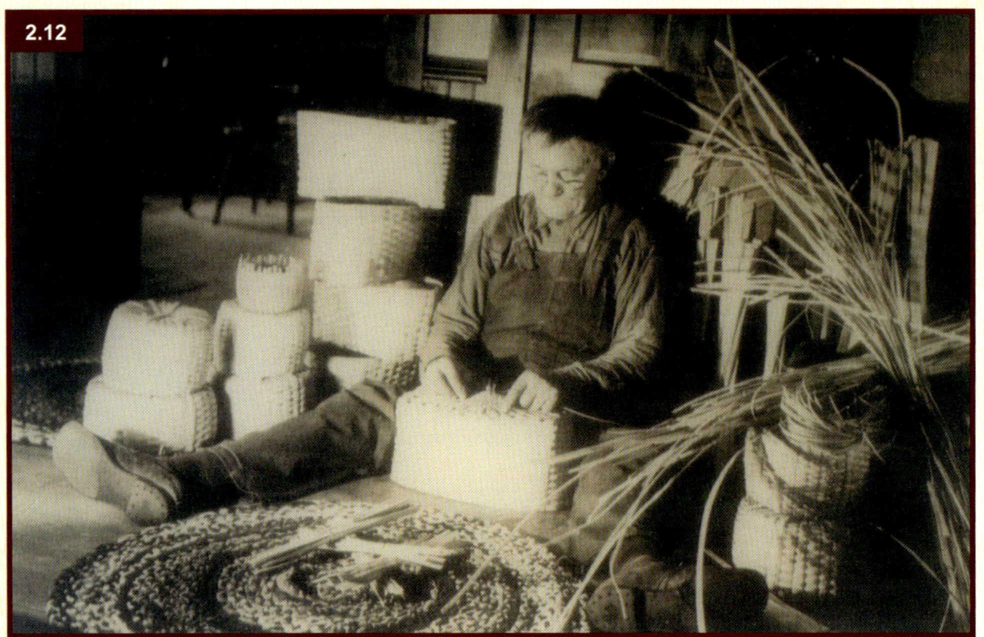

2.12. Yankee basketmaker Rowse Matterson of Saunderstown, Rhode Island, plaiting baskets with oak splints rived from neighborhood trees and reed brought from Connecticut, c. 1920.

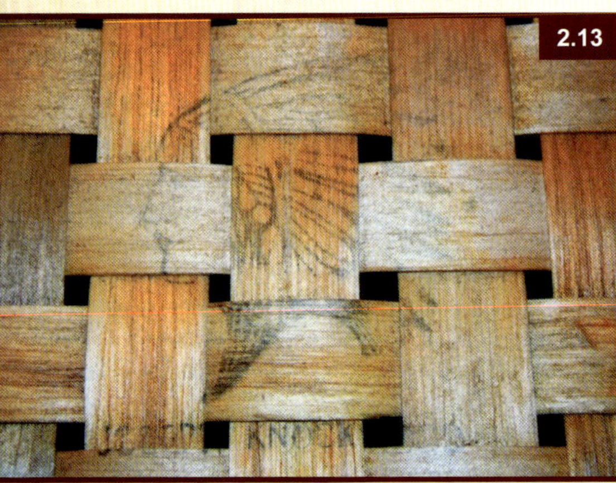

2.13. Some baskets are helpfully identified by a maker. Micmac (Mi'kmaq) maker Joseph Knockwood used a rubber "Indian head" stamp and black ink to mark his baskets, c. 1950–1960s.

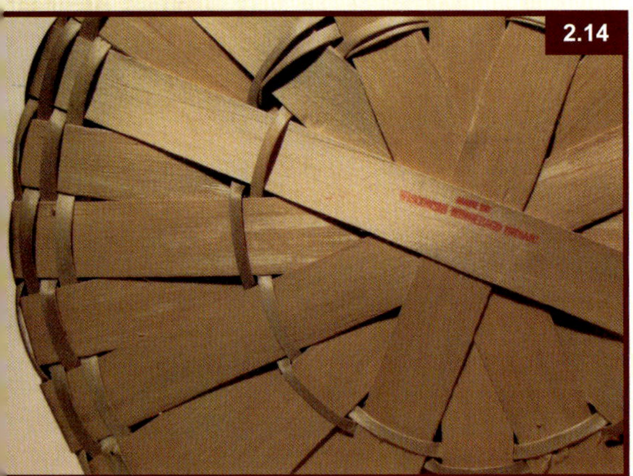

2.14. A 20th-century Ho-Chunk (Winnebago) maker stamped this woodsplint basket base "Made by Wisconsin Winnebago Indians."

and for many of the same purposes. This transcultural *fusion* of basketry traditions can lead to some *confusion* for basketry collectors when it comes to making firm attributions.

Probably many undecorated Native-made work baskets used on farms and in fields likely wore out beyond repair and are under-represented today. Furthermore, baskets were often exchanged, used, handed down, and preserved with little regard for their origins. Surely, among the many older unadorned plaited woodsplint baskets that have survived to the present day are those made by Northeastern Indians as well as by others—Yankees, Shakers, "Bushwhackers," Pennsylvania Germans, Appalachian folk, and even continental Europeans.

Attempts to sort out American Indian-made baskets from this larger pool of Northeastern woodsplint basketry are often frustrated. Many exceptions contradict the few commonly-repeated guidelines that are used to distinguish these wares.

Some say, for example, that Indian-made baskets tended to be constructed entirely without the use of nails, while Yankee-made and factory-produced baskets may have staples or brads to hold foundation elements in place at the start and, most often, to secure and finish off a rim. Yet, the presence or absence of metal fasteners is not a foolproof guide to attribution. As a case in point, members of the Sanipass family of Micmac Indian basketmakers in northern Maine have been plaiting woodsplint pack baskets for decades. Some of their baskets have splint-lashed rims, while others have nailed rims.

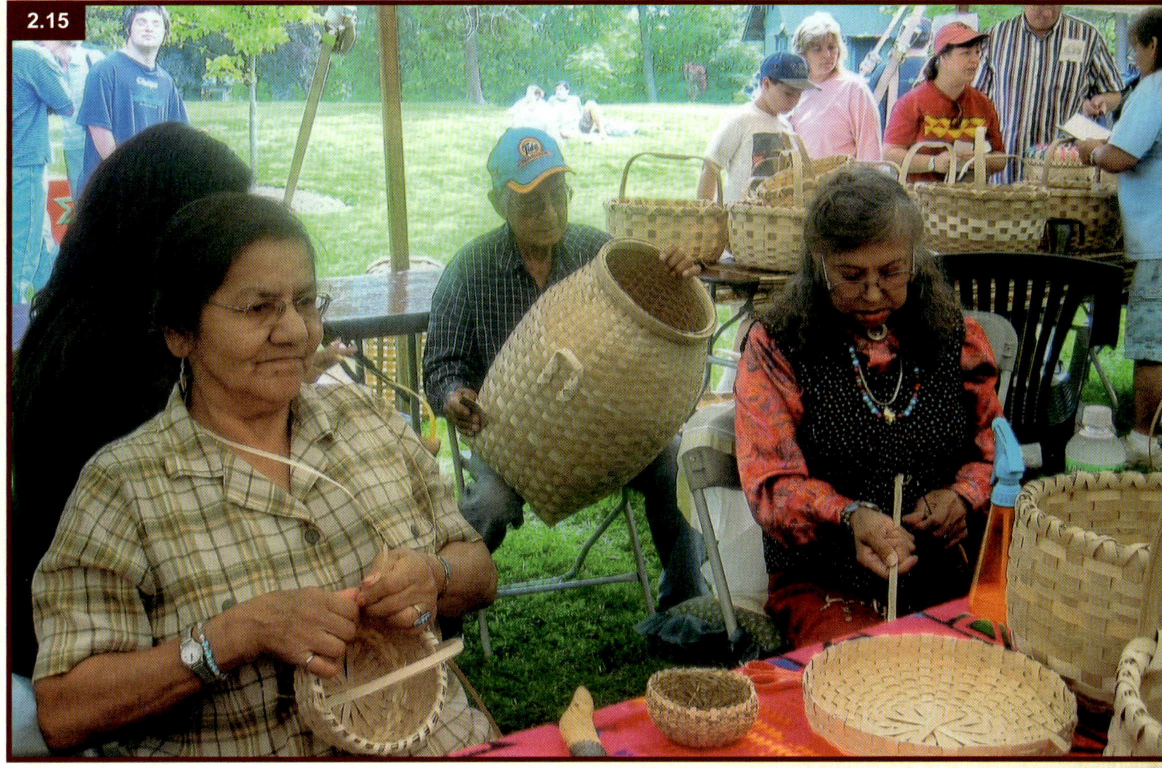

2.15. Members of the Sanipass family of Micmac basketmakers display a variety of baskets at a 2006 Maine Indian Basketmakers Alliance festival in northern Maine. Note that some of their basket rims are finished with lashed splints while others are nailed.

To further complicate matters, neighboring Native and non-Native basketmakers sometimes shared specialized components. Non-Native basketmakers might incorporate Indian-made basketry elements like carved handles or decorative trim into their own woodsplint baskets. From about 1850 into the 1920s, basketmakers in Maine's Sabbathday Lake Shaker community apparently purchased Maine Indian basketry materials and components like splint lacework for decorating their own Shaker-made sewing baskets and notions.

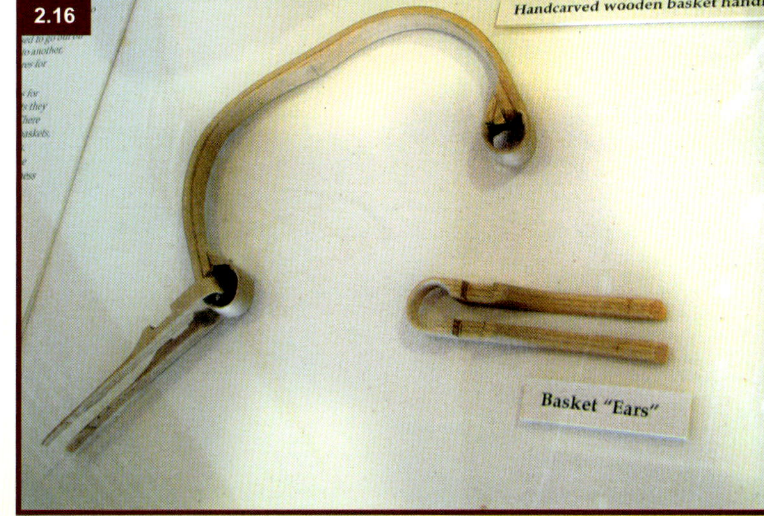

2.16. A basket handle and "ear" hand-carved by Newt Washburn, a Sweetser family member of western Abenaki and German heritage.

At the same time, other Euramerican basketmakers were supplying Indians with ready-made materials and products for plaiting into Indian-made work. Research by Gaby Pelletier found that Native basketmakers from the St. Francis Abenaki Reserve at Odanak, Québec, regularly bought prepared ash splints and sweetgrass lengths, as well as small sweetgrass and ash splint sewing accessories like thimble and scissors cases, from their French neighbors in the town of Pierreville. The St. Francis Abenaki then added these local, French-made products and materials to sewing baskets that are generally considered "Abenaki" today.

Likewise, historians credit French Ursuline nuns in Québec nearly three centuries ago with first applying steel needles and European embroidery techniques like satin-stitch to dyed moosehair on birchbark. The adaptation of these methods to Native

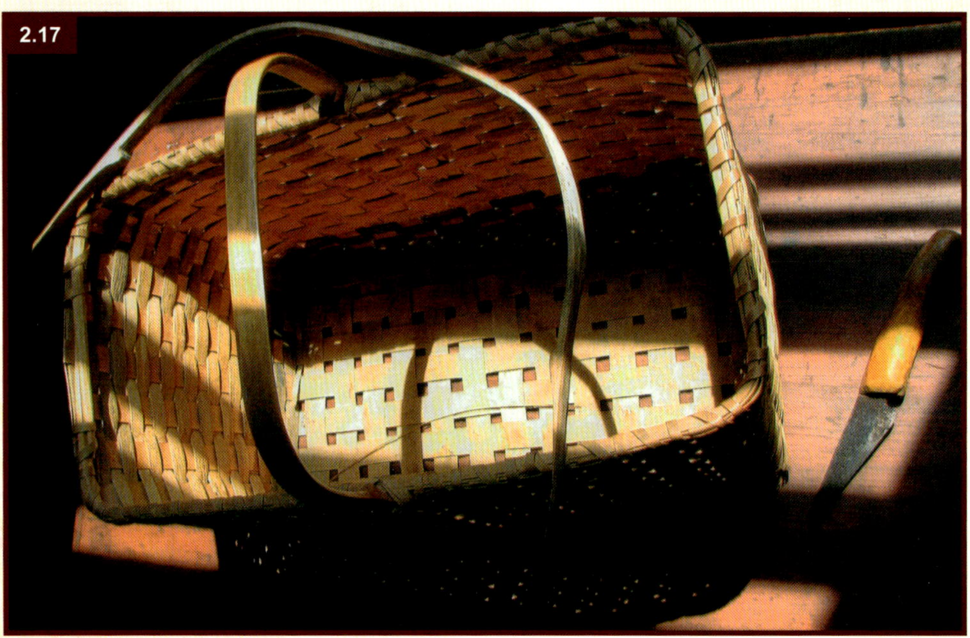

2.17. A Northeastern woodsplint basket with an extra carved handle and splint knife.

materials was taught to Indian girls in the convent schools and resulted in a hybridized craft. Later, through most of the 19th century, it was practiced exclusively by Indians. Distinctive moosehair-embroidered souvenir boxes and card cases made primarily by the Huron women of Lorette, near Québec City (and by a few Micmac and Maliseet), remained an important category of Native commerce until the close of the 19th century.

Many other instances of cross-fertilization in Northeastern basketry occurred as well. As a further example, several men of the German-American Sweetser basketmaking family of Québec and northern New England married Abenaki basketmakers. This family's work combined elements of both these woodsplint basketmaking traditions by the mid-1800s. Most recently, a fourth-generation descendant, Newt Washburn of Littleton, New Hampshire, continued the family enterprise into the 21st century, adding his own innovations to the craft while also teaching his skills to young non-Indian apprentices.

Useful and Pretty, Too

Many of the early baskets that are most obviously identifiable as having been made by Northeastern Indians are those embellished with Native decoration. Generally made for barter or sale, some of these same kinds of baskets, of course, also served the Native makers and their own families. But probably most were purchased, put to work, and sometimes preserved in the Yankee homes where they saw daily use, along with other containers like band boxes, hat boxes, and buckets and pails. After decades and even generations of service, most of the surviving early baskets found today are far from pristine.

By the late 18th and early 19th century, as some Natives resorted to their basketmaking craft as an essential economic enterprise, they adapted their own traditional skills for a new audience. Some of the motifs they commonly used for embellishing their basketry, such as the "medallion" device, have deep Native roots in the region. Certain of these American Indian basketry forms and decorative techniques continued to persist over a very long timespan in this new era, confirming their acceptance and popularity with Euramericans.

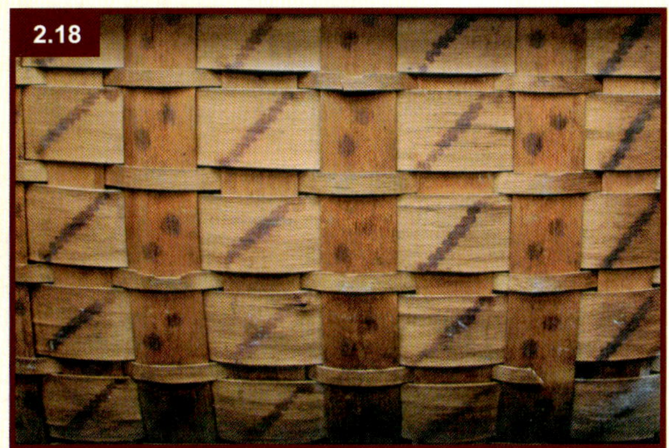

2.18. Detail of a probable Natick woodsplint basket with repetitive, typomorphic design elements, c. 1830s.

The baskets Native makers most commonly produced surely appealed to their consumers on at least two levels, the practical and the aesthetic. That these early basketry products were useful is obvious. But the embellishments that the makers added no doubt also contributed to the initial attraction and marketability of the baskets that endure in households and collections today.

A century ago, the pioneer Northeastern basketry researcher Frank Speck recognized what he defined as "typomorphic" layout. His term described repetitive dark-hued design elements on southern New England Indian baskets that produced surfaces superficially suggesting the look of early typeset broadsides and other printed matter. The familiarity of the aesthetic among both Christianized Native basketmakers (many of whom could read and one of whom was a printer's apprentice) and their Yankee customers may account, at least in part, for the ready acceptance of these early Native baskets in the marketplace.

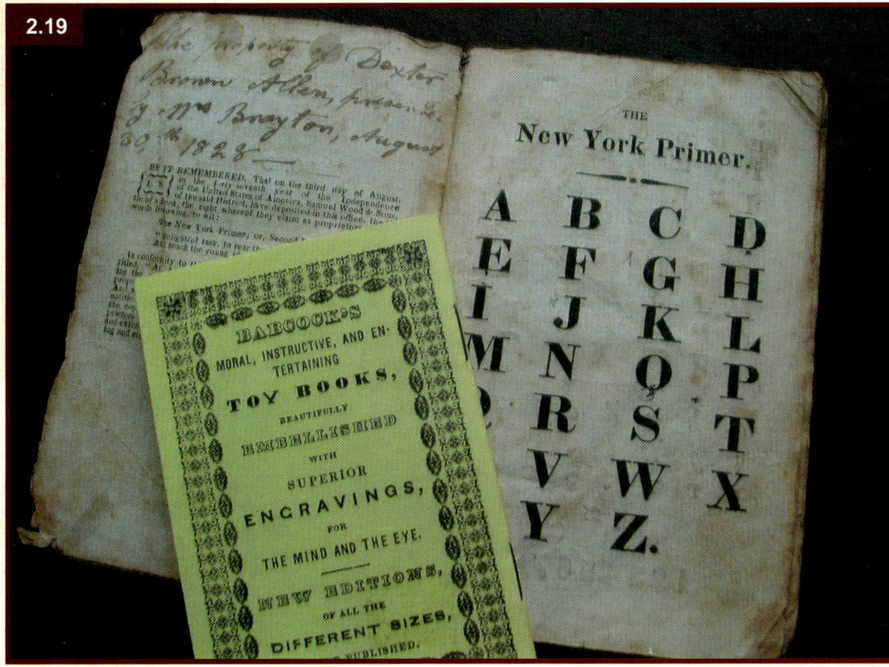

2.19. Examples of early printing, one inscribed and bearing a penned 1828 date.

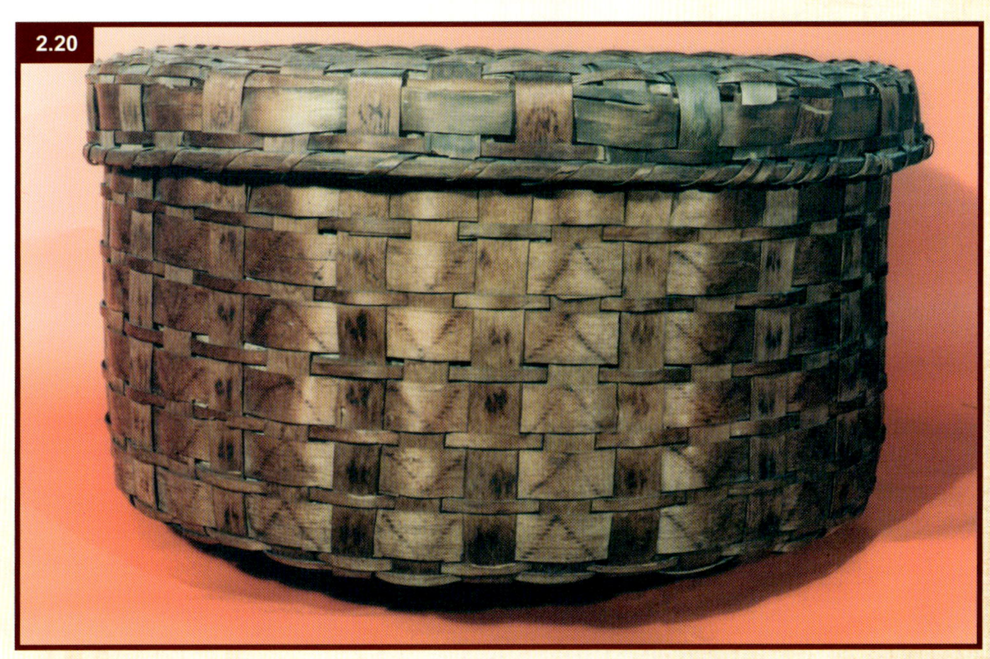

2.20. A probable Pennacook or Massachusett covered storage basket with hand-painted typomorphic black unit elements, c. 1830s.

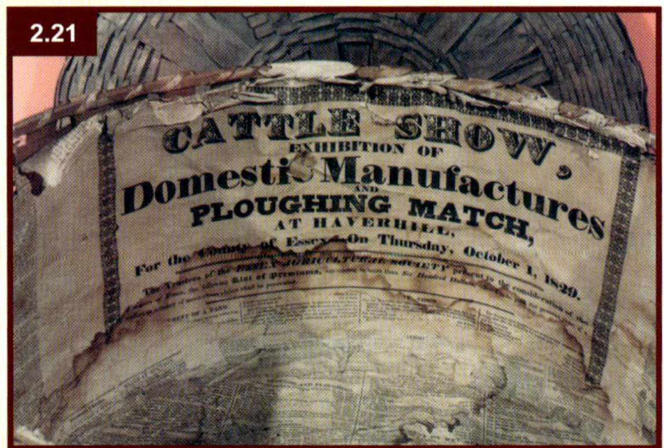

2.21. An 1829 *Boston Courier* newspaper lines the interior of the covered storage basket **(2.20)** and gives notice of the Essex Agricultural Society's exhibit at Haverhill, Massachusetts. The fonts and graphics resonate with the storage basket's block-like exterior decoration and plaited structure.

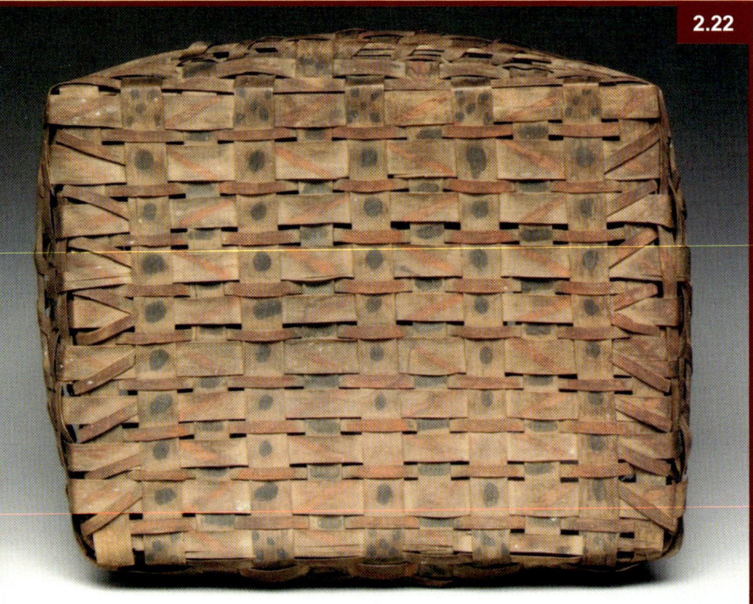

2.22. A southeastern New England rectangular storage basket cover, early to mid-1800s, displays repetitive unit painting.

Perhaps some of this basketry might even have aligned with Euramerican tastes on a subconscious level. For instance, dyes and paints, often compounded with a combination of Native and Euramerican ingredients, were applied to the early woodsplint baskets to create designs ranging from repetitive layouts to more free-ranging painterly compositions.

Either of these Native decorative approaches may embody design organizations that sometimes were shared with other domestic goods familiar in White households at the time. Is it really just a coincidence, for example, that certain early 19th-century decorative layouts and pigment colors enhancing southeastern New England woodsplint basketry both resembled and coordinated well with patterns found on loomed overshot coverlets and period block-stamped wallpapers?

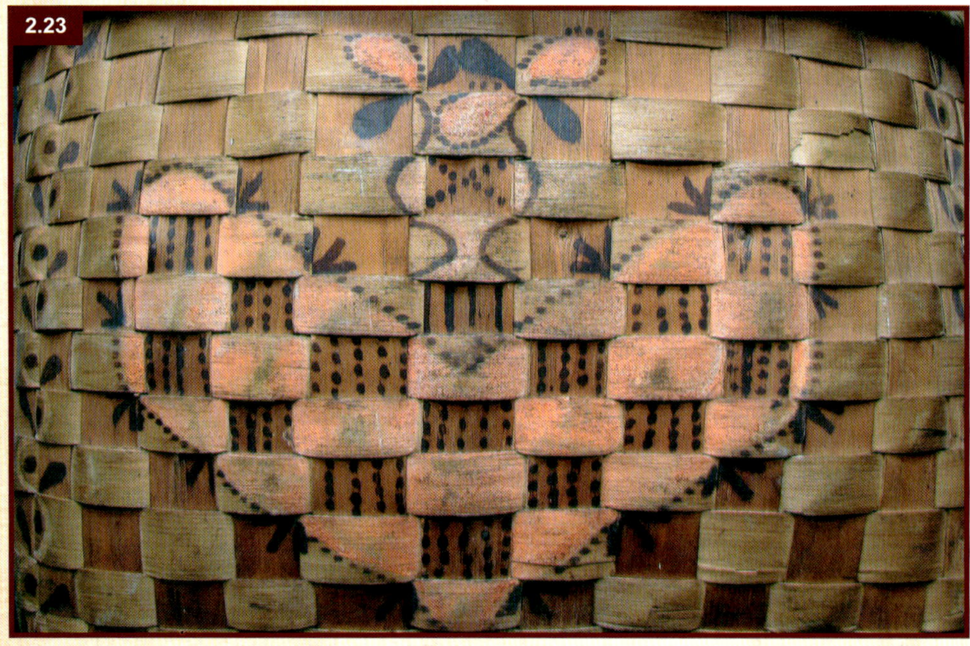

2.23. The wall of this Nipmuc basket, c. 1820-1830, was used like a canvas and painted with a heart and flower vase.

Many Meanings

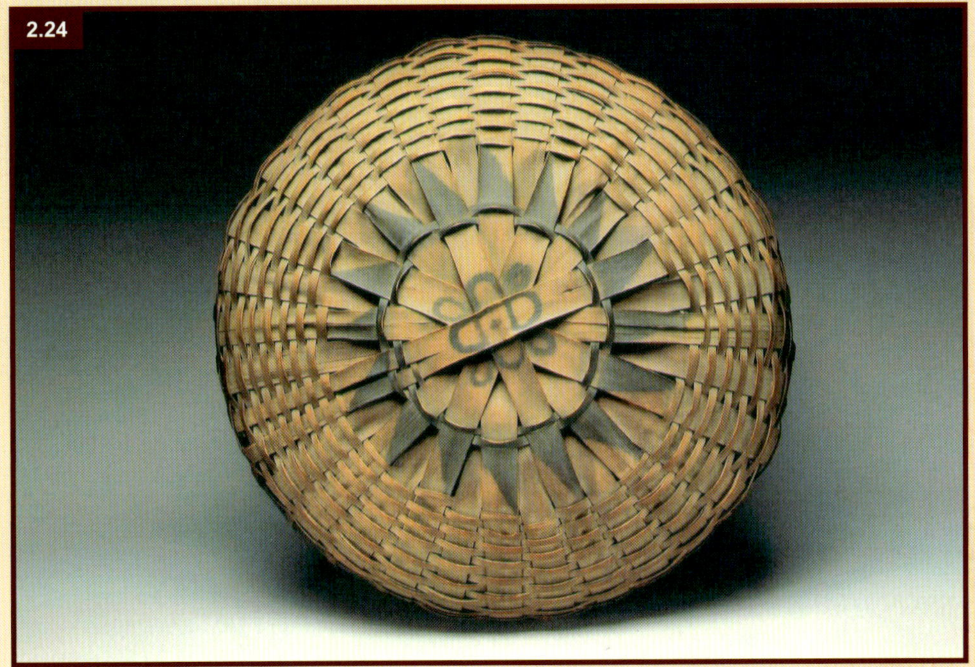

2.24. A hand-painted, four-lobed medallion centered on a Mohegan-style basket cover, c. 1850-1860.

The so-named "medallion" or "rosette" shown here is found on many Native woodsplint baskets that were used in early 19th-century Northeastern homes. It is a complex four-lobed device built with simple units like domes, dots, and curls. Basketmakers from a number of southeastern New England groups, most notably the Mohegan, painted the medallion on many of their late 18th- to mid-19th-century woodsplint baskets.

Ann McMullen has considered medallions as initially constructed from basic design units that were precisely combined in highly structured patterns—essentially following a conventional grammar, with both a vocabulary of symbols and rules of syntax—much like a well-constructed sentence. She observes that later, by the mid-1800s, painted baskets have designs with less precise layouts and more jumbled rosette elements, indicating that Native rules governing this symbolic vocabulary and compositional syntax were breaking down culturally in this region.

Thus, by the mid-19th century, this particular decorative basket "language" was being imperfectly learned or culturally lost. Medallion-based decorations applied less precisely, and even randomly, without knowledge of or regard for the proper rules, resulted in baskets that "read" much like a sentence that is not grammatical. This outcome suggests that complex cultural disruptions happening at the time were contributing substantially to a shift away from earlier, often deeply rooted Native conventions and decorative styles.

The medallion exemplifies how multiple meanings for a single symbol may coexist within contemporaneous communities or cultures. According to Mohegan informant Gladys Tantaquidgeon, the early 19th-century Mohegan basketmaker intended the medallion to symbolize the four divisions of the Mohegan people. Simultaneously, the Euramerican homemaker perhaps recognized the rosette as a representational floral design that resembled motifs on her woven coverlet or wallpaper. Today, a museum

FOCUS:

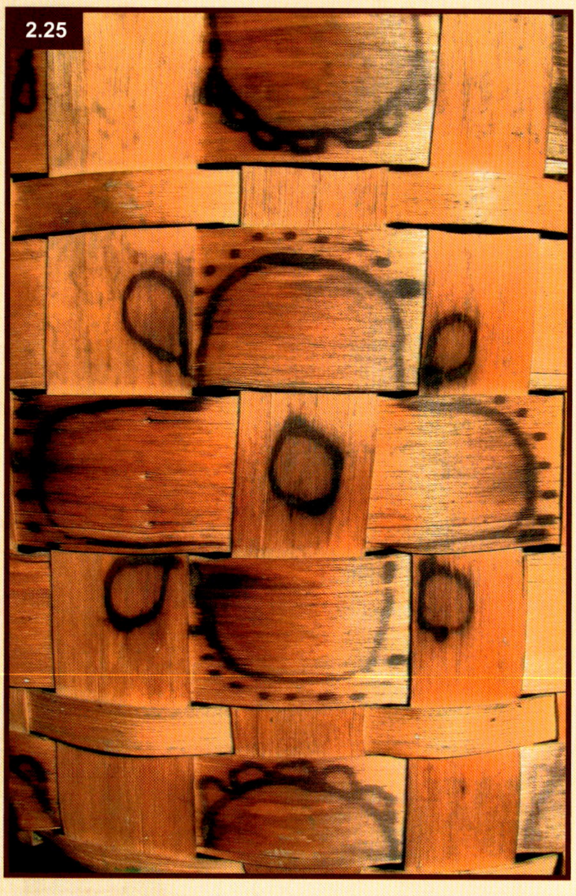

curator or art historian might initially describe the motif by classifying it neutrally as a quatrefoil or four-lobed element.

Throughout the Northeastern Woodlands, other common symbols too proved popular because they had meaning, though not necessarily the same meaning, to both Natives and Euramericans. In addition to the medallion in southern New England, motifs with alternate, highly charged meanings included diamond shapes and strawberry vines. In Northern New England and the Canadian Maritimes region, mid-19th-century porcupine-quilled design compositions on Micmac birchbark boxes depict timeless Algonquian elements that can resemble the compasswork of New England sailors and Euramerican folk art.

Another popular decorative element is the eagle. In the early to mid-1800s, this symbol commonly appeared on non-Indian decorative arts like appliqué quilts, band boxes, and imported Chinese porcelain tea services. Raptors also were worked into Tuscarora beadwork offered to tourists at Niagara Falls and were depicted on moosehair-embroidered birchbark objects from the Great Lakes region, where the thunderbird was a potent sacred being in Native life. Both American citizens and Native peoples viewed this avian form similarly as a powerful and dominant symbol, yet it also embodied other, distinctly different values and deeper meanings in each culture.

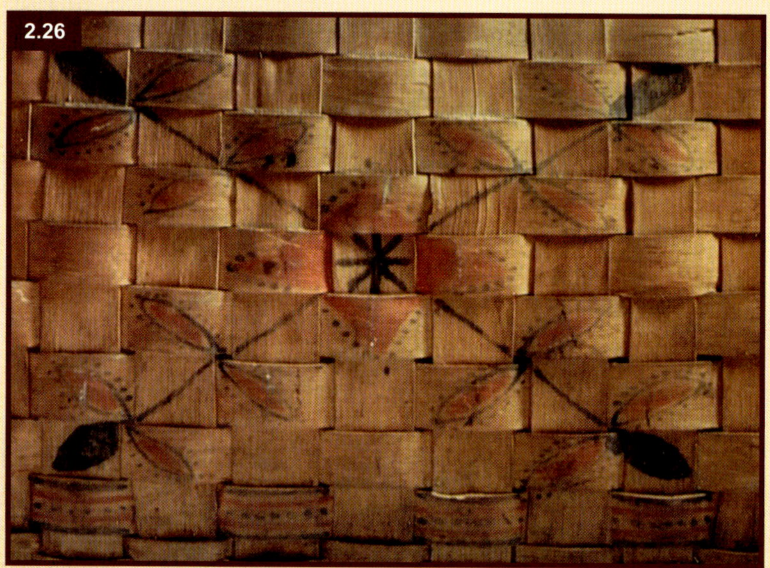

2.25–2.28. Early 19th-century decorative devices, layouts, and pigment colors on southeastern New England baskets may resemble patterns on overshot coverlets and block-stamped wallpapers. Here, one can compare (2.25) the hand-painted medallion on a Mohegan-style basket, and (2.26) the red and blue design on a probable Mohegan basket, c. 1820, with (2.27) the popular early 19th-century "Whig Rose" coverlet design and (2.28) the block-stamped "Charleston Rose" American wallpaper pattern.

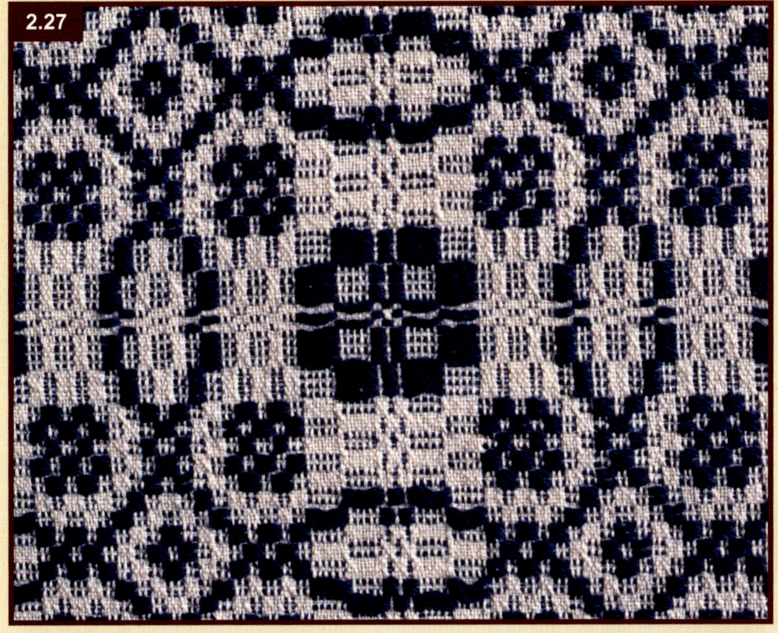

2.27

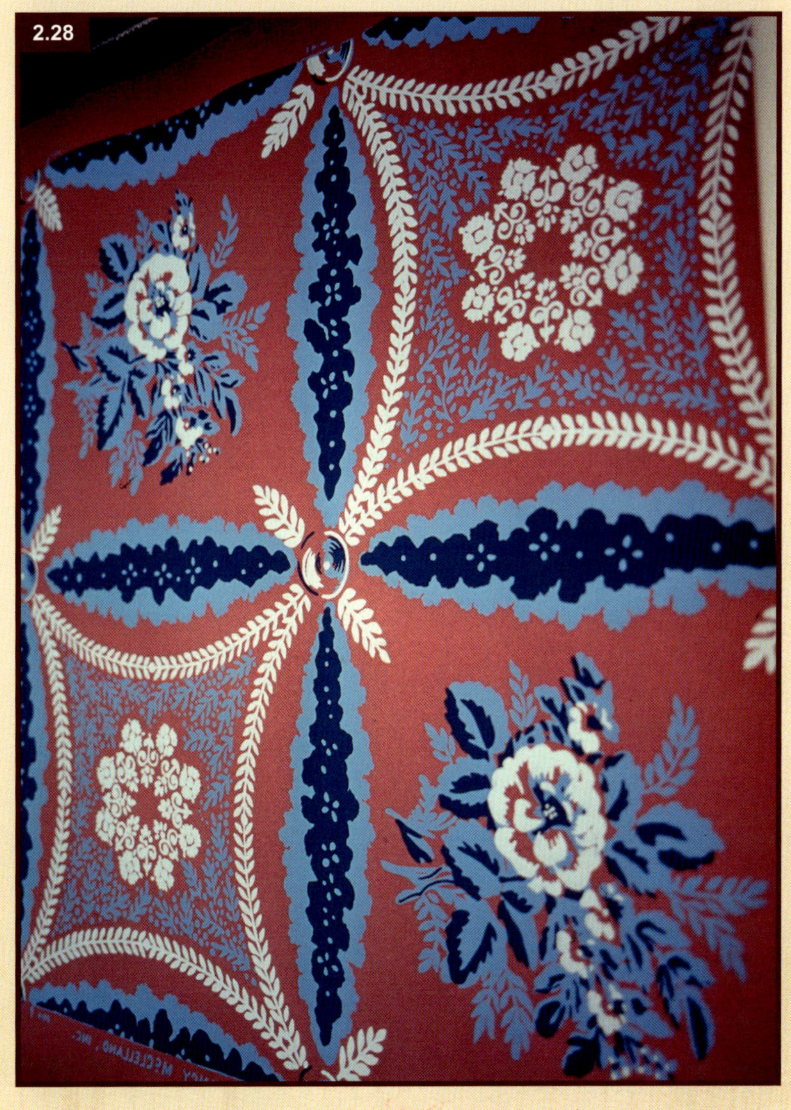

2.28

FOCUS:

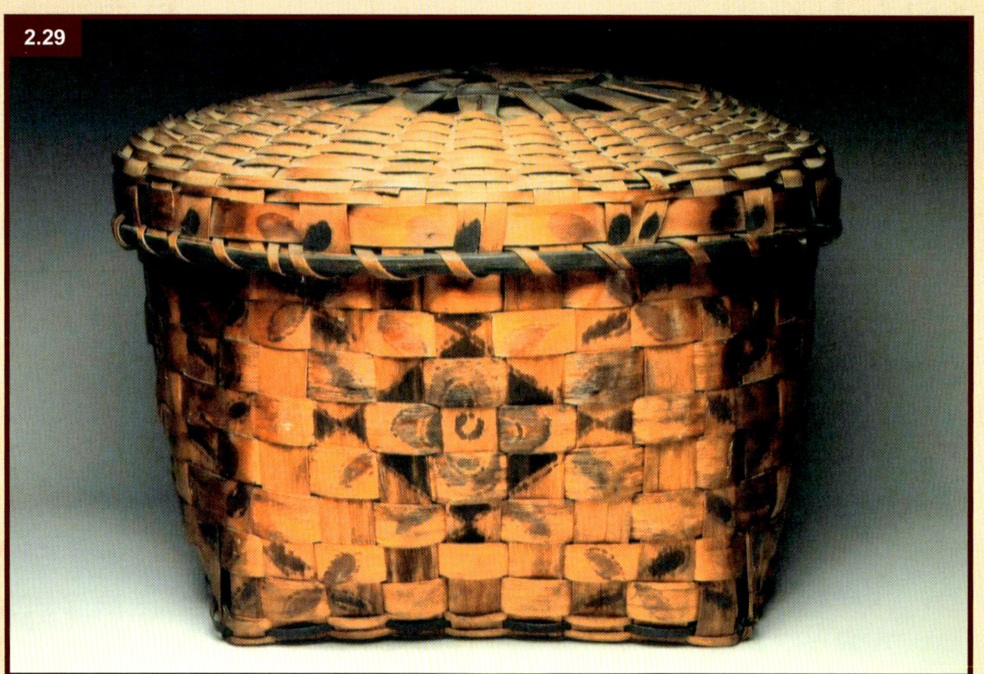

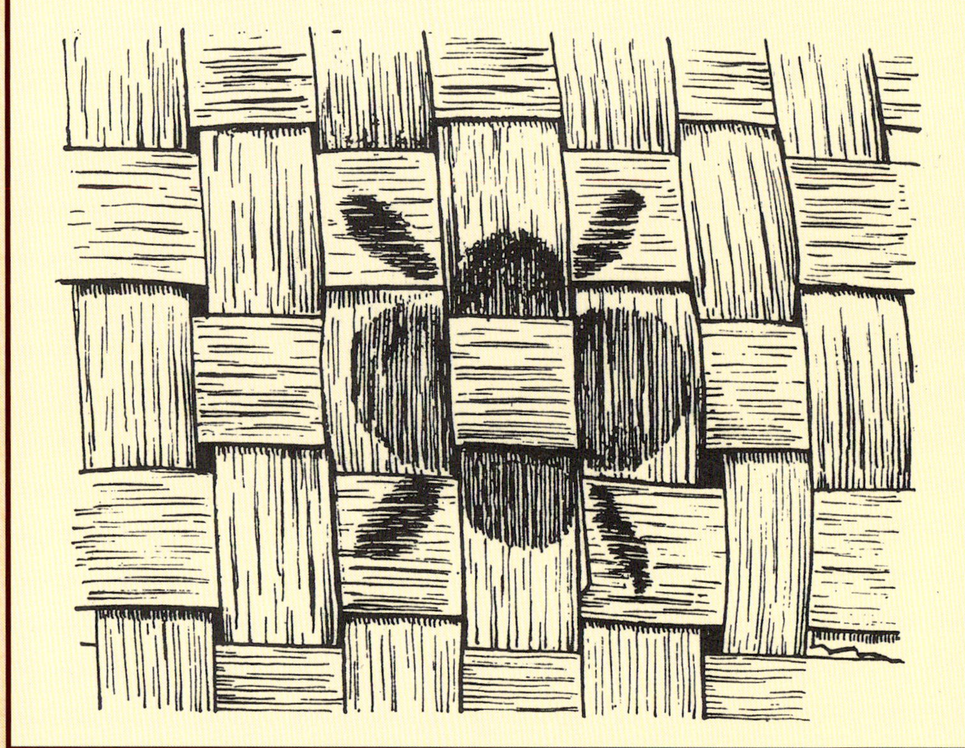

2.29. Mohegan-style covered storage basket, c. 1850-1860, with hand-painted devices including a medallion and "JHS" marked on the base.

2.30. Sometimes construction details are specific to a particular regional, tribal, or individual style. Traits that can vary, thus providing identification clues, include the ways in which weavers or weft splints are inserted or trimmed, how the start to a basket base is constructed, and how the start to a basket cover is begun. Plaiting with multiple rings of woodsplints (vs. with one continuous weft splint), as seen on the interior of this western Abenaki storage basket, is a very early technique.

2.31. These distinctively trimmed white oak standards, or warp splints, are diagnostic of the Yankee-style work of the late 19th-century Schaghticoke basket-maker Henry Harris.

2.32. Trimmed standards, or warp splints, forming star-like bases suggest the work of northern New England's basketmaking Sweetser family, or their apprentices.

Defining Regional Styles

A style consists of specific distinctive construction techniques or decorative elements that individually or in tandem point to a certain basketmaking group or location. By the early 1800s, several local Northeastern Indian woodsplint basketry styles were emerging. These styles are seen in the clustering of shared traits that may be recognized as one considers the geographic and cultural distribution of particular basketry types.

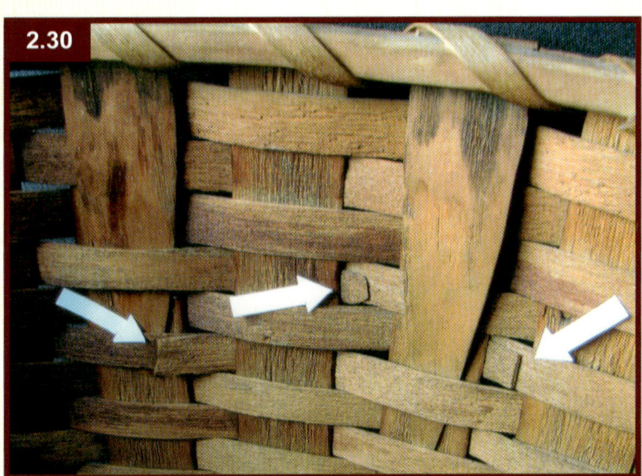

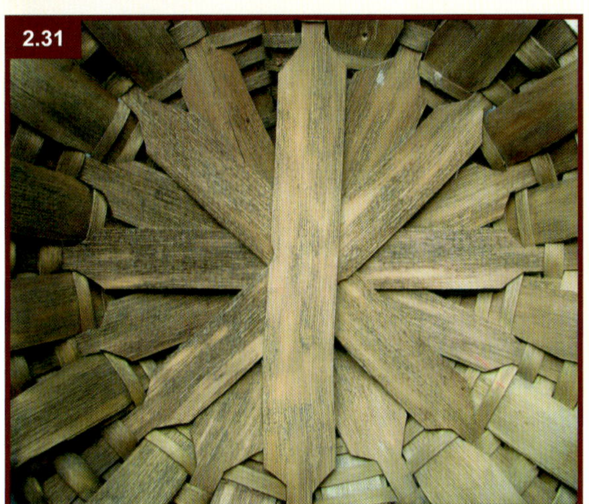

After several decades of examining Northeast Indian baskets, we suspect that some elements of "regional style" possibly grew out of individual or family conventions quite early on, probably in the late 18th to early 19th centuries. As their particular basket products took hold and were successfully marketed and used, the makers may have asserted "ownership rights," as has been the case among certain Native families in groups like the Wabanaki in more recent times. These basketmakers then concentrated on repeating their production in the next season. Some individuals specialized in making basket bases, rims, covers,

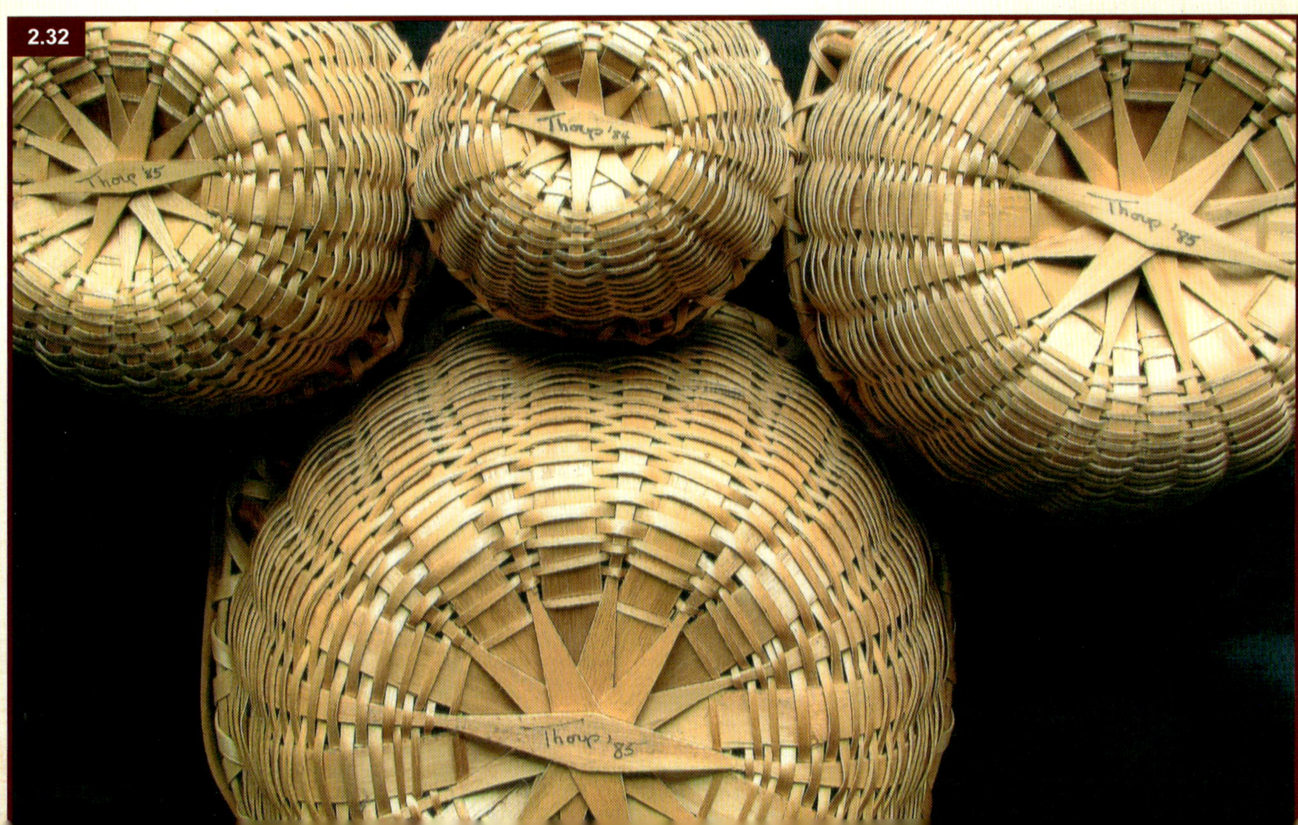

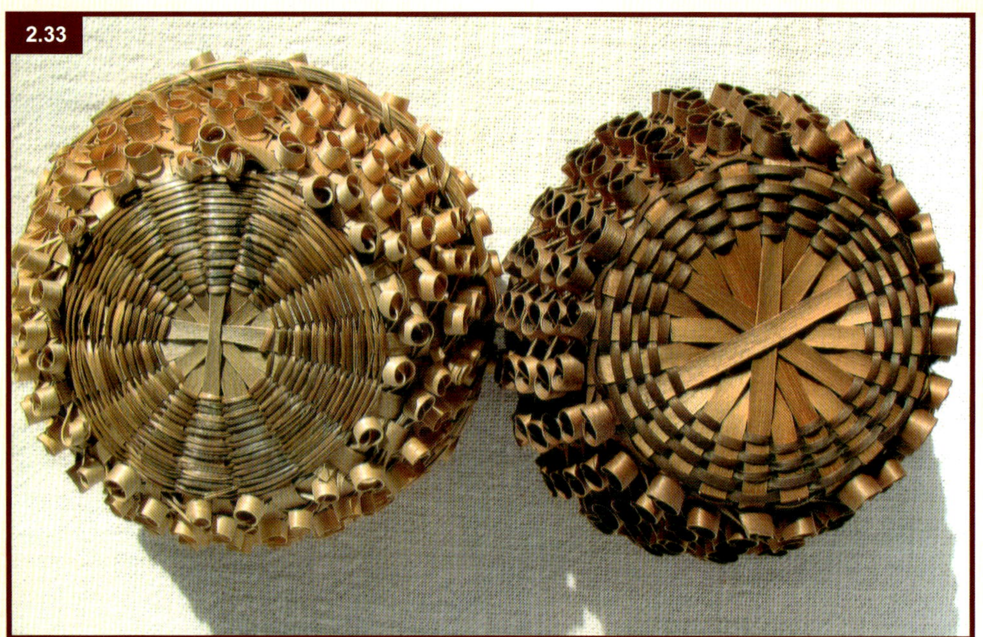

2.33. Basket starts either of ash splints or of ash splints plus sweetgrass likely are the product of different unidentified individual makers.

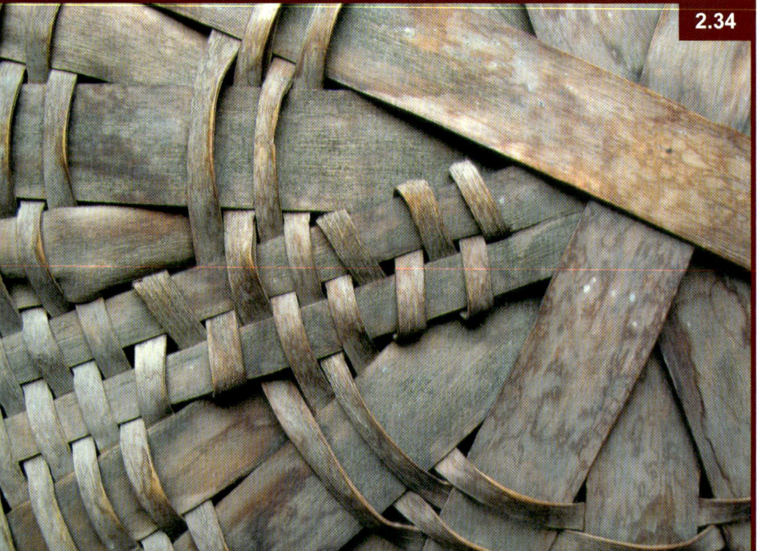

2.34. The start on this storage basket cover points to a likely western Abenaki basketmaker.

or other parts that became fairly uniform. Plus, an increasing reliance on tools like blocks and gauges after the mid-1800s may have further limited output variation.

Eventually the more successful creations, by now becoming standardized, were closely emulated by other local Native basketmakers, who adopted or adapted some of the same forms, techniques, decorative methods, or materials to their own basketry products. Thus, what may at times have begun as an individual or

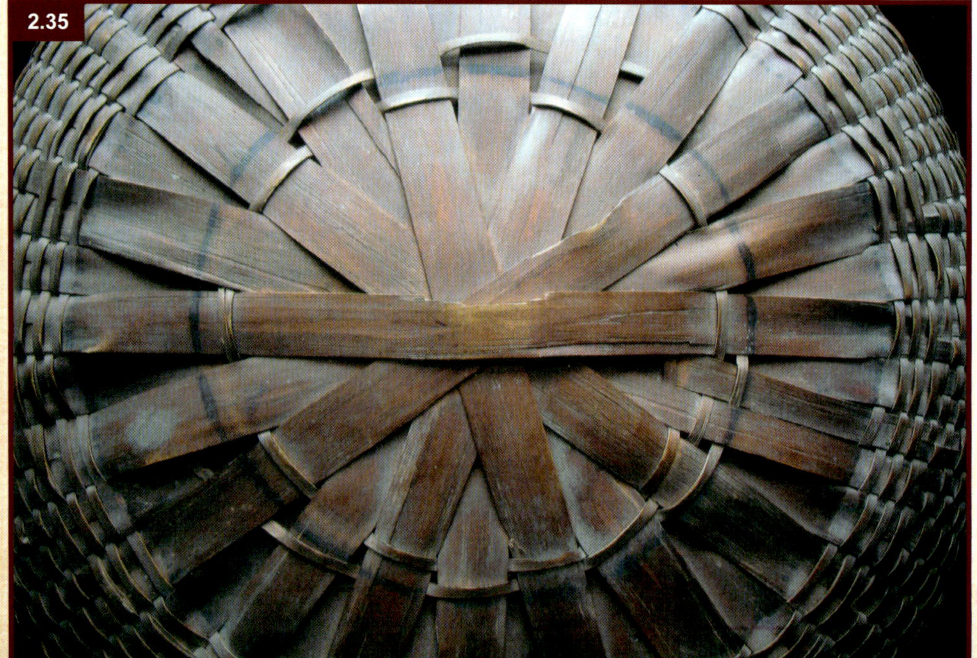

2.35. A southeastern New England basketmaker began this storage basket cover differently.

2.36. Some of the tools that have helped to streamline production while also standardizing finished forms include crooked knives, splint gauges, and blades for preparing ash splints for plaiting, from a Penobscot (Old Town, Maine) basketmaker's kit.

2.37. Simple wooden blocks were used for creating open shapes like the bottom of this covered button basket (left) and the completed woman's purse (right).

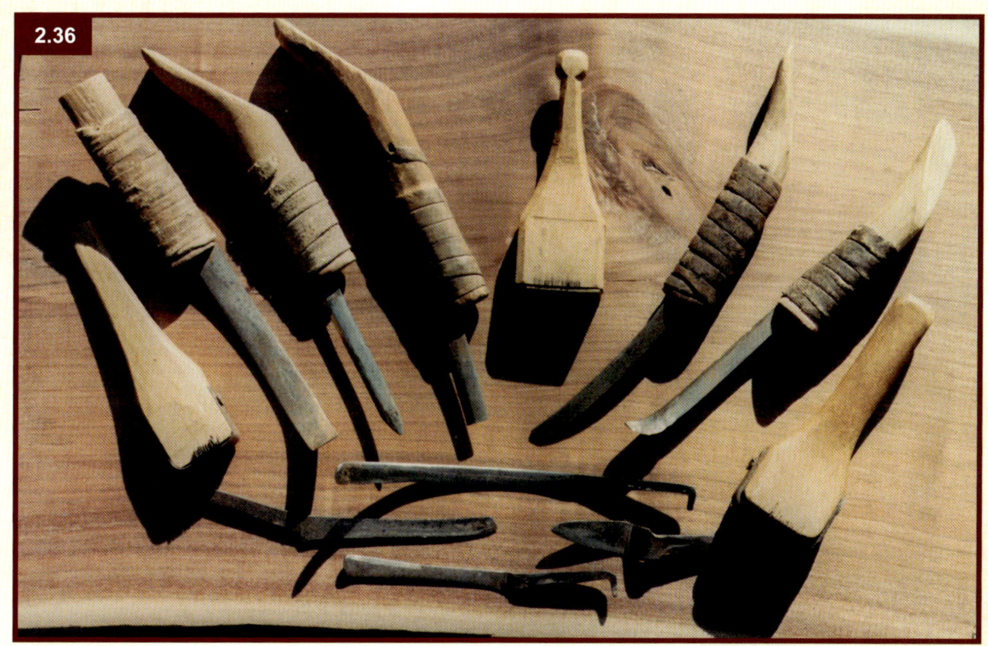

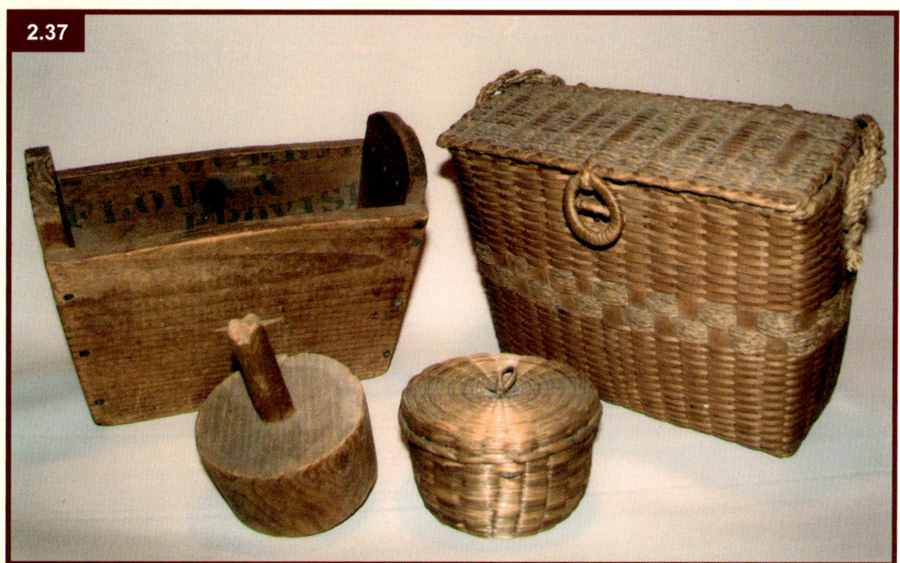

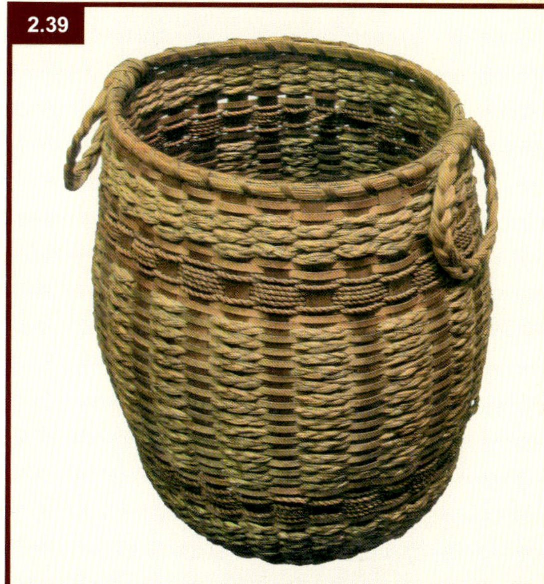

2.38, 2.39, 2.40. Compound wooden blocks or molds assembled of fitted sections **(2.38)** were used for weaving low bowls and for taller, incurving forms, like a barrel-shaped wastepaper basket **(2.39)**, plaited around a compound wooden block, later pulled apart for removal **(2.40)**.

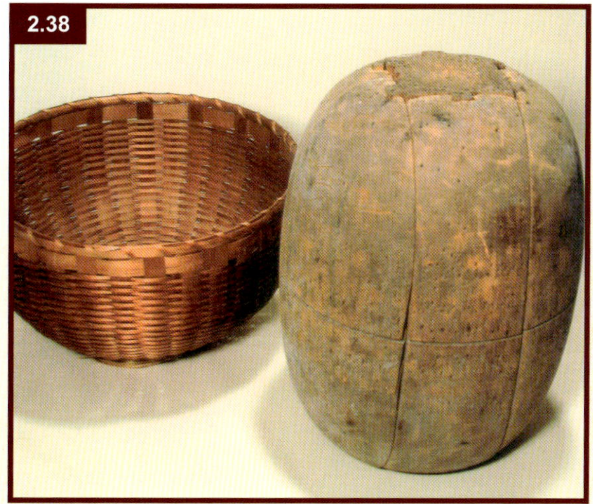

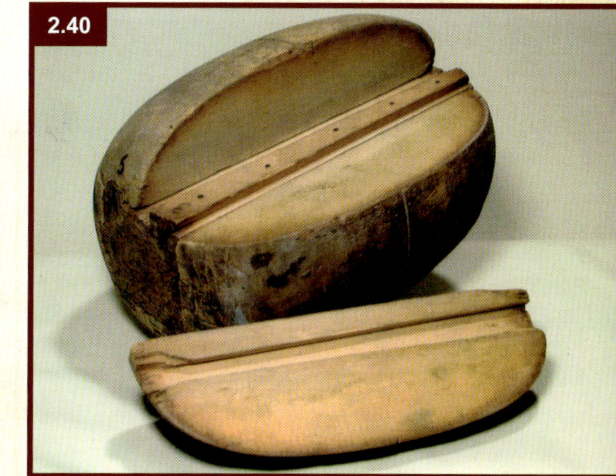

family preference was picked up by nearby basketmakers and eventually developed into what today may be recognized as a specific "style" associated with a particular region.

Though the Northeast can be divided into regions in different ways, for example by Native language groups, we consider four separate *basketry* regions in this discussion. While woodsplint baskets from across all four regions do share many of the same traits, Indian basketry across and within each of the several geographic and cultural regions of the Northeastern Woodlands exhibits some stylistic distinctions. Certain specific characteristics differ significantly enough to support the status of four separate regional styles. The four regional basketmaking divisions are:

- *Southern New England and Long Island*
- *Northern New England and Canadian Maritimes*
- *Upper New York State*
- *The Great Lakes*

2.41. Sometimes basketry trends can be corroborated by supporting information like historical documentation, United States census data, and Native oral histories. An example is this 1850 federal census return for Grafton, Massachusetts. It enumerates 19th-century members of the "vase painter" Arnold and Cisco family of Nipmuc basketmakers (see basket **2.23, 3.26**).

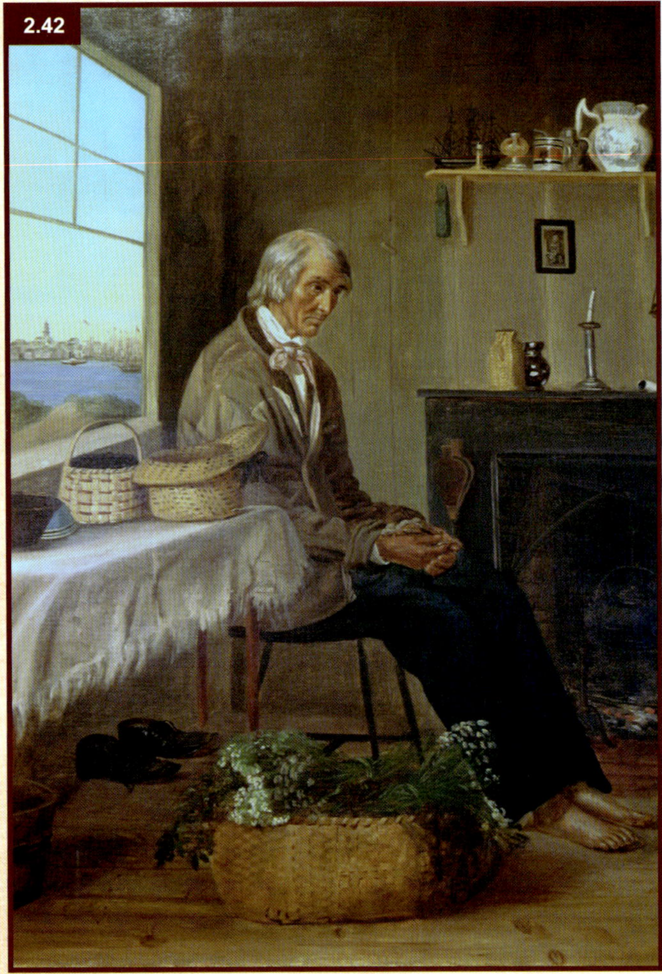

2.42. Abram Quary, a Nantucket (Wampanoag) Indian and basketmaker; oil portrait by Prussian-born artist Herminia Borchard Dassell, c. 1852.

SOUTHERN NEW ENGLAND AND LONG ISLAND

Although the Eastern Algonquians who occupy most of New England have spoken related languages and have long interacted with one another, certain distinctions characterize baskets made in Southern New England and Long Island versus those made in Northern New England and the Canadian Maritimes. This divergence began to appear early on, as basketmaking in each region was subjected to different influences and followed dissimilar routes. So, we discuss the Eastern Algonquian groups in the south and in the north separately as two divisions here.

Archaeological evidence reveals that twining with flexible materials to produce soft bags and baskets was widespread in the Northeast

2.43. This Mohegan *yokeag* bag for parched corn meal, c. 1650, survives as an example of mid-17th-century twined bags fashioned in southern New England. Twined of hemp cordage and porcupine quills, it is decorated with three horizontal bands of diagonal geometric elements. This layout persisted into 18th- to 20th-century southern New England basketry, despite a general technological shift from twining to plaited splintwork.

2.44. This small bag, about 8" high, woven of cotton and other plant fiber, belonged to Caleb Cheeshahteaumuck (Gay Head Wampanoag) from Martha's Vineyard, who was the first Native American graduate of Harvard College, Class of 1665. The bag inspires modern-day Wampanoag work (see 6.3).

2.45. A flexible Gay Head (Aquinnah) Wampanoag open-twined bag by Basha Occouch, 10.5" high, c. 1815-1816 or earlier (back left), rests beside two Mashpee Wampanoag plaited examples that date to c. 1870 (front left) and pre-1845 (right).

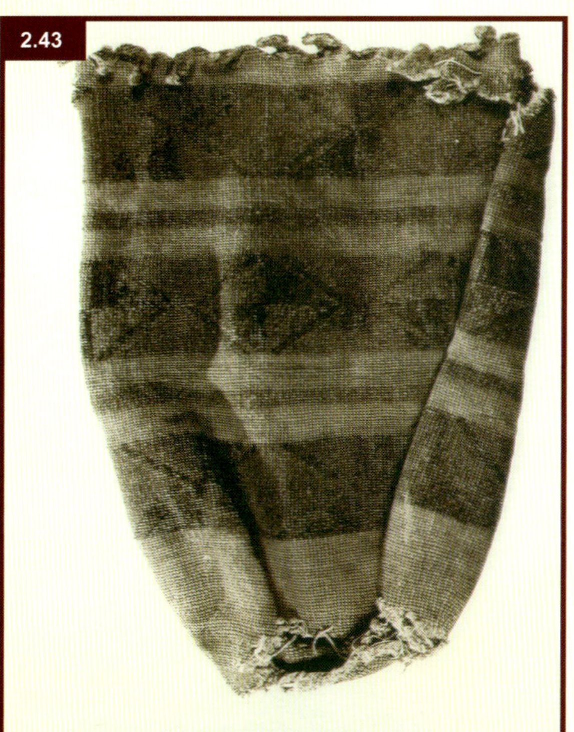

2.43

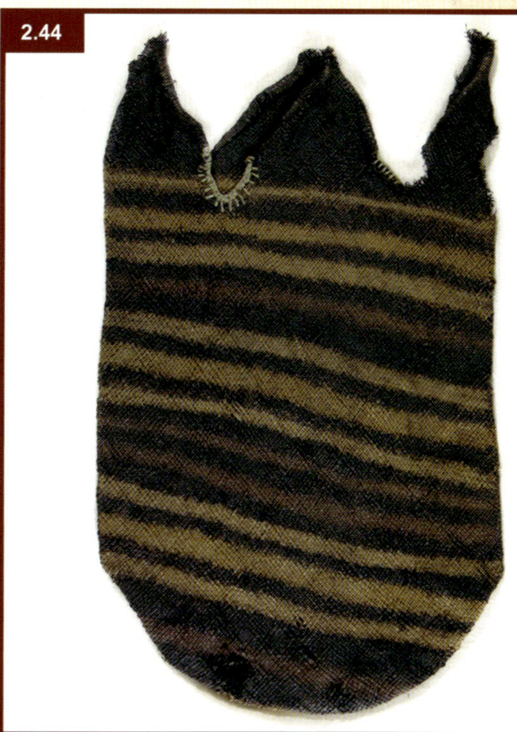

2.44

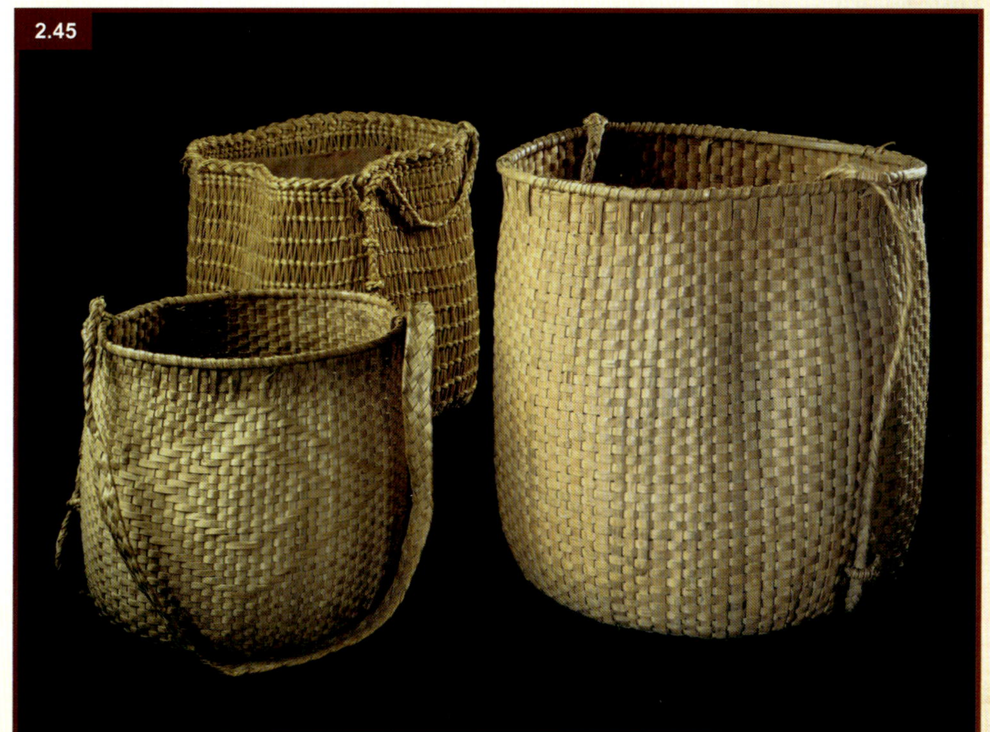

2.45

in pre-contact times. In Southern New England, twining continued into the late 17th century among the Mohegan, Narragansett, and others. A handful of bags twined during this period still survive.

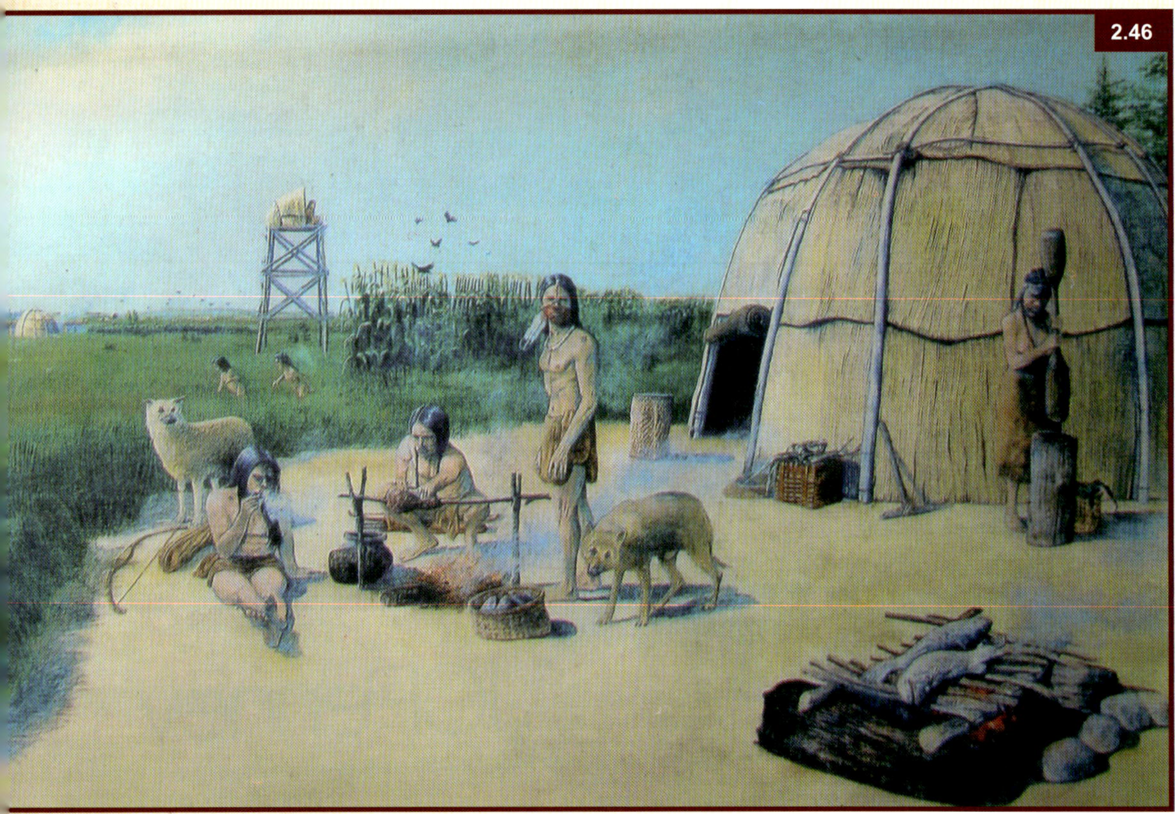

2.46. In their summer encampment near the sea coast, c. 1600, as envisioned by artist Robert Selby, Narragansett Indians have a variety of useful baskets close at hand.

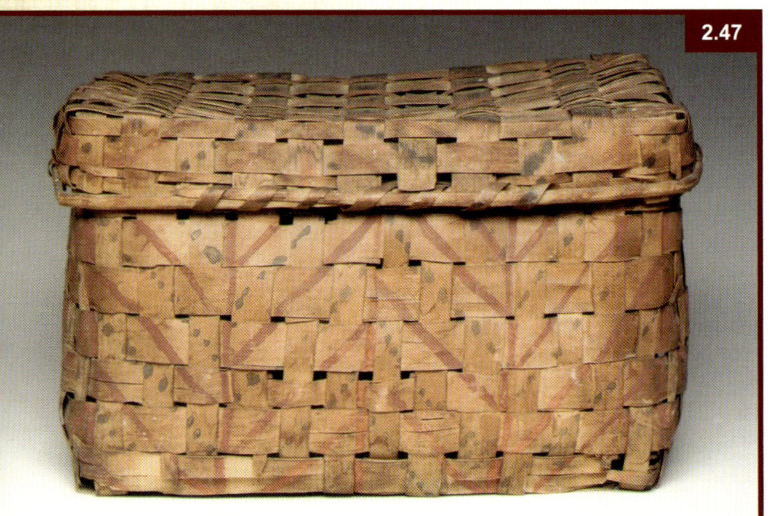

2.47. A rectangular storage basket from southeastern New England is hand-painted in a popular two-color combination of blue and Mohegan pink. Storage basket interiors often were lined with period newspapers that may provide clues to their origins and age, early 1800s.

Some basketmakers, like the Gay Head (Aquinnah) Wampanoag and Mashpee Wampanoag of southeastern Massachusetts, continued to twine or plait flexible bags into the 19th century. Eventually, though, twining and plaiting of flexible materials lost favor to the plaiting of woodsplints. Some contemporary Wampanoag basketmakers, however, recently have revived the twining technique.

For woodsplint plaiting, distinctions between Southern and Northern New England basketry are already apparent by the early to mid-19th century. These differences are especially noticeable in the large covered storage baskets that were common in both areas.

In Southern New England, early covered storage baskets often were decorated with stains or pigments. Basketmakers applied the color to woodsplints by hand-painting or stamping decorative elements, or by swabbing color onto just the exterior of splints.

The southeastern part of this basketry region extends from eastern Connecticut and Long Island eastward across Rhode Island to Cape Cod and the islands, including Martha's Vineyard and Nantucket, off southern Massachusetts. Here, wide woodsplints hand-painted with spare designs, typically in black only or in two-color combinations

2.48. Decorative characteristics of early to mid-19th-century southeastern New England baskets include hand-painted embellishments, like flowers.

2.49. "Medallions."

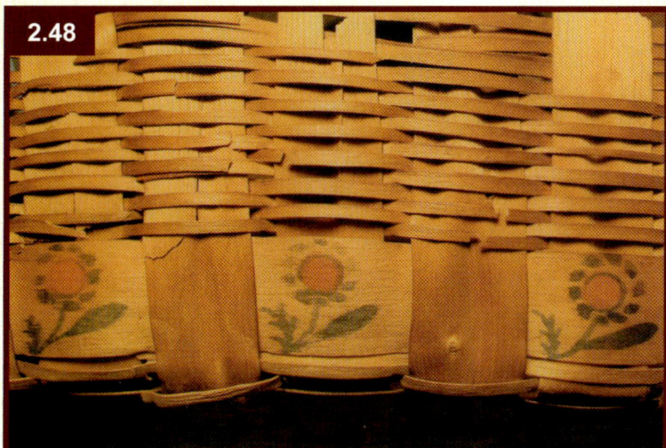

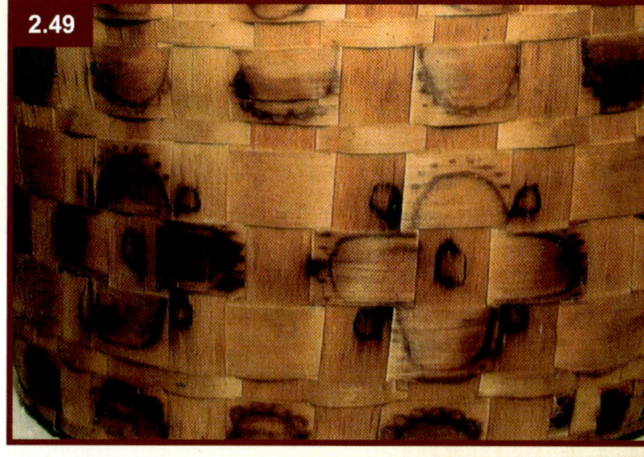

2.50. Diamond-shaped "stockade" elements.

2.51. Horizontal "trail" motifs.

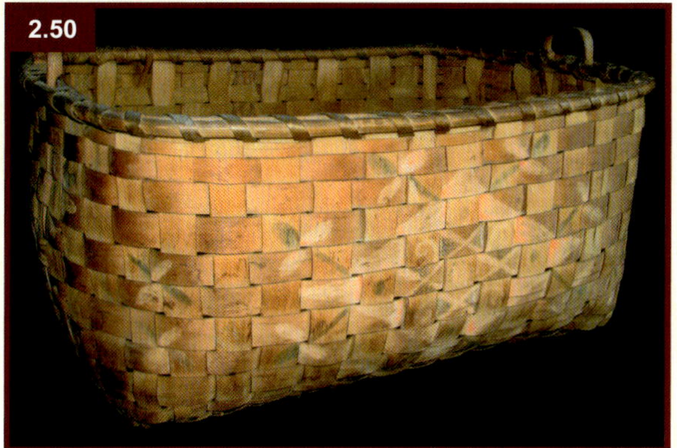

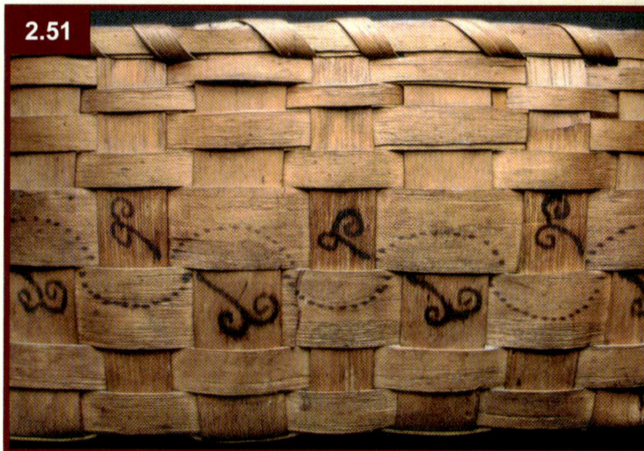

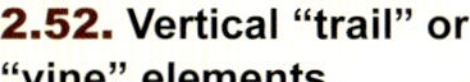

2.52. Vertical "trail" or "vine" elements.

2.53. Scorched punctate devices.

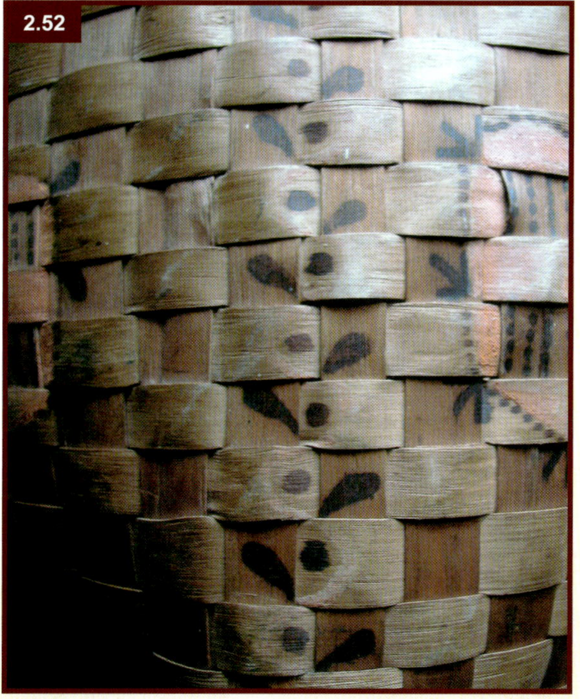

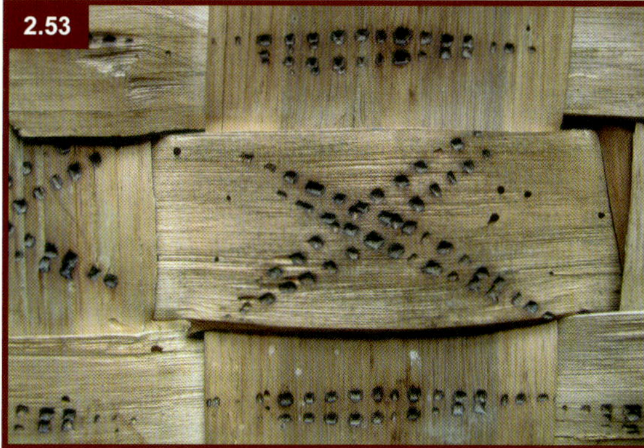

like "Mohegan pink" (orangish pink) and blue or Mohegan pink and brown, often grace the walls and covers of early to mid-19th-century storage containers.

By comparison, baskets look somewhat different if they have originated from the southwestern portion of the region. Southwestern New England extends across western Connecticut roughly to the border of New York (plus Long Island) and northward into adjoining counties of central-western Massachusetts.

Here, many covered storage baskets feature both wide and narrow splints that often were swabbed with pigments as their only decoration. Horizontal rows of one or more

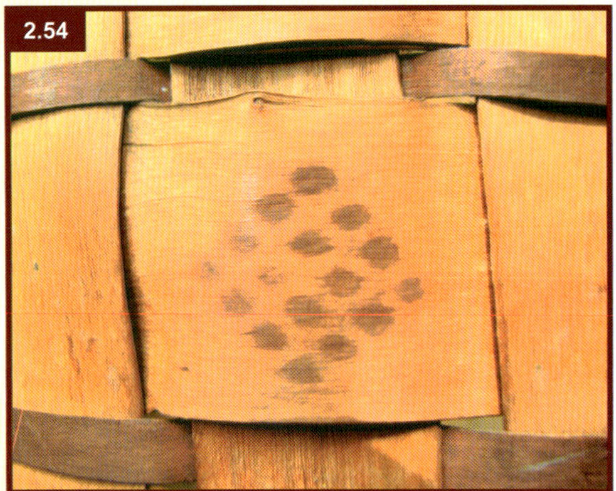

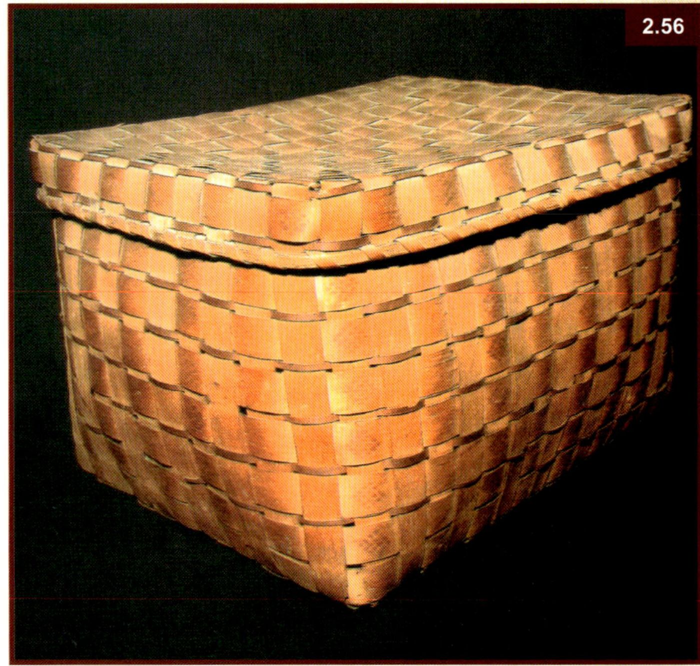

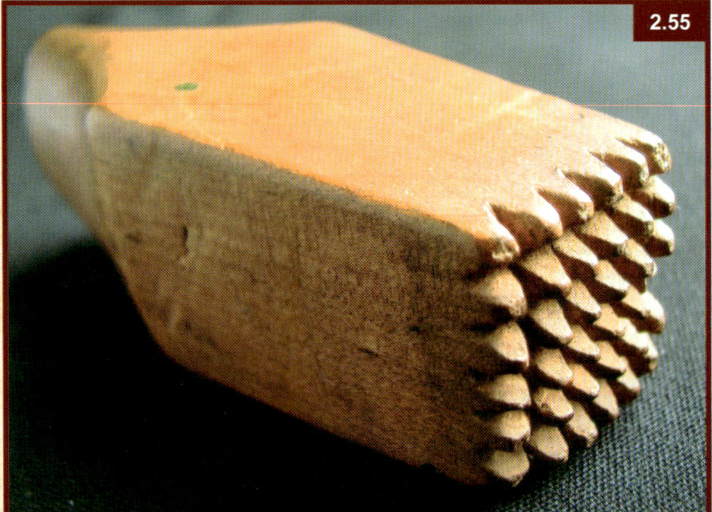

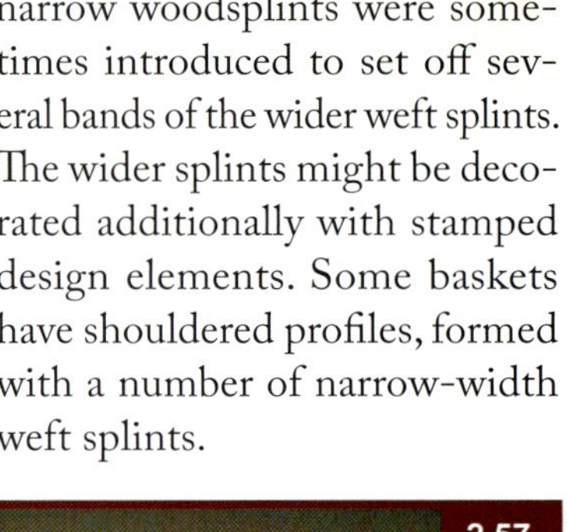

narrow woodsplints were sometimes introduced to set off several bands of the wider weft splints. The wider splints might be decorated additionally with stamped design elements. Some baskets have shouldered profiles, formed with a number of narrow-width weft splints.

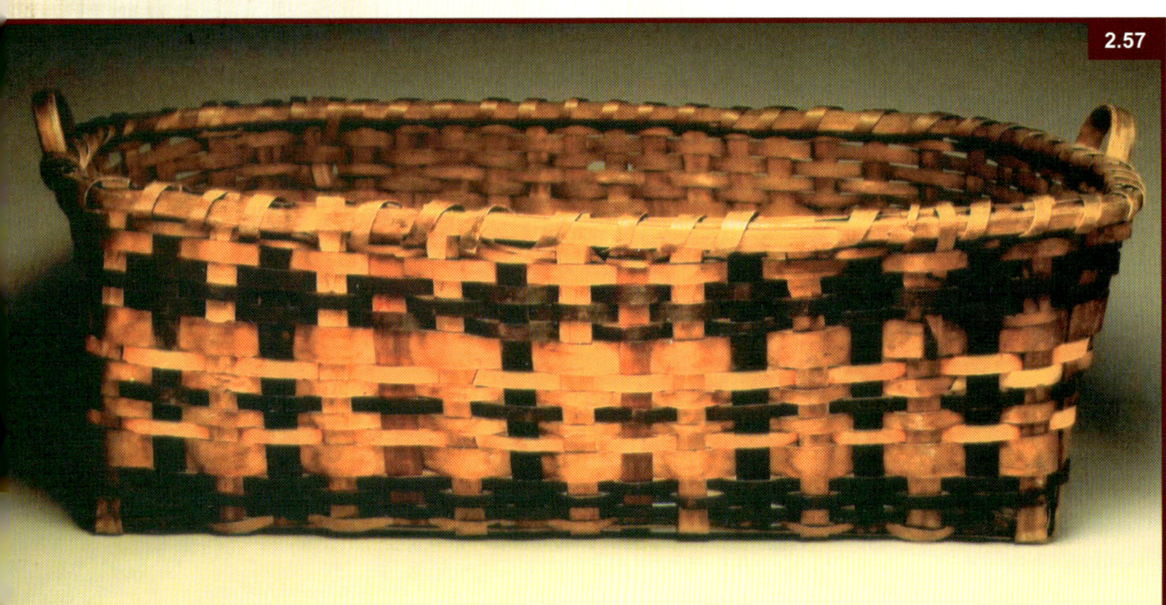

2.54, 2.55. A close-up view of the stamped motif on this basket (2.56) resembles the device carved into a 3-inch wooden block-stamping tool (2.55).

2.56. This covered storage basket, c. 1830s, is typical of southwestern New England with its swabbed narrow weft splints, stamped wide splints with dotted designs in Spanish brown and very faded laundry bluing, and an 1828 newspaper lining its interior.

2.57. Decorative characteristics of early to mid-19th-century southwestern New England baskets with wide and narrow splints include baskets with splints that are swabbed-only.

2.58. Southwestern New England baskets may have splints that are stamped-only.

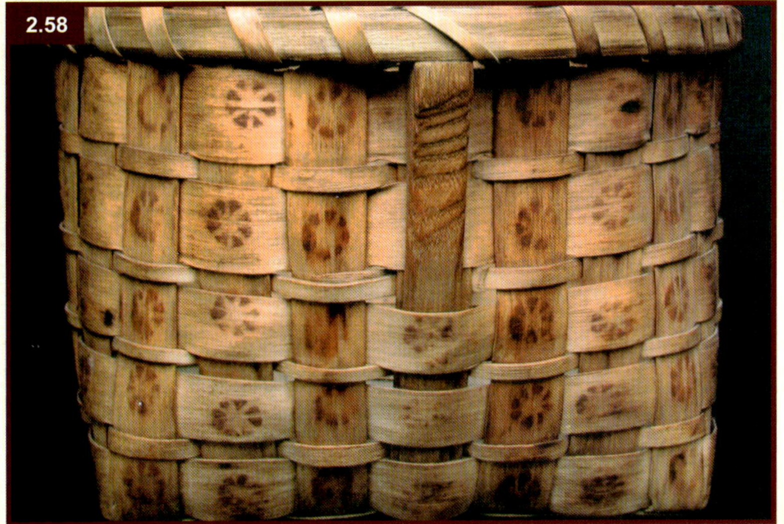

2.59. Baskets from this region more often have splints that are both swabbed and stamped.

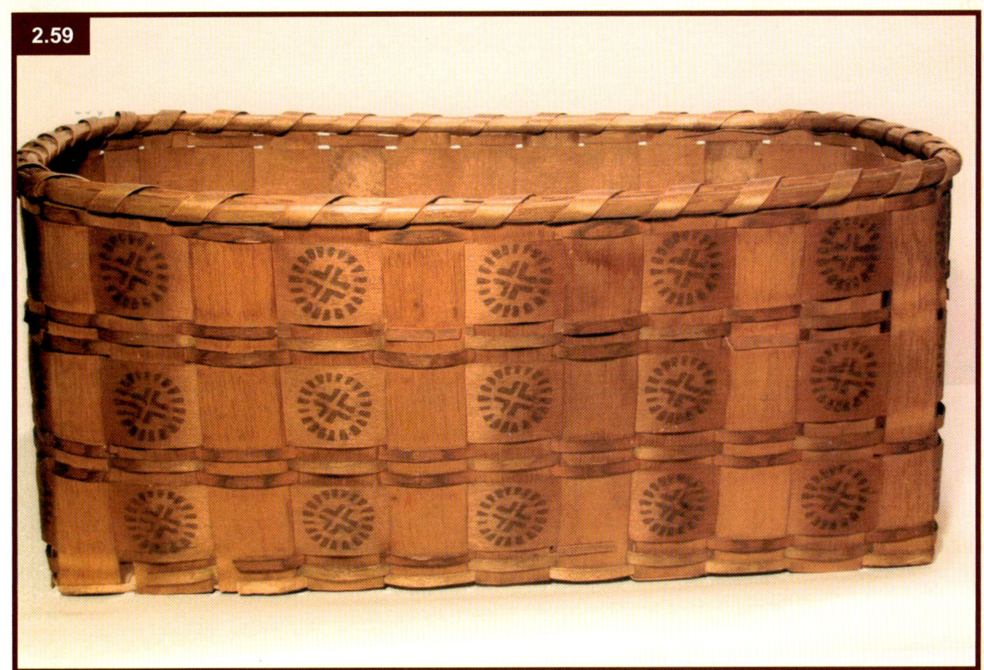

2.60. Many swabbed-plus-stamped motifs are created in two-color combinations like brown and faded Mohegan pink.

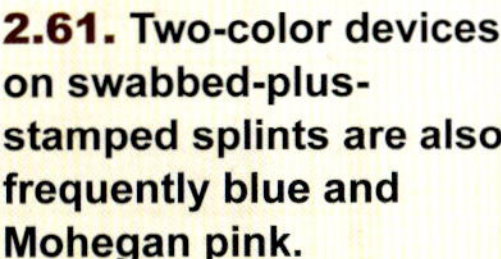

2.61. Two-color devices on swabbed-plus-stamped splints are also frequently blue and Mohegan pink.

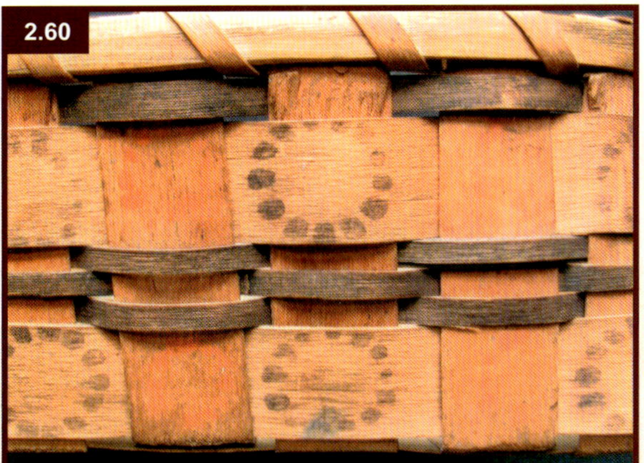

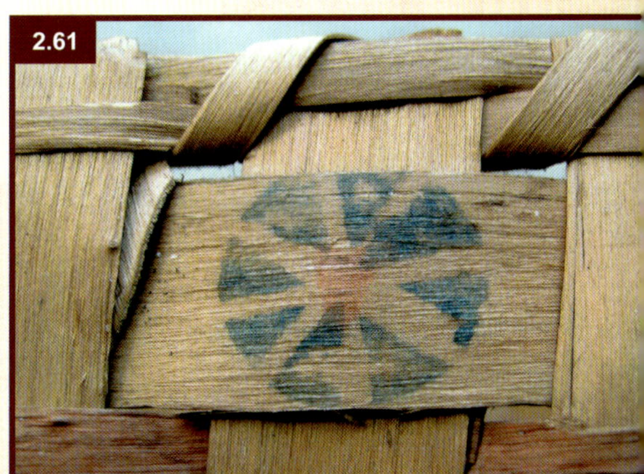

What to Look For

Look for these characteristics to help identify Southern New England and Long Island baskets:

Forms

- Some flexible twined bags
- Large plaited woodsplint storage baskets with covers and wide or wide-plus-narrow splints
- Smaller uncovered plaited woodsplint baskets with or without handles

Techniques

- Plain plaiting
- Some hexagonal plaiting or "hex weave"
- Some twining (in very early or very recent work)

Decoration

- Applied stains and pigments (including black, brown, orangish pink, blue, green, yellow)
- Wide woodsplints with hand-painted design elements (eastern Connecticut, Rhode Island, or southeastern Massachusetts)
- Woodsplints with swabbing
- Woodsplints with stamped elements (southwestern Connecticut, Long Island)
- Woodsplints with swabbing plus stamped elements
- Scorched punctate decoration (Gay Head Wampanoag)

Materials

- Usually ash splints
- Splints of hickory, oak, and other non-ash hardwoods, plus rye straw favored by Wampanoag

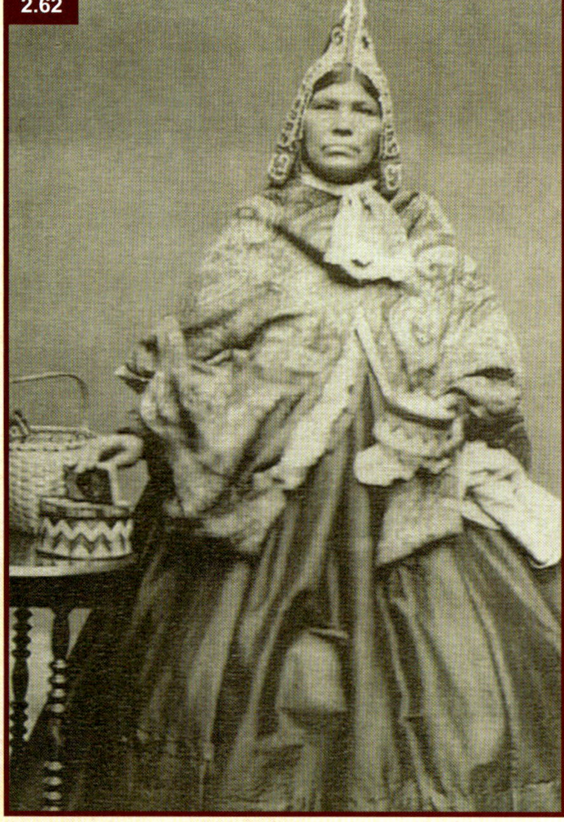

2.62. ***"A Mi'kmaq woman with quillwork box and basket,"* is possibly Mary Christianne Paul Morris of Chocolate Lake or Bella Marble of Shubenacadie, Nova Scotia, photographed by Joseph S. Rogers, c. 1863-1873.**

Northern New England and Canadian Maritimes

Mid-19th-century covered storage baskets created in Northern New England and the Canadian Maritime Provinces differ somewhat in appearance from comparable baskets made in Southern New England and Long Island. For instance, Northern New England examples lack hand-painted or stamped design elements. However, like some Connecticut-area examples from southwestern New England, they may have woodsplints that are swabbed with color.

Smaller, fancier woodsplint baskets made in Northern New England and the Canadian Maritimes and St. Lawrence lowlands during the late 19th

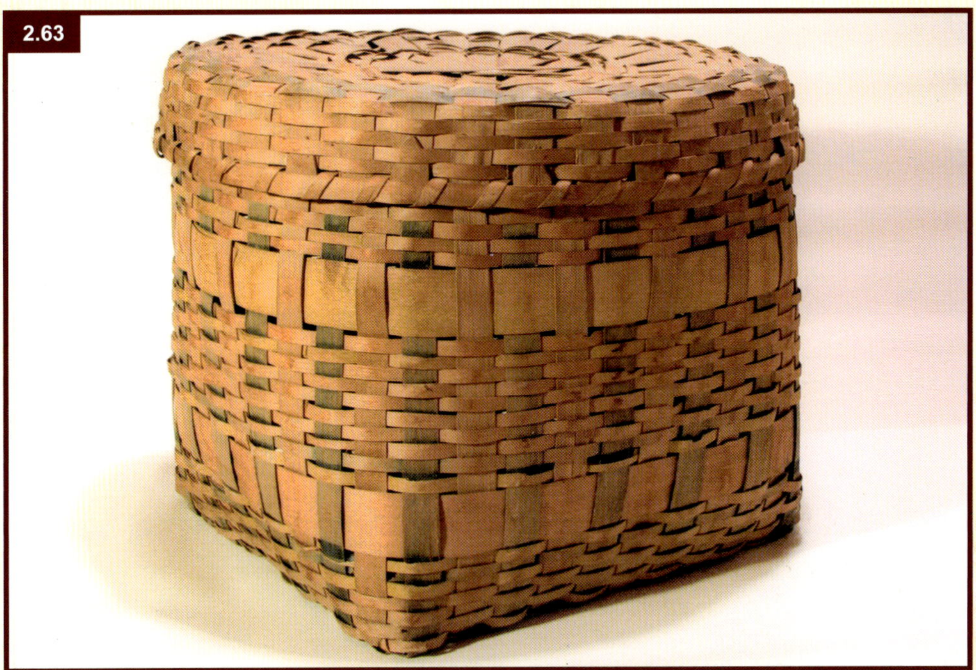

2.63. This typical covered storage basket from Maine is likely Penobscot. It has wide, yellow-swabbed weavers, or weft splints, and blue-swabbed warp splints, c. 1830-1860.

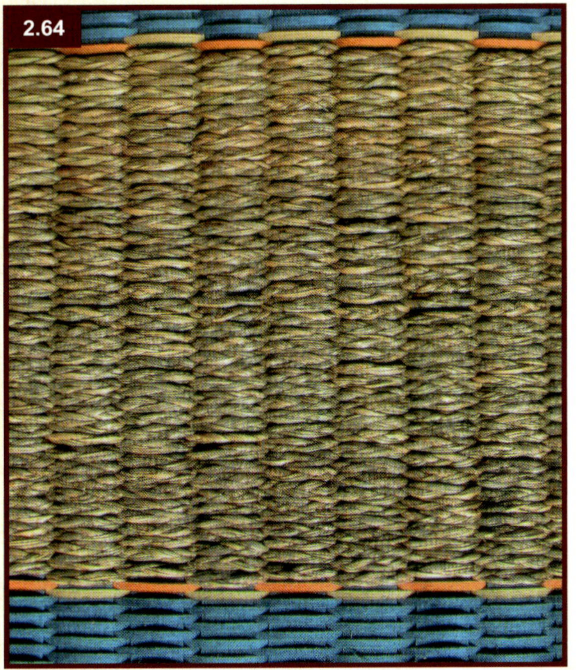

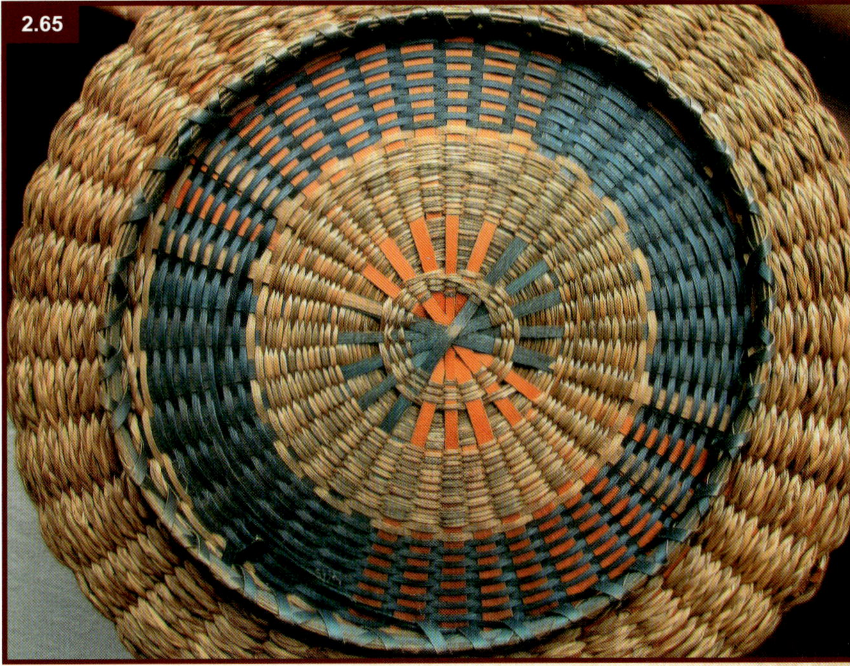

2.64. Baskets from Northern New England and the Canadian Maritimes often have brightly dyed woodsplints and braided sweetgrass.

2.65. The interior of this splint and sweetgrass basket remains brightly dyed, despite exterior fading.

century to early 20th century are highly embellished. They may dazzle the eye with splints that originally were brightly dyed with aniline colors. More often, though, these dyes may have faded away on exposed surfaces.

As the dyeing process permeates the entire splint, dyed splints have color visible on both interior and exterior surfaces, distinguishing them from swabbed examples. Woodsplints might be dyed with vegetal, mineral, or commercial aniline coloring agents like Diamond-brand dyes.

After about 1880, Eastern Algonquian craftspeople in Maine and southeastern Canada began interweaving lengths of fragrant sweetgrass into their ash splint products. Novel shapes that copied Euramerican domestic wares like yarn holders, lidded sewing

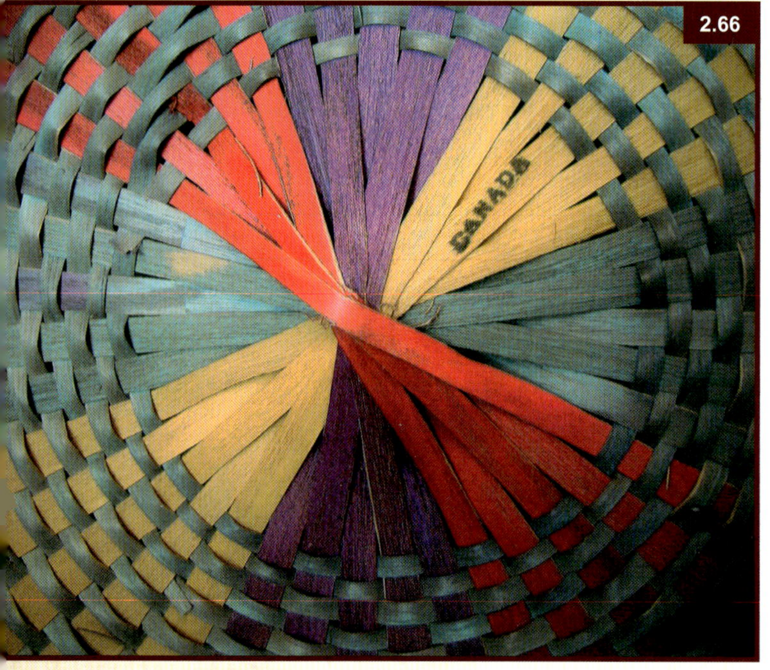

baskets, handkerchief baskets, hair receivers, fans, bookmarks, and wall pockets gained popularity as souvenir items for tourists in late Victorian times and were turned out in vast quantities.

Even today, Penobscot, Passamaquoddy, Abenaki, Micmac, and Maliseet makers are known for both their sturdy woodsplint utility baskets and their decorative fancy work. The northernmost peoples also have fashioned birchbark objects, some of which may be etched with curvilinear or geometric elements, or with forms copied from nature. Other birchbark objects may be decorated with porcupine quill work.

2.66. Diagnostic characteristics from Northern New England and Canadian Maritimes include many decorative methods, like plaiting baskets with multi-colored or "Roman-colored" dyed woodsplints.

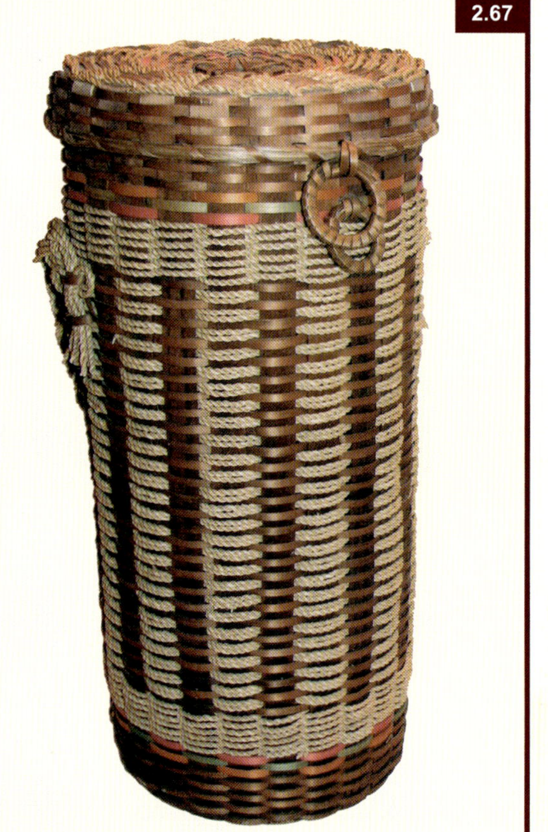

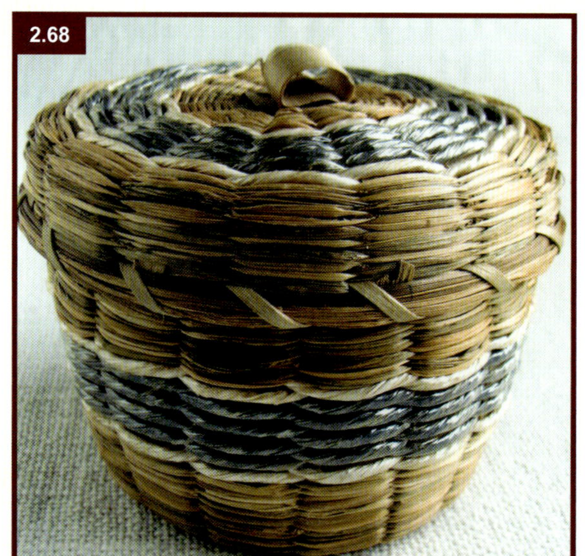

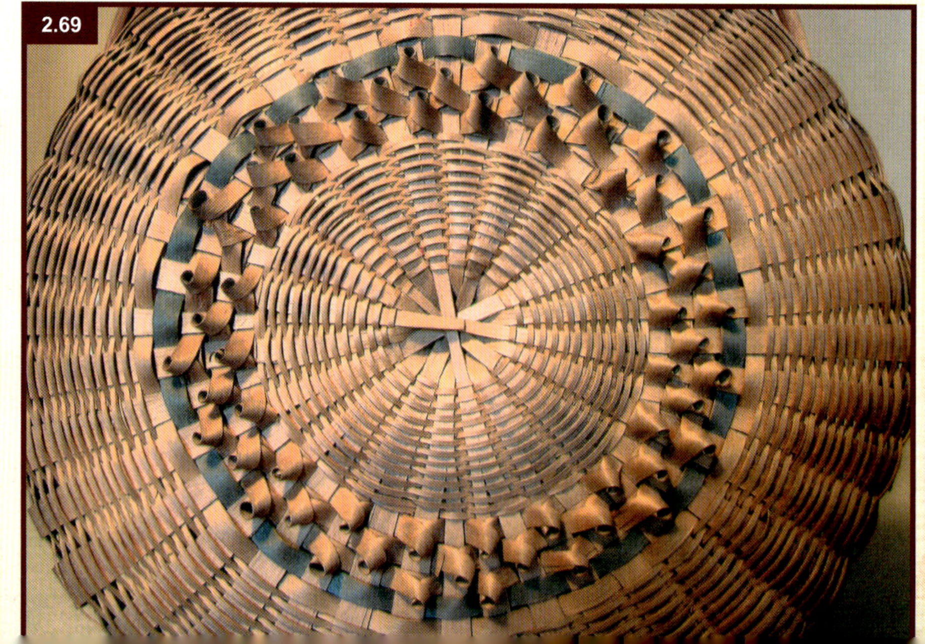

2.67. Baskets with ash splints, sweetgrass, plus Hong Kong cord.

2.68. Baskets with ash splints, sweetgrass, plus plasticized cord.

2.69. Curly splintwork.

2.70. Woodsplint lacework.

2.71. Frogs, like this example by Mary Mitchell Gabriel, Passamaquoddy.

2.72. Bound ring-handles of coiled woodsplints.

2.73. Etching on birchbark boxes.

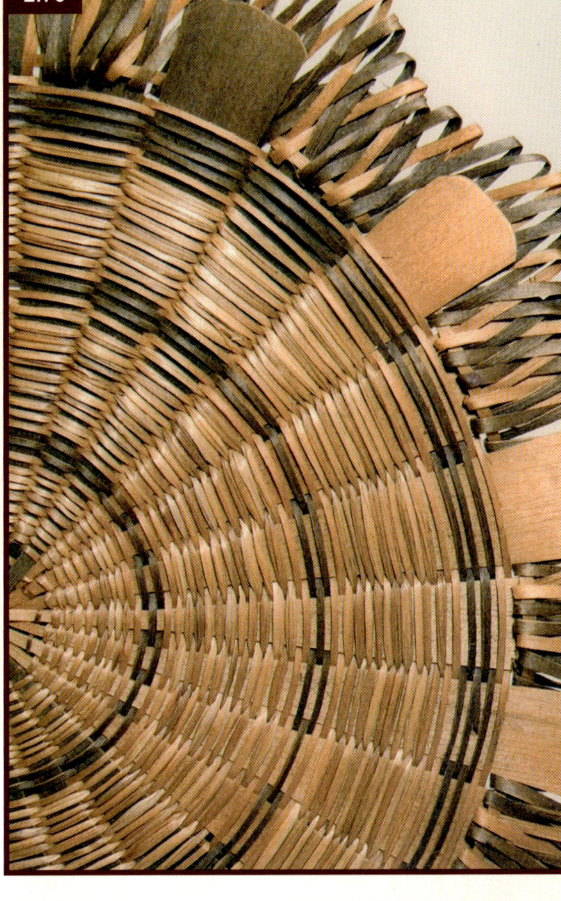

2.70

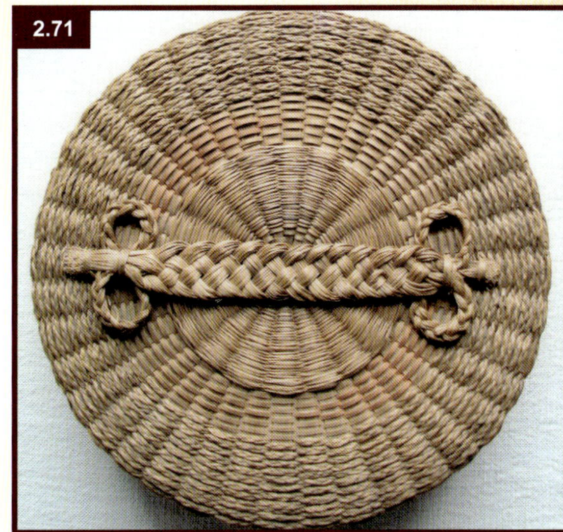

2.71

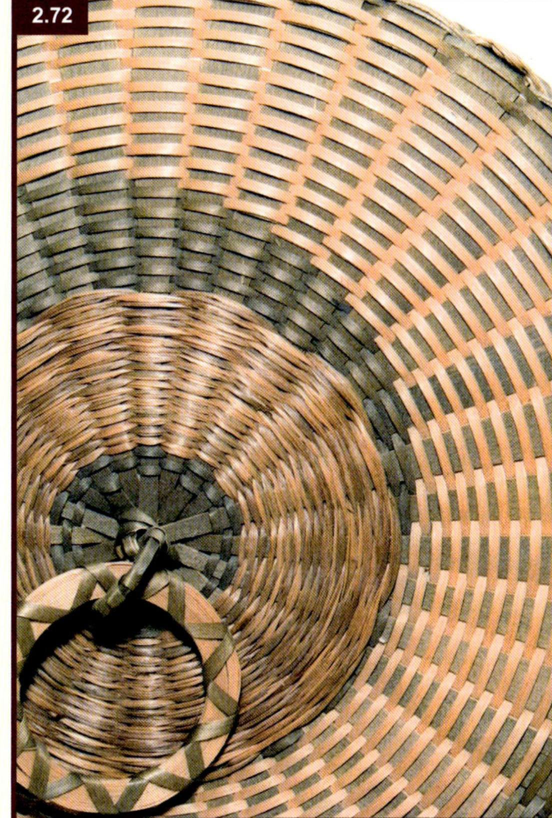

2.72

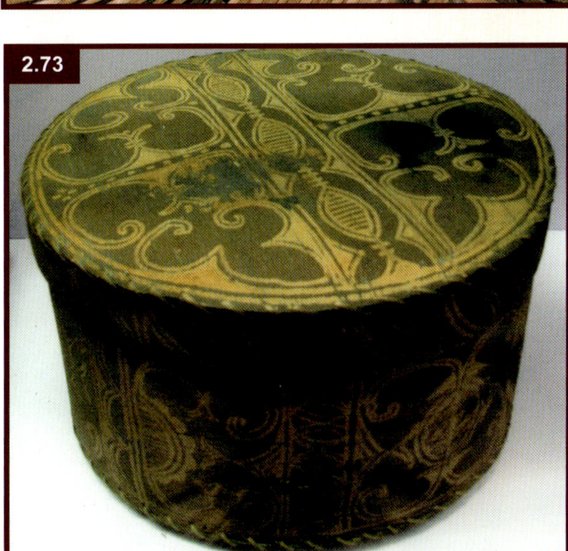

2.73

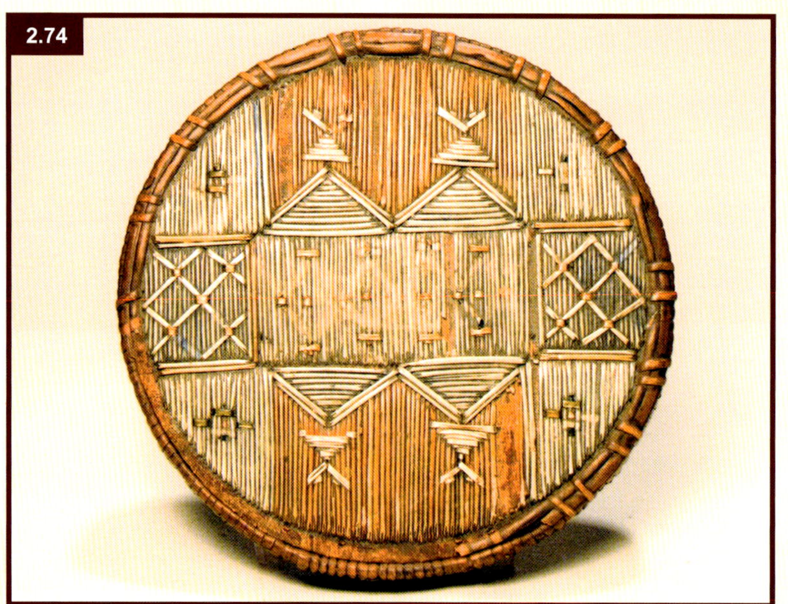

2.74. Porcupine quill decoration on a birchbark box.

What to Look For

LOOK FOR THESE CHARACTERISTICS TO HELP IDENTIFY NORTHERN NEW ENGLAND AND CANADIAN MARITIMES BASKETS:

FORMS

- Large plaited woodsplint storage baskets with covers and wide or wide-plus-narrow splints
- Plaited woodsplint baskets with or without handles
- Novelty basket forms and whimseys
- Birchbark containers, with or without decoration

TECHNIQUES

- Plain plaiting
- Hexagonal-plaited utility forms and small sewing basket inserts
- Some twill plaiting of baskets (especially in recent work)
- Many birchbark objects have rims bound with spruce root stitching and/or wrapping
- Some birchbark objects have rims edged with sweetgrass then bound with spruce root

DECORATION

- Applied pigments (including blue, green, purple, yellow, orange, red)
- Woodsplint bands with swabbing (early to mid-19th century)
- Dyed woodsplints with monochrome or one color (late 19th through entire 20th century)
- Dyed woodsplints with polychrome or several colors, called "Roman colored" (early 20th century)
- Structural manipulation of splints to form points, twists, and curls
- "Fancy" splintwork resembling lacework
- Woodsplint-lashed sweetgrass edging on some basket rims
- Etched double-curve or floral and faunal design elements on birchbark
- Dyed porcupine quill embroidery on birchbark
- Pull handles: loops or bound coils of rolled woodsplints
- Braided attachments or "frogs" of sweetgrass or "Hong Kong" cord

MATERIALS

- Ash splints
- Ash splints plus sweetgrass (in straight, braided, or two-ply twisted lengths)
- Ash splints plus "Hong Kong" twisted paper, grass, or plastic cord
- Applied feathers, pine cones, other materials (in very recent work)
- Birchbark objects, some with porcupine quill decoration

Upper New York State

Iroquoian basketmakers include the Mohawk, Oneida, Onondaga, Cayuga, Seneca, and Tuscarora. Together, they comprise the Six Nations Confederacy (also known as Haudenosaunee). These groups are concentrated in central New York state and along the St. Lawrence River in Ontario and Québec. The archaeological record has shown that Iroquoian peoples have been plaiting woodsplint utility baskets for their own use since well before 1700, and they were probably plaiting other materials from much earlier times.

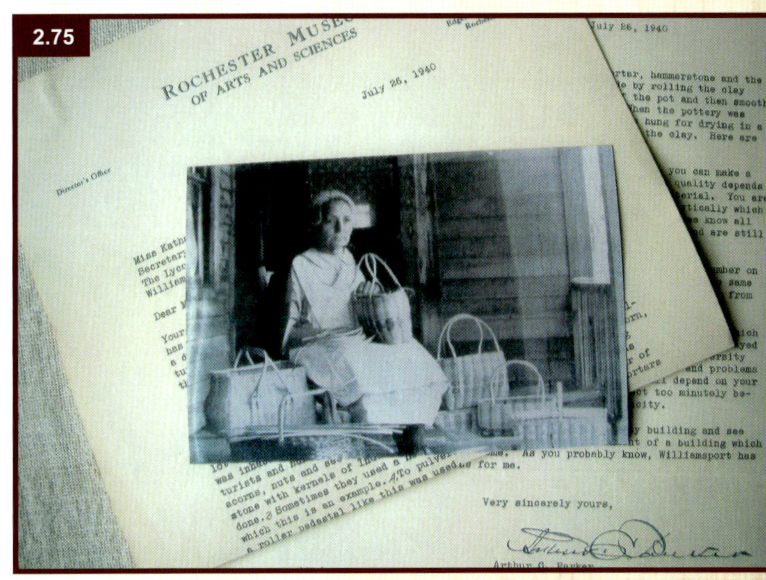

2.75. Archaeologist and museum director Arthur C. Parker, an Iroquois man from a prominent Seneca family, helped to revive his tribe's Native crafts when he oversaw a federal WPA program during the Great Depression. Workers like Seneca basketmakers earned fifty cents an hour to produce traditional products for museum exhibits that documented Iroquois culture.

Corn or maize has been the main agricultural crop of these Iroquoian groups for centuries. Not unexpectedly, their woodsplint work baskets include a number of specialized forms like sieves, trays, corn-washing baskets, and pack baskets for processing corn and hominy. Although fashioned originally for Native use, by the late 1700s baskets also were being sold to local farmers and other non-Indians. By the 19th century, covered storage baskets and other utility

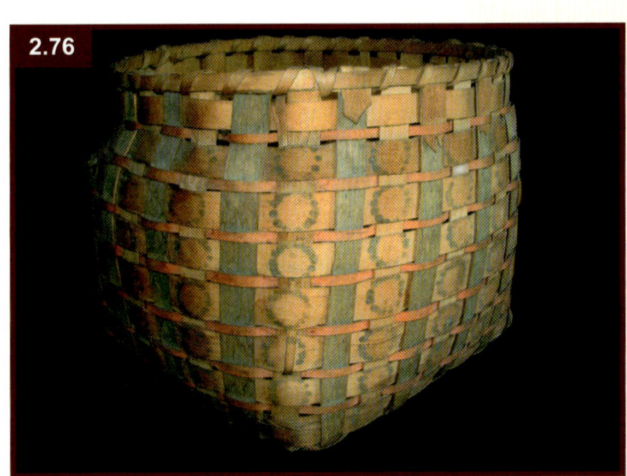

2.76. Typical forms include an Iroquois swabbed and stamped storage basket, now lacking its cover, c. 1850, 13" rim diameter.

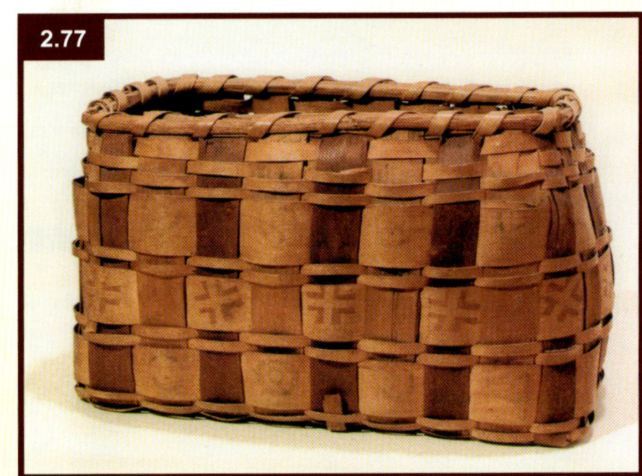

2.77. Seneca swabbed and stamped work basket, missing its handle, c. 1870, 9" long.

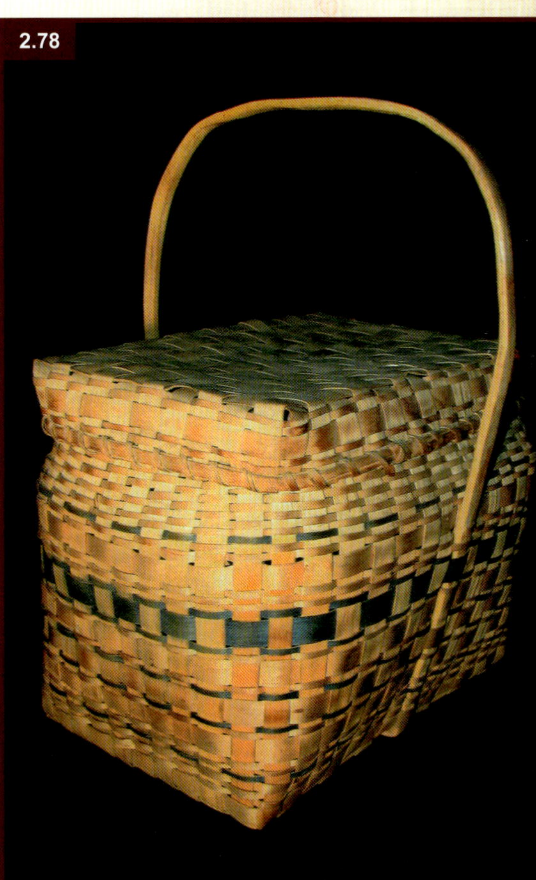

2.78. Seneca covered storage basket, with handle and blue swabbed splints, which may have been a product of the 1930s Seneca Arts Project, 11" long.

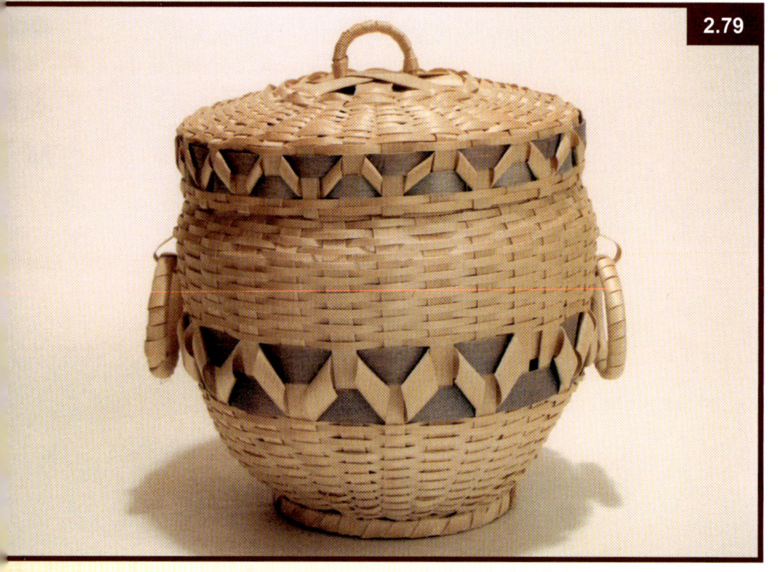

forms for use within the home also were made and might be decorated with swabbing and/or stamped designs.

By around 1900, some Akwesasne Mohawks near St. Regis on the St. Lawrence River were supplying the nearby trading post, among others, with plaited woodsplint baskets and whimseys that closely resemble those made by Algonquians from Northern New England and the Maritime Provinces. These souvenir basketry products became highly standardized as the basketmakers catered to the commercial outlets and to early 20th-century jobbers who supplied the mail-order houses. Iroquoians, as well as neighboring Eastern Algonquian basketmakers, provided quantities of these wares. They all favored ash splints with decorative aniline dyes, curly splint weaves, and fragrant sweetgrass that appealed readily to tourists.

Iroquoians have been alone, though, in creating distinctive cornhusk products. The Seneca have twined cornhusks into small,

2.79. Vacationers to upstate New York have always appreciated Iroquoian ash splint baskets, which often are colorfully dyed and may be given distinctive wrapped pull handles or knotted or appliquéd knobs. This Oneida Iroquois covered basket with blue-dyed horizontal weft splints has a wrapped pull ring, and its base has been signed by its maker, Katie Sickles, 1980s, 6" high.

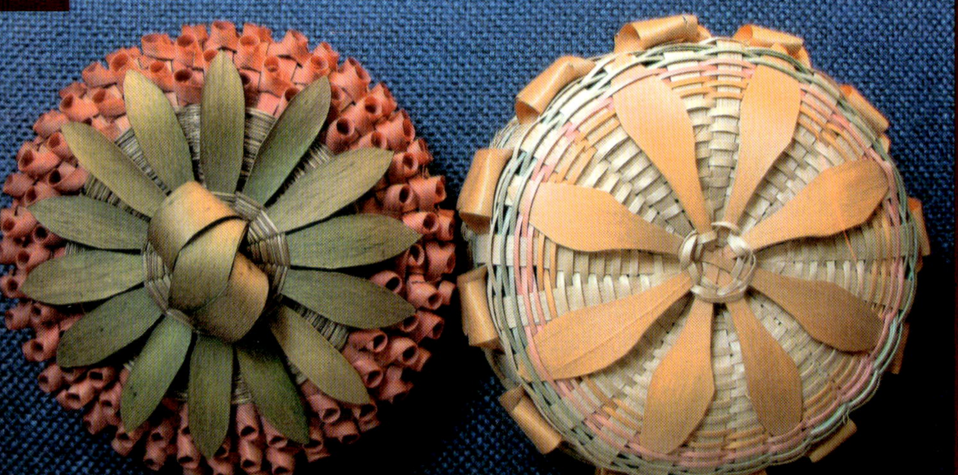

2.80. Appliquéd leaves or petals may surround knobs or pulls or central starts on covers from this region.

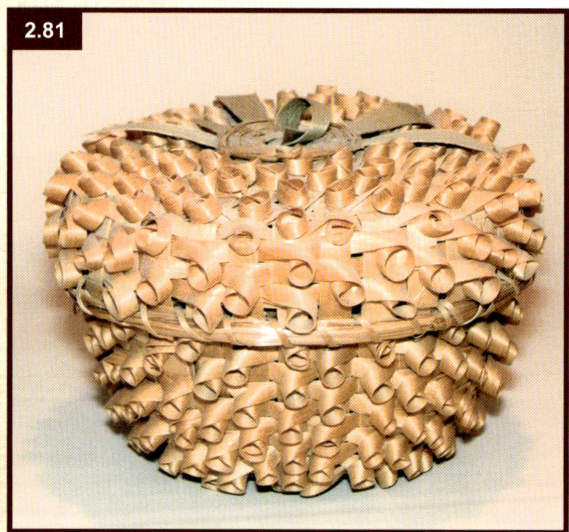

2.81. Curly splintwork and fragrant sweetgrass are used in upper New York state, as elsewhere.

2.82, 2.83. Cornhusk masks, or fringed "bushy heads," represent spirits who instructed the Iroquois to grow maize. Though many have been woven for sacred use and are not displayed out of respect, these two examples with original tags were made for sale to travelers in the mid-20th century. **2.82** is 4" high.

2.84. A Tuscarora or Onondaga maker coiled and stitched braided cornhusk into a salt or tobacco basket before adding a corncob stopper, early to mid-20th century, about 3" high.

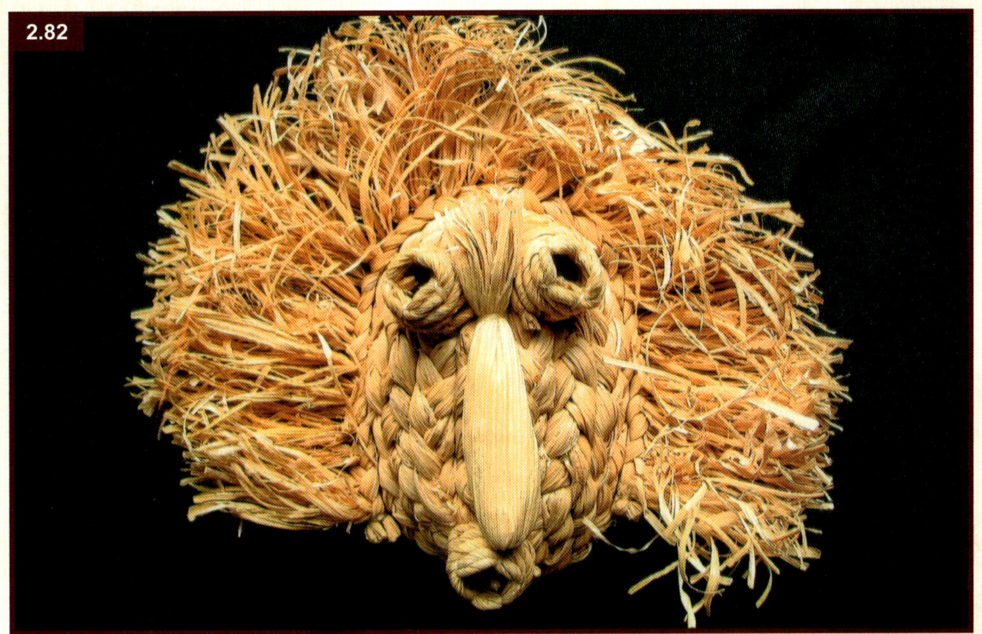

2.82

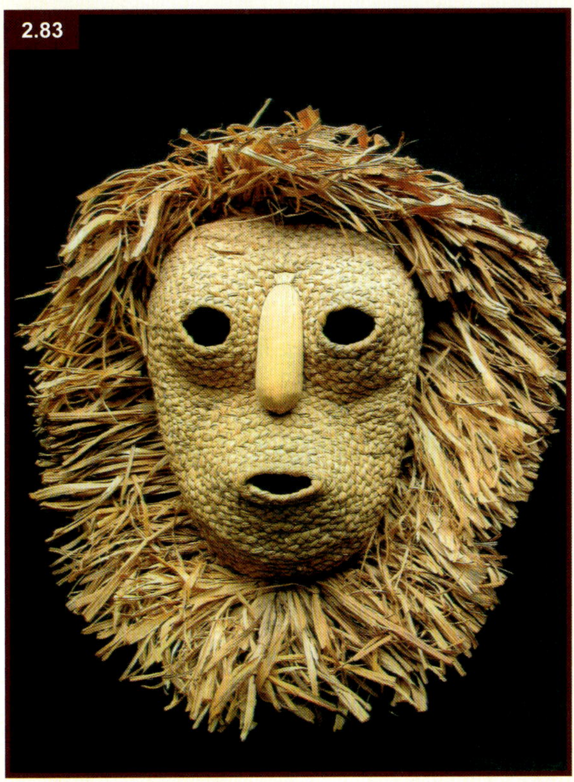

2.83

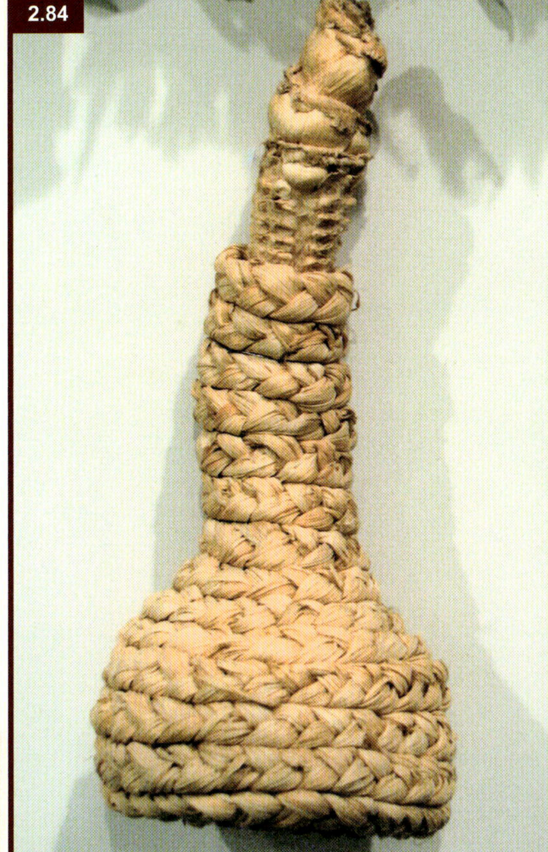

2.84

useful salt bottles, tobacco containers, and even moccasins. They also have twined cornhusks into masks both for Native ceremonial use and for sale. By contrast, other Iroquoian groups like the Tuscarora and Onondaga have used a different technique, coiling and stitching lengths of braided cornhusk into moccasins, Husk Face masks, and other forms.

What to Look For

LOOK FOR THESE CHARACTERISTICS TO HELP IDENTIFY UPPER NEW YORK STATE BASKETS:

FORMS

- Plaited woodsplint utility baskets for processing hominy or corn
- Many novelty basket forms and whimseys
- Twined cornhusk moccasins, masks, small bottles (generally Seneca)
- Braids of cornhusks coiled into masks, small bottles (generally Tuscarora, Onondaga)

TECHNIQUES

- Plain plaiting
- Some hexagonal plaiting or "hex weave"
- Twill plaiting
- Twining of cornhusks (Seneca)
- Coiling of braided cornhusks (Tuscarora, Onondaga, and some Seneca)

DECORATION

- Combined wide and narrow woodsplints with swabbing
- Applied stains and pigments (including yellow, blue, green, red, orange)
- Swabbed and/or stamped designs, often in three- or four-color combinations
- All-over stamped decorative elements
- Brightly dyed woodsplints
- A single wide swabbed or dyed (often blue) weft splint placed slightly below rim
- Structural manipulation of splints to form points, twists, and curls
- "Fancy" splintwork resembling lacework
- Appliqué splint petals or curls
- Pull handles: appliqué splint petals or curls cluster around a central knot or ring

MATERIALS

- Ash splints
- Ash splints plus sweetgrass (straight or braided lengths)
- Cornhusks

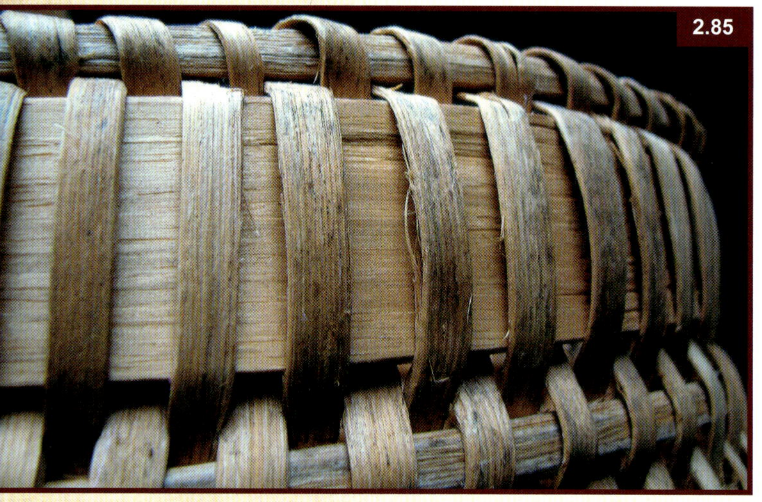

2.85. This distinctive Rappahannock rim finish is a style also shared with Appalachian basketmakers.

Algonquians like the Delaware in the mid-Atlantic region and their kinfolk in Oklahoma also have produced some plaited woodsplint baskets. Most of their forms resemble Iroquoian hominy or corn processing baskets. But mid-Atlantic basketmakers generally have used a wider range of materials, such as oak, cornhusk, mulberry, and honeysuckle. Nanticoke and Rappahannock baskets may feature distinctive rim finishes.

THE GREAT LAKES

In the westernmost region of the Northeast, the Siouan-speaking Ho-Chunk (formerly Winnebago) and Central-Northern Algonquian-speaking groups living around the Great Lakes have used twined bags, twill-plaited mats, and stitched birchbark vessels more often than they have relied on woodsplint baskets. Wild rice, a primary staple gathered from local lake shallows, generally was stored and even prepared in flexible basswood fiber bags or birchbark containers made for Native use.

2.86. Three Ojibwe (Chippewa) basket makers near Saginaw, Michigan, plait a variety of woodsplint baskets, c. 1900.

2.87. This southeastern Ojibwe basswood-fiber bag is a flexible type that has been widely used in the Great Lakes region for carrying and storing goods like wild rice, c. 1900, 15.25" high.

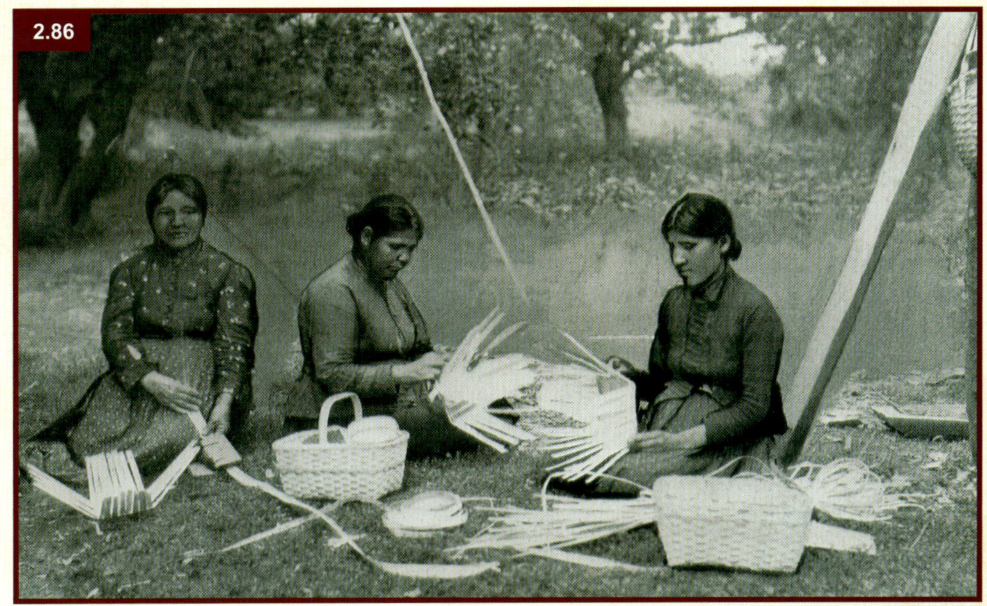

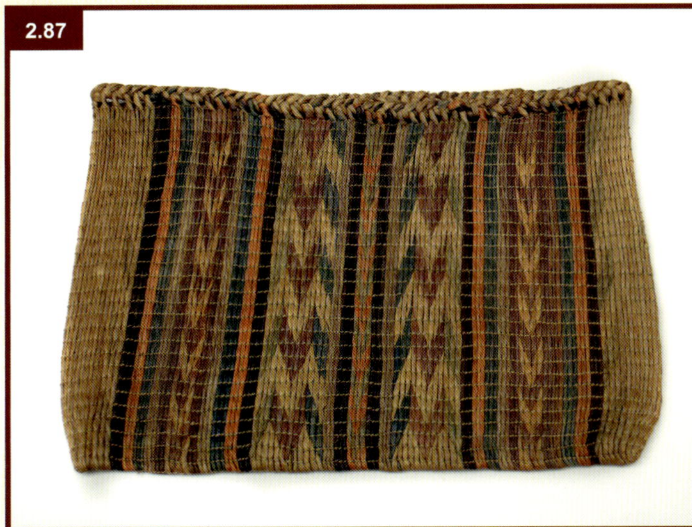

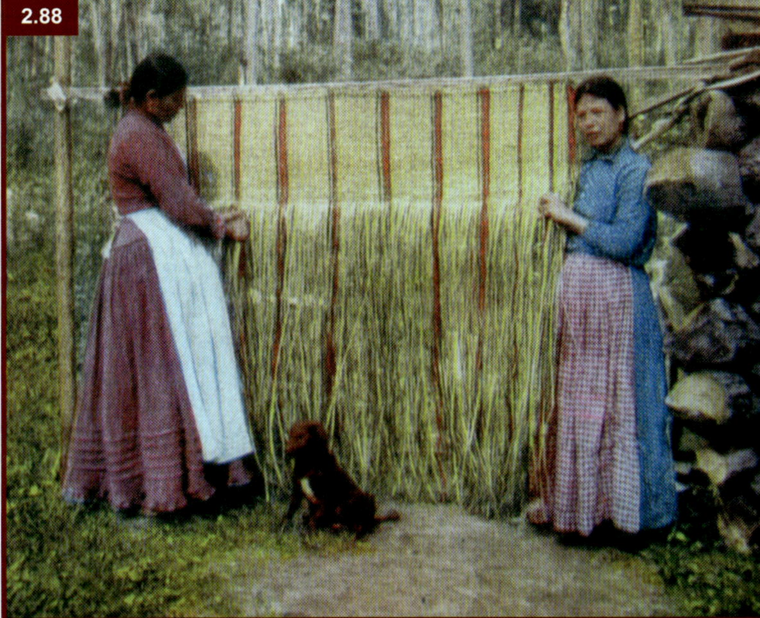

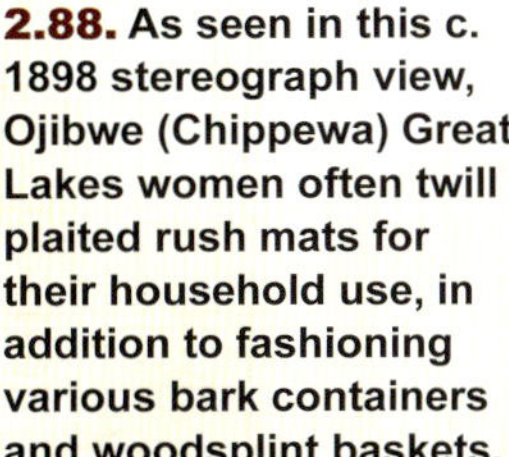

2.88. As seen in this c. 1898 stereograph view, Ojibwe (Chippewa) Great Lakes women often twill plaited rush mats for their household use, in addition to fashioning various bark containers and woodsplint baskets.

2.89. Examples of birchbark vessels from the Great Lakes include a mid-20th-century etched Huron *mokuk*, signed "Max le Gros Huron," 6" long.

Customary forms, such as bark *mokuks* used for storage, quickly found their way into the market economy as curios and souvenirs. Decorative techniques like etching, dyed moosehair embroidery, and porcupine quillwork, along with sweetgrass edging at rim borders, often ornament birchbark vessels made for 19th- and 20th-century tourists.

Great Lakes peoples have plaited some ash splint baskets, as well. The Oneida and Stockbridge may have initially introduced the plaiting technique to

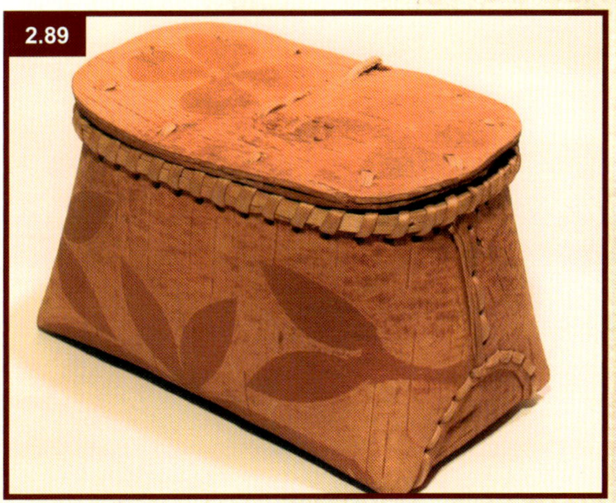

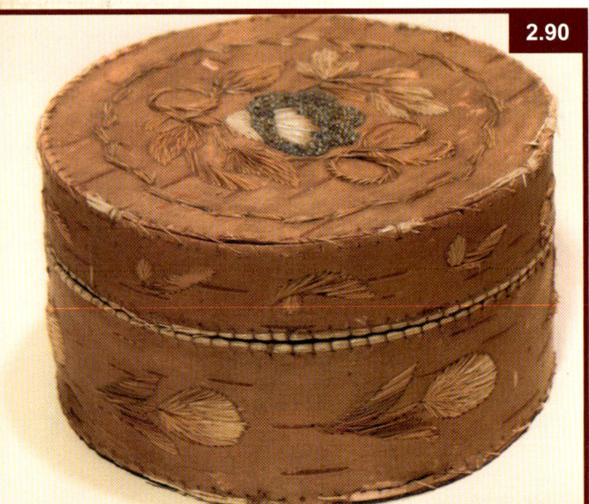

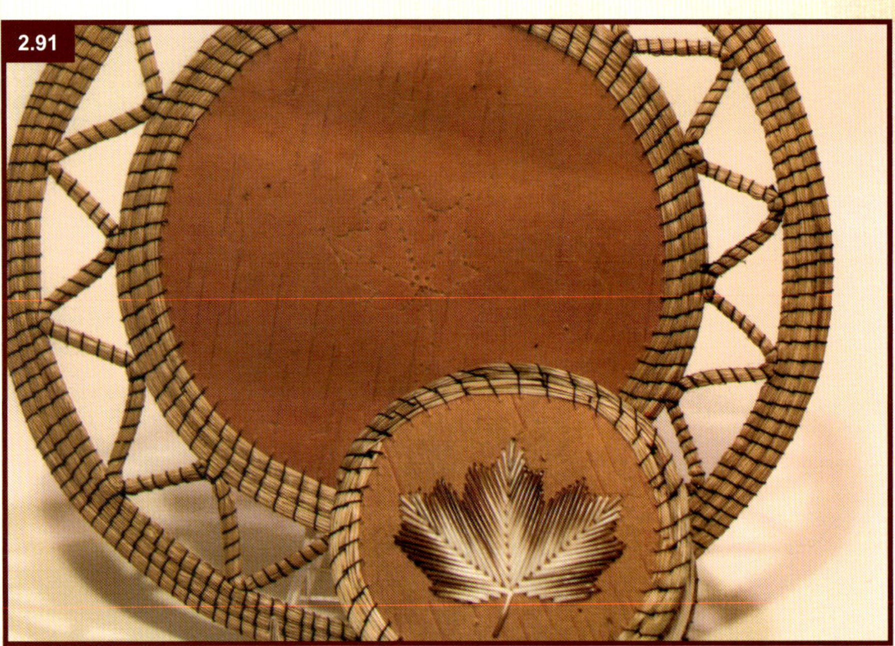

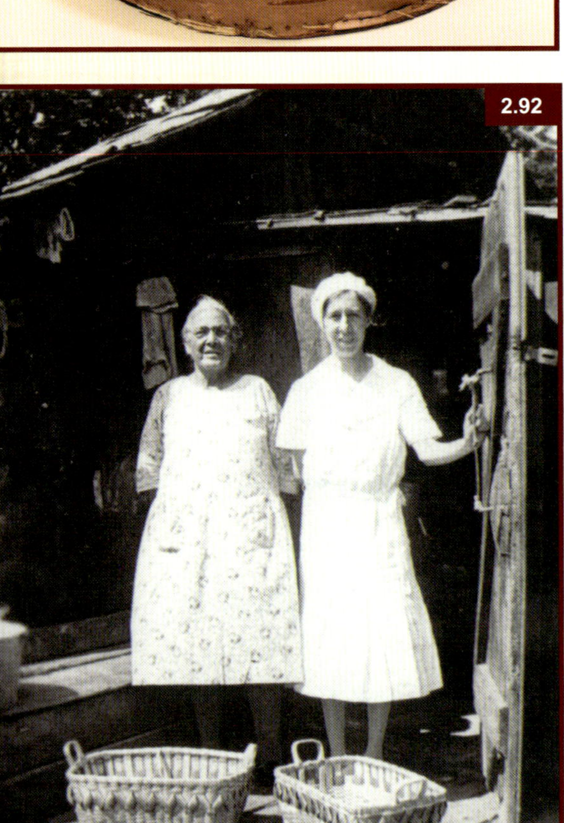

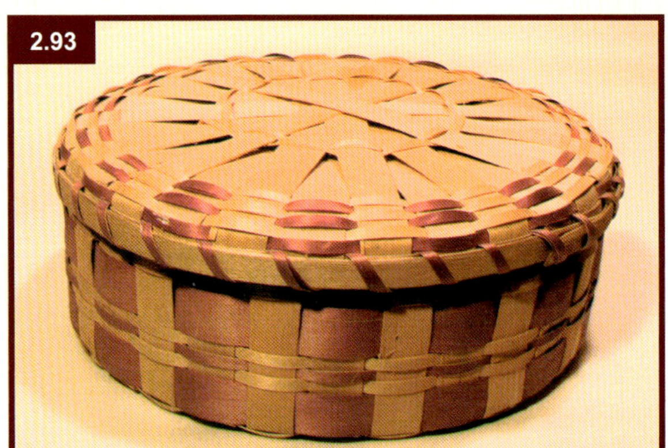

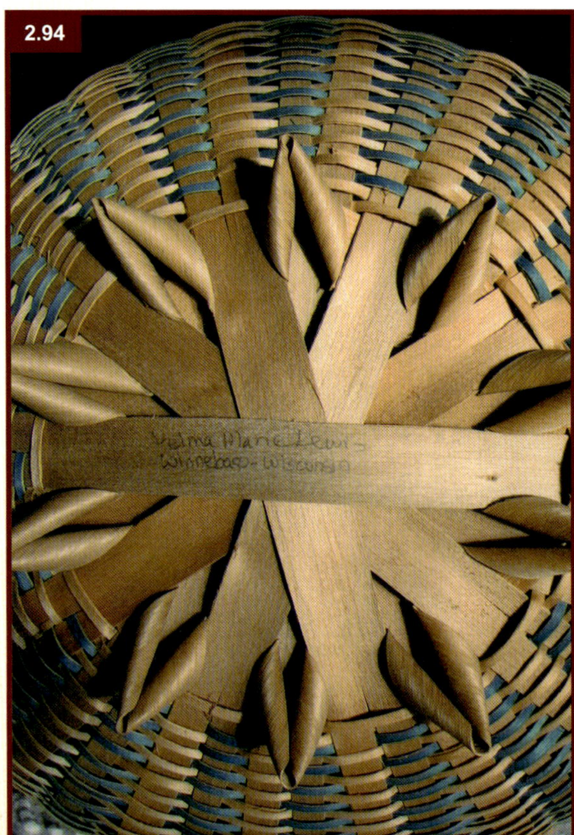

2.90. A covered Great Lakes birchbark box embellished with moose or caribou hair embroidery, c. 1830-1860, 4" diameter.

2.91. Mid- to late 20th-century mat, plus a box enlivened with porcupine quillwork, both edged with sweetgrass stitched with black cotton thread. Note the pierced outline of a leaf, where quills (now gone) once also embellished the larger mat.

2.92. Mrs. Indian Paul (left) of Michigan offered baskets for sale to tourists like Mrs. Mary Lindenthal Kline (right), c. 1947. Her baskets are decorated with dyed woodsplints and curly splintwork.

2.93. Distinctive decorative or structural characteristics from this region include various methods like dyed wide and narrow woodsplints.

2.94. Pointed "porcupine twist" curly splintwork on basketry base.

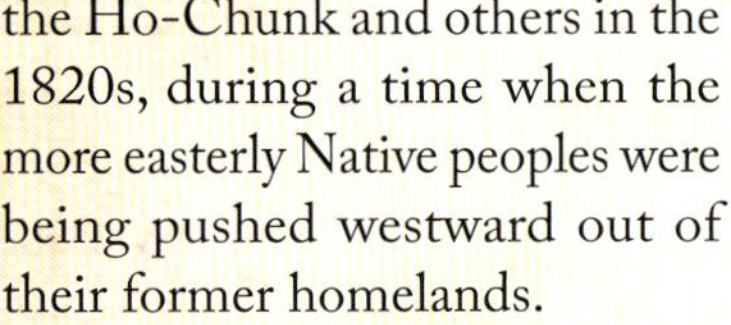

the Ho-Chunk and others in the 1820s, during a time when the more easterly Native peoples were being pushed westward out of their former homelands.

A number of basketmakers living near the Great Lakes, again emulating those Iroquoian groups further to the east, have added

2.95. Twill-plaited base on rectangular- or square-shaped basket.

2.96. Swing-handle basket.

2.97. Continuous "S" or "figure-8" shaped swing-handle attachment.

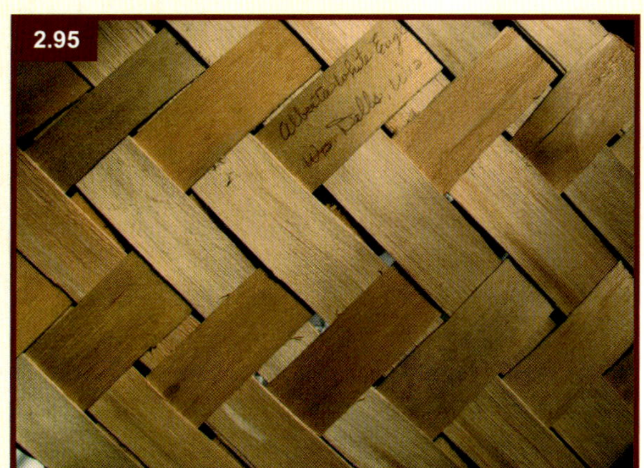

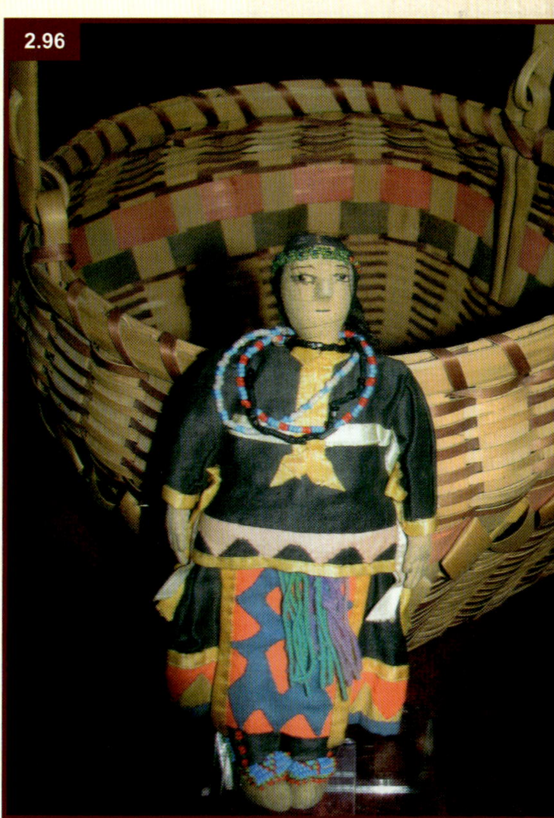

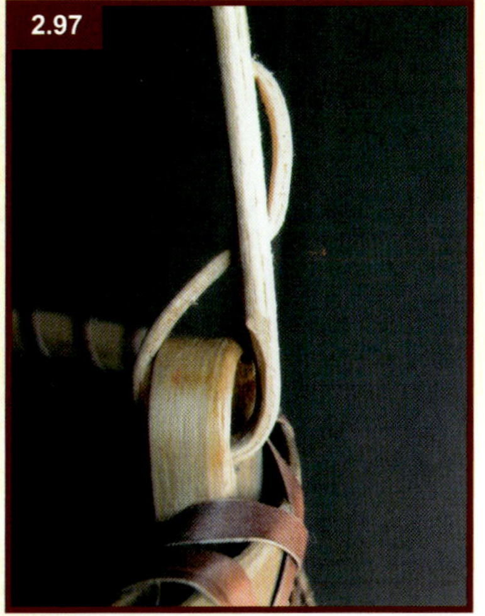

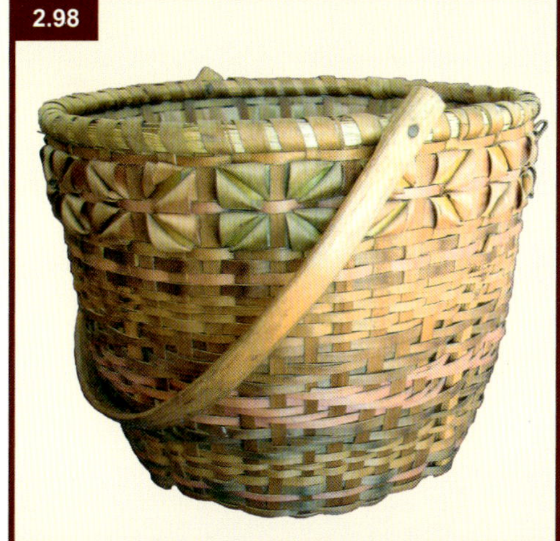

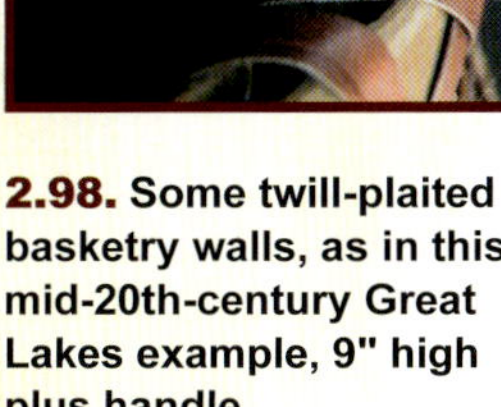

2.98. Some twill-plaited basketry walls, as in this mid-20th-century Great Lakes example, 9" high plus handle.

2.99. Ash splints plus sweetgrass, as seen in this covered Ojibwe basket.

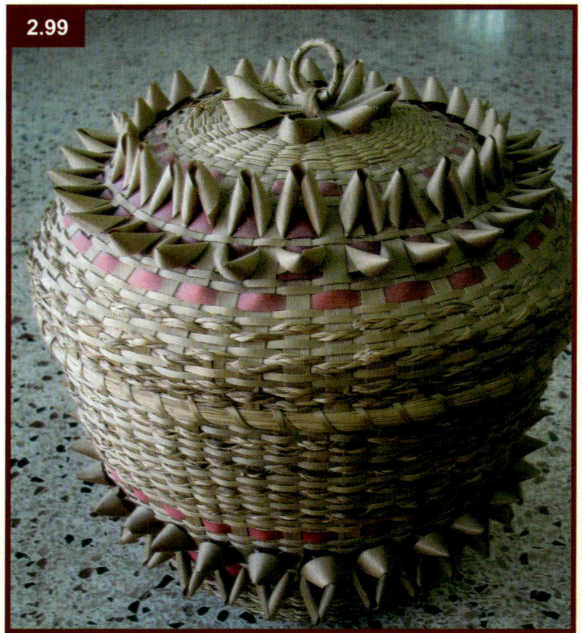

dyed splints and curly details as decorative elements on plaited woodsplint baskets. Some of their baskets, for instance, may display one colored weft splint in the upper portion of the basket, resembling those made by their Oneida teachers of New York state.

Other Great Lakes makers, like the Ho-Chunk and the Sac and Fox, have fashioned woodsplint baskets with distinctive features that differ from similar forms made further to the east. Bases of these baskets are often twill plaited. Their drop- or swing-handle attachments frequently may be steam-bent and looped back on themselves to form a distinctive "S" or figure-8 shaped closure without the aid of metal fasteners. As in other regions, colorful aniline dyes and curly "diamond" twisted splintwork add to their appeal and marketability.

Small bundle-coiled sweetgrass baskets, usually stitched with commercial black thread, like those by Ojibwe and Potawatomi (Anishinaabe) basketmakers, are another

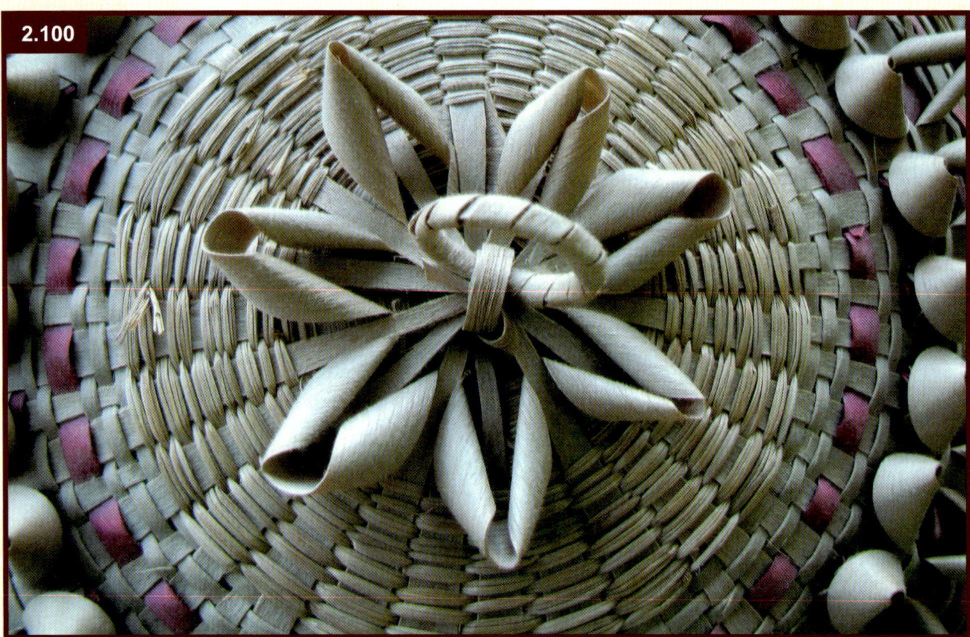

2.100. Curly splintwork clustering around a central wrapped ring.

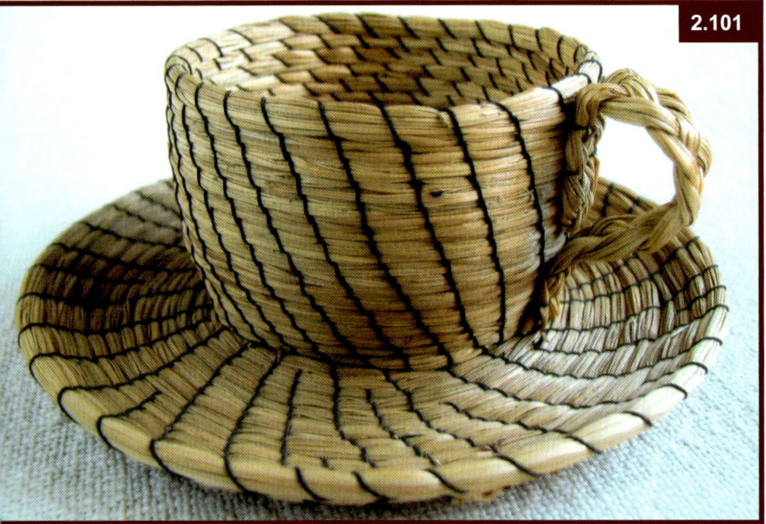

2.101. Bundle-coiled novelties include this sweetgrass teacup and saucer, 4.5" diameter.

distinctive product from this region. They have been—and continue to be—a popular and modestly priced contribution to the western Great Lakes tourist trade.

Some Great Lakes tribes were wholly or partially removed to other locations. Groups including the Sac and Fox, Potawatomi, and Delaware (Lenape) nations, as well as the Ottawa and Seneca-Cayuga tribes, are represented today in the state of Oklahoma (formerly Indian Territory). Numbered among these Native peoples are some individual basketmakers, a few of whom continue to maintain connections and share basketmaking traditions with their Northeastern Woodlands kinfolk.

2.102. Birchbark picture frames edged with stitched bundles of sweetgrass were popular mid-20th-century souvenirs of Great Lakes vacations, 6.5" maximum width.

What to Look For

Look for these characteristics to help identify Great Lakes area baskets:

Forms
- Folded elm-bark utility vessels
- Flexible twined basswood fiber bags and commercial yarn bags
- Plaited woodsplint baskets with or without handles
- Twill-plaited mats
- Birchbark containers with or without decoration
- Small bundle-coiled sweetgrass whimseys

Techniques
- Folding and stitching of bark and birchbark
- Plain plaiting
- Twill plaiting of basket bases is common
- Bundle coiling of sweetgrass, stitched with commercial black thread
- Birchbark objects may have rims bound with spruce root stitching
- Birchbark objects may have rims edged with sweetgrass bound with black thread

Decoration
- Etched floral and faunal elements on birchbark objects
- Applied moosehair or porcupine quill work on birchbark objects
- Thread-stitched sweetgrass edging on rims of many woodsplint baskets
- Thread-stitched sweetgrass or moosehair edging on rims of many birchbark boxes
- Brightly dyed woodsplints
- Structural manipulation of splints to form points and "diamond" curly twists
- Swing-handles with "S"-shaped or figure-8 shaped attachments
- Pull handles: curly splintwork clusters around a central wrapped ring

Materials
- Elm bark
- Birchbark
- Ash splints
- Sweetgrass
- Commercial black thread

Extending the Legacy

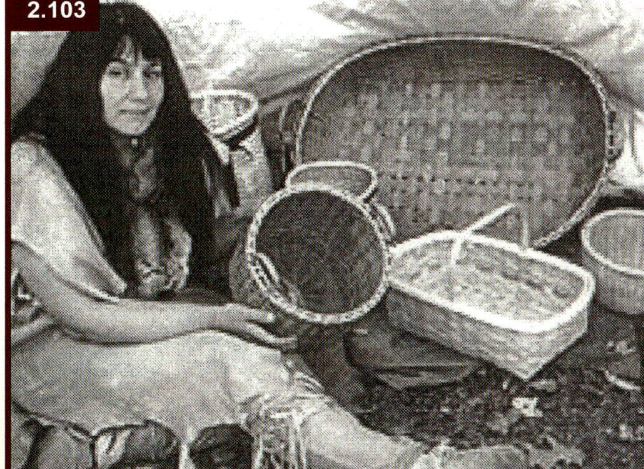

2.103. Strong Woman, Julianne Jennings, is a cultural anthropologist and member of the Nottoway tribal community of Virginia. For more than fifteen years, she has been promoting the cultural history of Native peoples through programs and workshops on ash splint basketmaking.

Since the late 20th century, Native Northeastern basketmaking has continued to change rapidly in new directions that still are nurtured by earlier roots. Today's Native woodsplint baskets frequently transcend regional divisions and styles.

Though some modern-day baskets may still "look Indian," others stylistically appear more abstract or cosmopolitan. In addition to creating fine examples of long-familiar forms, certain Native basketmakers in the Northeast are taking their craft in different directions. Techniques, forms, and designs are being combined in innovative ways using both customary and contemporary materials to create artistic baskets that are highly individualistic. This diversity is exciting. Basketmakers now value their craft as a creative outlet but also as a legacy of enduring Native identity and heritage. Their contemporary basketry has become a metaphor for the resilience of a traditional culture in a modern world.

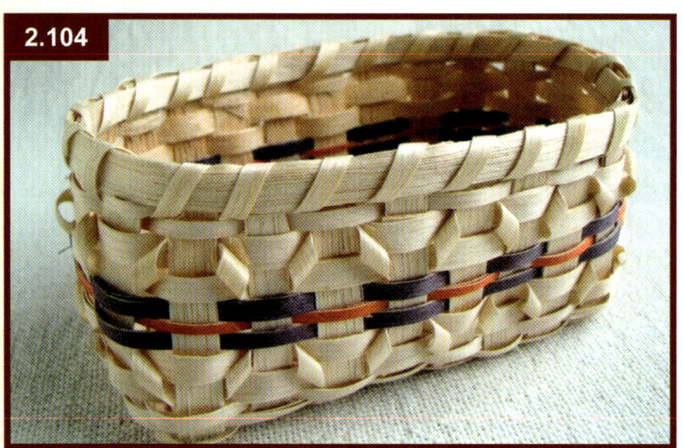

2.104. Barbara Robidoux of Santa Fe, New Mexico, is a Native basketmaker who exemplifies many of the changes impacting her craft today. She self-identifies as Cherokee but makes ash splint and sweetgrass baskets that share characteristics common to the Northeastern Woodlands craft. Barbara learned the basics of basketmaking while living on the Passamaquoddy reservation in Maine. She has embellished this small basket for holding business cards with dyed splints and curly splintwork.

Native peoples across the northern regions covered in this book share numerous cultural connections. Though they speak different languages and dialects, many of these groups have told similar stories of a giant culture-hero, a protector and transformer who shaped the Native world. They refer to him by various names (each with various English spellings). For example, the Ojibwe know him as Nanabozho, their Cree neighbors as Wesakechak; tribes across southern New England call him Maushop or Wetucks; and among the Wabanaki groups of northern New England and eastern Canada he is Glooskap. One Passamaquoddy legend recounts how Man emerged from the bark of ash trees as Glooskap struck the trees with his arrows. From the ash and other elements of the giant's realm, the people fashioned their baskets. With that association in mind, we present "Glooskap's Gallery" as a tribute to Northeastern Woodlands basketmakers and their work in the following section.

SECTION TWO

GLOOSKAP'S GALLERY

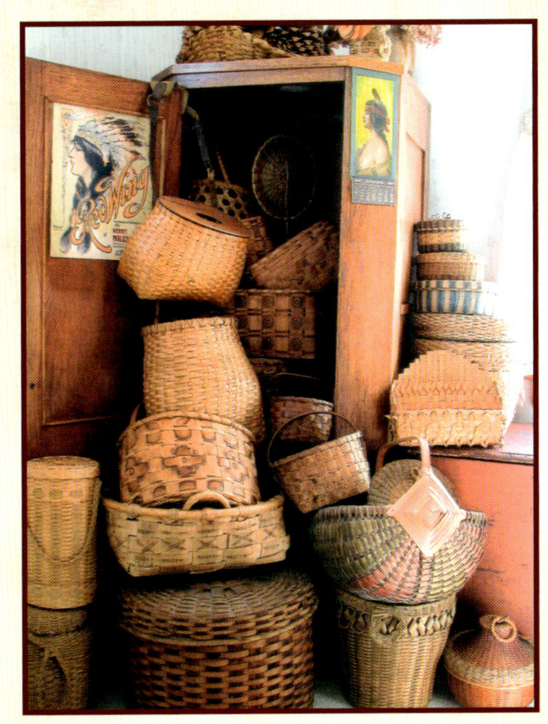

CHAPTER 3

USEFUL BASKETS FOR FARM & HOME

For generations, woodsplint work baskets have been indispensable to daily life on the farm and in the fields. Undoubtedly most Northeastern examples were heavily used and eventually wore out. Yet, a number have survived, and some continue to be used in homes today. Sturdy forms such as the seed-sowing or apple-picking basket; eel trap; fish-scale basket; practical baskets for gathering, carrying, or storage; potato baskets; pack baskets for the harvest or for carrying hunting or fishing gear on one's back; fishing creels; and feather baskets are typical examples.

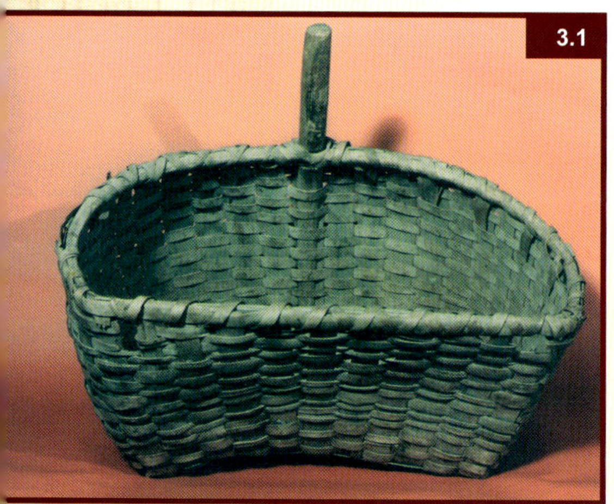

3.1. Seed-sowing basket of oak splints, probably Micmac, c. 1880-1900, 10" high plus handle.

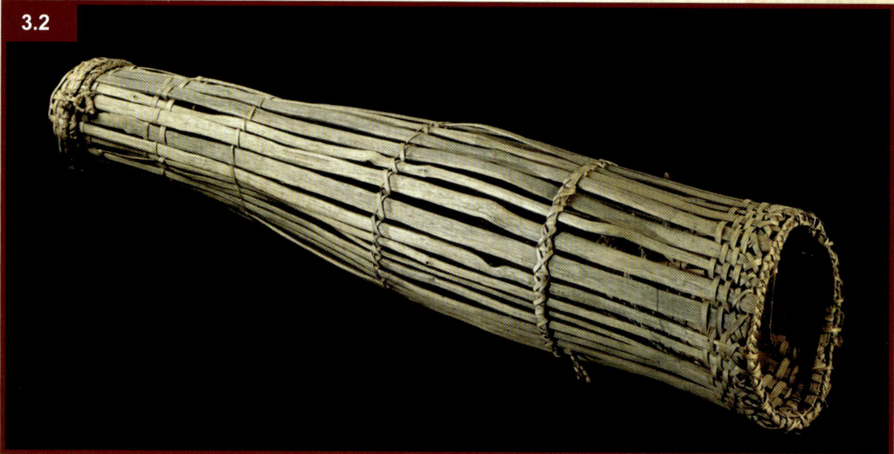

3.2. Cylindrical eel trap, Wampanoag, c. 1900, about 48" long.

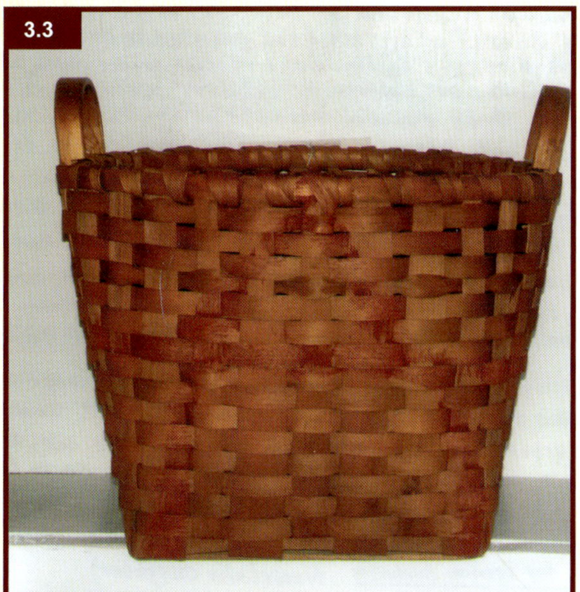

3.3. This fish-scale basket, with large painted letter "A" that indicates to which family or fishing boat it belonged, was used in herring and sardine processing plants for collecting fish scales to make into nail polish, cosmetics, and fertilizer; Passamaquoddy, c. 1950, 14" high.

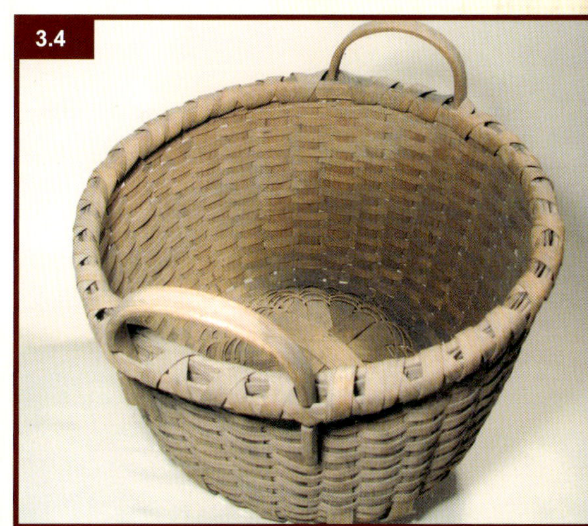

3.4. Rugged work basket plaited with the white oak splints preferred by Henry Harris, Schaghticoke, c. 1880-1890, 14" diameter.

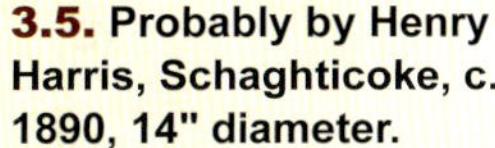

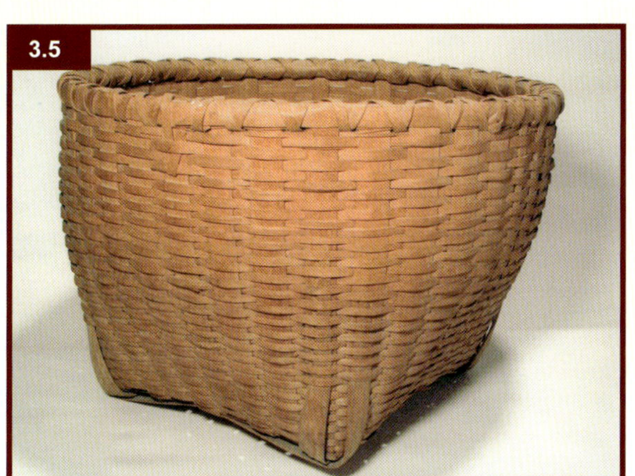

3.5. Probably by Henry Harris, Schaghticoke, c. 1890, 14" diameter.

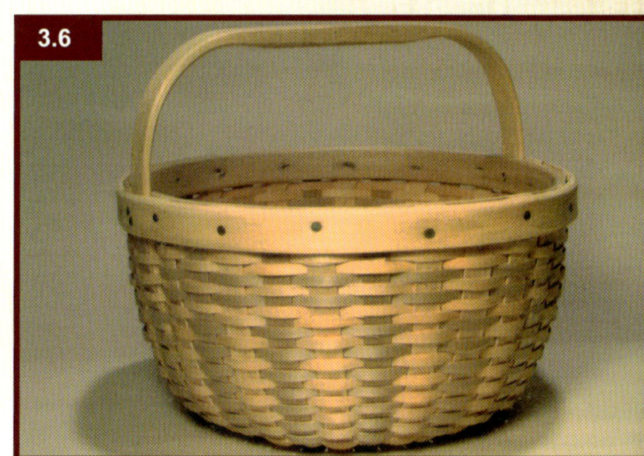

3.6. Potato-harvesting basket by Eldon Hanning, Micmac, 1980s, 8.5" diameter.

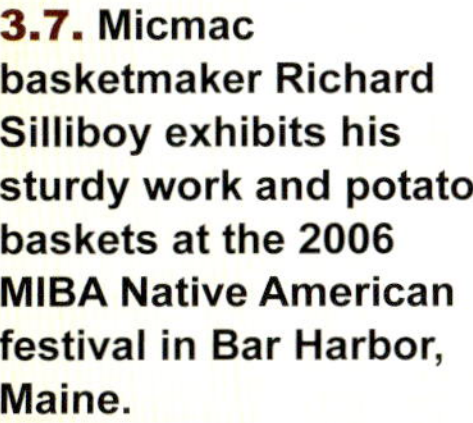

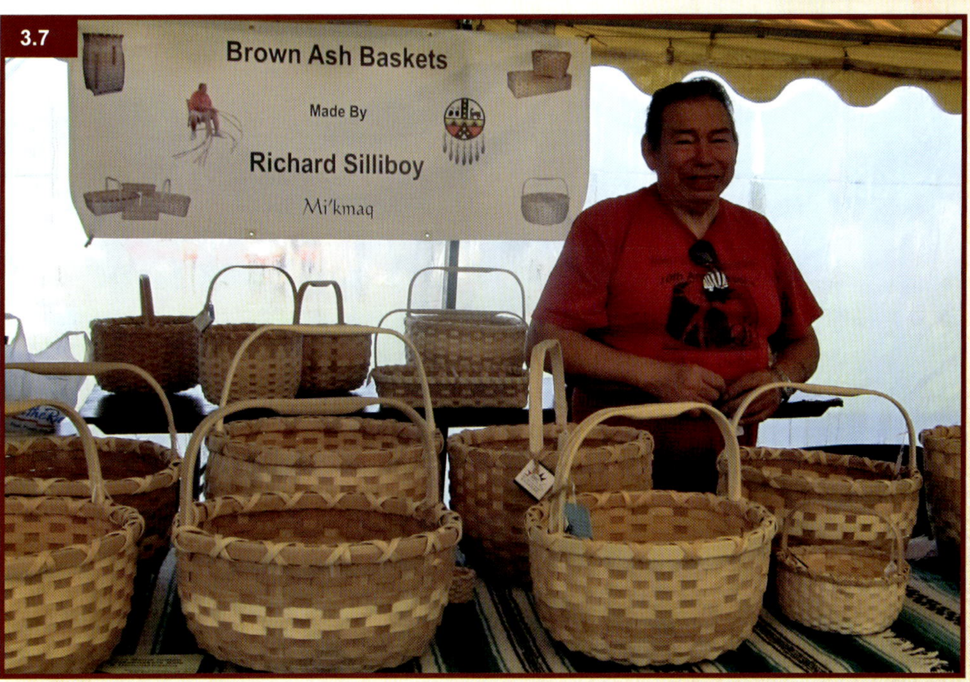

3.7. Micmac basketmaker Richard Silliboy exhibits his sturdy work and potato baskets at the 2006 MIBA Native American festival in Bar Harbor, Maine.

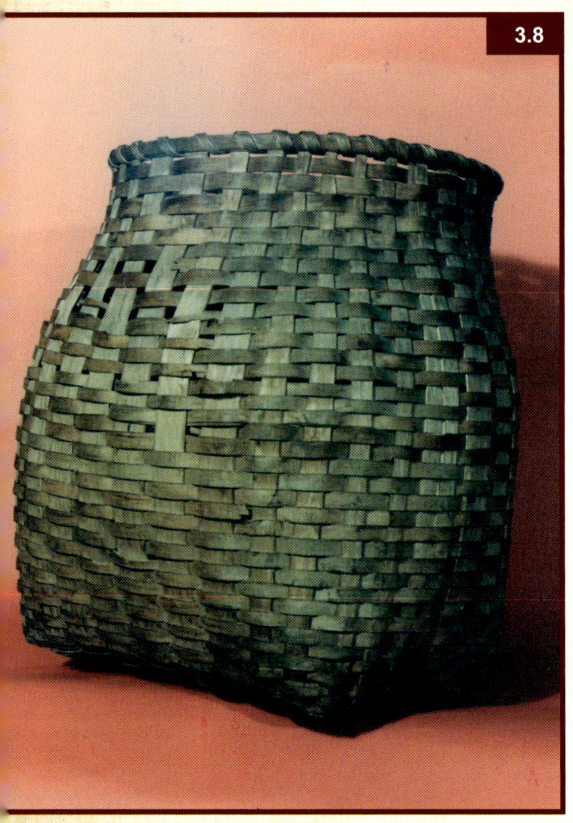

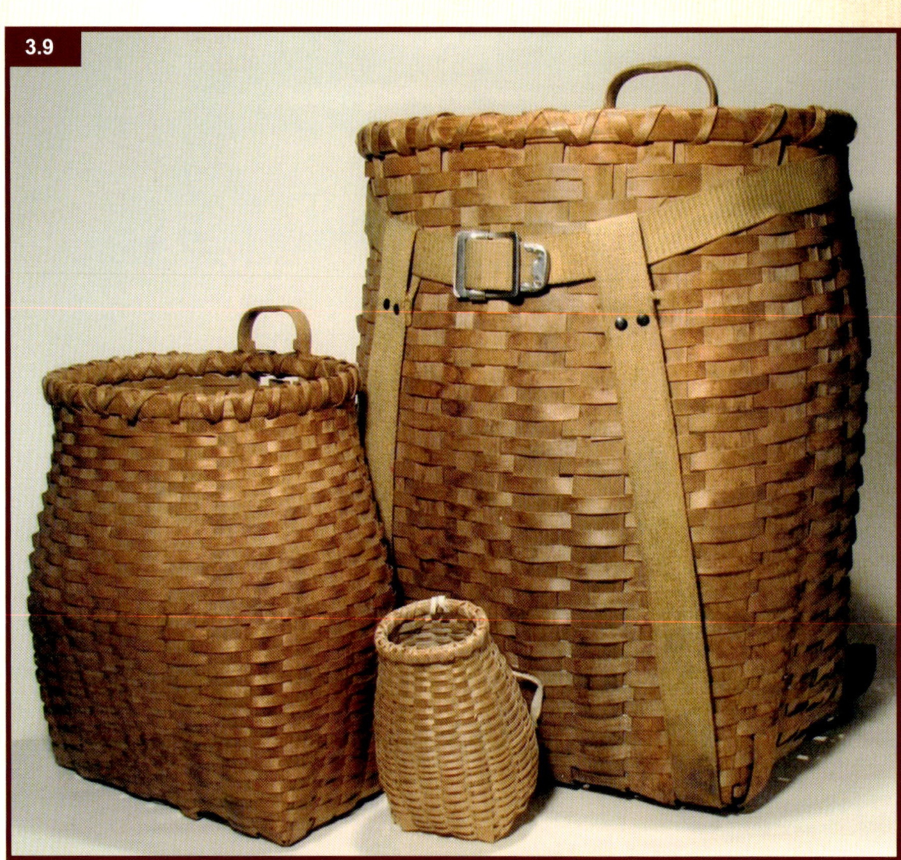

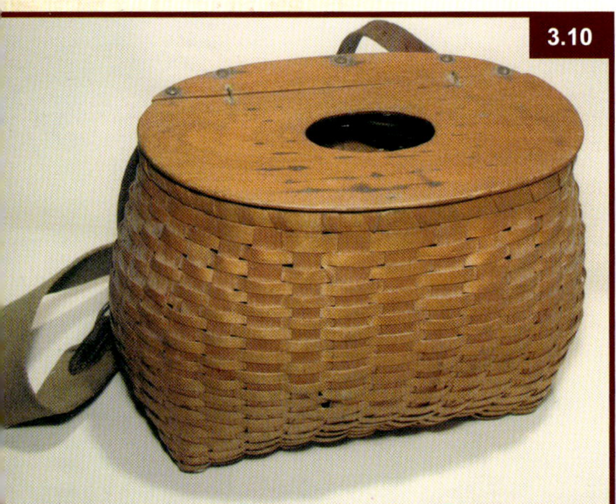

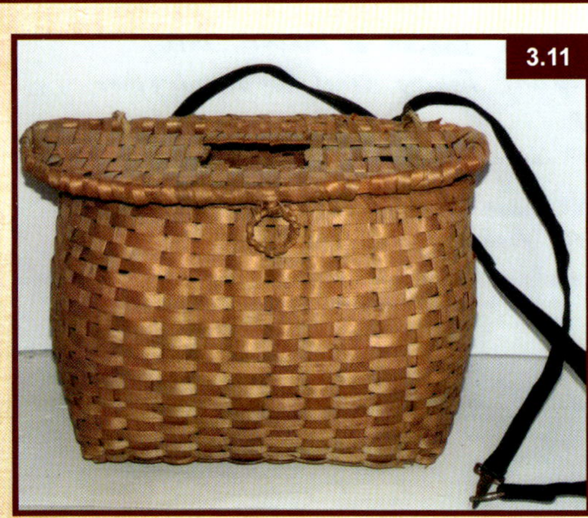

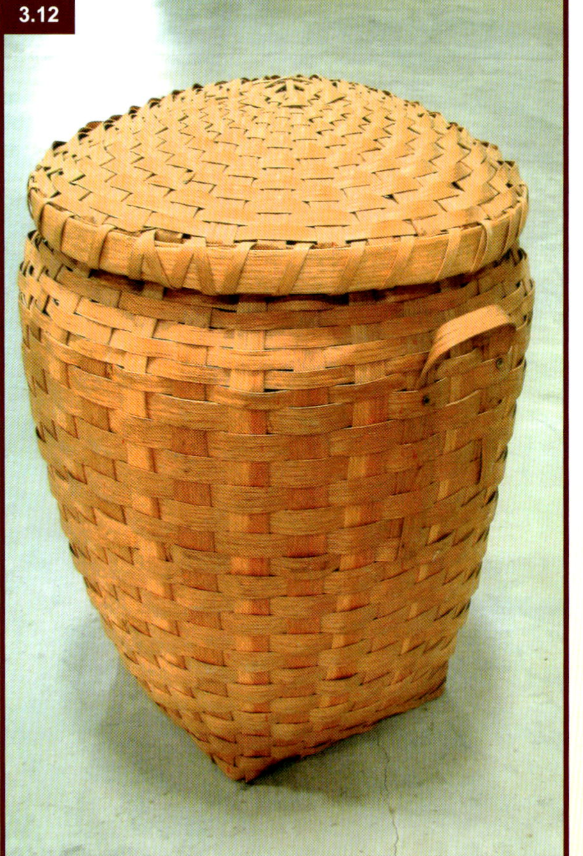

3.8. Pack basket, Iroquois, c. 1880-1900, 15" high.

3.9. Pack baskets served like knapsacks to carry heavy loads and have been created in a range of sizes, including miniatures. These examples are from northern New England, mid-to late 1900s, (right) 19.5" high.

3.10. Fishing creel, Passamaquoddy or Micmac by Elisée Gaudet, early 1900s, 9" high.

3.11. Penobscot fishing creel, c. 1910, 8" high.

3.12. Hamper or feather-storage basket with twill-plaited base, Great Lakes, mid-1900s, 32" high.

3.13. Feather-storage basket with slotted cover that slides up the handle, permitting the plucker of a chicken or goose to stuff in the feathers before they blow away, New England, c. 1890, 13.5" high.

3.14. Hamper or feather-storage basket, probably Maine or Canadian Maritimes, early 1900s, 22" high.

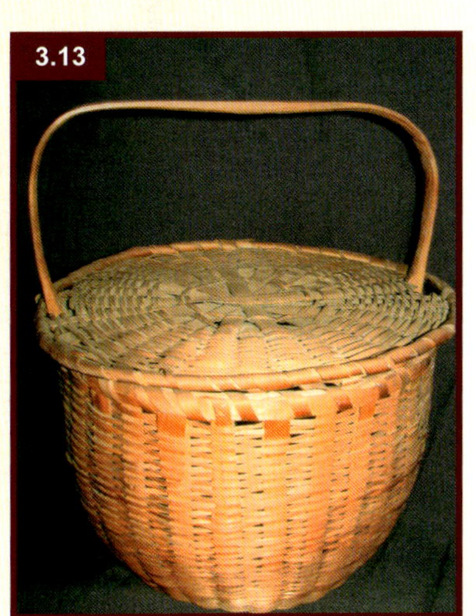

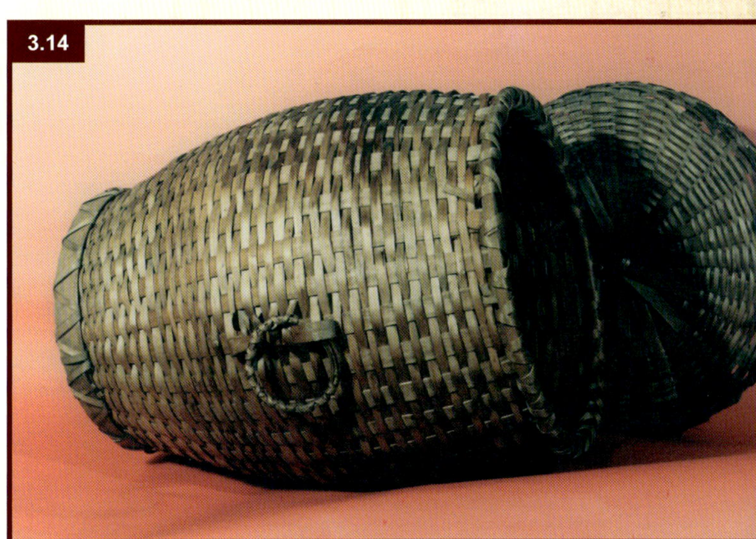

SETTING:

A Southern New England Farmyard

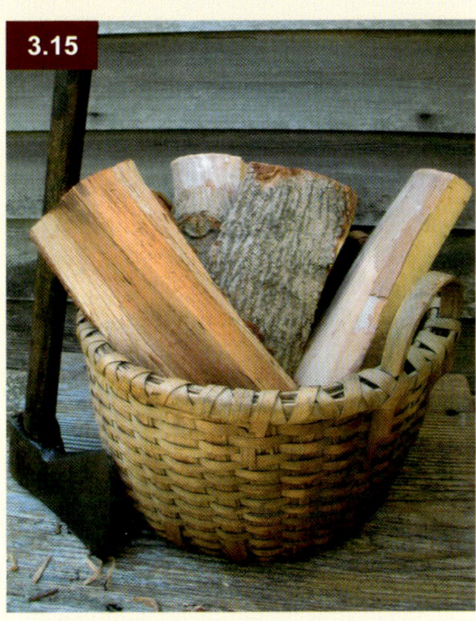

3.15. A sturdy farm basket makes a heavy load more manageable, Schaghticoke, c. 1880-1890.

Bees droned steadily as they gathered pollen from profuse purple blossoms on the lilacs growing beside the clapboarded farmhouse. The busy workers streamed back and forth between the lilacs and three newly-made basketry bee skeps guarding the edge of the cornfield.

Nearby, the big gray workhorse Misty whinnied in his pasture. He was hoping for a special ration of oats, an occasional treat, especially when he had been working as hard as he had been this spring. But the farmer's ax shrilled rhythmically without pausing, as Francis, its owner, drove his metal wedge into the next oak log, forcing it apart. He tossed the split hardwood quarters into a large woodsplint farm basket. With each pitch, the firewood thunked forcefully against the dense splints.

Francis reduced several more log sections to stovewood and at last reached the bottom of his pile. He set the ax against the wall of the barn, beside cords of wood, now fully seasoned, that he had stacked a year earlier. Bracing his waist with a sinewy hand, the farmer straightened his back and stood fully upright. As he pushed a wide-brimmed hat back from his forehead and mopped his perspiring brow, he assessed the capacious splint basket, now full of wood.

The farmer knew his wife would use up this basket of fuel shortly. Today was her day for baking their week's supply of bread. The load would be ample enough, though, to keep the woodstove stoked and adequately hot to finish the day's baking. He caught a whiff of fragrant loaves that were starting to brown, and his stomach rolled in anticipation.

With renewed vigor, Francis carried the heavily-laden basket into the kitchen. He placed it near the cast-iron oven. Then, heading out to tackle the next chore, he returned to the barnyard. First, he would give Misty a few oats.

Along the way, the farmer paused and took up another sturdy woodsplint basket.

Work baskets for the home and household interior served in capacities where sturdiness was less critical. Native basketmakers often embellished these products in appealing ways. Forms that were intended for use at home include covered storage baskets, trunks, and hat boxes; open work baskets for holding vegetables, balls of yarn, sewing and mending supplies, or other sundries; and smaller handled baskets for gathering eggs and toting produce or game or fish between the garden or shore and the kitchen or market.

3.16. A typical covered storage basket or trunk of average size at 19" long and 11.5" high, with red swabbing and blue stamping, mid-1800s.

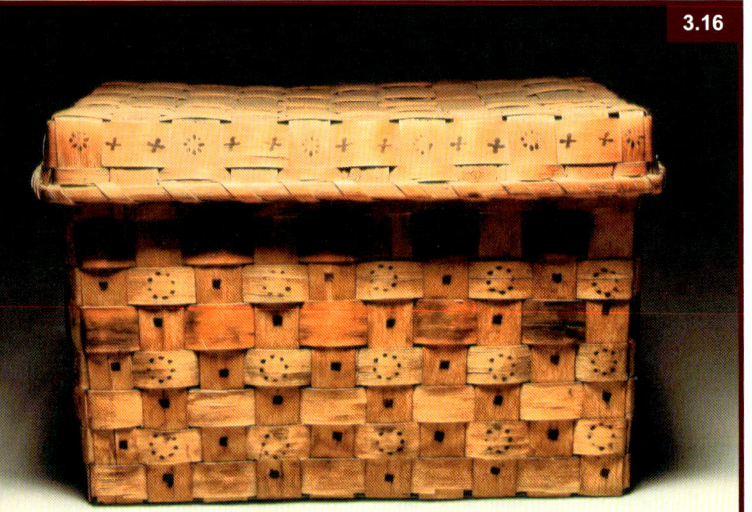

3.16

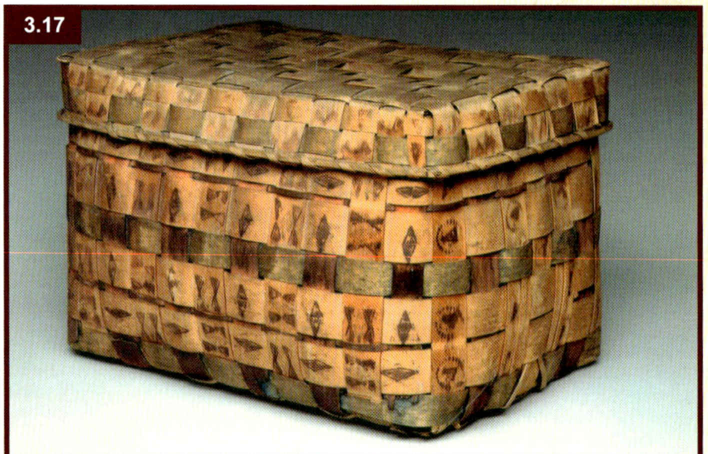

3.17

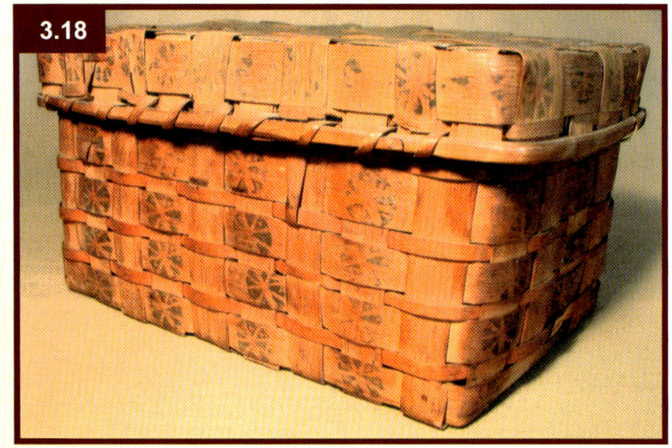

3.18

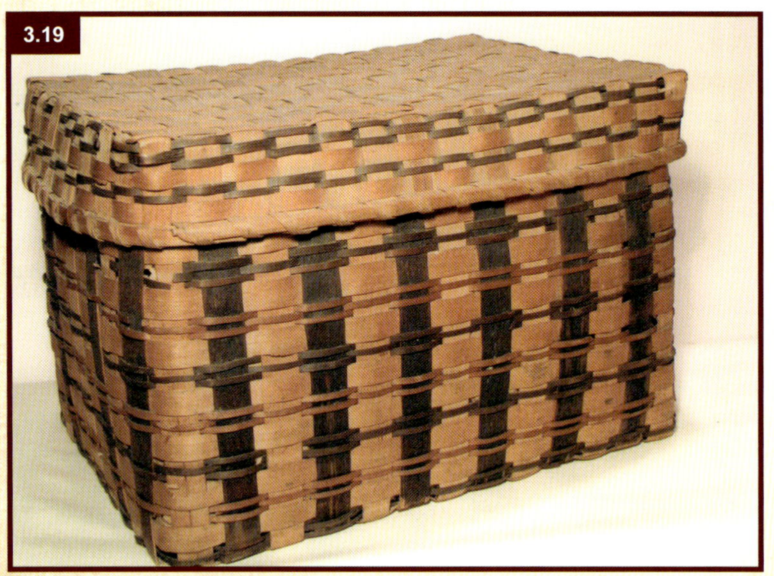

3.19

3.17. Covered storage basket, blue swabbing and brown stamping, mid-1800s, 15" long, 9" high.

3.18. Small covered storage basket, swabbed red weft elements and red and blue stamping, c. 1860, 10" long.

3.19. Covered storage basket with Spanish brown swabbing, probably Mahican (eastern New York) or Schaghticoke (western Connecticut), c. 1860, 15" long.

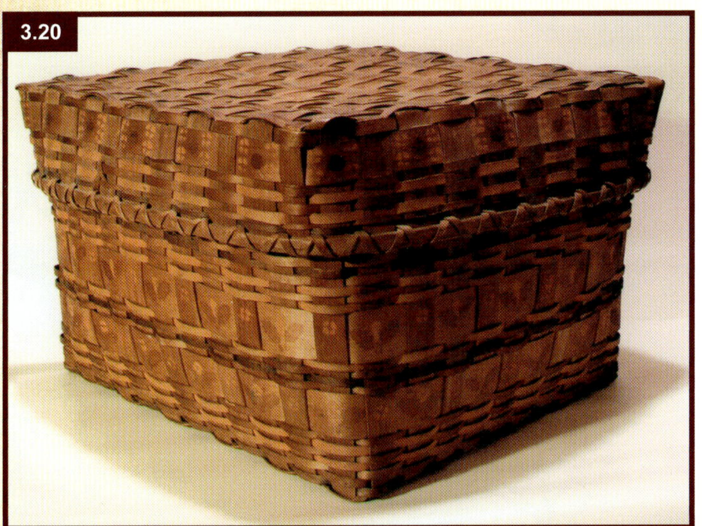

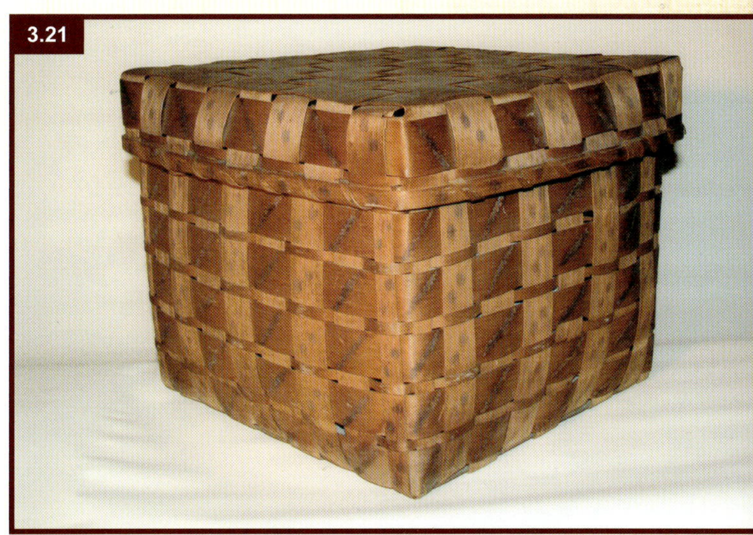

3.20. Connecticut covered storage basket with swabbing and stamping in Spanish brown—an inexpensive and popular primer in its day—plus a pinkish mixture of red lead and white lead called Mohegan pink, c. 1850, 14" long.

3.21. Covered storage basket with stamped brown and pinkish elements, possibly Natick, c. 1830s, 12" long.

3.22. Covered round storage baskets often served as bonnet or hat boxes, early to mid-1800s, 18" diameter.

3.23. Western Abenaki covered storage basket, mid-1800s, 18" diameter.

3.24. Two covered storage baskets, c. 1840-1850; probable Wampanoag example (left) is 17.5" diameter.

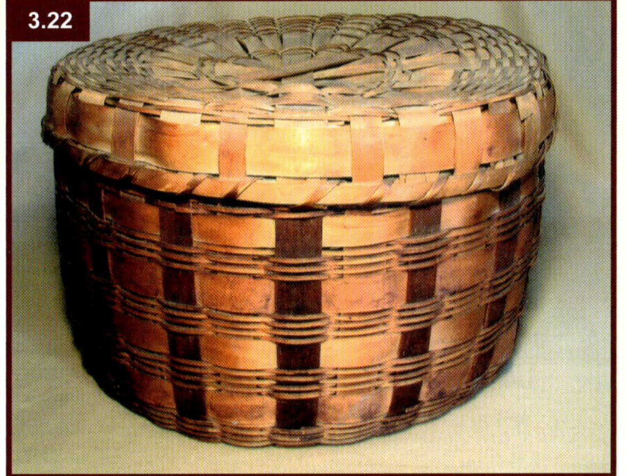

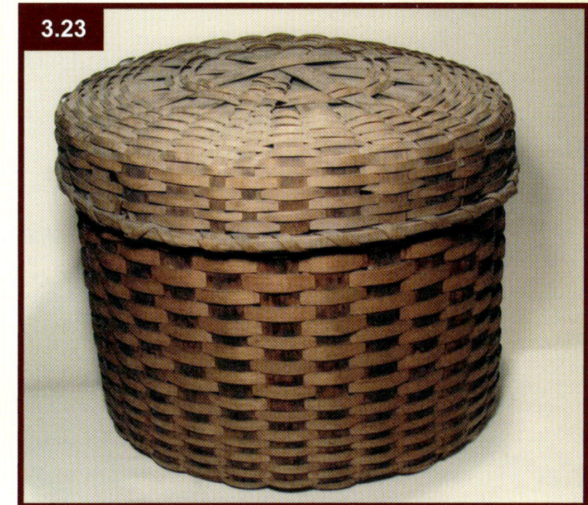

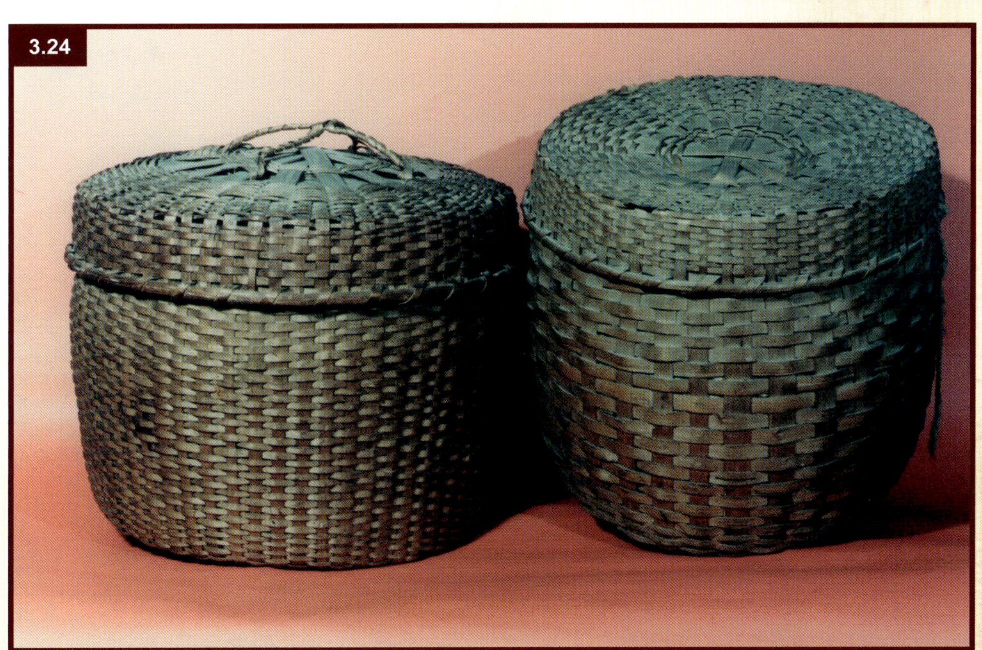

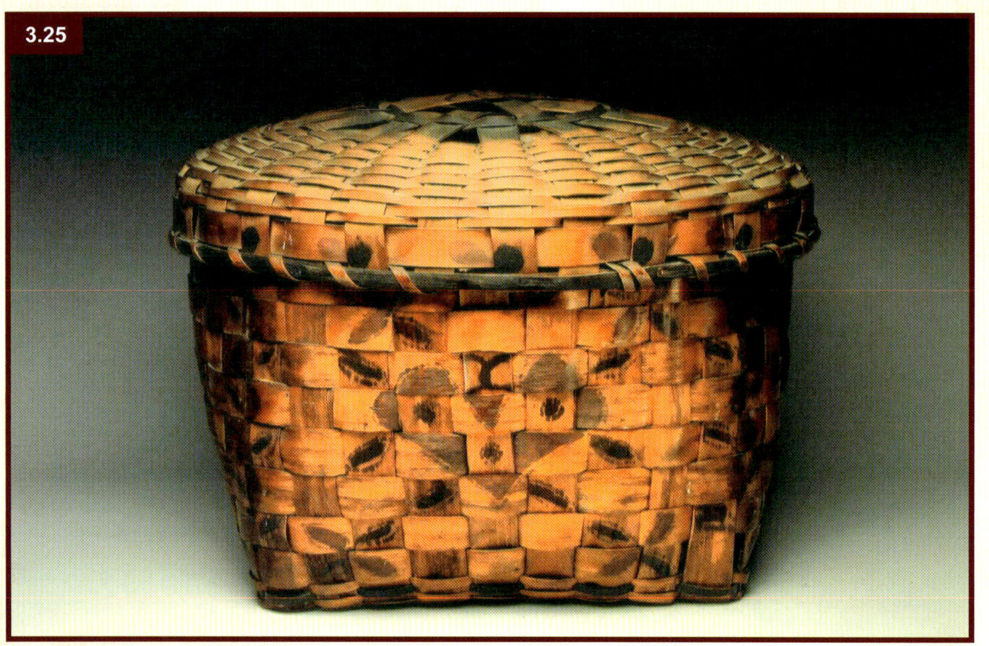

3.25. Covered storage basket, c. 1850-1860, marked "JHS," likely by an itinerant Native basketmaker. Baskets with this marking reveal a personal style reflecting various influences from several communities including Mohegan and Oneida basketmakers at Brothertown, New York, and Schaghticoke at Kent, Connecticut.

3.26. Covered storage basket attributed to the "vase-painter" Arnold basketmaking family of Hassanamesit, the Nipmuc "praying Indian" community near Grafton, Massachusetts, c. 1820-1830, 15.5" rim diameter.

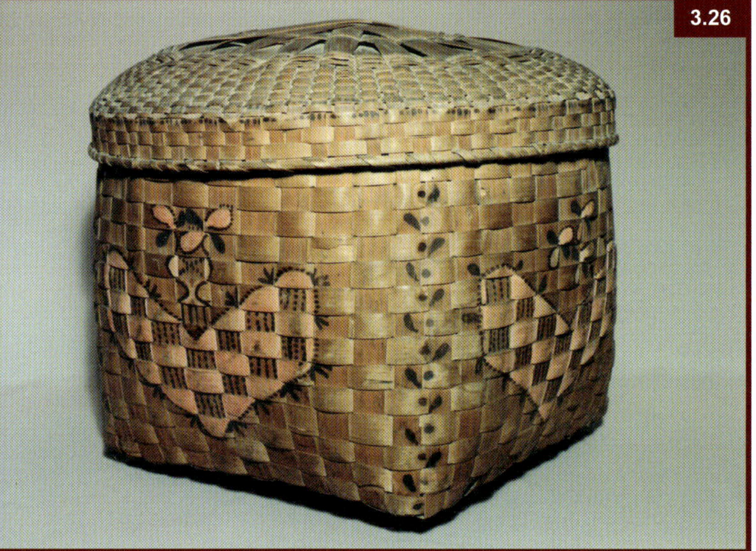

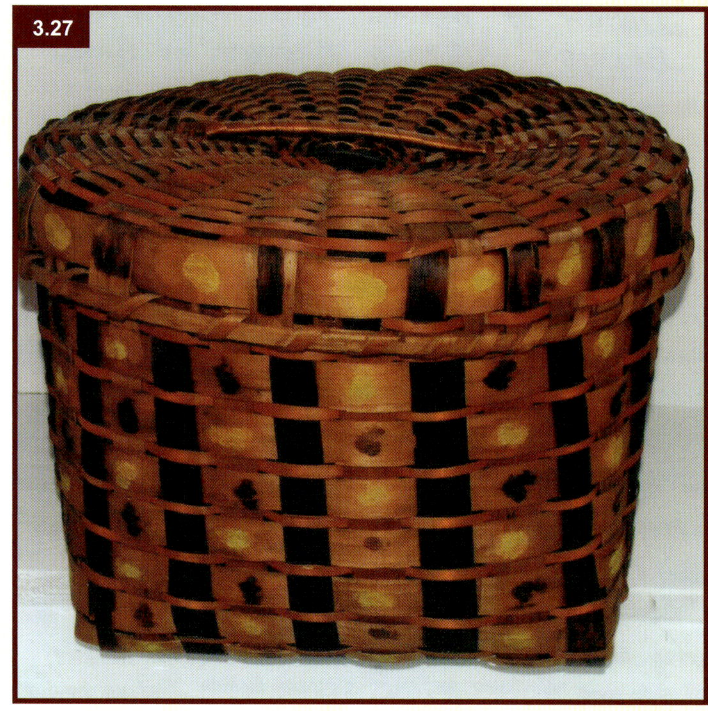

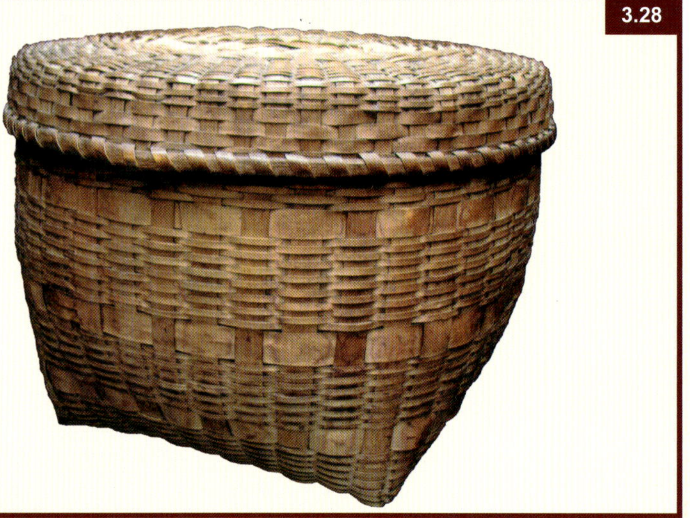

3.27. Covered hat- or bonnet-storage basket, mid-1800s, 13.5" square base.

3.28. Covered storage basket with three wide weft splints that lend a decorative effect, mid-1800s, 17" square base.

SETTING:

A Southern New England Homestead

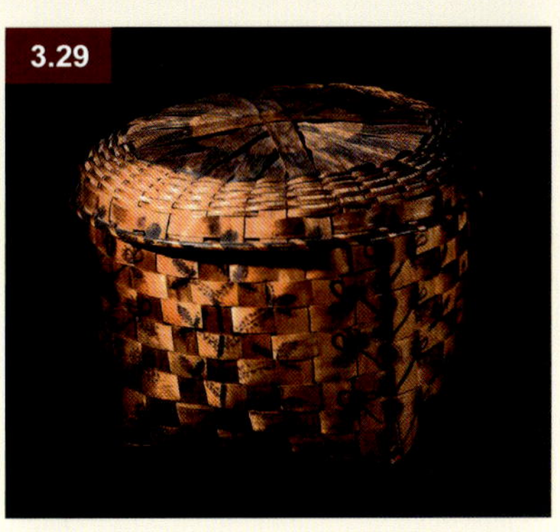

3.29. A storage basket or hat box painted in blue and Mohegan pink, c. 1850-1860, marked "JHS."

The aroma of jonnycakes smothered with fresh maple syrup and bacon seared on a heavy, cast iron griddle lingered in the air of the tidy farmhouse. It mingled with the pungent scent of fireplaces struggling to remove the raw early morning chill.

The Connecticut farmhouse was quiet now, except for the Guernseys lowing in the distance. The children already were making their way across the cow pasture to their one-room schoolhouse, and the dairy farmer had returned to his morning chores in the barn.

In the bed chamber above the kitchen, his wife, Molly, placed her corn broom near a well-worn side chair. A freshly plaited seat of pale woodsplints gleamed brightly from its distressed old frame. Several market baskets of various shapes and sizes, some with splints painted with simple dark designs, hung by their handles from pegs in an exposed wooden ceiling beam.

Molly started to tidy up the room. She straightened the bed linens and tucked them around her horsehair mattress, then flung the hand-woven overshot coverlet with its blue and white pattern across the four-poster bed.

As she smoothed out the coverlet, Molly glanced toward her tall wardrobe, now topped with a large, covered storage basket. A local Mohegan Indian basketmaker had plaited it of ash splints and painted its sides with a blue and red design. Molly smiled with satisfaction and pride. It coordinated nicely with her coverlet's pattern, as well as with the decorative stenciled motifs on the whitewashed plaster wall.

Molly had just lined the Indian basket with pages of a recent *Worcester Daily Courant*. The newspaper made the inner surface smoother and splinter-free. It would help to protect her fancy high-crowned bonnet with its feathers and ribbon trim where it rested inside. She pulled a dust cloth from her apron pocket as she circled the bed.

Molly reached up to brush off her basket's pretty cover.

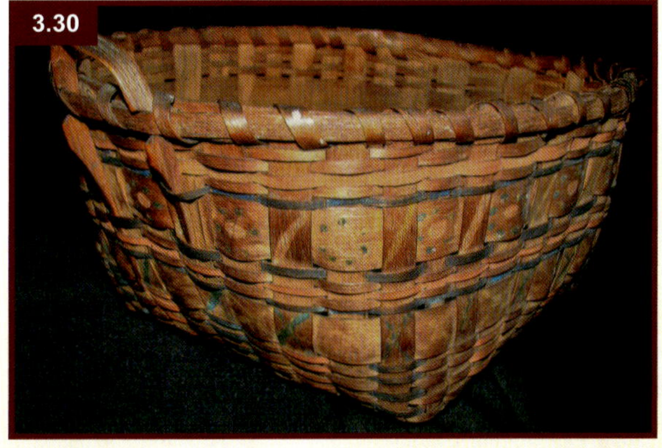

3.30. Open work baskets held varying contents from vegetables to socks in need of darning. Eastern Connecticut (likely Mohegan) basket, with pinkish and blue (aged to green) swabbed and hand-painted splints, marked "Clara Levalley" and "1851" in pale blue on base, 10" x 11" long.

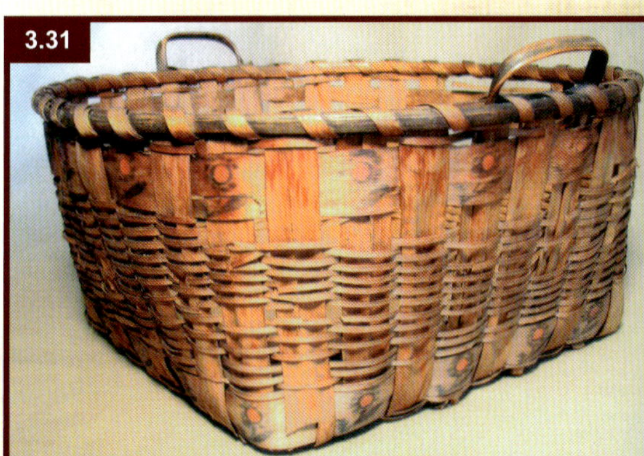

3.31. Open work basket with hand-painted pinkish and blue flowers, its rim swabbed with blue (a trait often associated with "JHS" baskets, but this one is unmarked), 1850-1860, 10" long.

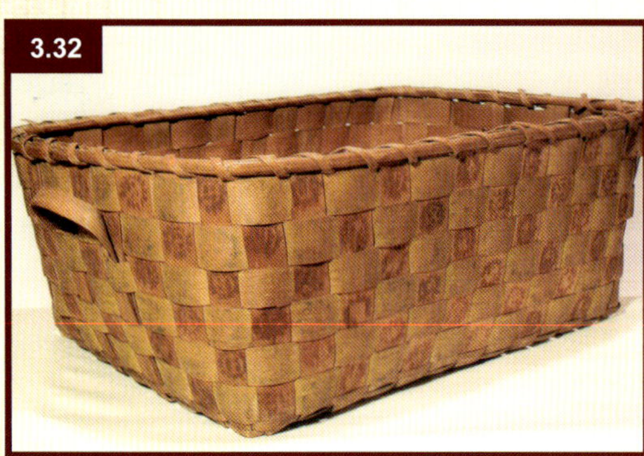

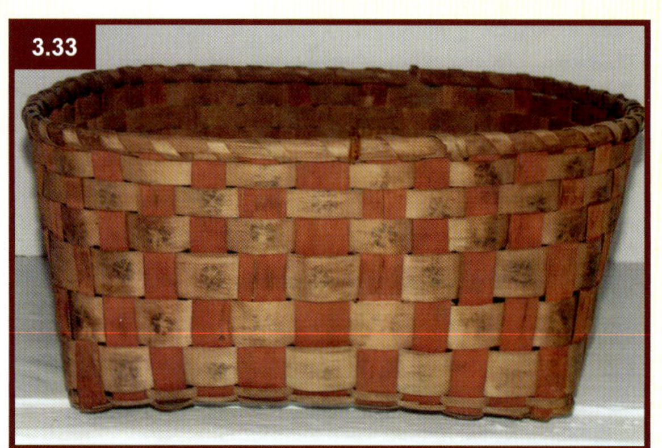

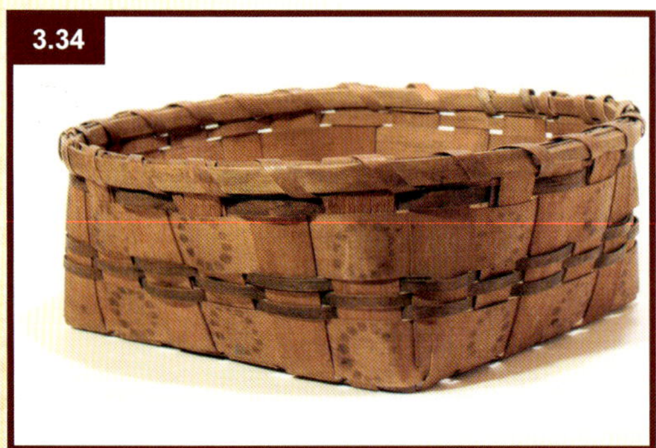

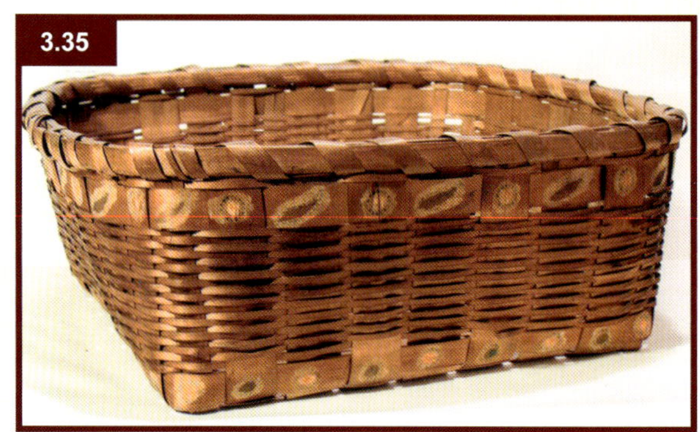

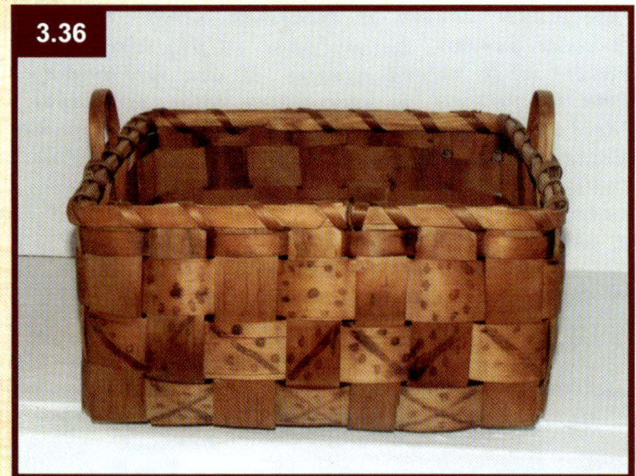

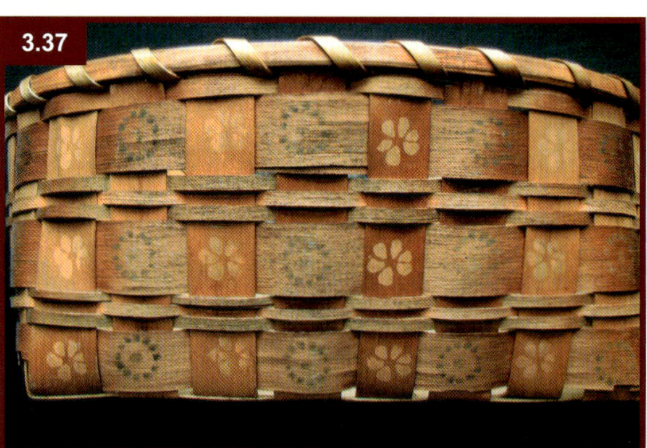

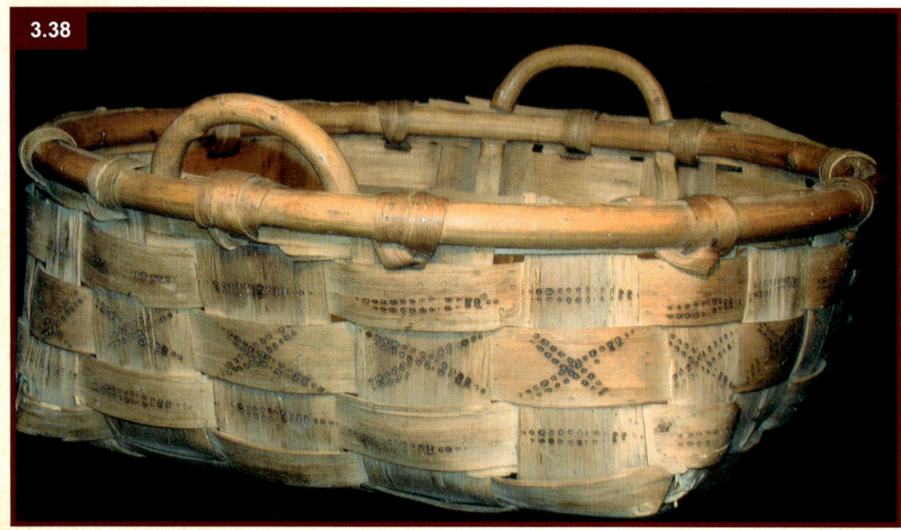

3.32. Work basket with chrome yellow, or lead chromate-swabbed splints (often a marker of Stockbridge, some Schaghticoke, and Iroquois work), accented with blue and reddish brown stamped all-over elements, c. 1860, 12.5" long.

3.33. Open work basket embellished with swabbing and stamped elements, attributed to the Paugusset of western Connecticut, c. 1830, 10" square.

3.34. Western Connecticut-style utility basket with swabbing and stamping in Mohegan pink and brown, c. 1850, 9.5" rim diameter.

3.35. New York state (possibly Stockbridge or Schaghticoke) work basket with yellow, Mohegan pink, and blue painted and stamped elements, c. 1860, 13" x 13.5" rim diameter.

3.36. Open work basket, with devices hand-painted with walnut stain, possibly Mohegan, c. 1830-1840, 11.5" square.

3.37. Western Connecticut-style utility basket with swabbing and stamping in Mohegan pink and blue, c. 1850, 12" x 13" rim diameter.

3.38. Sturdy open work basket plaited with wide splints decorated with scorched punctate designs, Gay Head (Aquinnah) Wampanoag from Martha's Vineyard, Massachusetts, c. 1890, 15" rim diameter, 7" high.

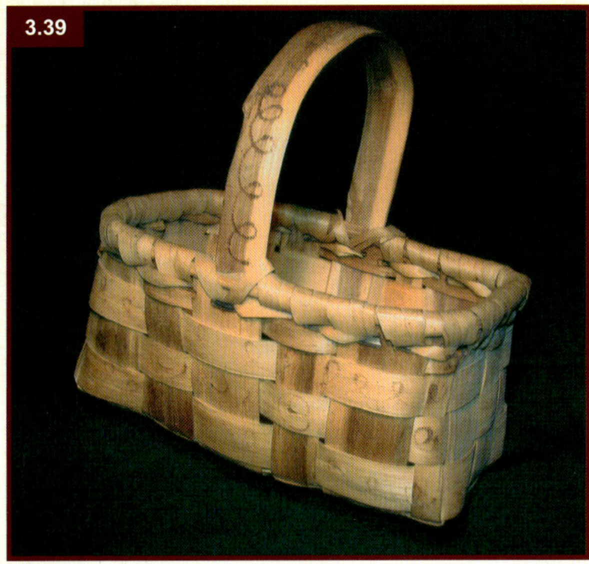

3.39. Mineral stains in some Gay Head (Aquinnah) Wampanoag handled baskets suggest they were used while digging or carrying colored cliff clays for making souvenir Gay Head pottery, c. 1890, 4" high plus handle.

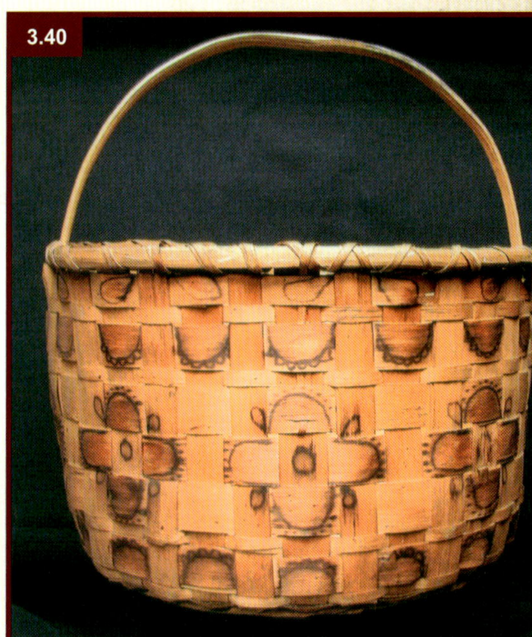

3.40. Open work baskets were used for holding household sundries, gathering eggs, and toting produce, Mohegan or Pequot, c. 1820-1830, 13" rim diameter.

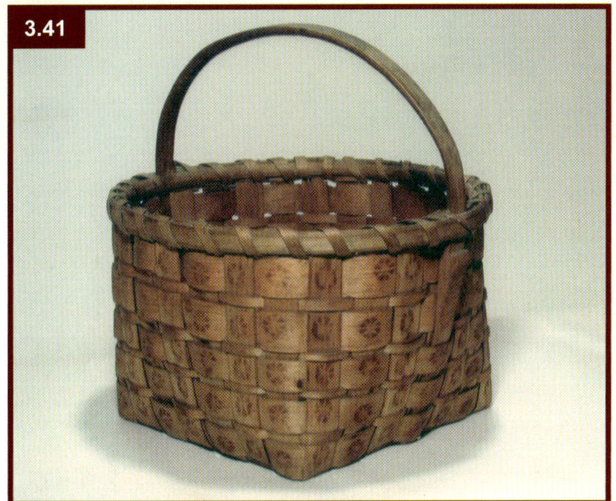

3.41. Carrying basket decorated all over with brown stamped elements, typical of the work of Connecticut makers familiar with Iroquois basketry, c. 1850-1860, 8" rim diameter.

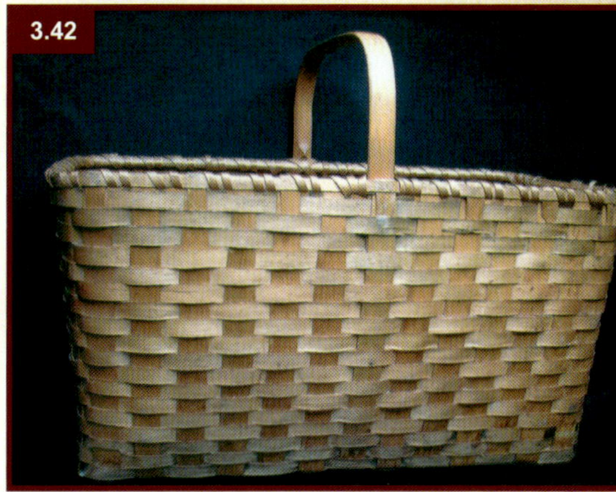

3.42. Sturdy carrying basket with faded blue-dyed splints, 16" long.

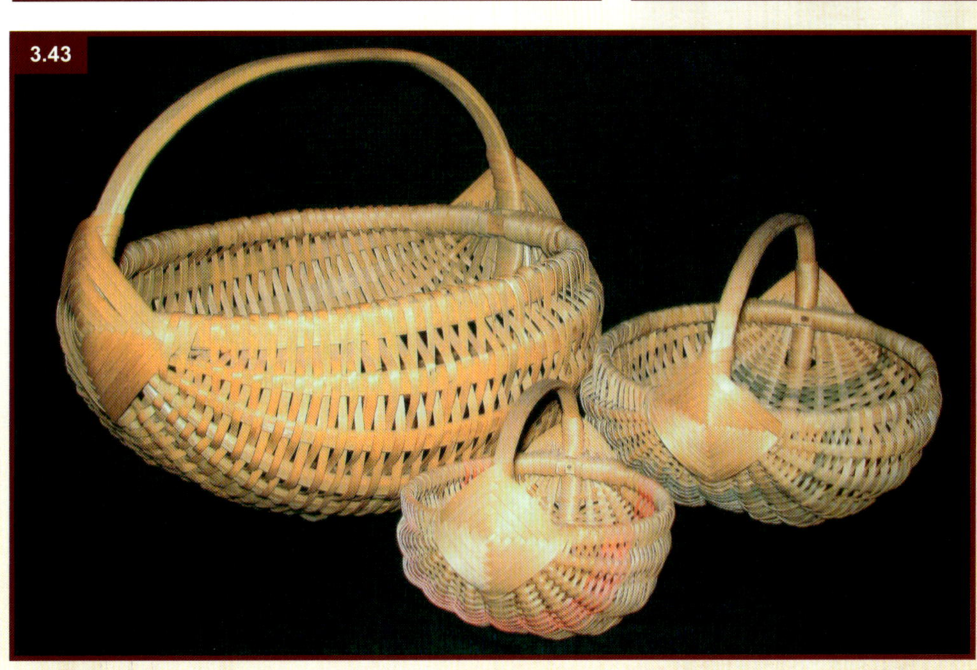

3.43. Heavy-duty melon-shaped oval "beaver" baskets with dyed splints and "God's-eye" handle finishes. Bilingual tags explain that the oval beaver-pelt shape symbolizes First Nations (aboriginal peoples of Canada) industry and harmony with the natural world, Micmac, c. 1970s, (right) 10" x 11" diameter.

FOCUS:

How to Handle a Basket

Early baskets made by Native Americans for their own use seldom had attached handles. Europeans, of course, had separate basketmaking traditions, and many of their products were mounted with handles. Their descendants in America also preferred the convenience of handles on certain containers, like egg carriers and market baskets. Native basketmakers quickly accommodated their customers with a variety of handle styles, including set-in handles, ear handles, strap handles, lug handles, side handles, bail handles, flop or swing handles, frogs, and ring pulls.

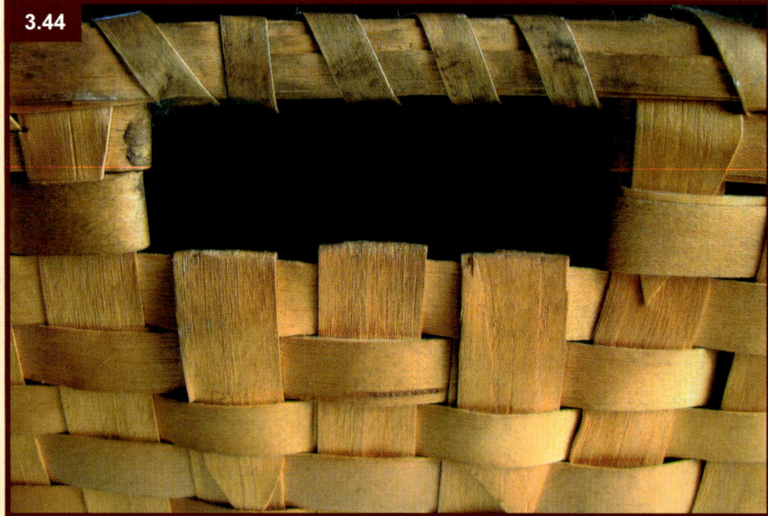

3.44. Set-in handle, which is a cut-out hole.

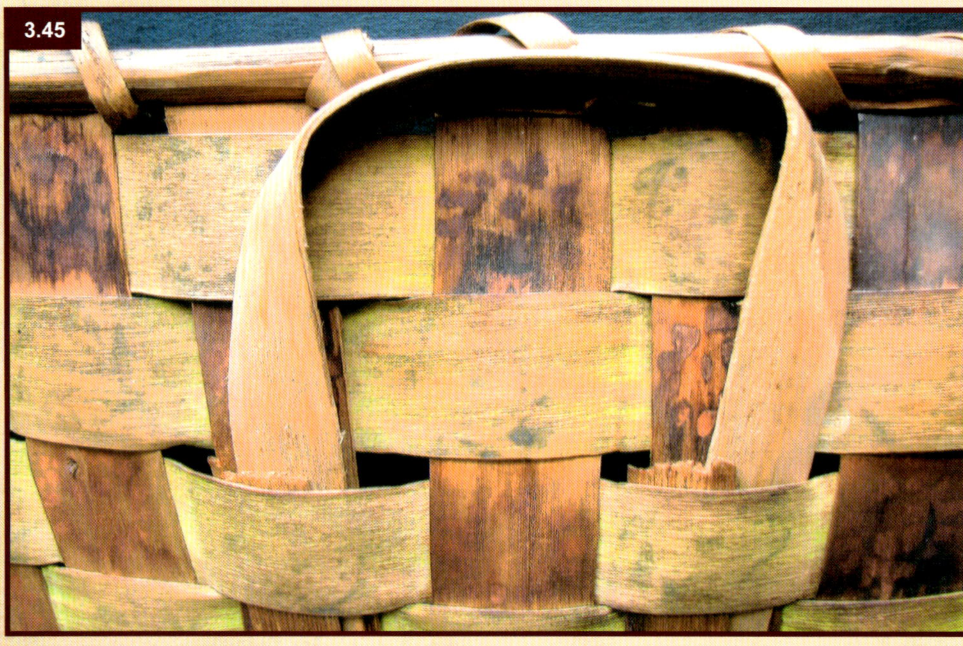

3.45. Ear handle, which is a splint tucked into the side wall.

3.46. Strap handle, which is a splint lashed to the side wall.

3.47. An unusual handle style formed with a bound bundle of sweetgrass.

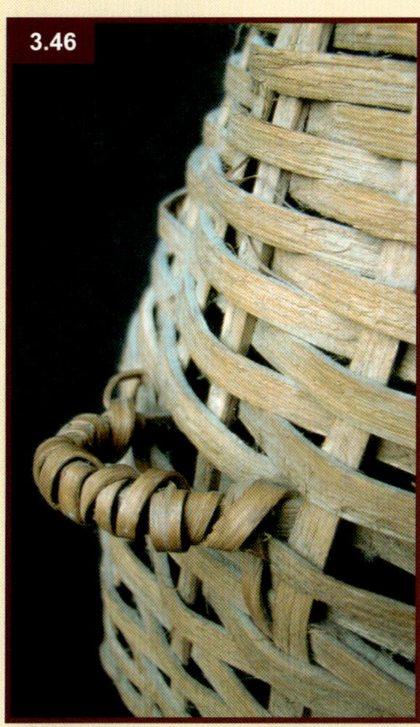

3.46

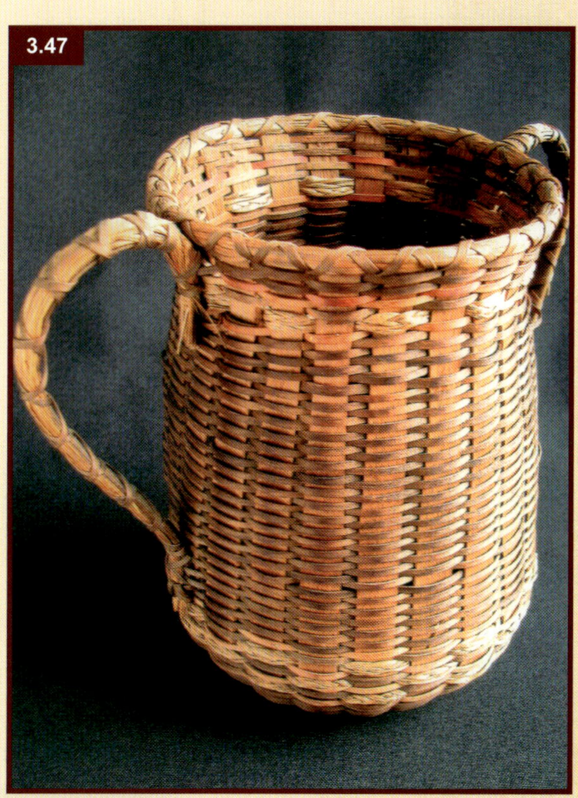

3.47

3.48. Lug handle, which is a splint or rod that is punched into the side wall and bound.

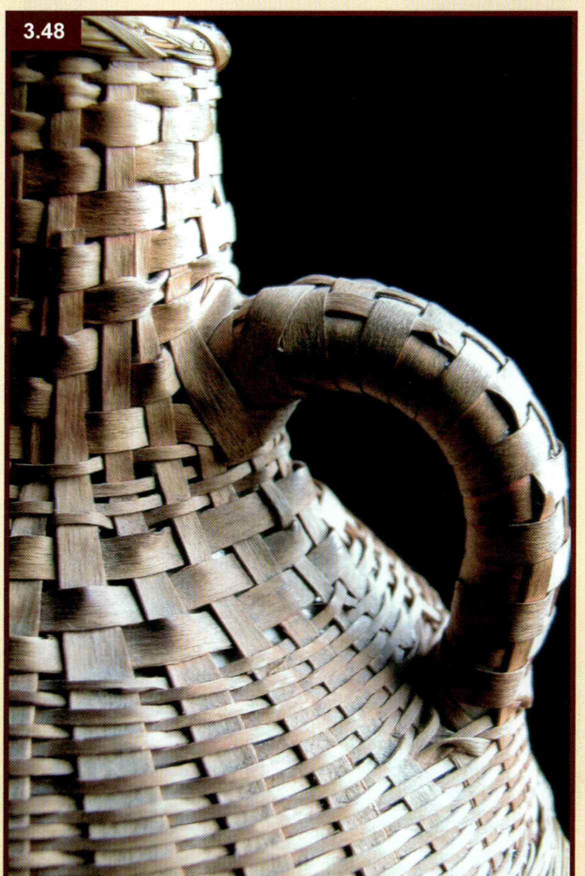

3.48

FOCUS:

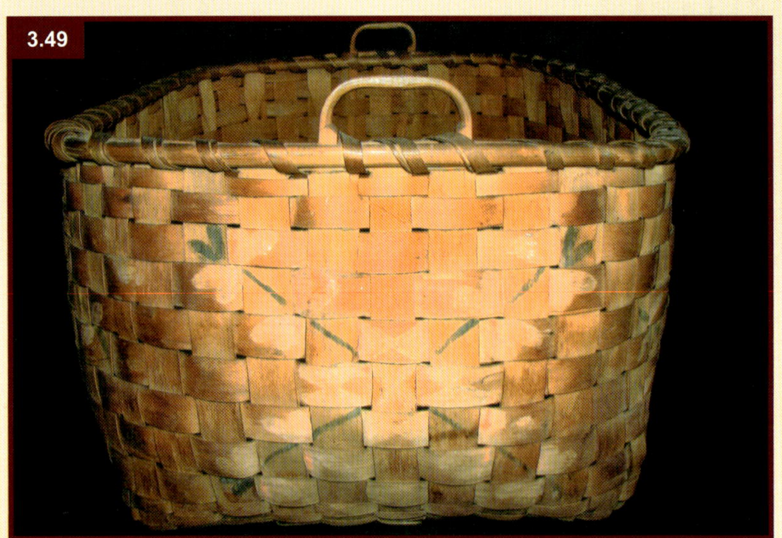

3.49

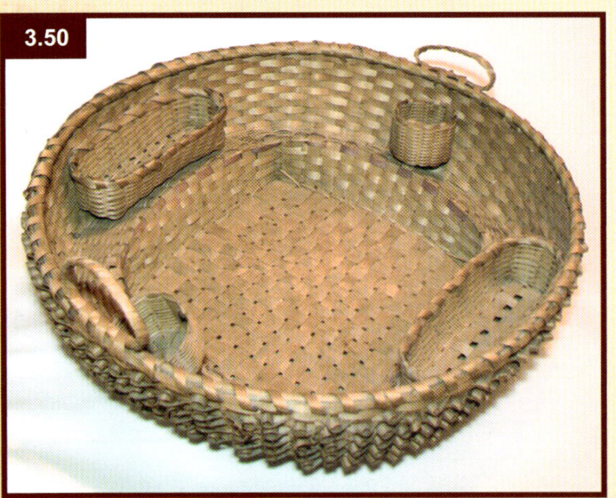

3.50

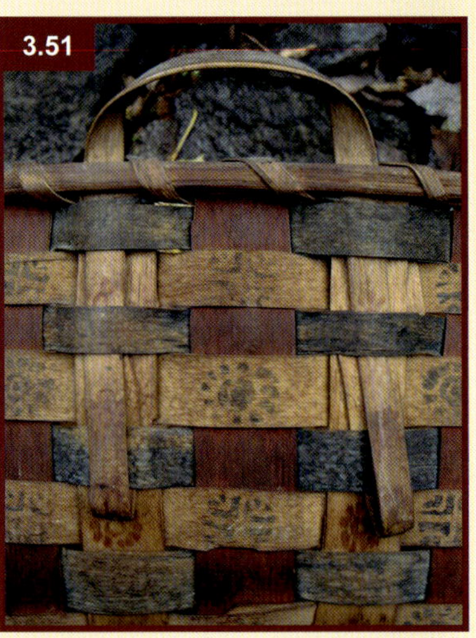

3.51

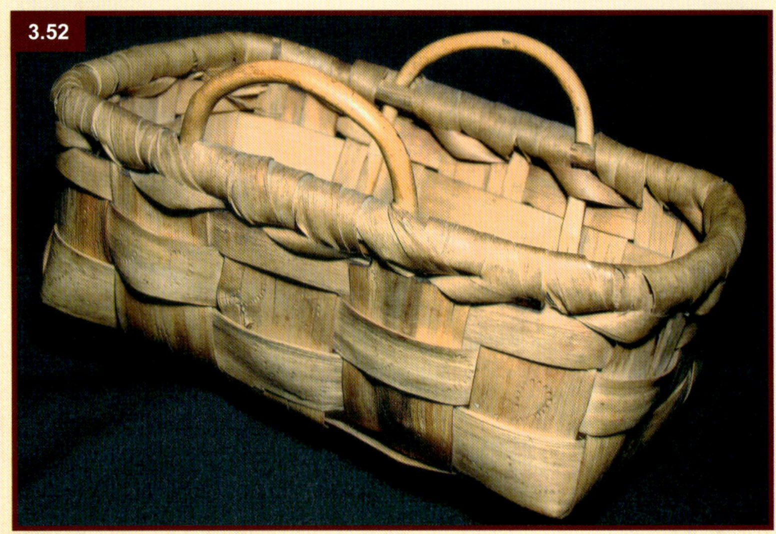

3.52

3.49–3.52. Side handle varieties, some of which are carved and notched.

3.53–3.58. Bail handle varieties, which are fixed or steady handles that are often notched, include so-called "God's-eye" finishes.

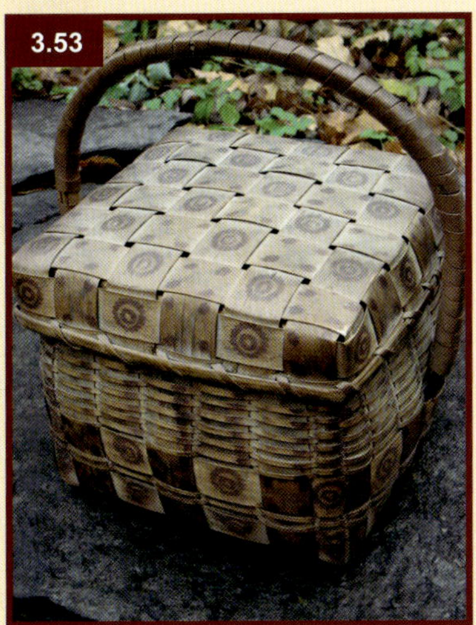
3.53

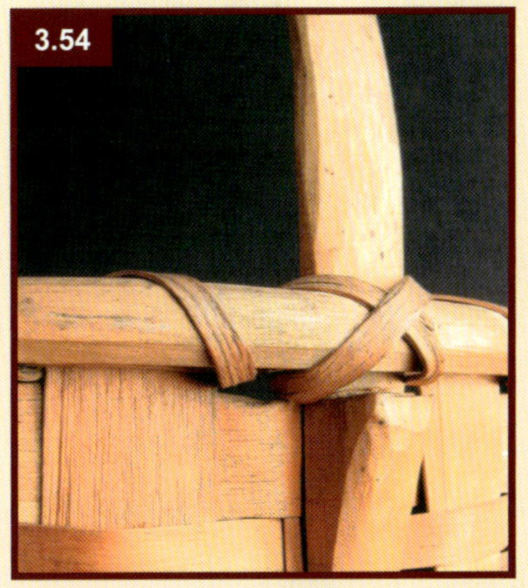
3.54

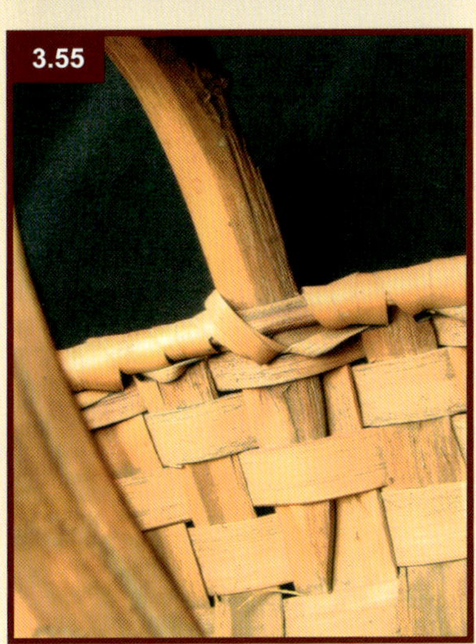
3.55

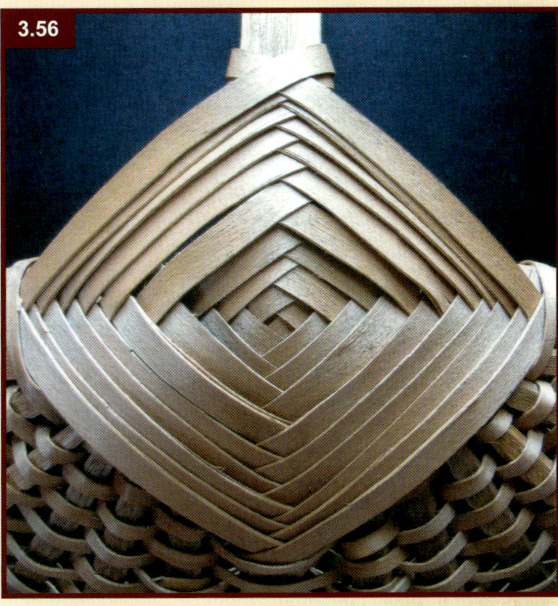
3.56

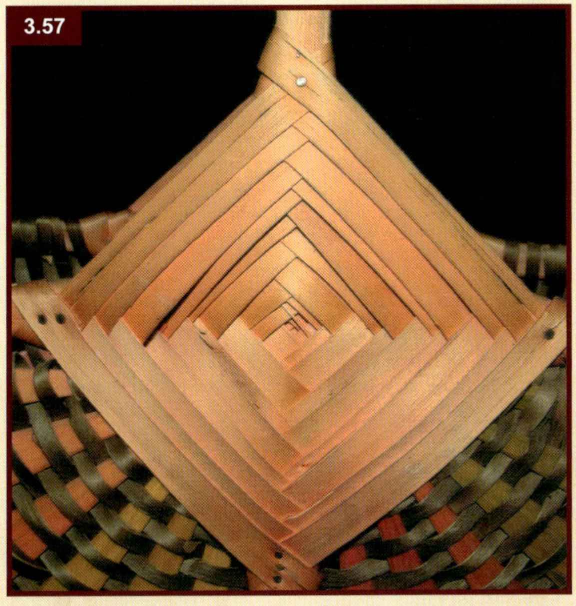
3.57

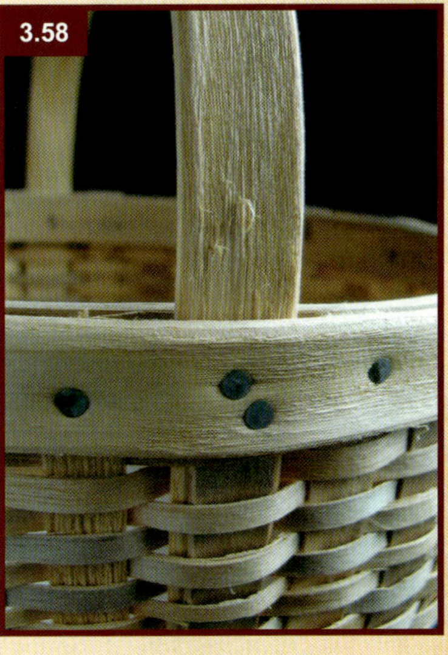
3.58

Focus:

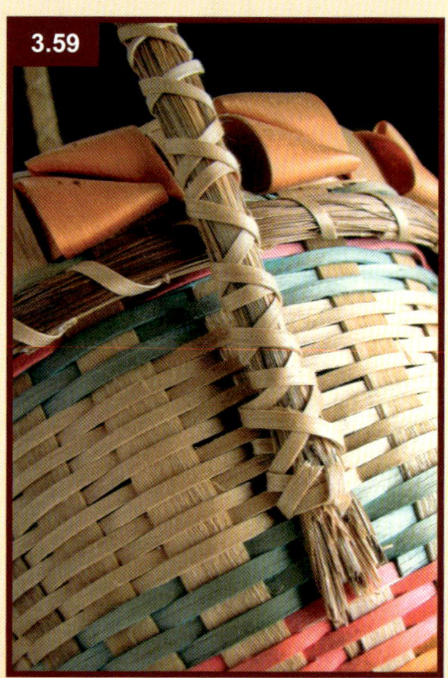

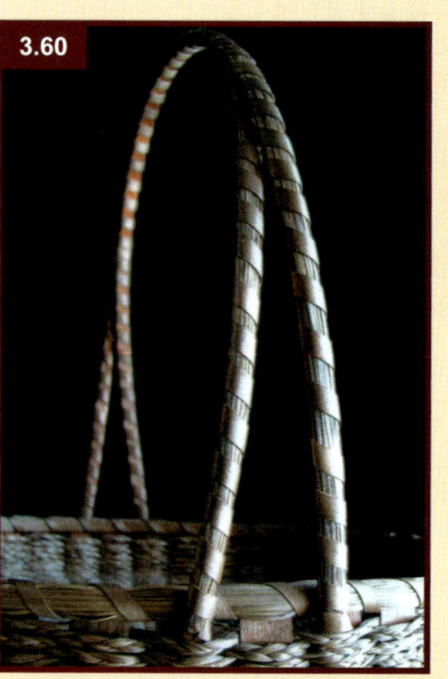

3.59–3.60. More bail handles.

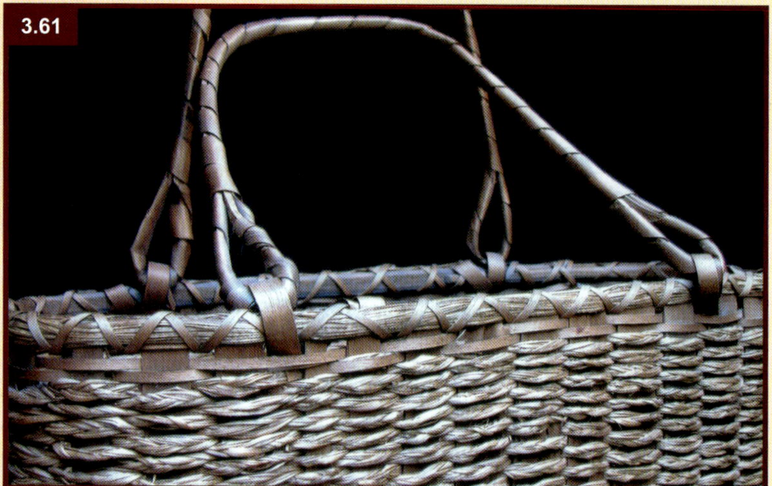

3.61–3.66. Flop handle or swing handle varieties, which are movable and usually arch over a basket.

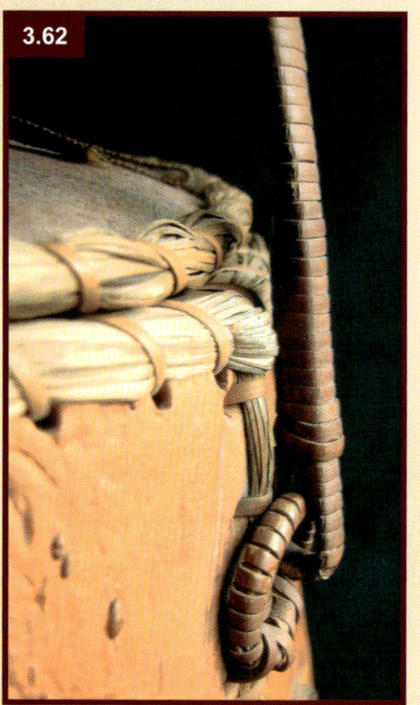

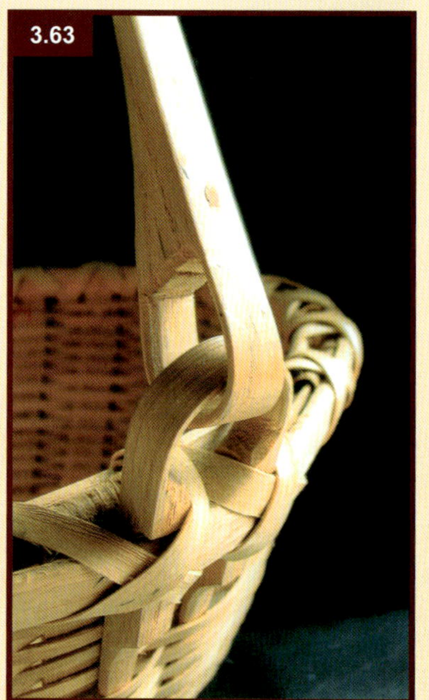

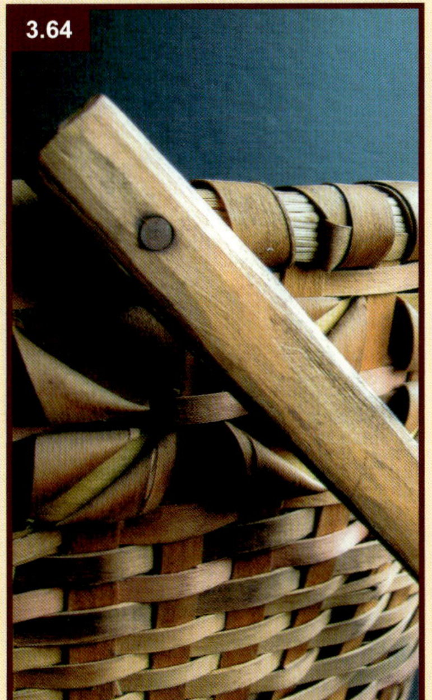
3.64

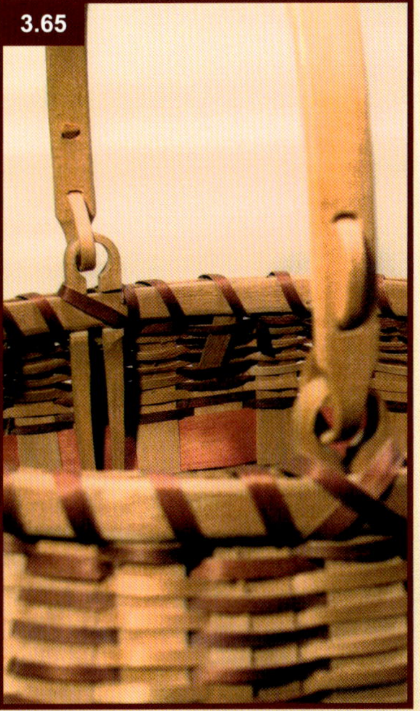
3.65

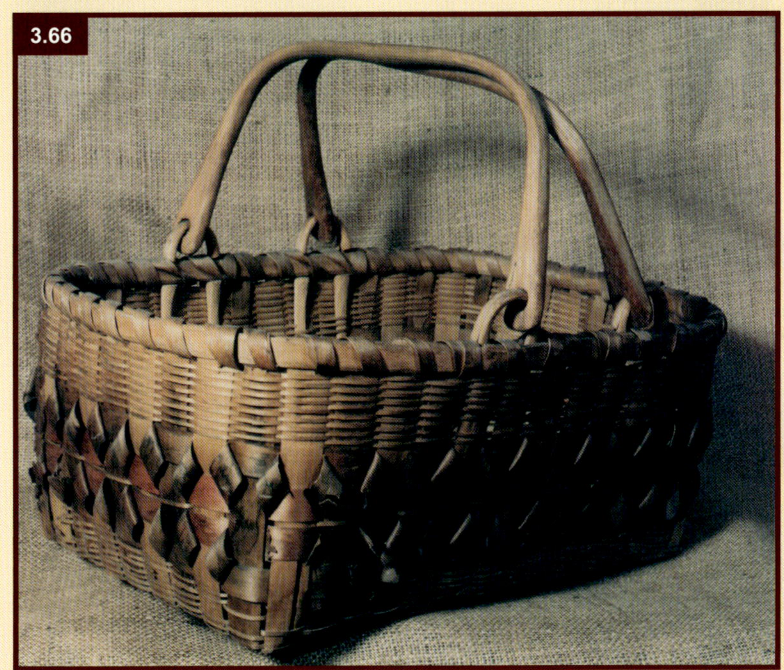
3.66

Focus:

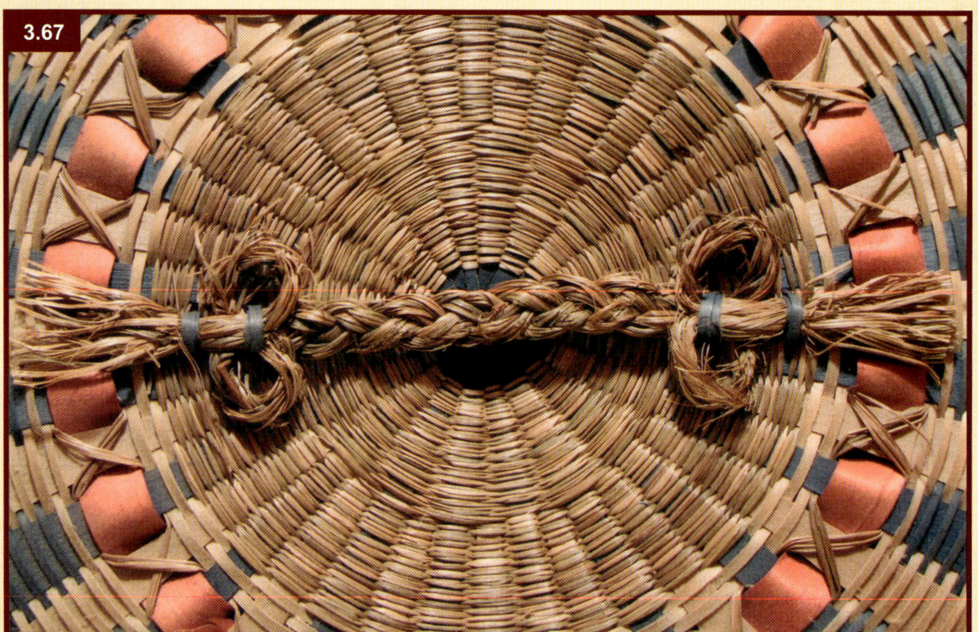

3.67. Strap-like "frog" handle.

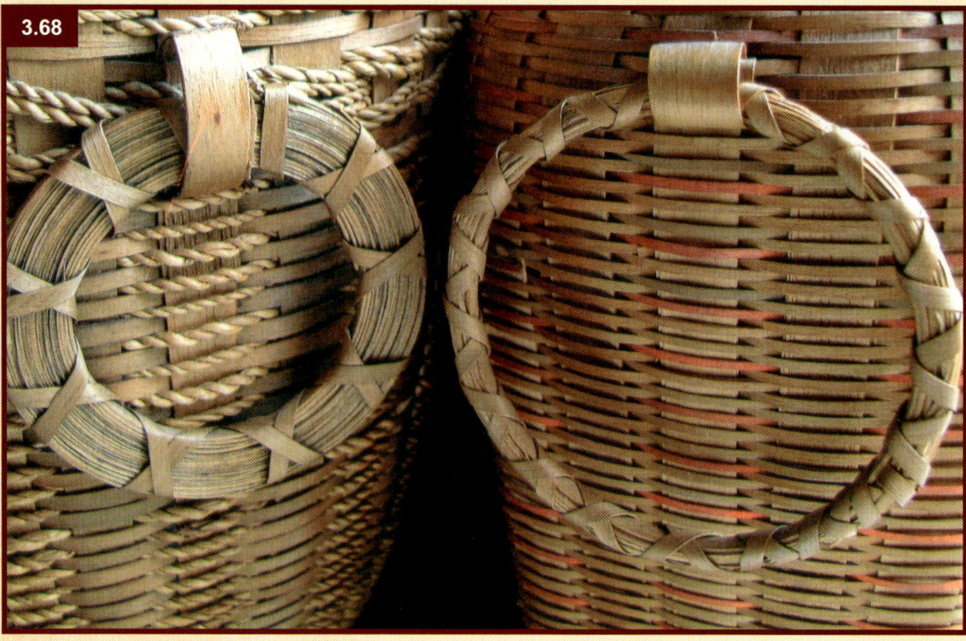

3.68. Pull handles or ring pulls, which are formed with bound coils of rolled woodsplints or bundled sweetgrass.

FOCUS:

Beautifying the Basket

The ingenuity of Northeastern Native American artisans is evident in the many ways that they have devised to decorate their woodsplint baskets. After all, without any creative details, plaited woodsplint baskets could look pretty drab. Various decorative methods encompass hand-painting, block-stamping, swabbing, punctate scorching, and dyeing of woodsplints. The inclusion of sweetgrass, "Hong Kong" and other twisted cord, appliqué elements, and handles and pulls, plus structural manipulation of additional splints inserted during the plaiting process to form twists, curls, and lacework are further examples.

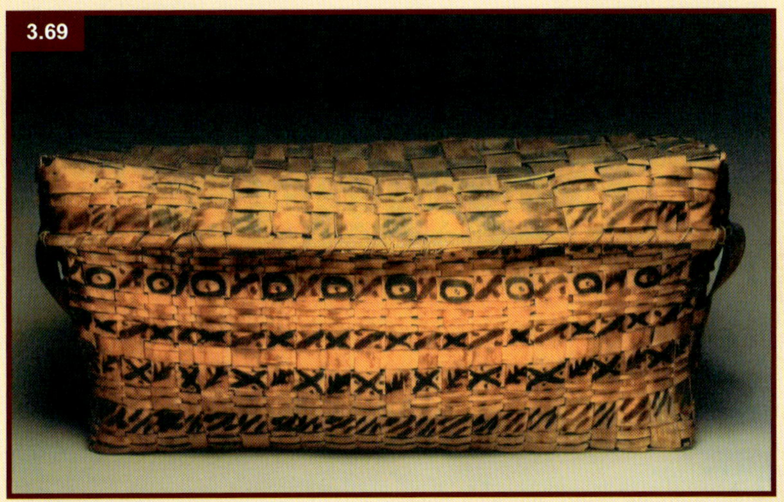

3.69. Hand-painting customarily is found only in the southern New England region, as on this early covered storage basket with ear handles and dark laundry blue and red (pokeberry?) decorative elements, 1810-1840, 24" long.

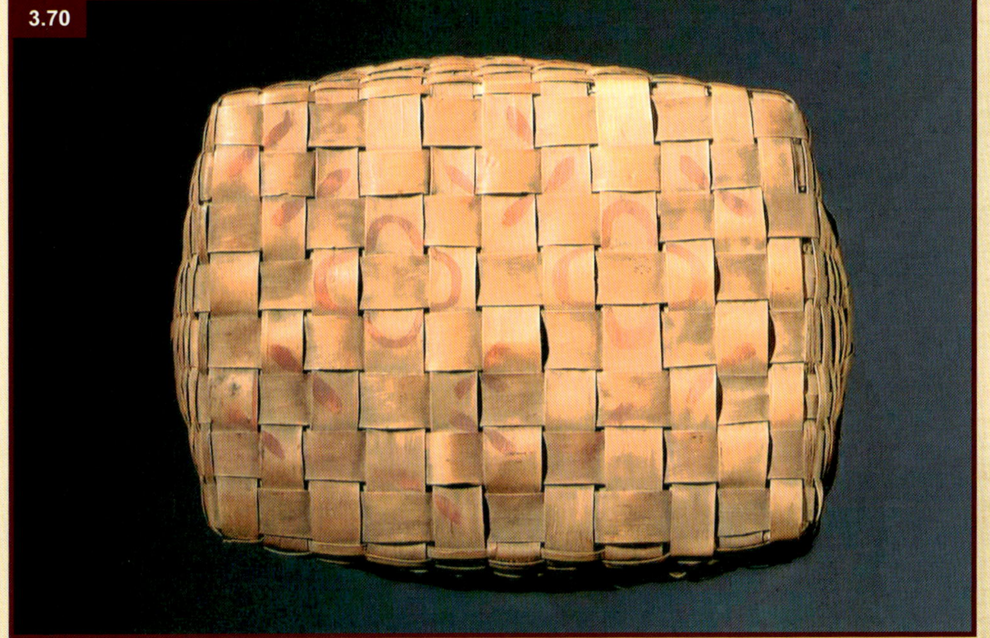

3.70. Painted medallions and leaves, likely Mohegan, c. 1830-1840, 15" long.

FOCUS:

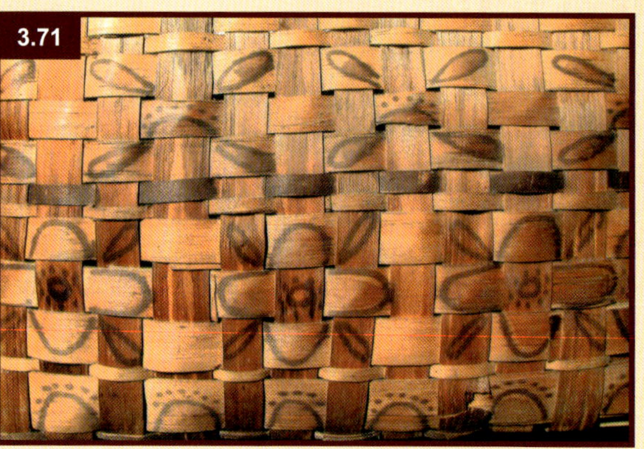

3.71. More hand-painted medallions.

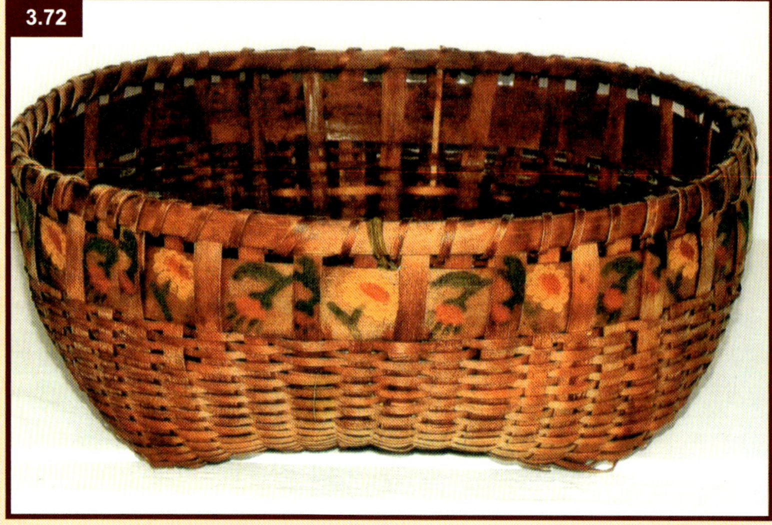

3.72. Painted flowers.

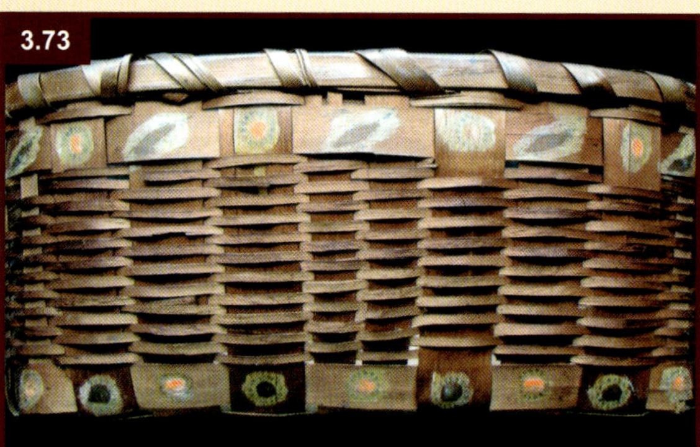

3.73. Green stampwork applied over hand-painted yellow leaf and flower outlines with alternating orange and green centers (most green has flaked off), New York state, c. 1860, 13" rim diameter. Pencilled note on base says this basket was purchased from Mr. Wood, Burdett, NY, for 35 cents.

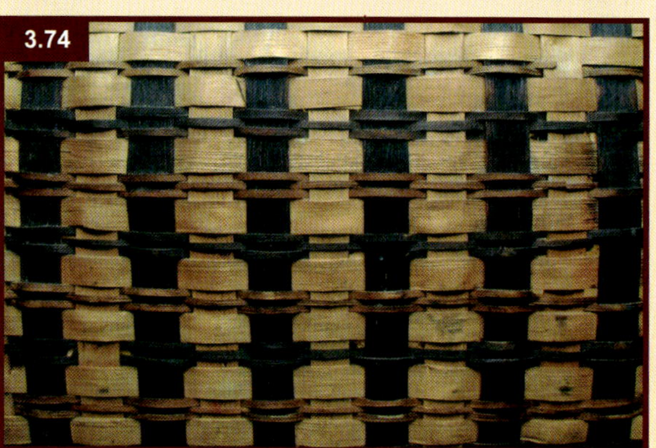

3.74. Swabbing only, on both warp and weft elements.

3.75–3.78. Swabbing plus stamping.

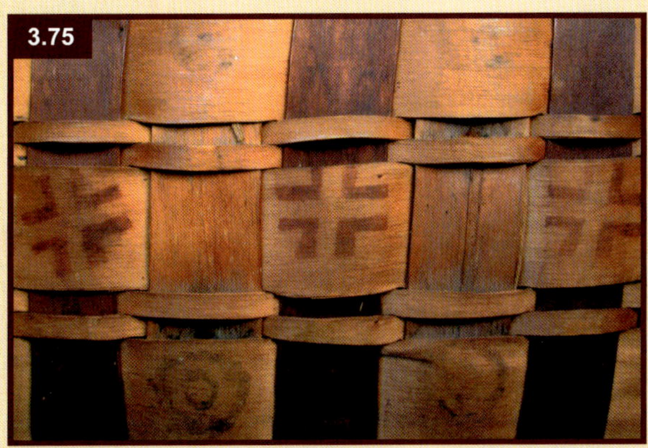
3.75

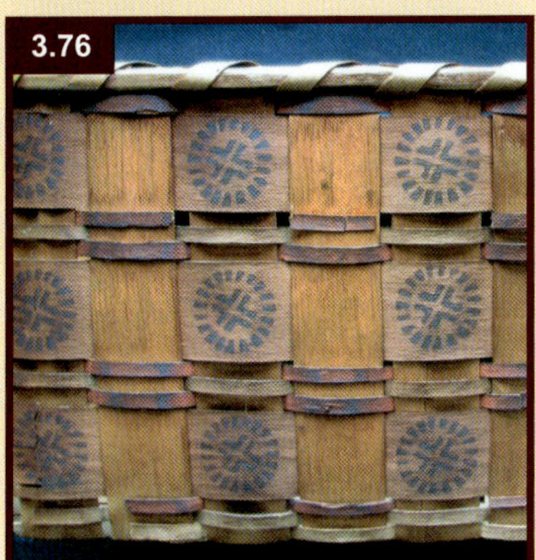
3.76

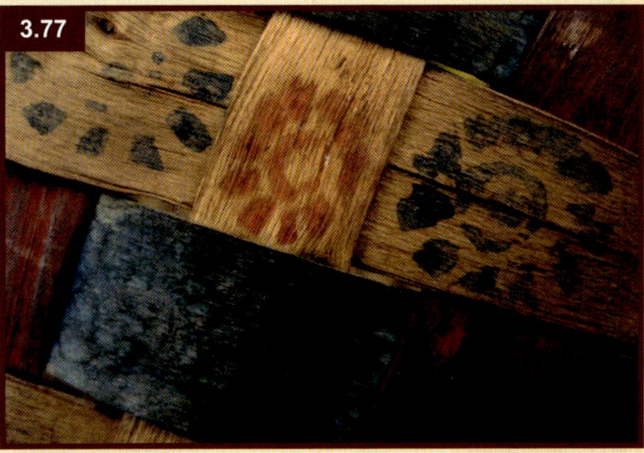
3.77

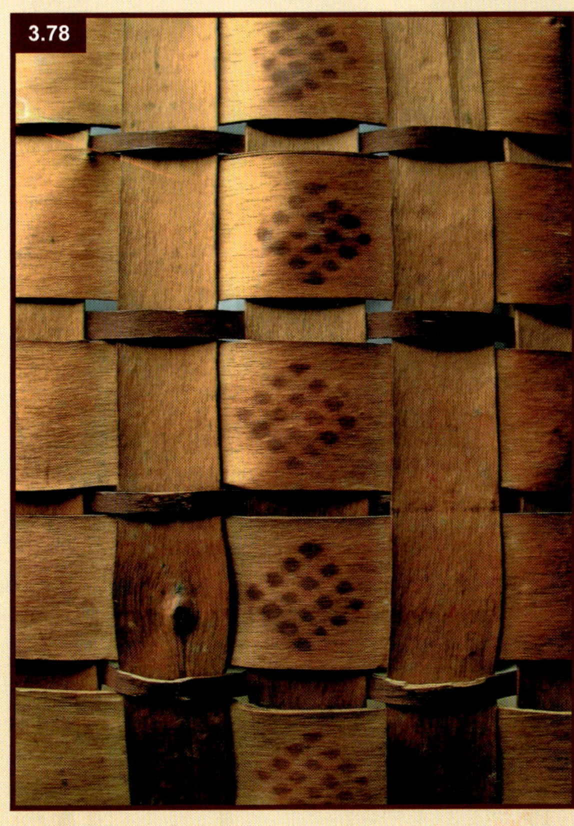
3.78

FOCUS:

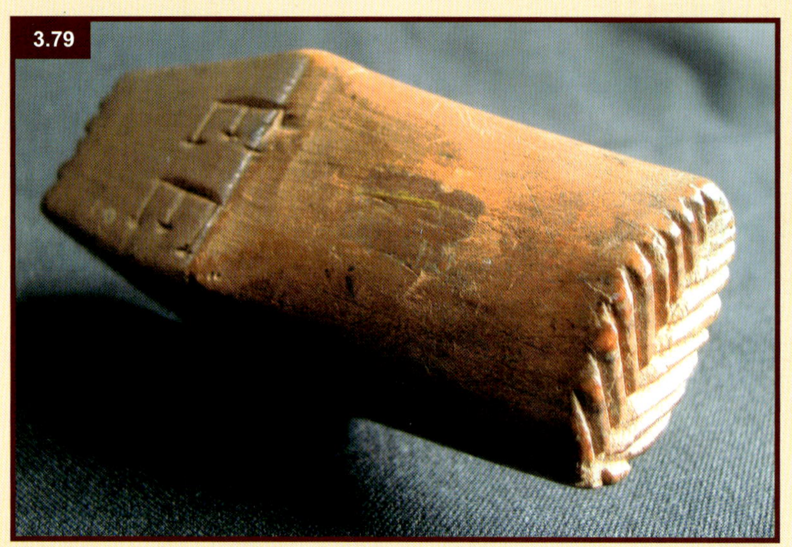

3.79. Carved wooden stamp.

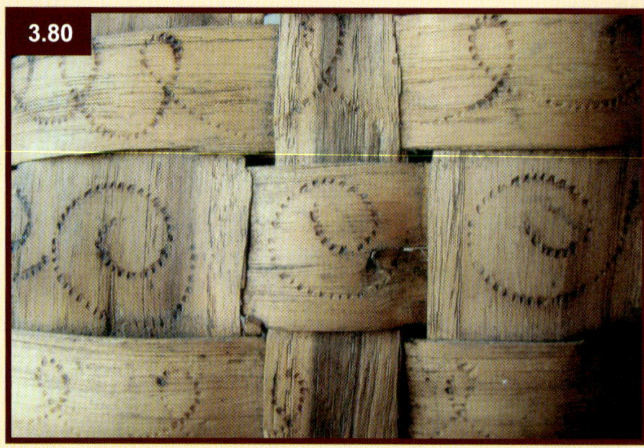

3.80. Scorched punctate decoration, uniquely Gay Head (Aquinnah) Wampanoag, c. 1890.

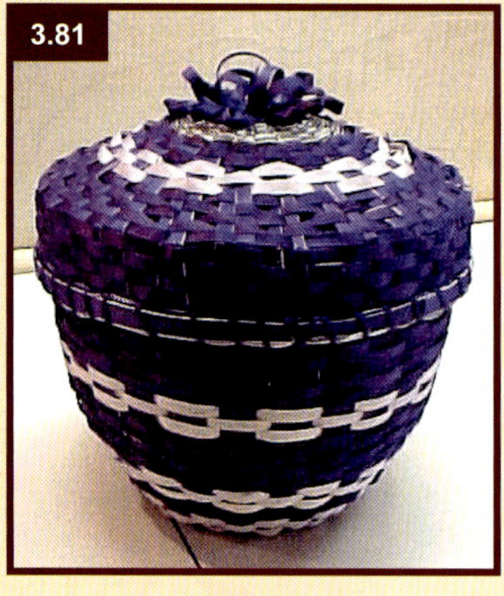

3.81. Contemporary basket with dyed splints, by Robin Lazore (Mohawk).

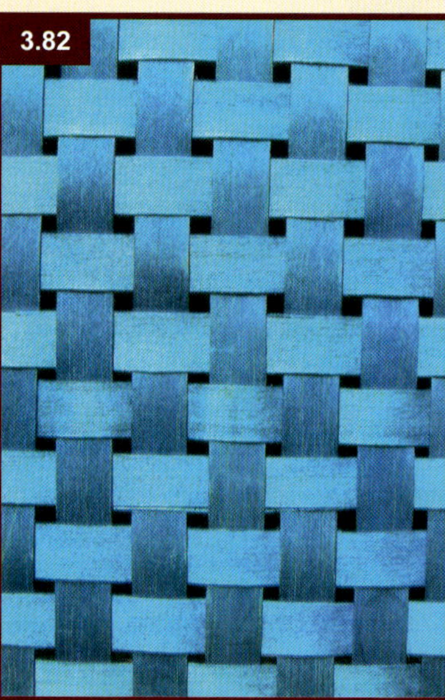

3.82. Dyed woodsplints are seen usually in northern New England, New York state, and Great Lakes baskets.

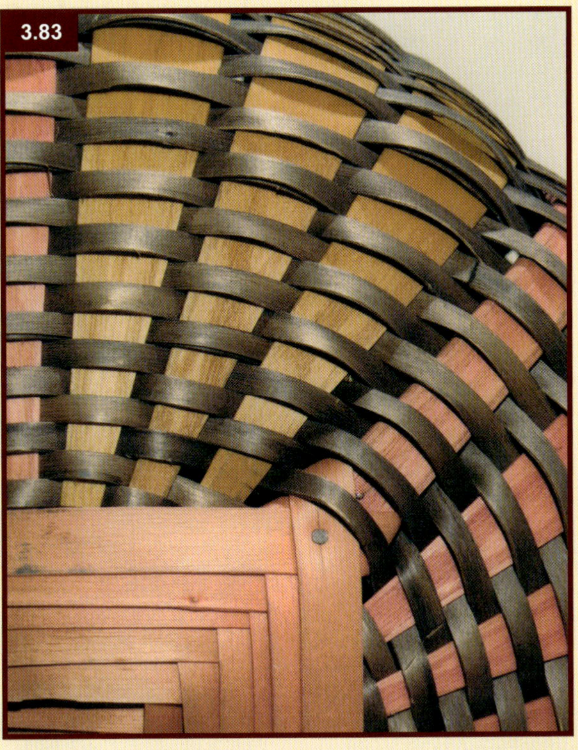

3.83. Rainbow-hued dyed splints.

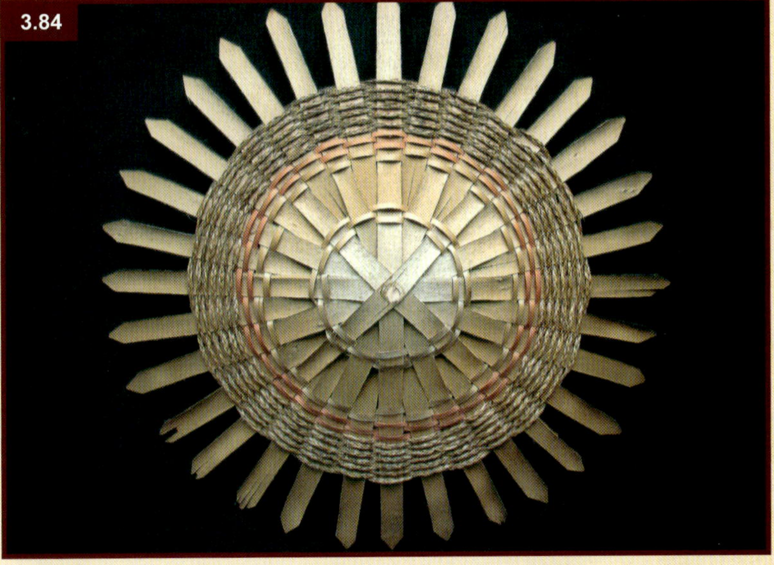

3.84. Sweetgrass lengths may be braided.

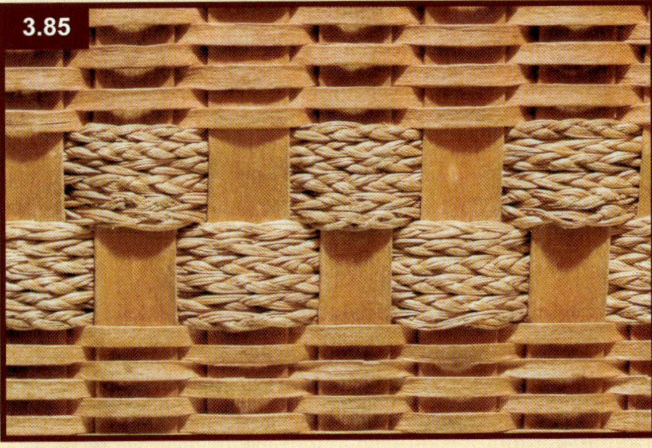

3.85. Detail of braided sweetgrass.

FOCUS:

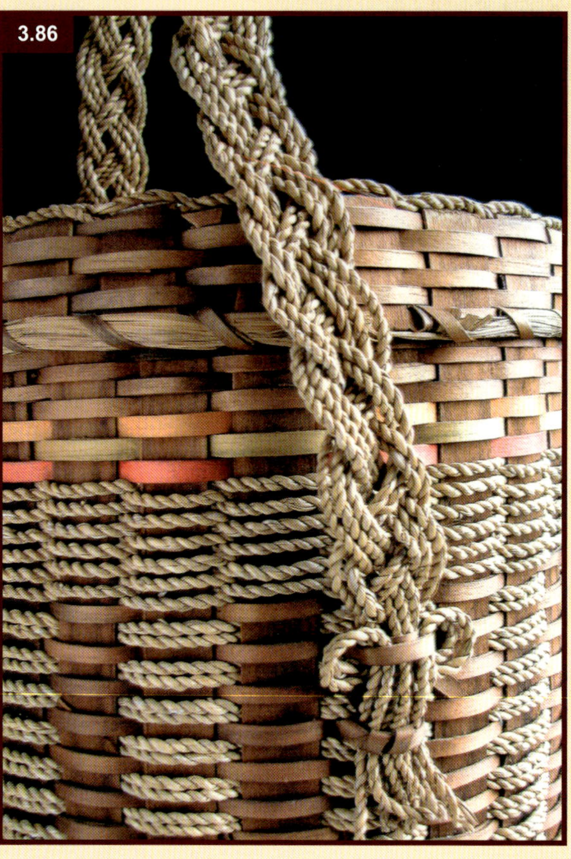

3.86. Detail of Hong Kong cord.

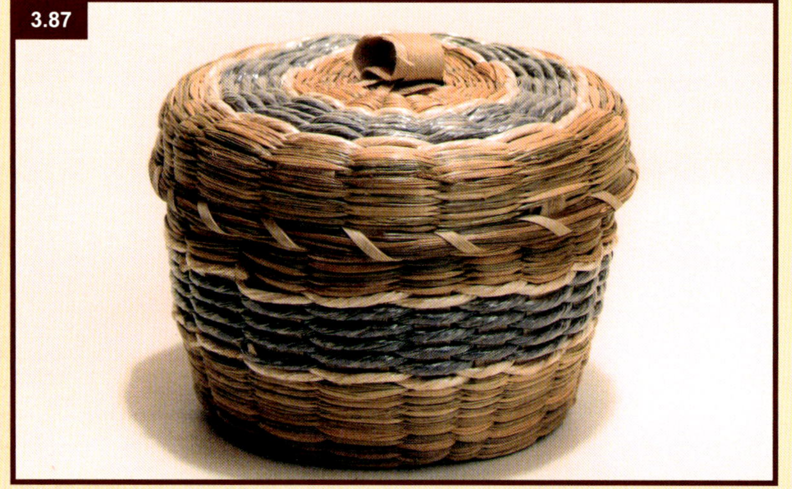

3.87. Plasticized cord.

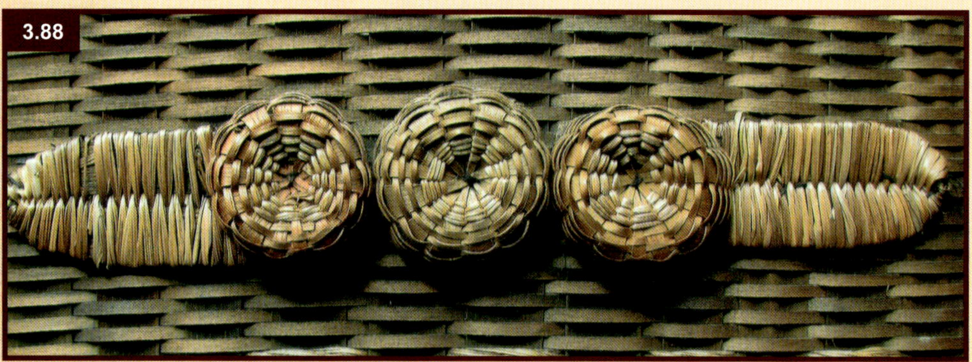

3.88. Appliqué splintwork elements.

3.89. Appliqué splint leaves or petals.

3.90. Handles include bound coils of rolled splints.

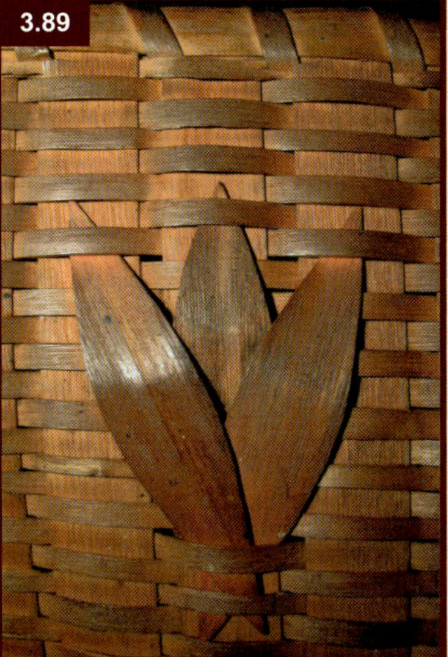

3.89

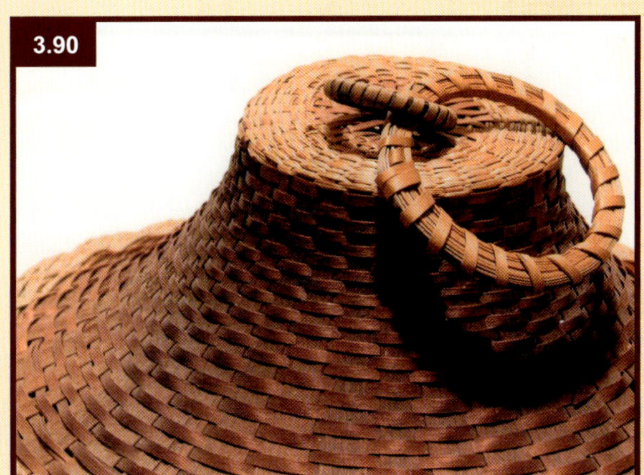

3.90

3.91. A "frog" or decorative braided handle of sweetgrass.

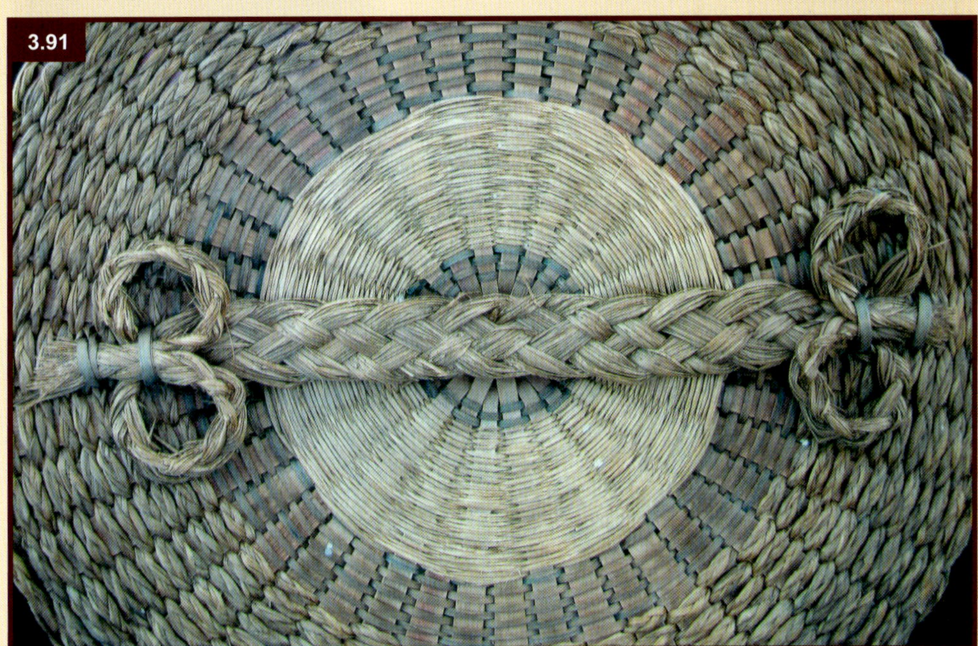

3.91

3.92. Curly splintwork.

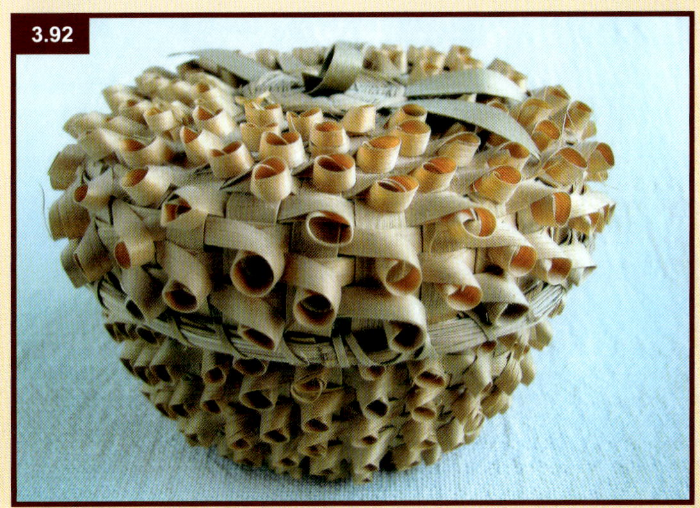

3.92

In addition to producing a familiar range of useful forms, Native basketmakers were usually willing and able to design new basketwork items that appealed to receptive homemakers. They also readily filled special orders for one-of-a-kind requests. Coveted forms like flower vases, wastebaskets, and baskets for entertaining and dining at the table, like the tea caddy, covered bottles, coasters, trivets, sandwich trays, and flower and fruit baskets, remain in use today.

Sheaths or cases for protecting delicate glass tumblers, as well as lunch pails, pie baskets, and picnic baskets were utilized while traveling, working, or attending church suppers and social gatherings. Numbered among other uncommon household baskets are lamps and basketwork for young children like rattles, beds, cradles, and toy dolls' cradles.

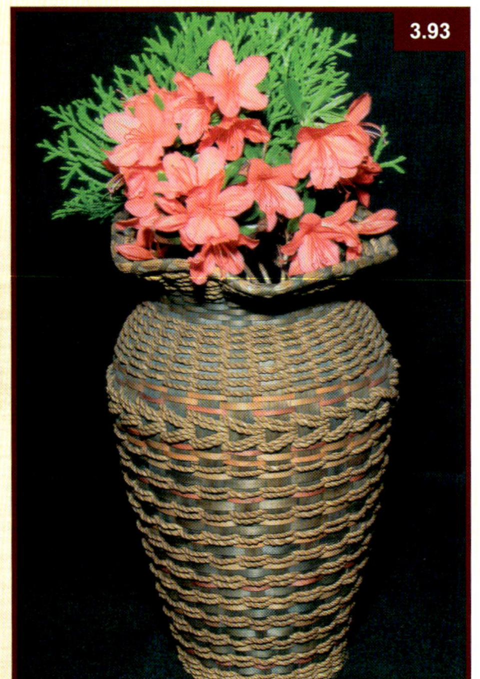
3.93

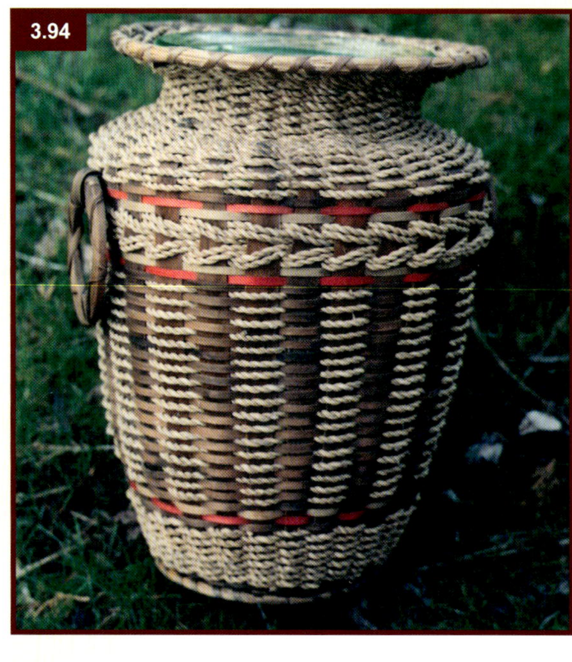
3.94

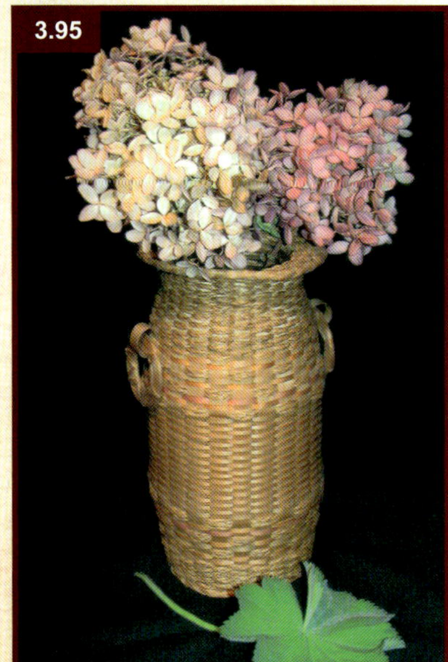
3.95

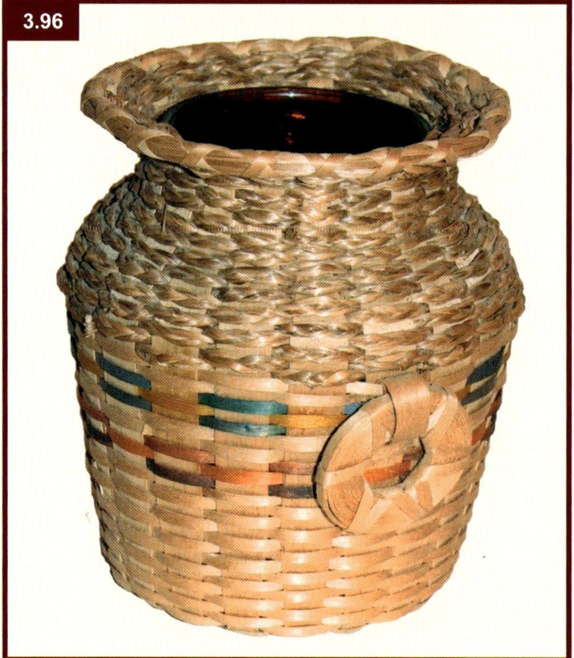
3.96

3.93–3.96. Urn-shaped basketry flower vases, plaited around glass jars with dyed ash splints and Hong Kong cord or sweetgrass, sold well in resort areas, 1920s–1950s.

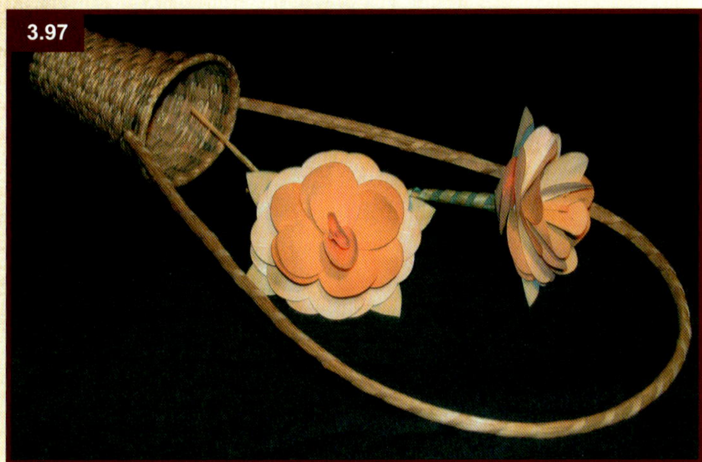

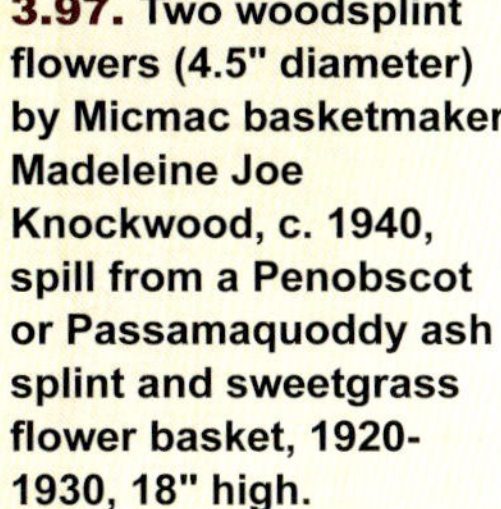

3.97. Two woodsplint flowers (4.5" diameter) by Micmac basketmaker Madeleine Joe Knockwood, c. 1940, spill from a Penobscot or Passamaquoddy ash splint and sweetgrass flower basket, 1920-1930, 18" high.

3.98. Wastebasket with curly splintwork and Hong Kong cord trim and ring handles, 1920-1940, 12" high.

3.99. Barrel-shaped wastebasket, plaited around a compound block or mold, sold for $14.00 per dozen in the 1920s, probably Penobscot, 13" high.

3.100. Probable Penobscot or Passamaquoddy covered caddy, perhaps for holding loose tea, c. 1900-1920, 5" high.

3.101. Stoneware bottle covered with ash splint and sweetgrass basketwork, Nova Scotia (likely Micmac), early 20th century, 7" high.

3.102. Ash splint plus sweetgrass coasters, mats, and trivets for the table have long been useful souvenirs, 5" diameter.

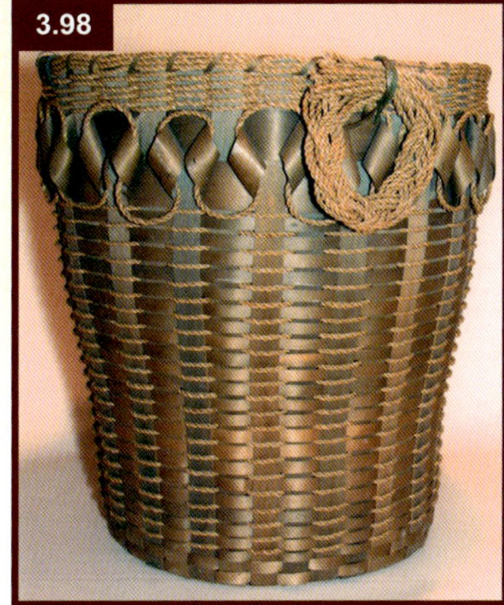

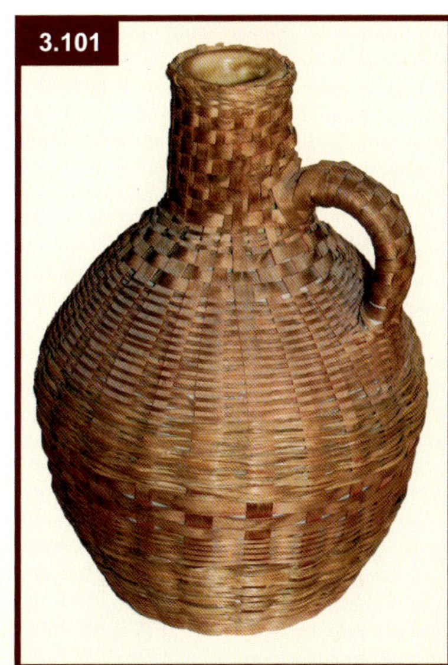

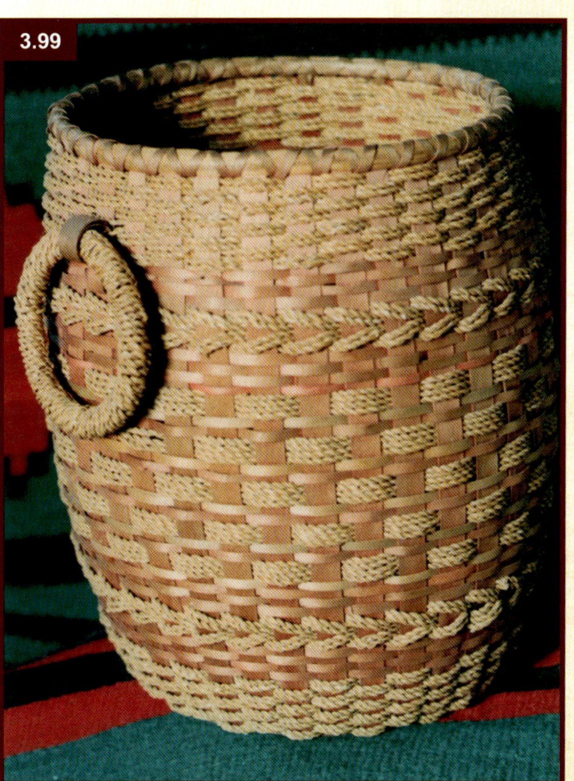

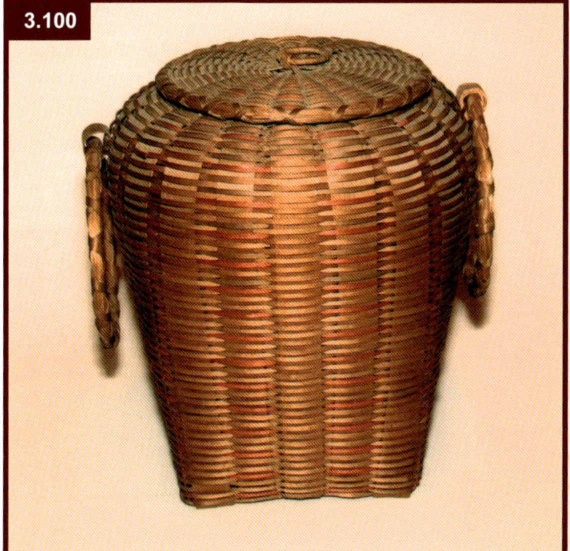

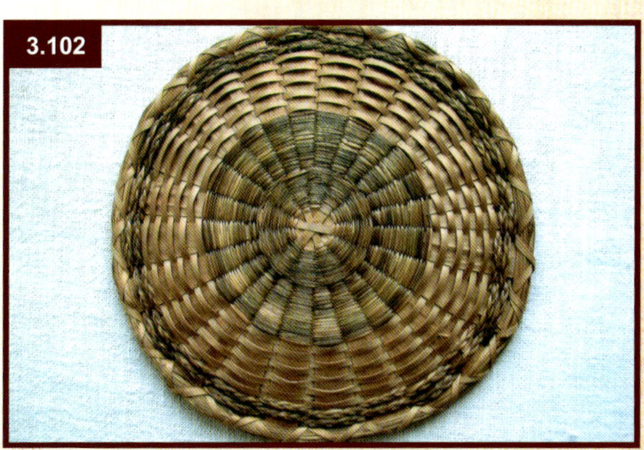

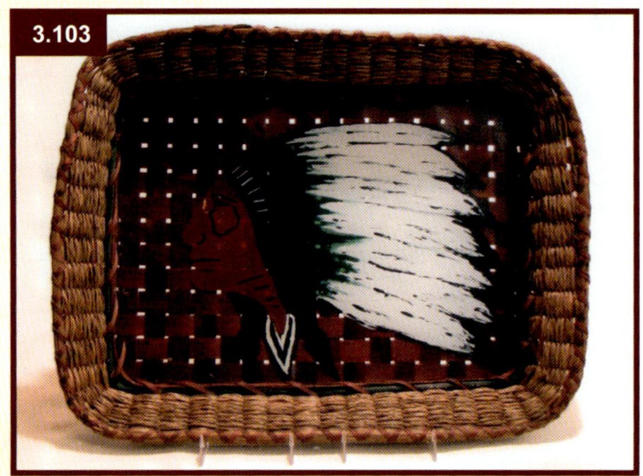

3.103

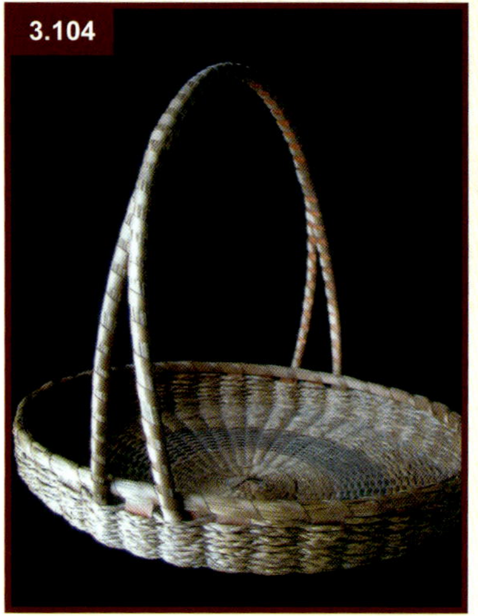

3.104

3.103. Basketmakers like the Penobscot of Maine occasionally fashioned tablewares like this dyed ash splint and sweetgrass tray with reverse painting on its glass insert, c. 1920, 14" long.

3.104. The tall handle towers above this shallow tray, early 1900s, 10" diameter.

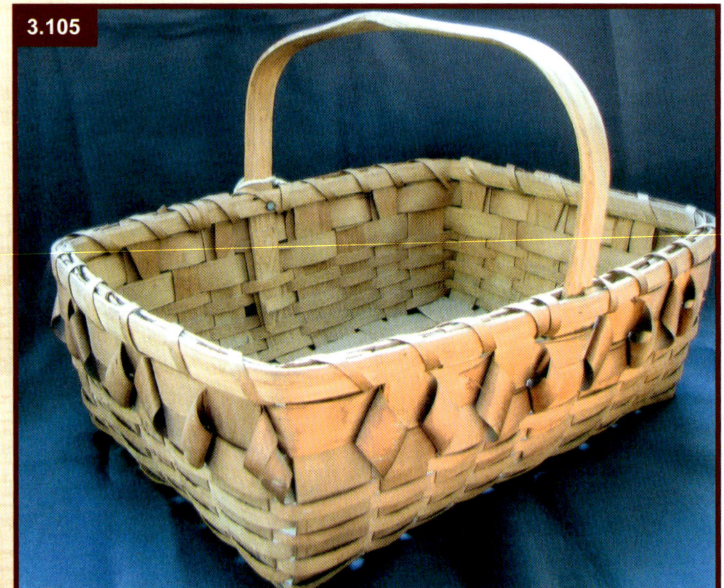

3.105

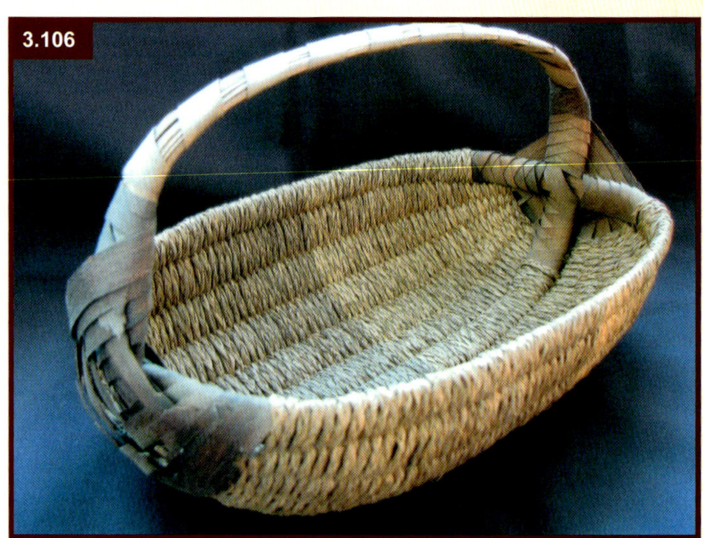

3.106

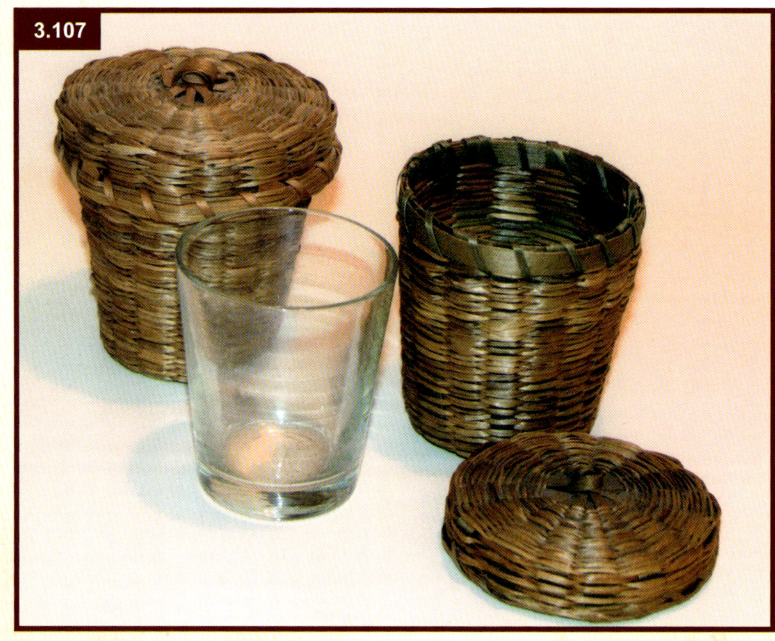

3.107

3.105. The owner of this basket has used it for garden cuttings, Christmas greens, and fruit, "1917" pencilled on base, 8.5" high with handle.

3.106. Maliseet-style melon-shaped fruit basket with a "God's-eye" handle attachment, early 1900s, 9.5" long.

3.107. Ash splint and sweetgrass sheaths or cases for cushioning delicate glass tumblers during travels, c. 1900, 3" high.

3.108. Covered lunch pail of ash splints and braided sweetgrass with braided Hong Kong cord handles, Passamaquoddy, 1930s, 9.5" long.

3.109. Pie or cake basket with copper rivets attaching the handles, attributed to the Micmac, 1940s, 12" diameter.

3.110. This pie basket **(3.109)** separates into two sections, each holding its own cake or pie. The top basket of this particular example may be inverted to serve as a "stand" for displaying contents.

3.111. Plaited ash splint picnic basket with faded purple-dyed wefts has been a popular form for more than a century, Maine, 20" long.

3.112. Ash splint and Hong Kong cord table-lamp base and shade, c. 1930-1940, 14" high.

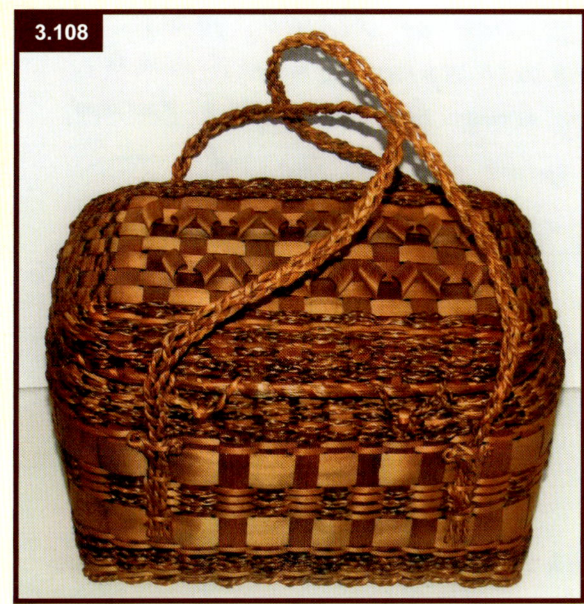

3.108

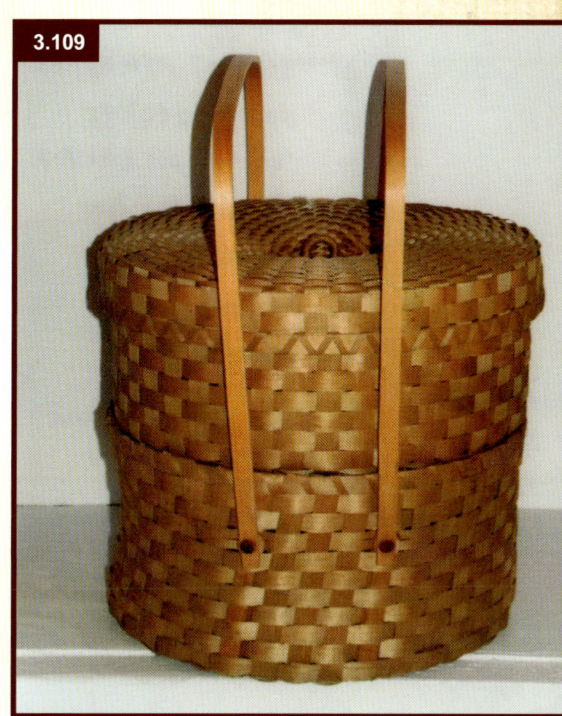

3.109

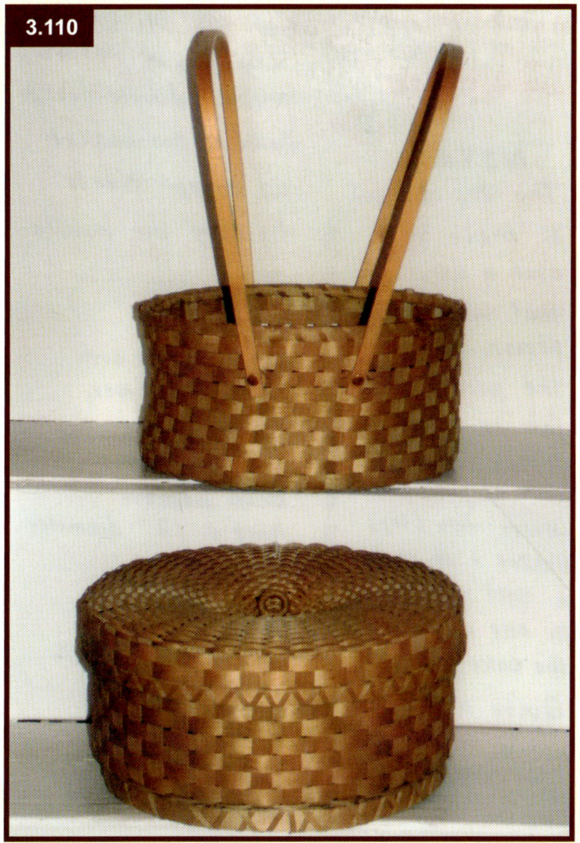

3.110

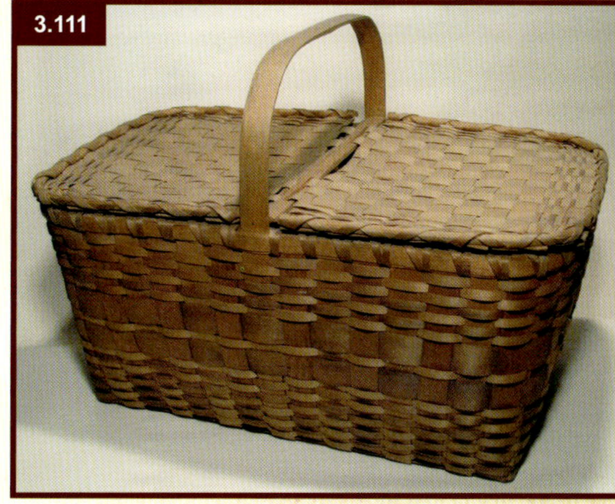

3.111

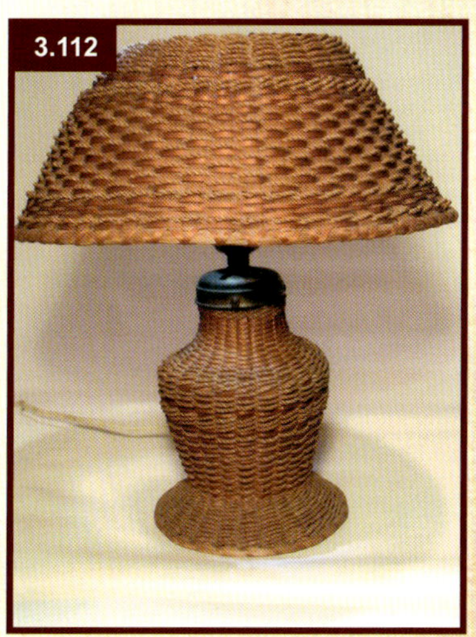

3.112

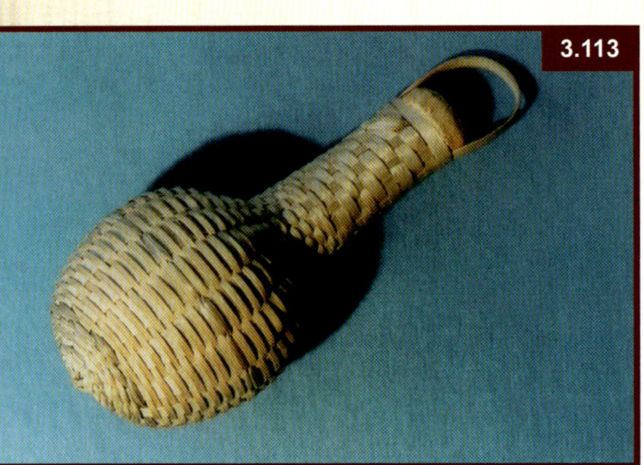
3.113

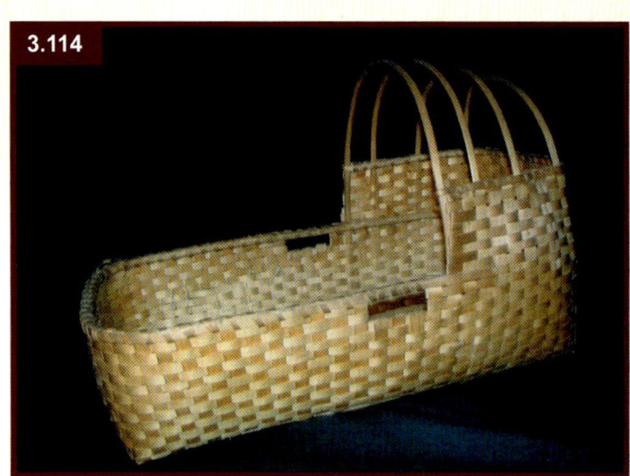
3.114

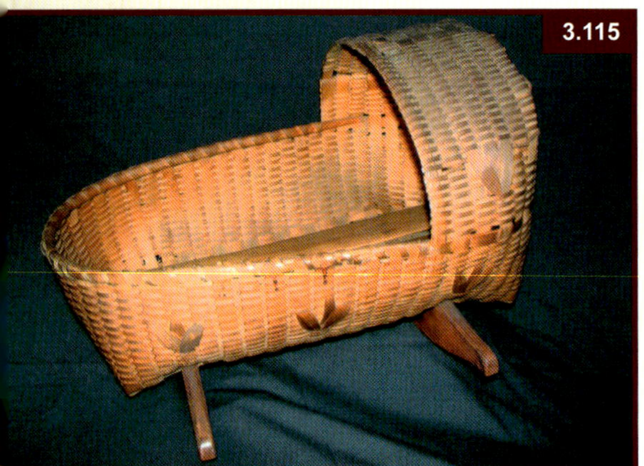
3.115

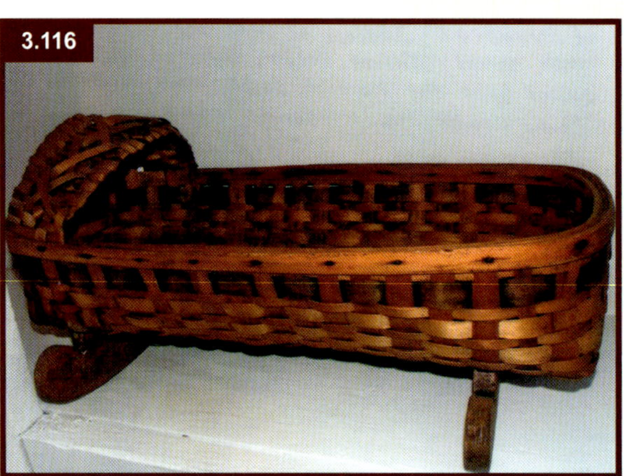
3.116

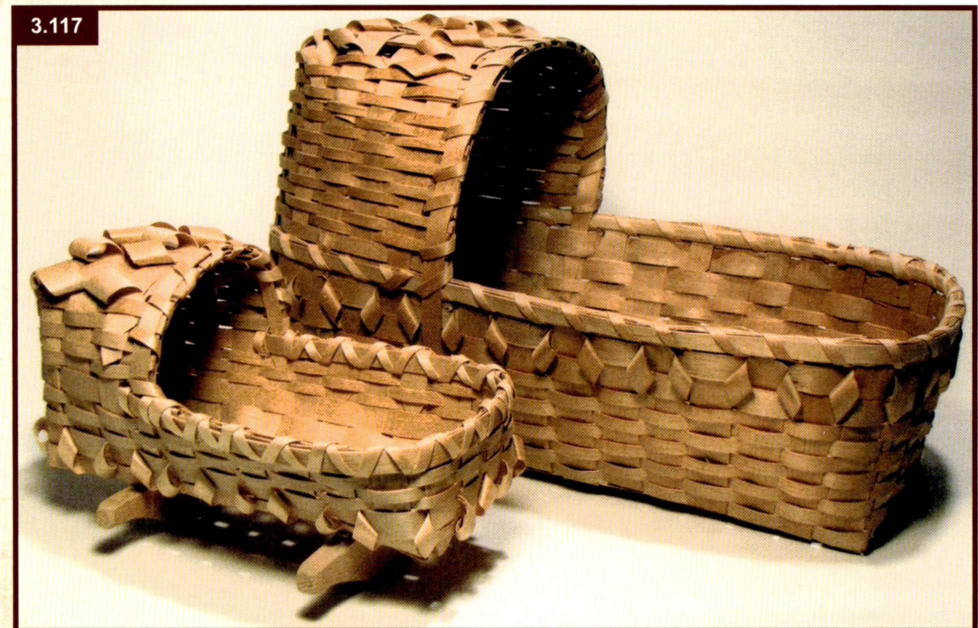
3.117

3.113. Ash splint and sweetgrass baby rattle with a carved wood stopper, Iroquois (Mohawk), 1970s, 5.75" long.

3.114. Full-sized infant's bed, without rockers, has four carved hoops forming an open frame to support a cloth shade over a child's face, Abenaki, early 20th century, 28" long.

3.115. Full-sized Iroquois (Seneca) infant's cradle with carved wooden rockers, reinforced inside with three rived slats attached to the splint basketwork with square-headed nails. Eight tulip-like splint overlays and early red paint embellish the sides and hood, 1860, 30" long.

3.116. Penobscot ash splint infant's cradle with hood, carved wooden rockers, and a nailed rim, c. 1920, 24" long.

3.117. Miniature cradles and beds for dolls often have decorative curly splintwork, (right) signed "Mary Goo Goo Mic Mac," 9.5" long.

CHAPTER 4

SPECIAL BASKETS FOR HER & HIM

By the late 19th century, Native crafters plaited specialized woodsplint baskets for women and for men. Calling card trays as well as wall pockets for holding small items like combs or bobbins, household keys, or letters readied for the RFD post were receptacles used by either men or women. Certain baskets for men held starched linen or celluloid shirt collars. Both sexes adopted covered rectangular baskets that were marketed as veil boxes, but which frequently served as photograph or stationery boxes atop desks.

Other basketry products were associated with women's roles and women's dress. Native makers and distributors created them and marketed them specifically with women in mind. Basketry handbags and shoppers and market totes followed trends in women's fashion magazines. So did glove boxes and handkerchief boxes. Decorative covered jewelry or sundries boxes and hair receivers might be found on a woman's personal dresser or vanity.

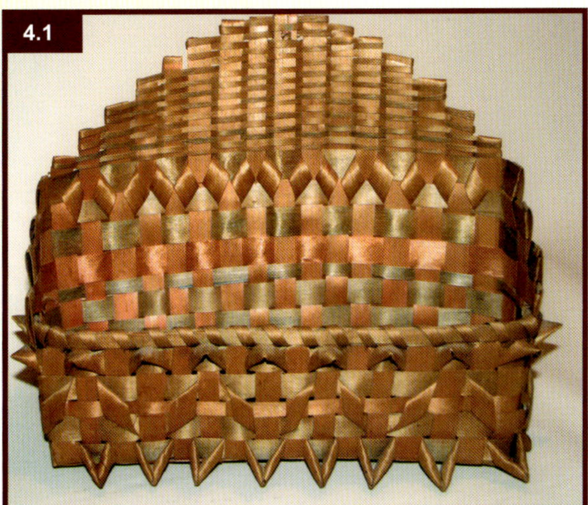

4.1

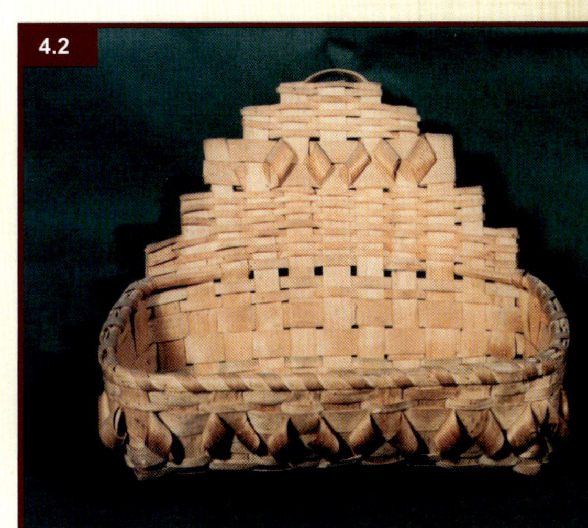

4.2

4.1, 4.2. Plaited splint comb holders or wall pockets enhanced with curly splintwork.

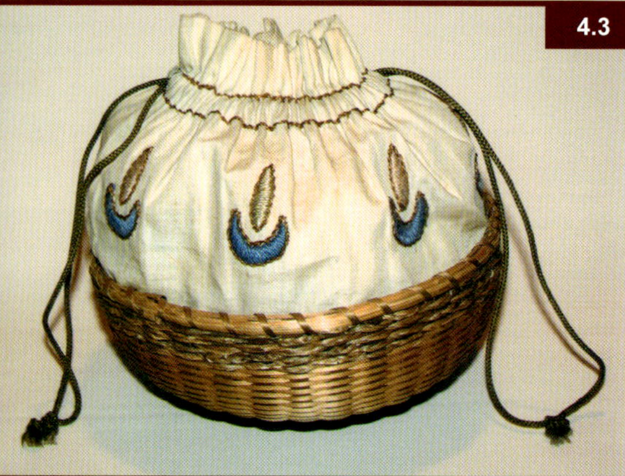
4.3

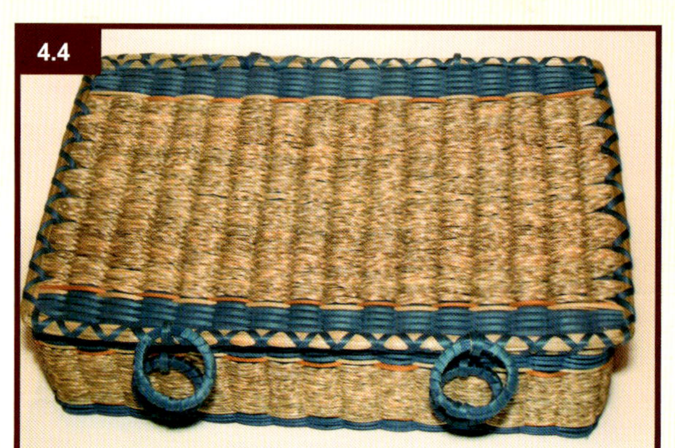
4.4

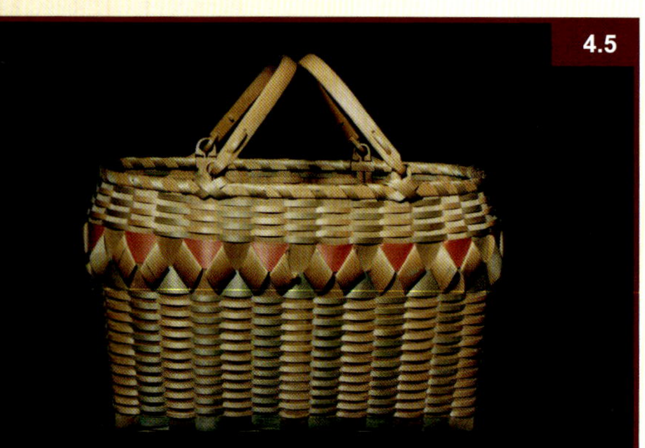
4.5

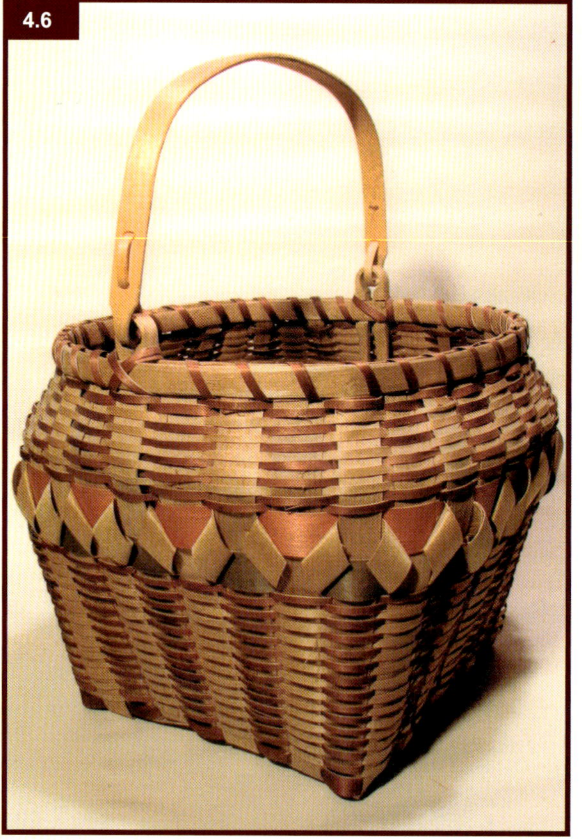
4.6

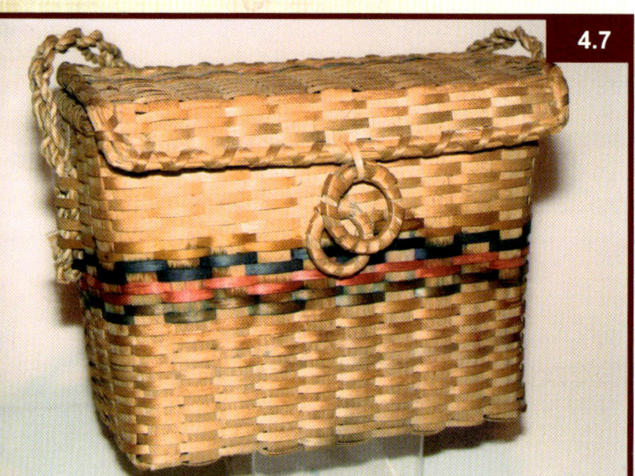
4.7

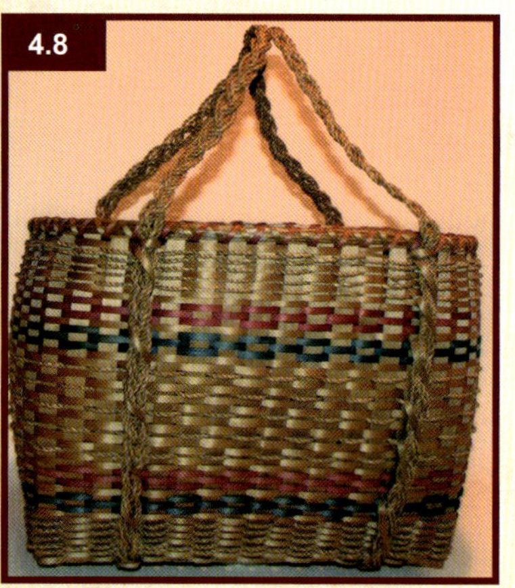
4.8

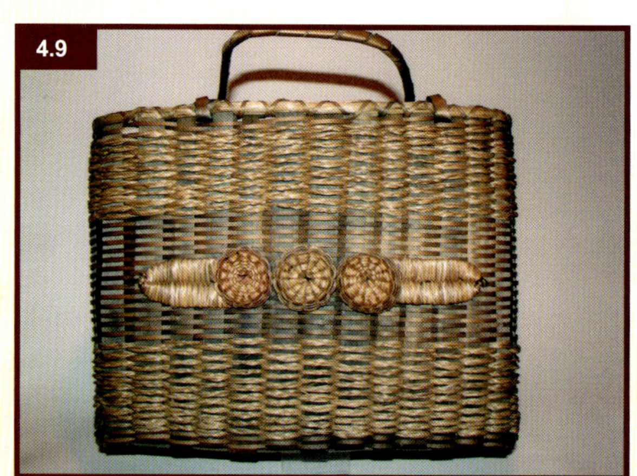
4.9

4.3. Ash splint and sweetgrass basket for holding men's celluloid collars also doubled as a woman's sewing or handiwork basket. An earlier owner during the American Arts & Crafts Movement embellished it with the embroidered top and drawstring closure.

4.4. Rectangular basket for holding veils, photographs, or stationery, probably Penobscot, c. 1920, 9" long.

4.5–4.12. Handbags, shoppers, purses, and market totes from the early 1900s came in many sizes and shapes and often followed the fashion of the day. The two swing-handle examples are Ho-Chunk from Wisconsin (**4.5, 4.6**), while the remainder are Wabanaki Confederacy (Abenaki, Maliseet, Micmac/ Mi'kmaq, Passamaquoddy, or Penobscot), c. 1900-1950.

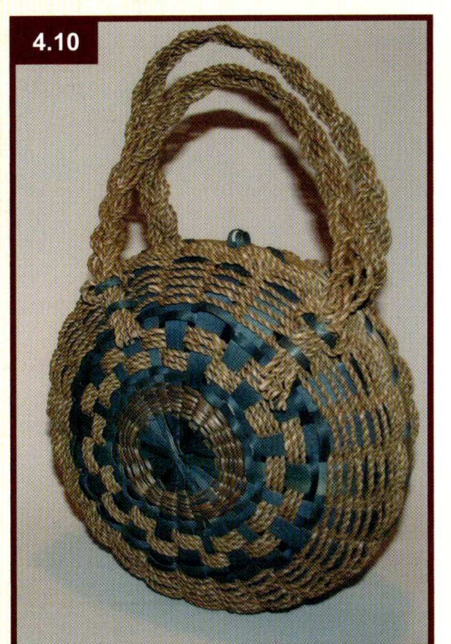

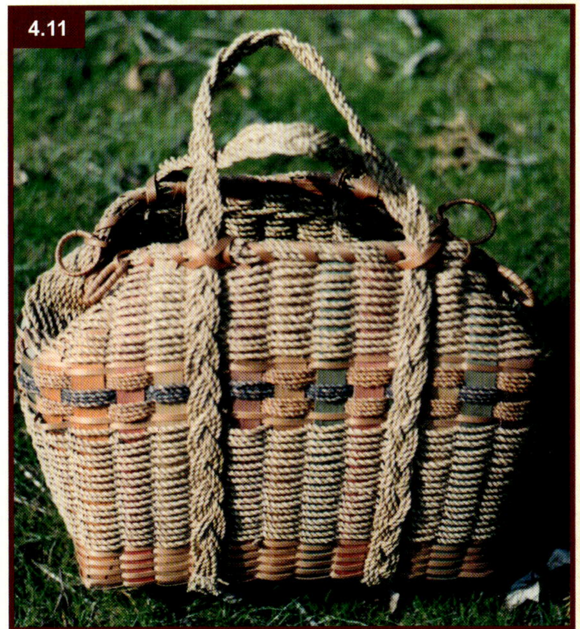

4.13. Basketry case holding an embroidered clutch handbag, Penobscot or Abenaki (Odanak), c. 1930, 12" long.

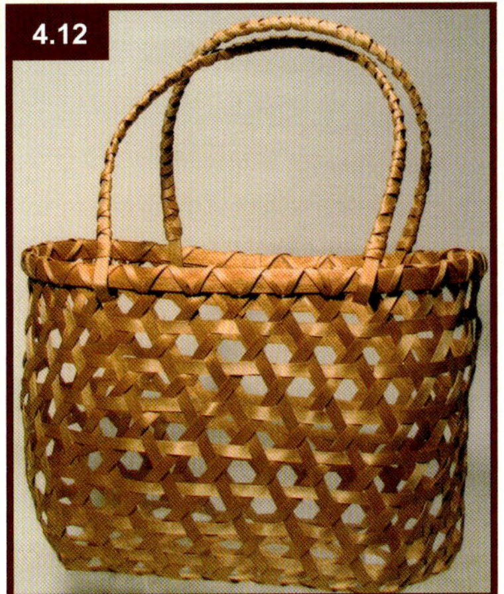

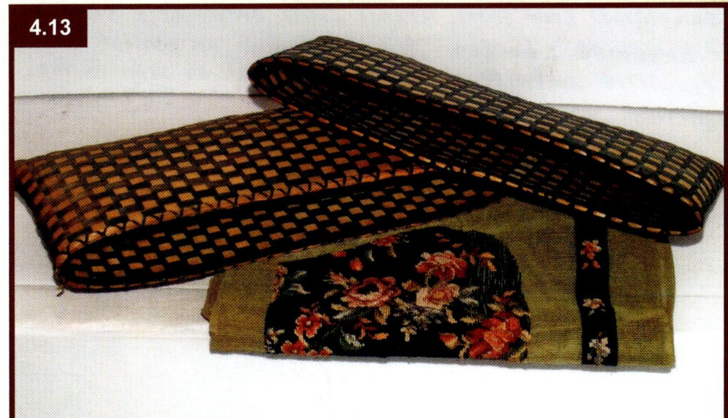

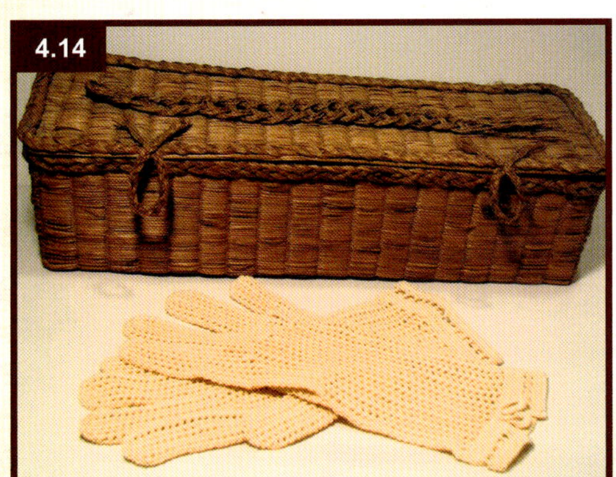

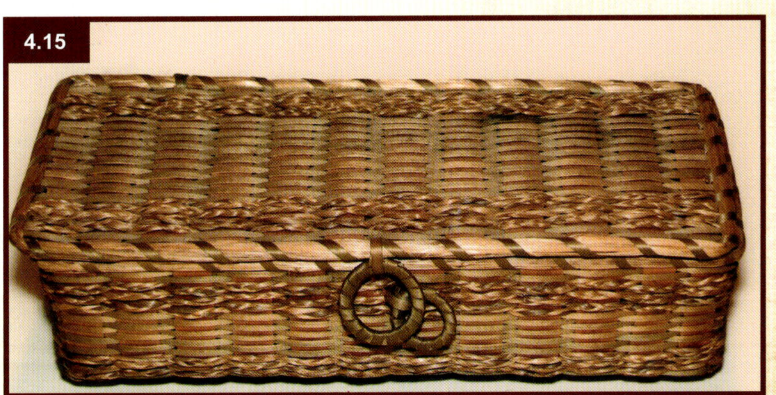

4.14, 4.15. Long, covered ladies' glove boxes, Penobscot or Passamaquoddy, early 1900s. **4.14** is 13" long.

4.16

4.16. Some women acquired closely matching sets of baskets for their homes, like this glove box and handkerchief box, stamped "Made in Canada," probably Abenaki, c. 1920, (right) 5" square.

SETTING:

Back Home Again

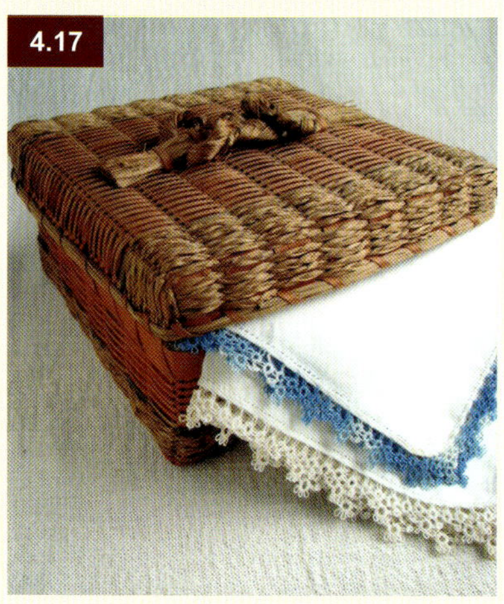

4.17. A basketry hankie box can lift one's spirits with its aromatic vanilla-scented sweetgrass and cheerful dyed ash splints, Abenaki, c. 1920s, 6" square.

Cora turned toward her battered steamer trunk with a sigh of resignation. She had put off unpacking it for almost a week. As the young woman reached for its lid, she paused. The lonely call of a loon on the lake across the road drew her to the open window. Its forlorn cry mirrored her spirits.

The early September day was sunny, but tendrils of mist were curling up from the cooling surface of the lake, and she sensed a nip of autumn in the brisk air. Leaves here at home already were starting to turn, with yellows and flaming reds showing here and there.

Cora looked wistfully toward pale blue mountains rimming the horizon. They now appeared low and indistinct. Had it been only a few days ago, she wondered, that the train had brought her home through those very peaks from her grandmother's island in Alexandria Bay? How high and rugged the Adirondacks had seemed as the engine labored through the narrow passes. Her spirits slumped further at the memory of watching those idyllic days of summer recede, along with the bay and the crags, with every chug of the coal-burning steam engine.

On the lake, the loon cried once more. Cora now had little more than another long, cold, dark winter to anticipate before she might return to Thousand Islands. Cora sighed again. She drew away from the window and moved toward her battered old trunk. She braced its lid against the wall. A layer of whimseys and baskets rested on top of her clothing: little pine-scented balsam pillows and beaded moccasins, several ash splint fans and miniature birchbark tipis for her friends at school, a shopper purse for her mother, and a cheerful rainbow-hued lunch basket for her father.

A lidded splint handkerchief box trimmed with sweetgrass had proven so useful, though, that Cora had decided to keep it for herself. The pleasing vanilla-like perfume of sweetgrass and black ash splints greeted her, reminding Cora that the baskets, too, had come home from the bay. As she started to unpack the baskets, filled with the scent of summer and her memories of sunbeams, the young woman's spirits began to lift.

Cora brought her fragrant handkerchief basket closer to her face and, with a small smile, drew in a deep breath.

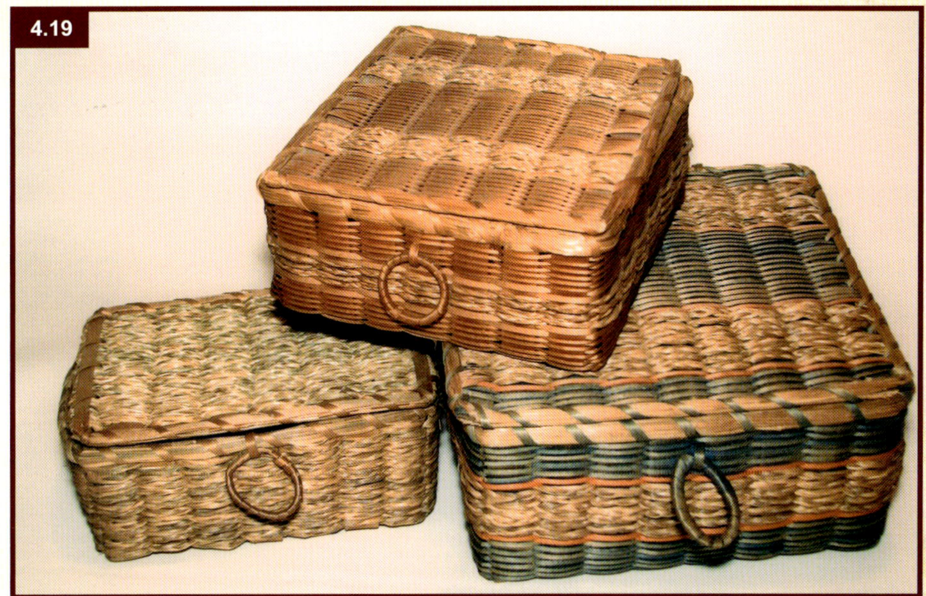

4.19

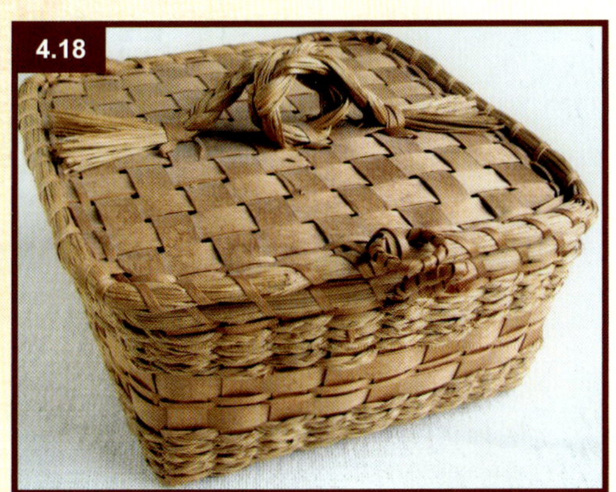

4.18

4.18–4.20. Covered handkerchief boxes were the early 20th-century homemaker's version of paper facial-tissue boxes.

4.21–4.23. Pillow-shaped boxes with attached covers cushioned freshly ironed and starched linen hankies when traveling, Penobscot and Abenaki (right), early 1900s.

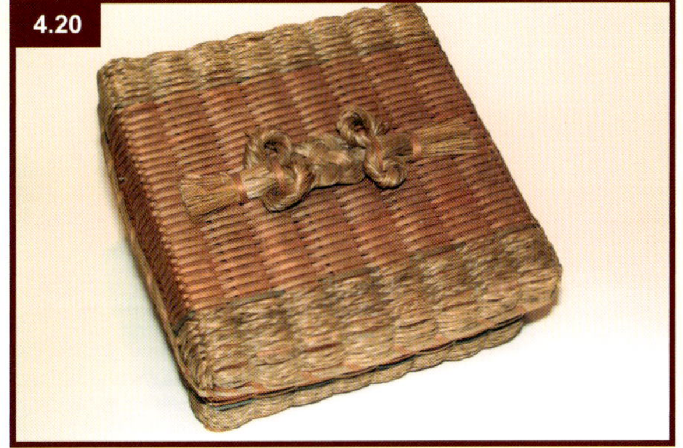

4.20

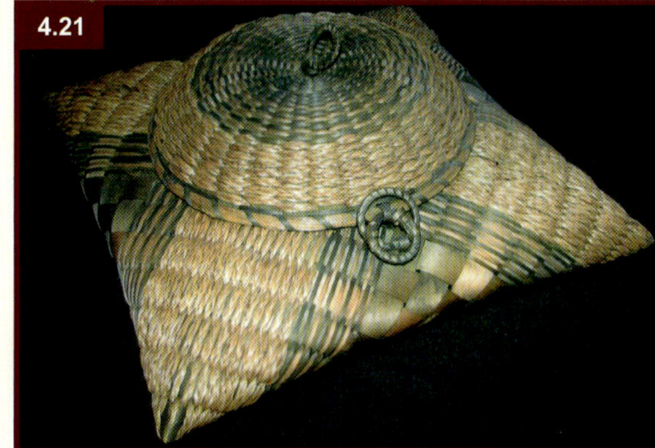

4.21

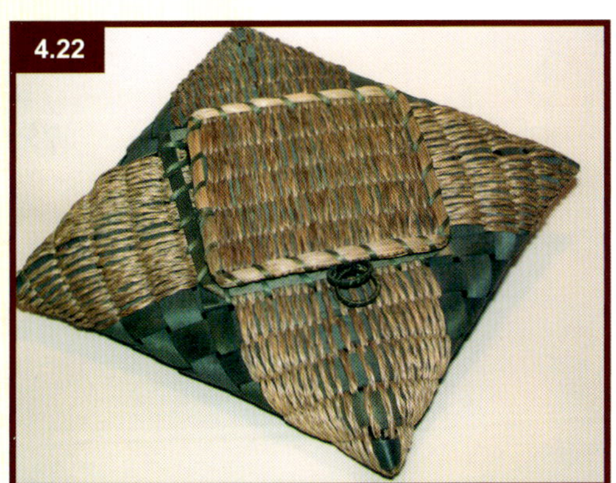

4.22

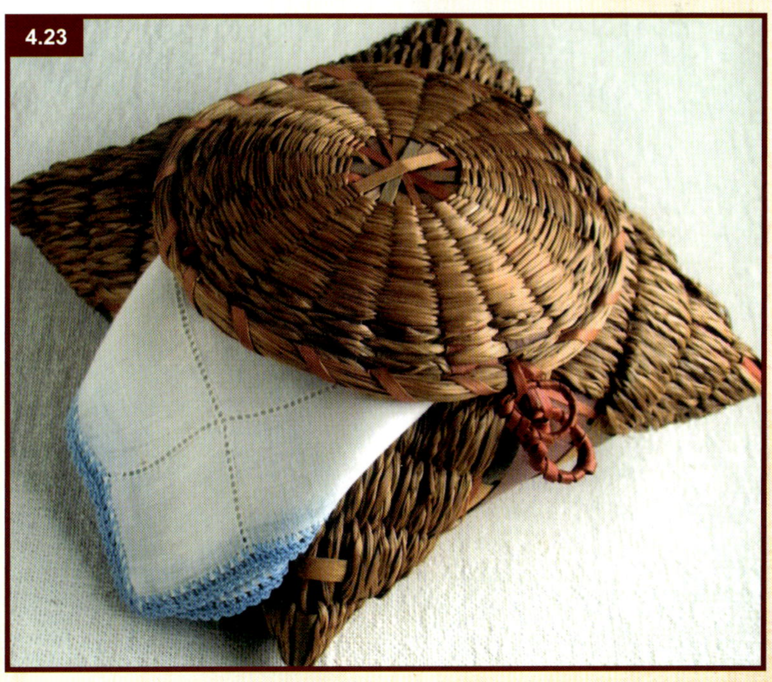

4.23

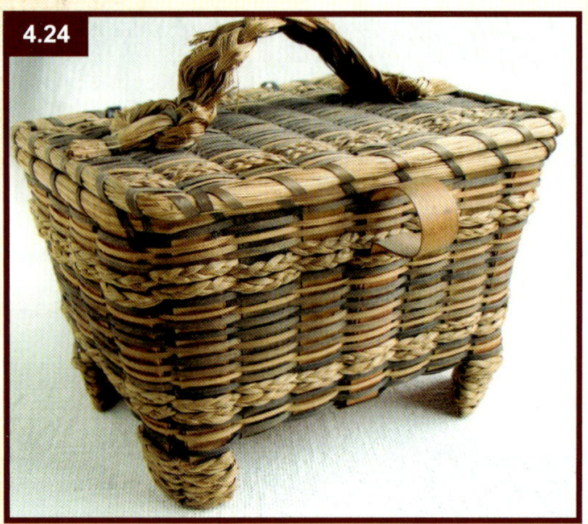
4.24

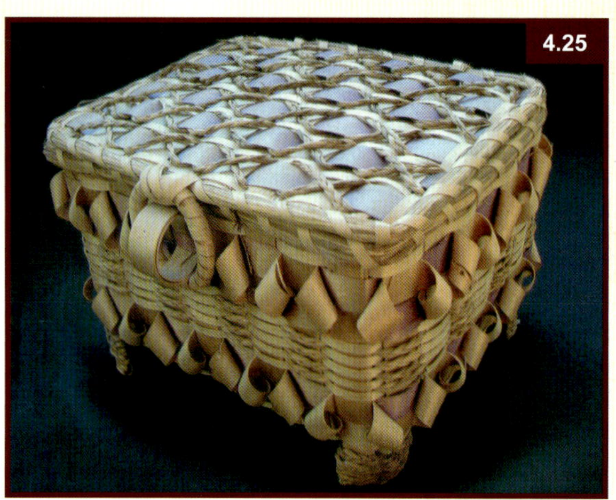
4.25

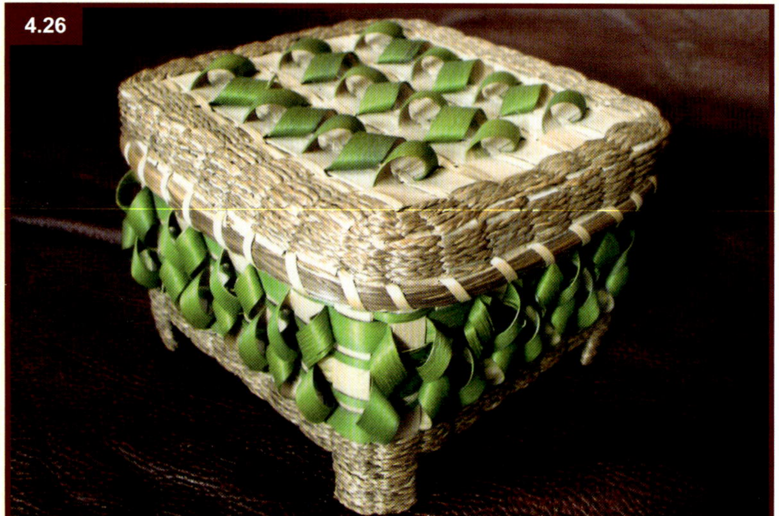
4.26

4.24–4.26. Footed covered jewelry boxes survived on dressers, bureaus, and vanities where they generally were gently used. Although women usually plaited the finer ash splint baskets in the Northeast, men also began to weave them in the late 1800s as this commercial market expanded. Penobscot Leslie Ranco ("Chief To-Me-Kin") may have created the two jewelry boxes embellished with curly splintwork (**4.25, 4.26**), 1970s. He likely sold them in his Moccasin Shop on Route 1 in York, Maine.

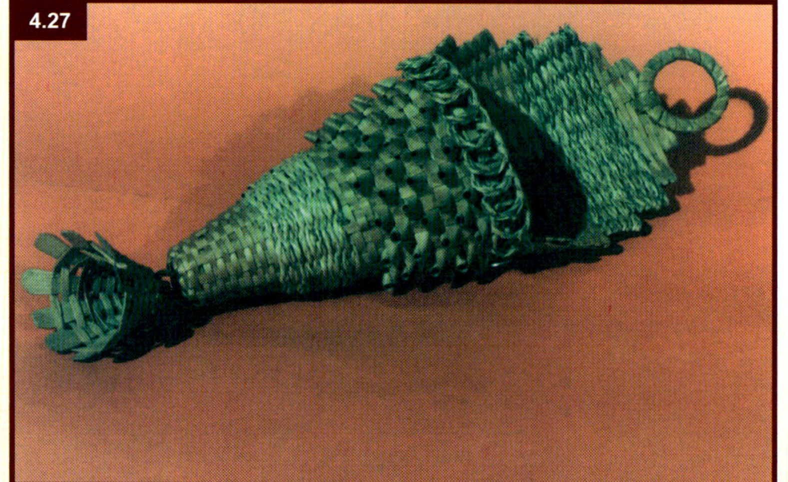
4.27

4.27. A fancy form seen rarely is the hair receiver, a wall pocket or receptacle for holding the gleanings from a brush or comb. This classic late Victorian period example, with its bell-shaped basketry tassel, was made for the tourist trade, c. 1900, 10.5" long.

FOCUS:

A Chorus of "Frogs"

A "frog" refers to an ornamental looped closure that is sometimes associated with "Mandarin"-style clothing, as well as cloaks and certain uniforms. Frogs became especially popular by the early 20th century, and commercial versions are still readily available from fabric stores. Native basketmakers have long used braided sweetgrass or "Hong Kong" twisted cord to create their own individual interpretations of a "frog"-like handle to ornament their work baskets. Like their cousins in nature, these "frogs" come in many species and varieties, some of which may be identified to individual basketmakers.

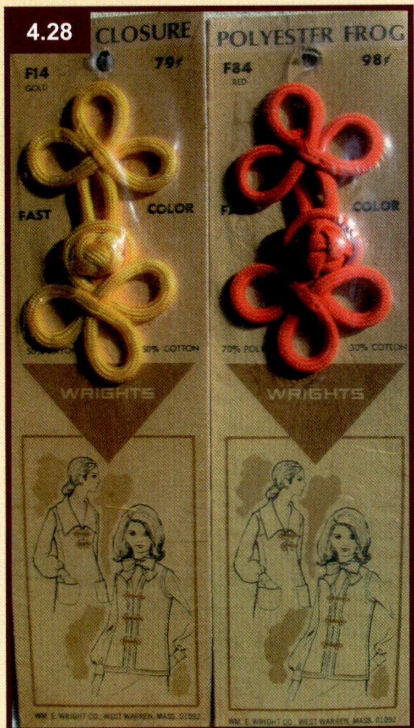

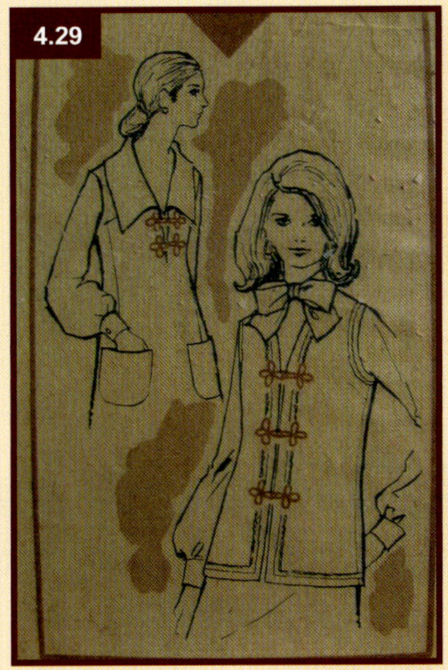

4.28, 4.29. Commercial frog closures, which could be used in place of buttons, were sold to seamstresses.

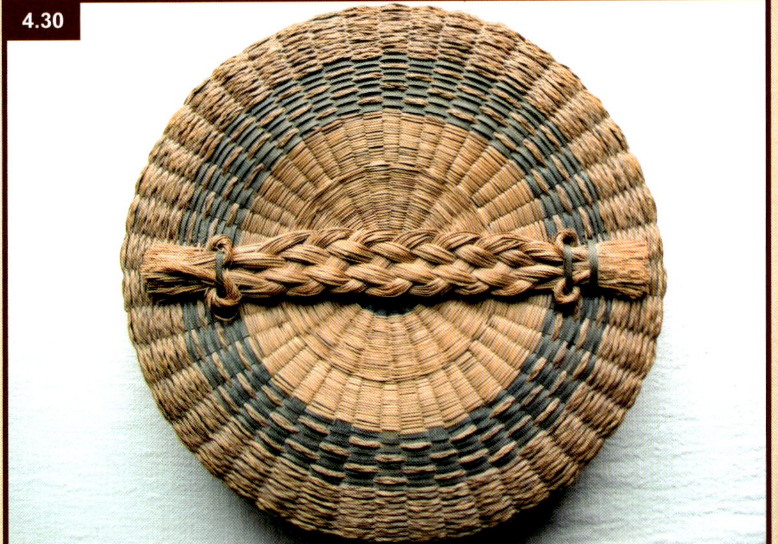

4.30. Sewing basket with a braided frog handle of sweetgrass.

FOCUS:

4.31

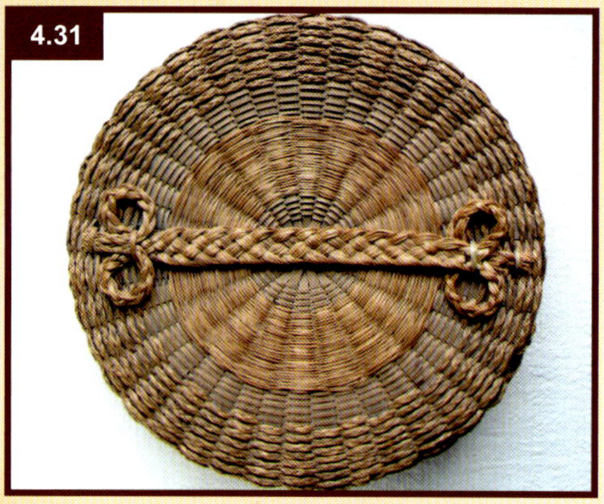

4.32

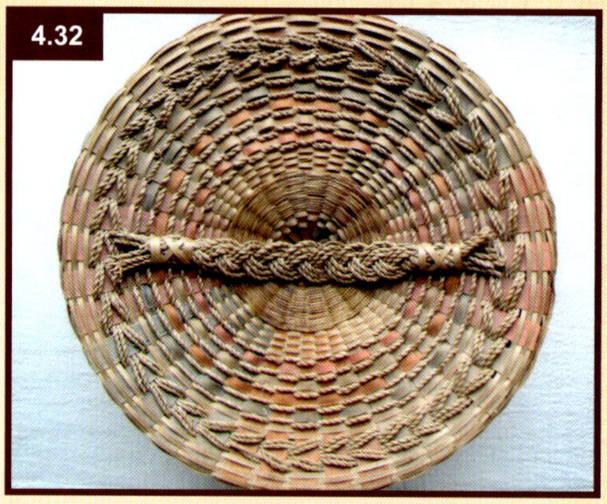

4.33

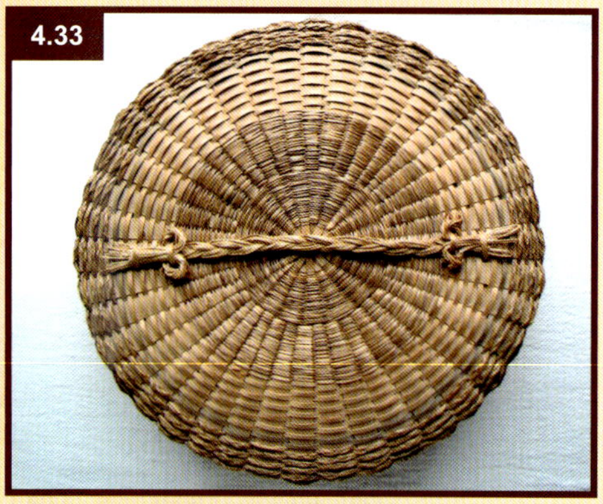

4.34

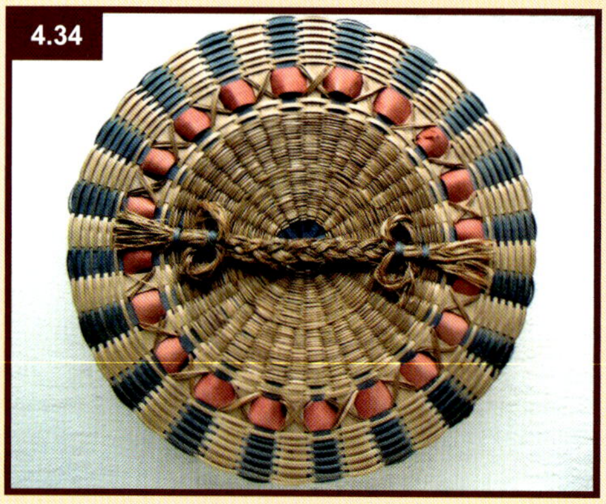

4.35

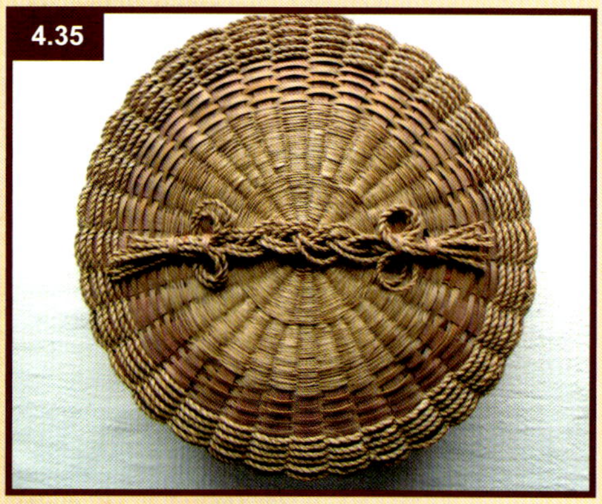

4.36

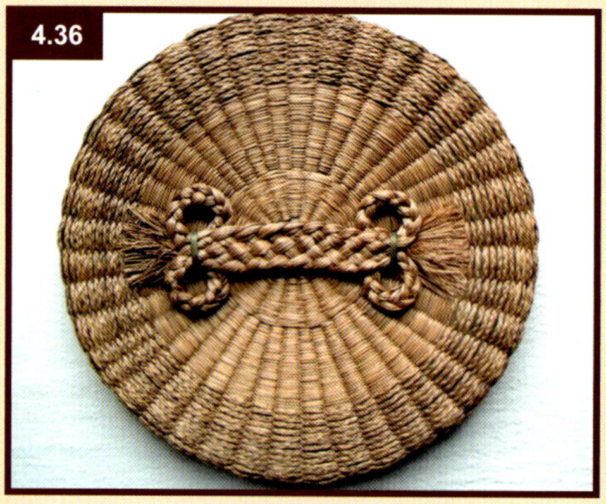

4.37

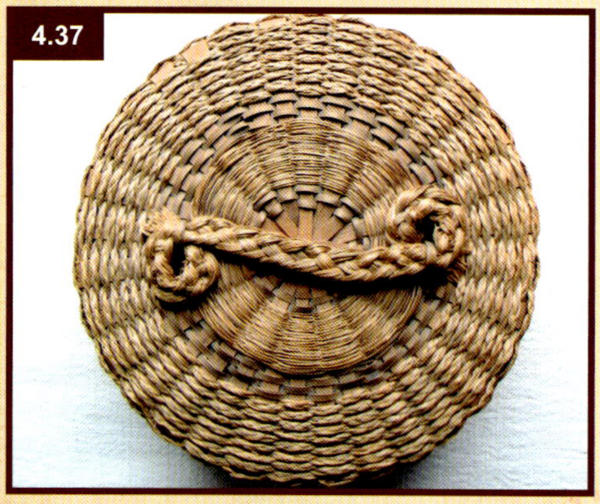

4.38

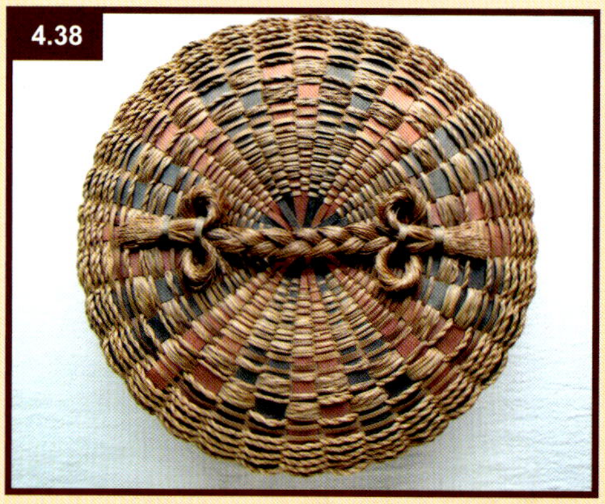

4.31–4.42. A dozen varieties of frog handles.

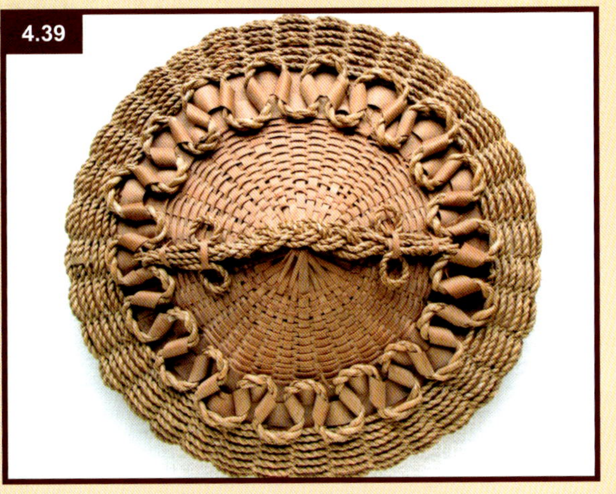
4.39

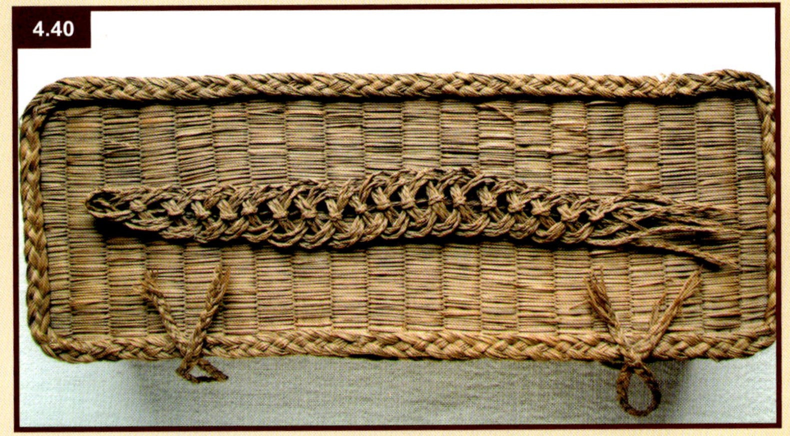
4.40

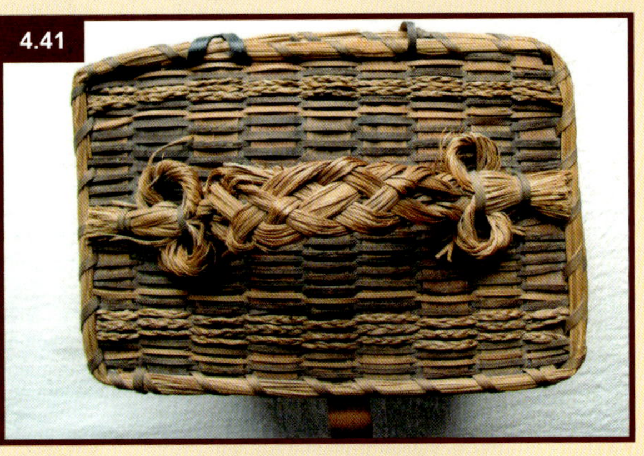
4.41

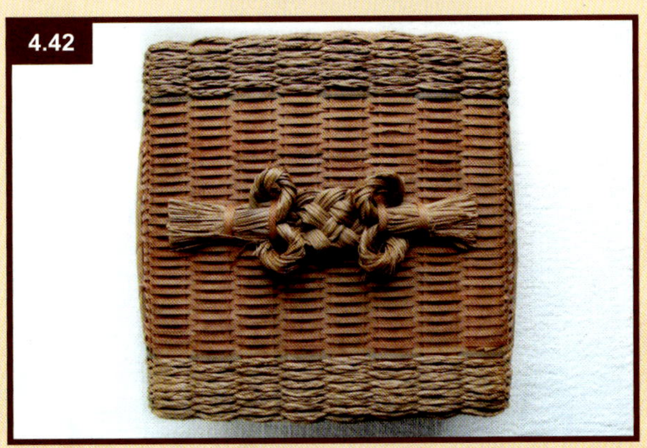
4.42

Perhaps the most prolific style of woodsplint basketry created with the homemaker in mind has been made for handiwork purposes. Sewing baskets and small basketry inserts for notions like cases for needles, thimbles, and sewing scissors were highly popular in the late 19th and early 20th centuries. Baskets that met knitting, tatting, and crocheting needs were also well received. Small work baskets and button baskets are likewise common, among other handiwork forms.

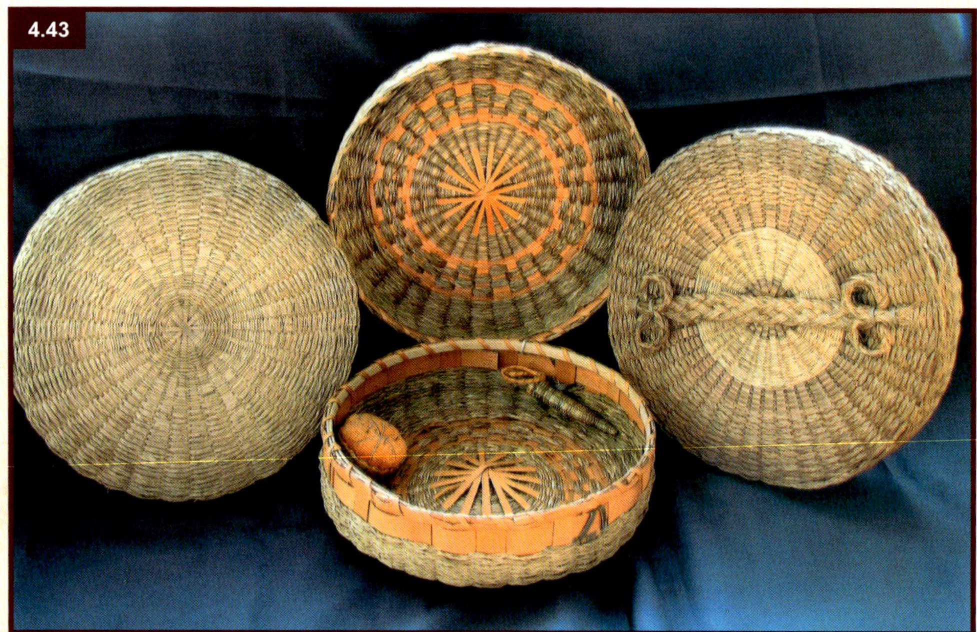

4.43. Low covered sewing baskets, called "flats" or "flat arm" baskets, some with additional baskets inside for holding notions, could be tucked under one's arm or slipped into luggage. They were the most popular ash splint and sweetgrass form sold out of mail-order catalogs, early 1900s. C. N. Saba of Toronto sold "flat arm" work baskets in sizes up to 13" diameter.

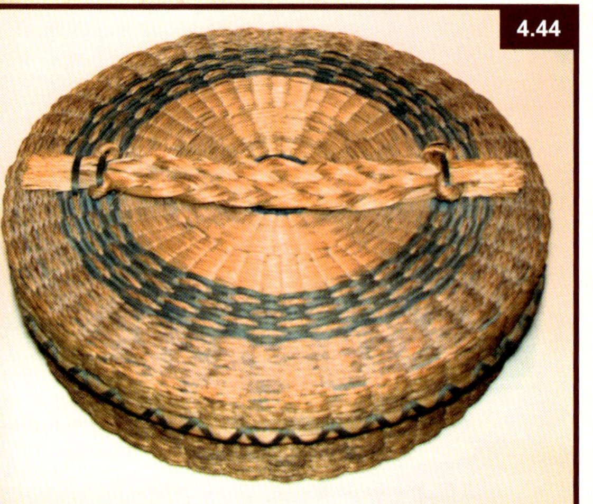

4.44. Sewing basket with braided sweetgrass frog, c. 1940s. Basketmakers collected, cleaned, and braided hundreds of yards of sweetgrass for a single average flat.

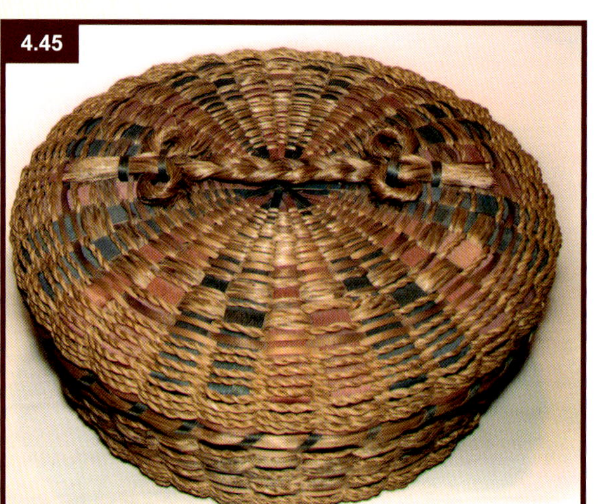

4.45. Deep, covered sewing or handiwork basket, mid-1900s, 4.5" deep, 10" diameter.

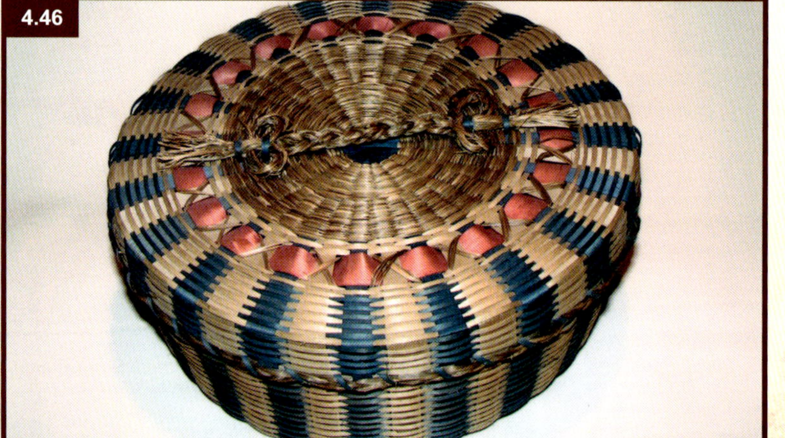

4.46. Colorful sewing basket, c. 1950-1970, 8.5" diameter.

4.47. Penobscot or Abenaki sewing basket or flat, c. 1910, 8" diameter.

4.48. Passamaquoddy sewing basket, 1970s, 9" diameter.

4.49. Ho-Chunk (Winnebago) covered sewing basket, plaited in the style of Margaret Decorah, with its base stamped "Made by Wisconsin Winnebago Indians," purchased at Wisconsin Dells, mid-1900s, 10" diameter.

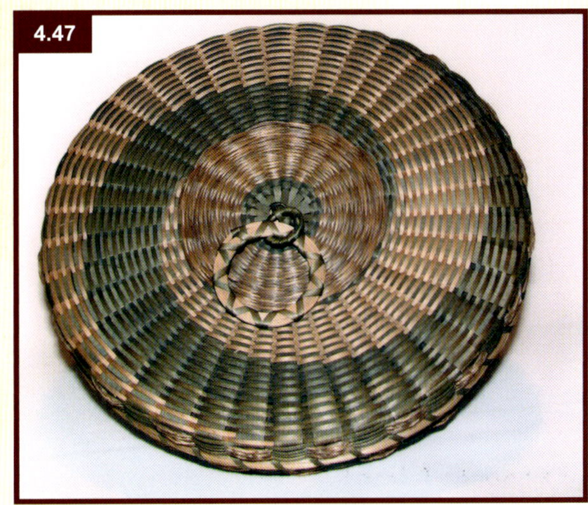

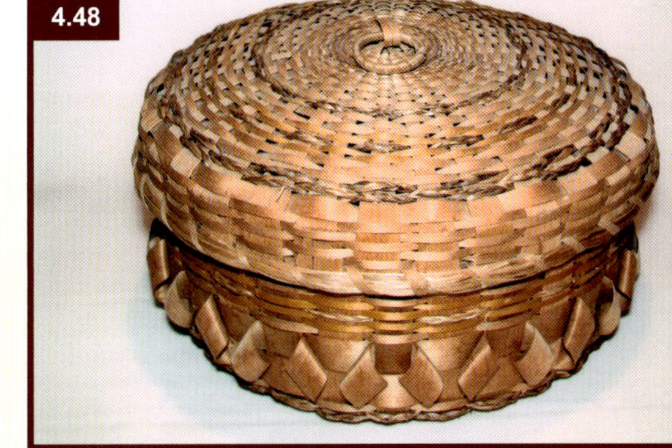

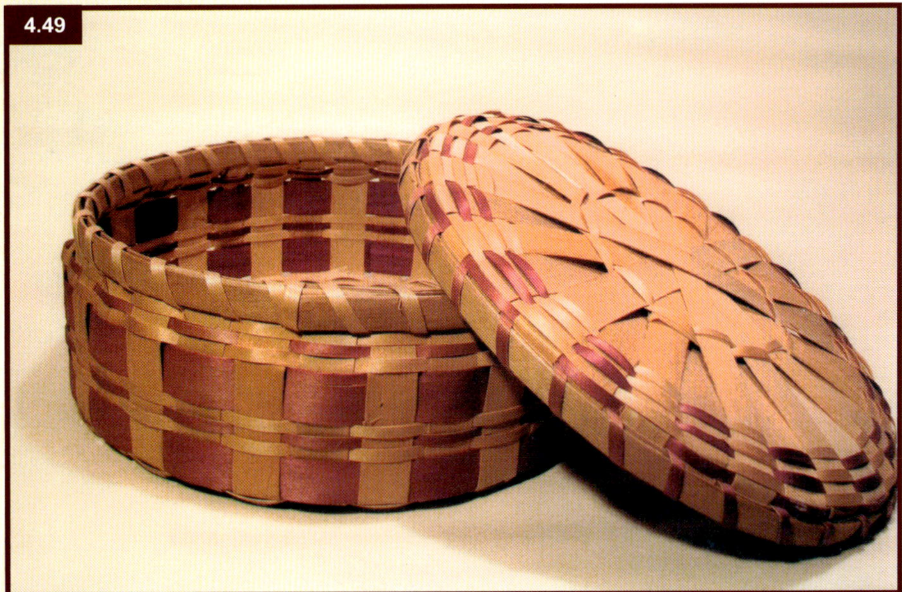

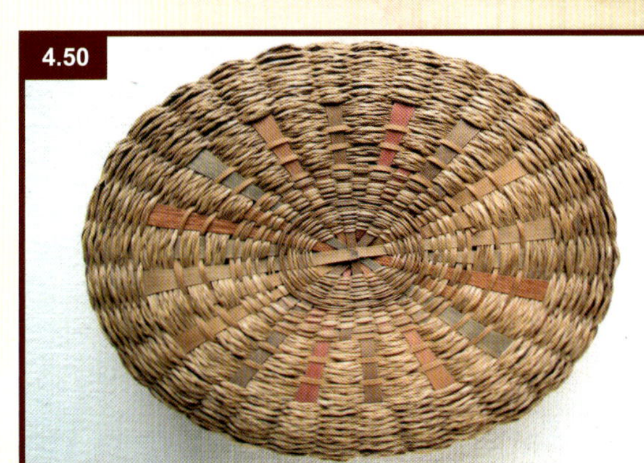

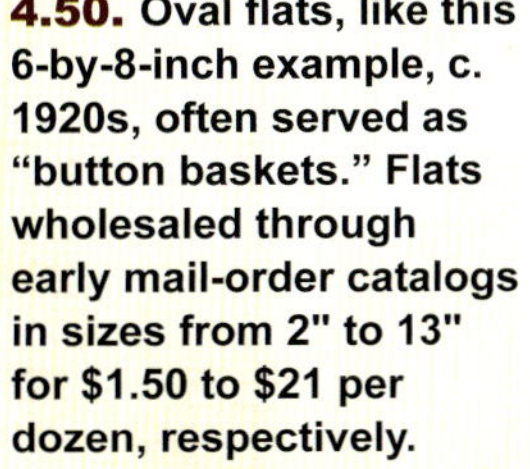

4.50. Oval flats, like this 6-by-8-inch example, c. 1920s, often served as "button baskets." Flats wholesaled through early mail-order catalogs in sizes from 2" to 13" for $1.50 to $21 per dozen, respectively.

4.51. Passamaquoddy deep sewing basket, with "shell" curly splintwork and a whirling pattern of purple-dyed splints, c. 1984, 10" high.

4.52. Interior has two inserts or pockets for holding sewing notions.

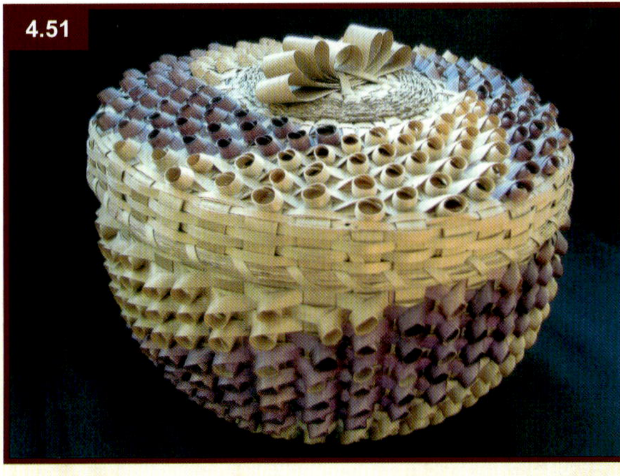

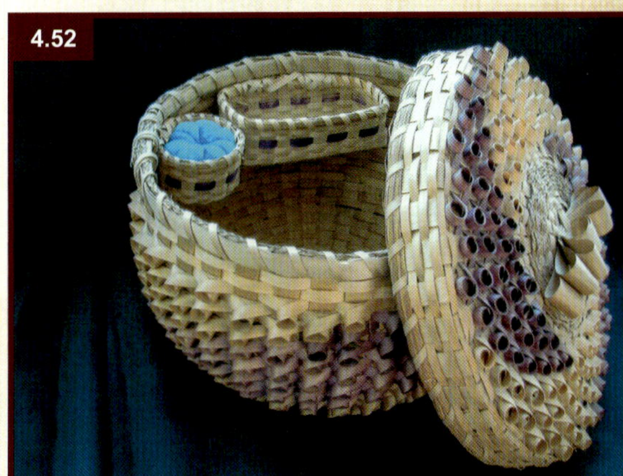

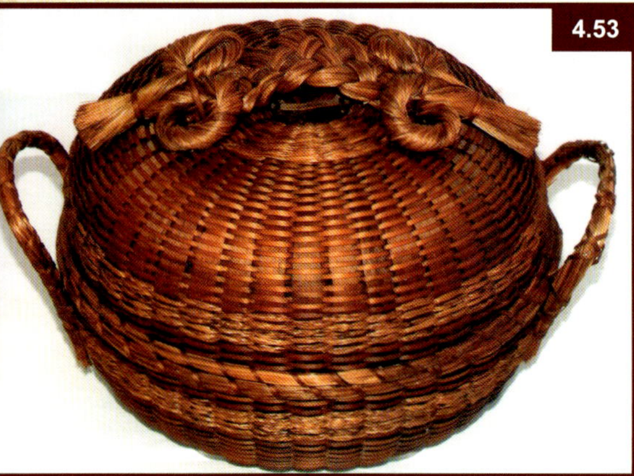

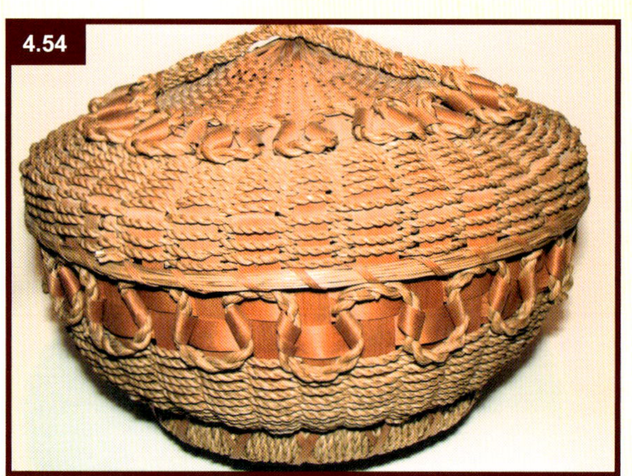

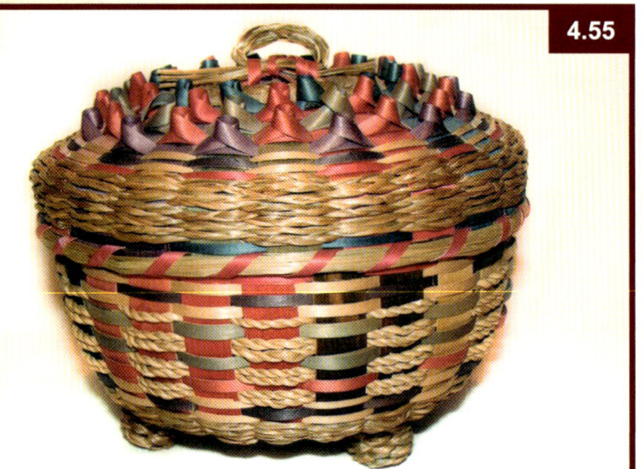

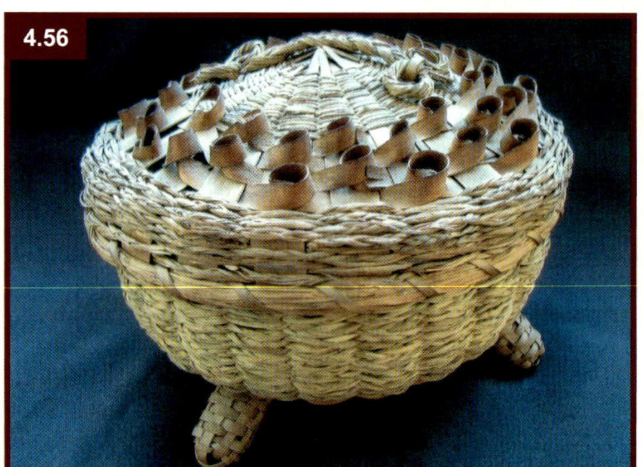

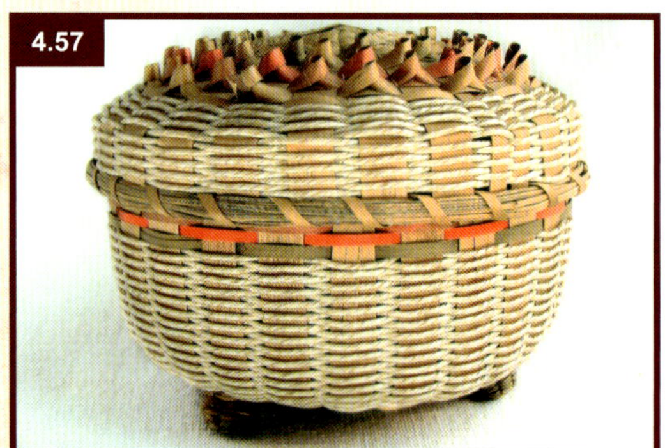

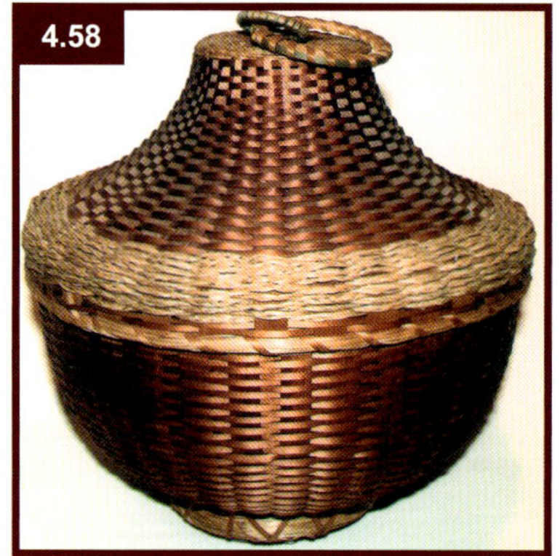

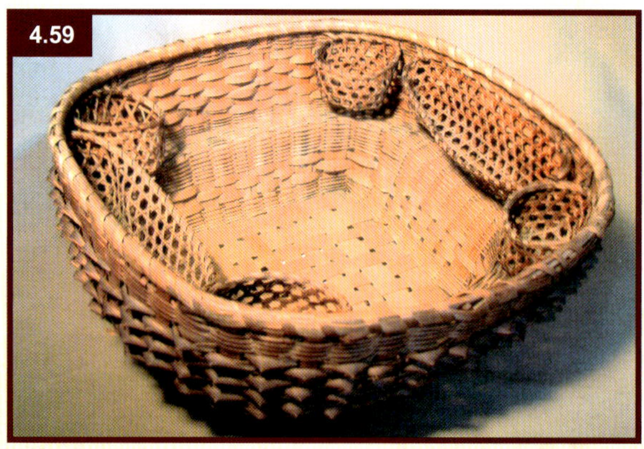

4.53. Deep, so-called "soup tureen-style" covered handiwork or sewing basket with a thick, braided sweetgrass frog, made by the accomplished basketmaker Mary Mitchell Gabriel, Passamaquoddy, honored as a 1994 NEA National Heritage Fellow, c. 1940s, 8" maximum diameter.

4.54. Covered deep work basket, elevated with a base ring and ornamented with orange-dyed ash splints plus Hong Kong cord, Abenaki, c. 1940s, 10" diameter.

4.55–4.57. Some Abenaki describe small kettle-like sewing baskets, supported on three miniature basketry feet, as "marmites," the French term for round covered pots on legs used for cooking soup. Because this form is plaited over a basketmaking block, the basketry marmite varies little in shape or size; these are early to mid-1900s and 7.5" diameter.

4.58. Abenaki basketmaker Yvonne Robert of Odanak is credited with first making this form of handiwork basket with its bell-shaped cover, early 1900s, 9" high.

4.59. Six basketry compartments or pockets for holding accessories, plaited in hex weave. Sharp "porcupine twist" or "thistle" curly splintwork, and red-orange dyed ash splints (now faded), have made this open sewing basket a delight to use, northern New England, c. 1890, 11" diameter.

4.60. Double-decker covered sewing basket partitions storage space into two sections. Curly splintwork lends the two-tiered rectangular form an elaborate wedding-cake appearance, Micmac, 1950s, base 9" wide by 12" long.

4.61–4.63. A sewing stand was a coveted piece of decor in 1920s to 1930s northern New England homes. The two-tiered examples (**4.62, 4.63**) are Micmac, 1918, and are 22" to 24" high. Splints used for plaiting the Passamaquoddy single-tiered stand (**4.61**) were dyed blue originally, though they are now faded, c. 1935, 26" high.

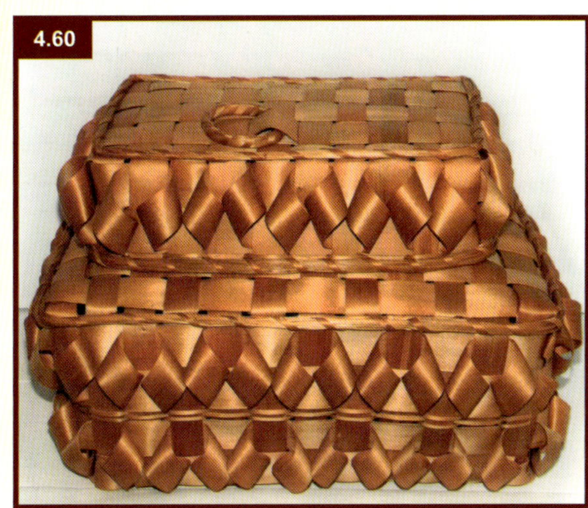

4.60

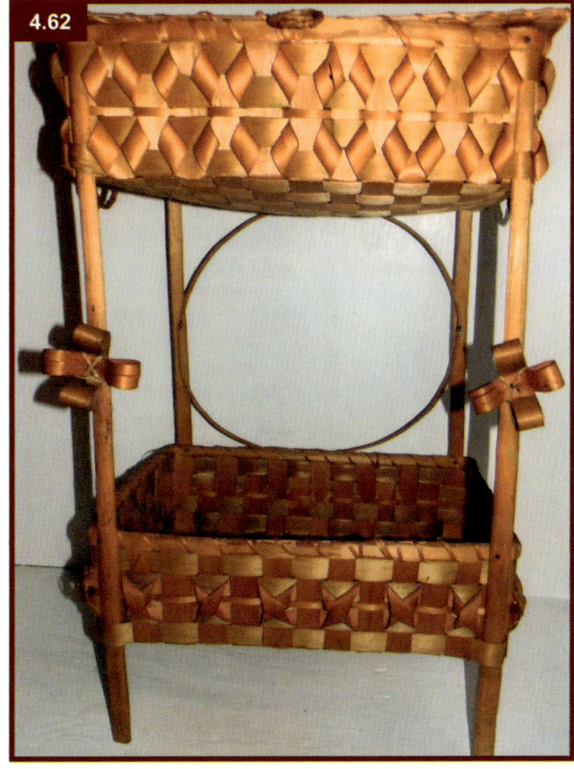

4.62

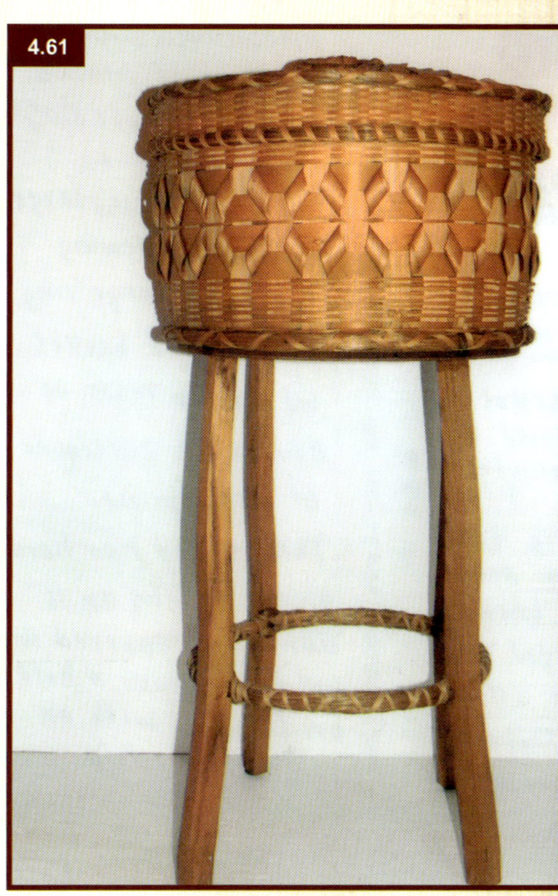

4.61

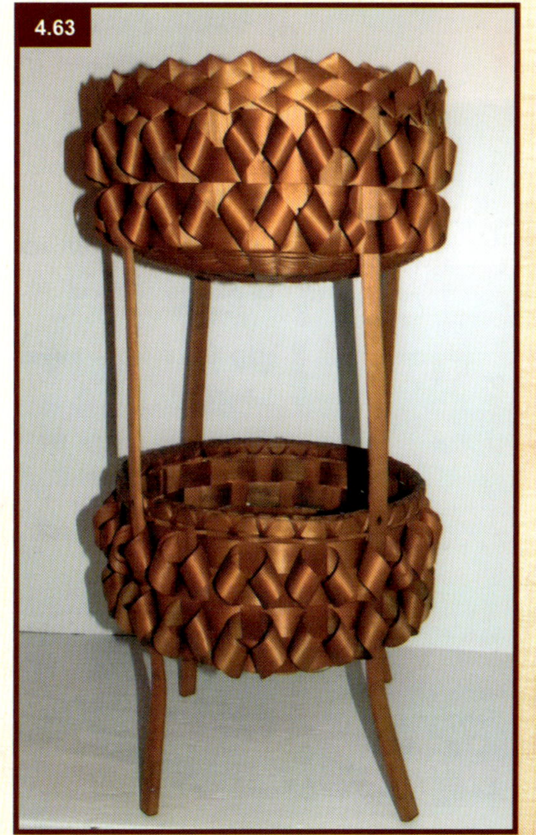

4.63

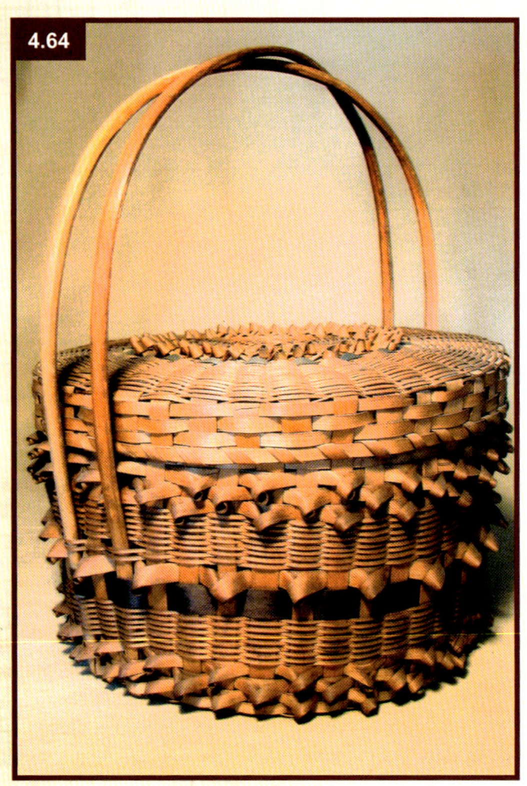

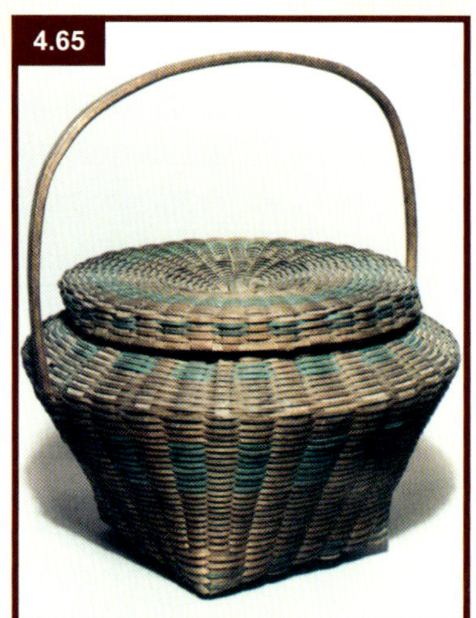

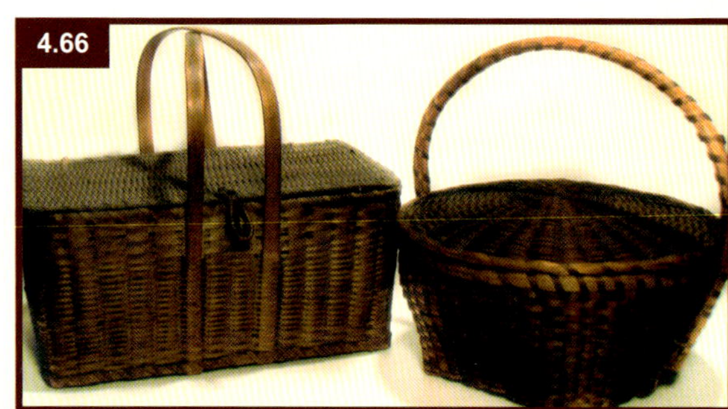

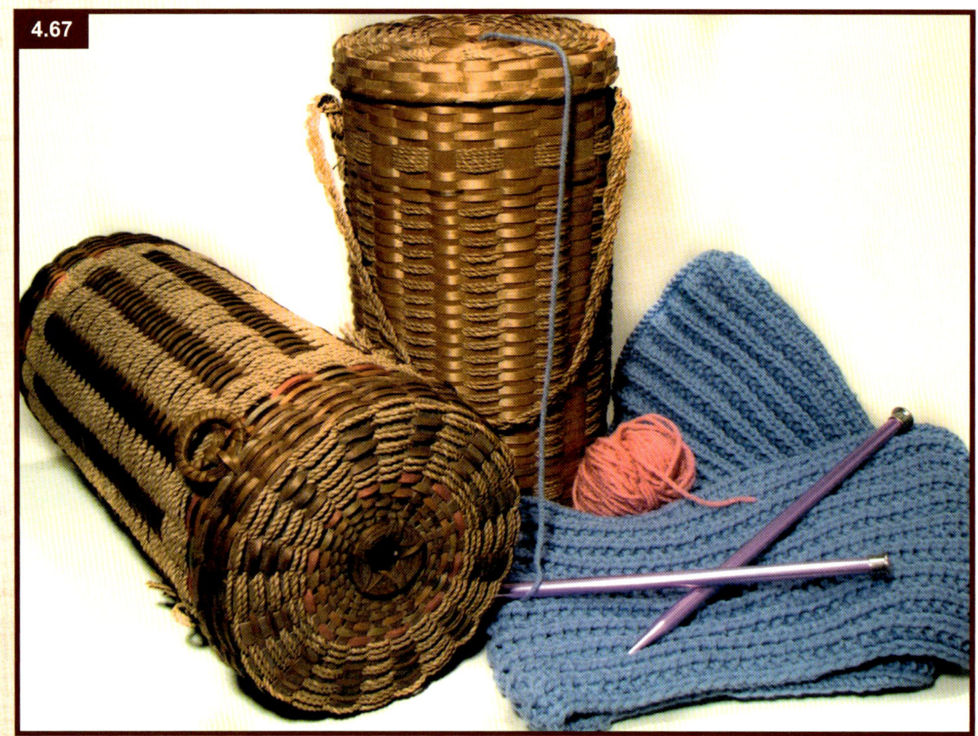

4.64. Early covered handiwork basket with double bail handles and curly splint work, c. 1890, 8" diameter.

4.65. Covered woman's handiwork basket with a carved bail handle, plaited over a compound block using narrow gauge-cut splints, some with greenish-blue swabbing, c. 1880, 4" square base.

4.66. Two Northeastern covered work baskets made on blocks and given bail handles. These forms were versatile and could have been used for multiple purposes, such as for lunch boxes, c. 1900, (right) 9" diameter.

4.67. Tall covered baskets with openings for drawing yarn from a skein have been used from Victorian times to the present day. Native Northeastern peoples have plaited distinctive styles on blocks, sometimes substituting stronger Hong Kong cord for sweetgrass handles and trim, c. 1920-1950, (right) 11" high.

4.68. Tall covered skein basket plaited with ash splints and sweetgrass, northern New England or Canadian Maritimes, c. 1920s, 16" tall plus handle.

4.69. Covered crochet or tatting baskets held supplies like cotton crochet thread and crochet hooks. Though plaited with ash splints and fragrant braided sweetgrass, this Penobscot basket was given a strong handle of Hong Kong cord, c. 1920s, 6" high.

4.70. Penobscot or Passamaquoddy acorn-shaped yarn or string basket was plaited over a wooden block, which sped production and produced an evenly woven, uniform product, c. 1920s, 5.5" high.

4.71. Acorn-shaped baskets of ash splints and sweetgrass held a small ball of yarn, string, or crochet thread for a variety of household and handiwork uses, c. 1920s–1940s, 5" high plus handle.

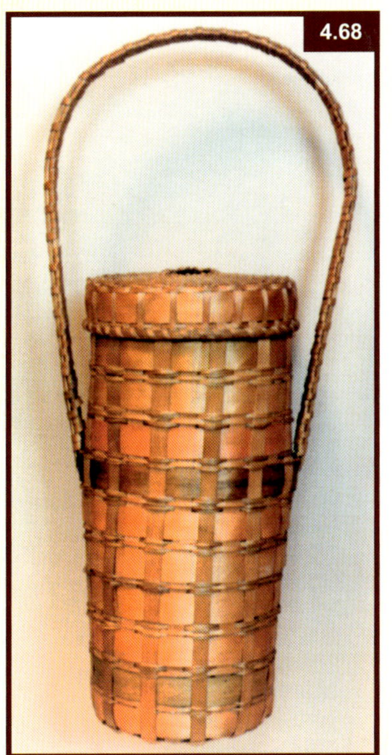
4.68

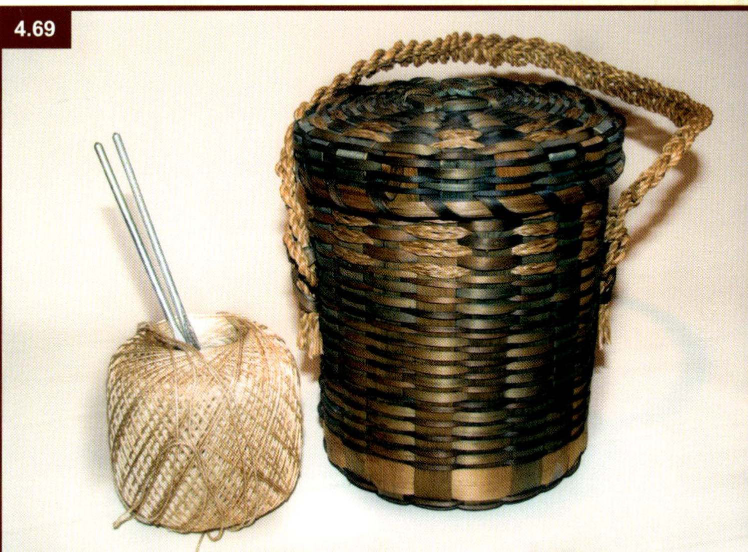
4.69

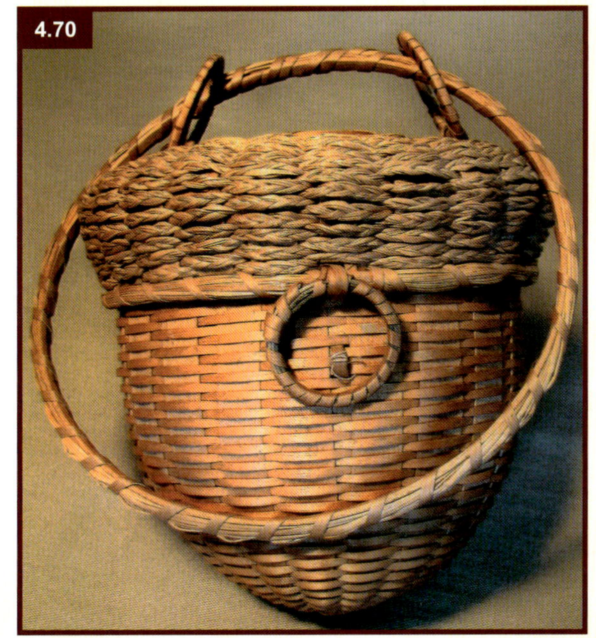
4.70

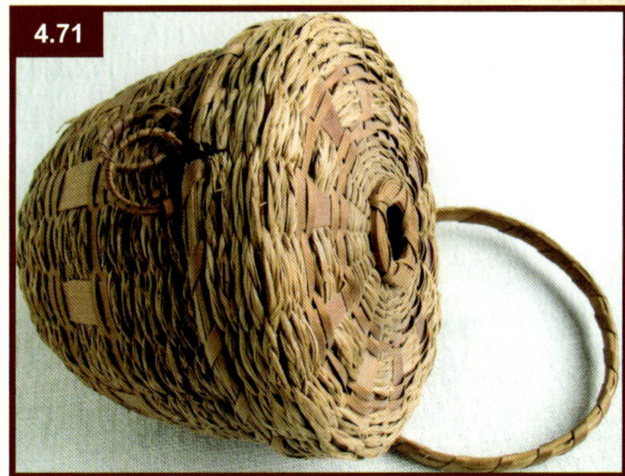
4.71

SETTING:

A Northern New England Town Home

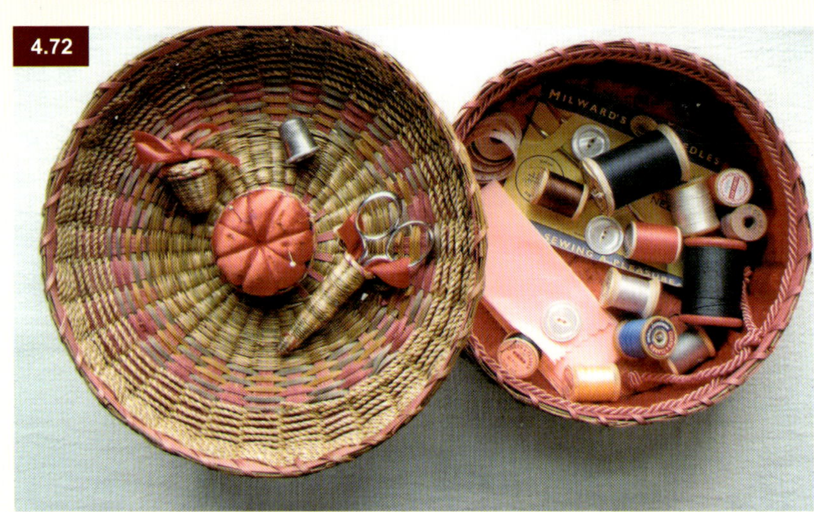

4.72. This Native "flat arm" basket with brightly dyed ash splints, red satin lining, and assorted accessory baskets made the homemaker's inevitable chores of darning and mending more pleasurable, c. 1920s–1930s, 8.5" diameter.

Ruth finished washing the dinner dishes and stacked them in the drainboard to dry. The housewife extinguished the kitchen gaslight. Wrapping her shawl around her shoulders against an evening chill, she moved down the long front hall to rejoin her scholarly husband. He already had retired to the library in their elegant Georgian-style home, nestled on a quiet shaded street near the academy where he taught.

Tidy rows of leather-bound classics lined the library walls from ceiling to floor. Only gas wall sconces, several old family portraits in gilt frames, and two curtained front windows interrupted the otherwise continuous shelves. Most evenings after dinner, while her husband puffed on his pipe and reflected on the works of Virgil or Horace, Ruth did her mending or indulged in knitting. But tonight was different. She thought happily that her evenings filled with darning old socks would never again be quite the same.

Ruth kept a chicken coop behind the house. She sold the eggs locally and had been saving up her money for something special. This afternoon, while attending an agricultural exhibit near the school, she had dipped into her proceeds. Ruth had come home with an Indian sewing basket plaited with colorful dyed ash splints and sweetgrass.

A set of matching accessory baskets, attached to a bright satin ribbon, came with it. For the rest of the day, as she went about her chores, Ruth had been thinking about how best to arrange the tiny notion baskets. All were so small that she decided to safeguard them by stitching each one onto the red satin lining the sewing basket's cover.

The housewife settled into a low rocking chair facing her husband. She picked up her delicate sewing scissors and reached for the ribboned basketry chatelaine. Ruth snipped carefully, first freeing the small covered thimble holder, then the pin cushion, the needle case, the scissors holder, and finally the lidded thread basket. She pulled her bright new sewing basket closer and lifted its lid.

Ruth picked up the tiny thimble case and, with a threaded needle in hand, began to stitch.

4.73. Many Native basketmakers plaited their own small thimble cases of ash splints and sweetgrass for inserting in Native-made handiwork baskets. But, according to Gaby Pelletier, some Abenaki basketmakers at Odanak, Québec, found it more economical to purchase the tiny sweetgrass accessories from French basketmakers in neighboring Pierreville, early 1900s, all about 1" high.

4.74. Unusual thimble case worked with curly splintwork, early 1900s, 1" high.

4.75. This small basket holds a spool of thread.

4.76. Small covered baskets, 2 to 4 inches in diameter, held buttons, watches, and trinkets, early 1900s.

4.77. Pin cushions might be used alone or inside covered sewing baskets, early to mid-1900s.

4.78. Needle cases, early to mid-1900s.

4.79. Thread winders.

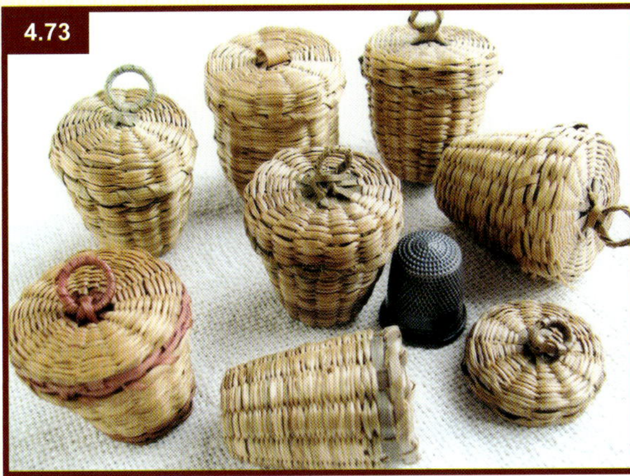

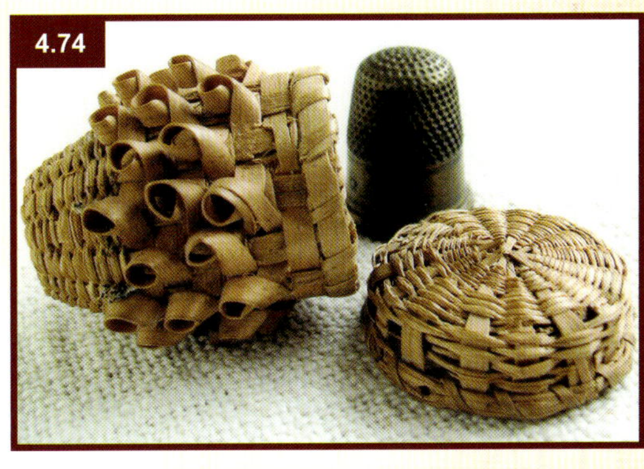

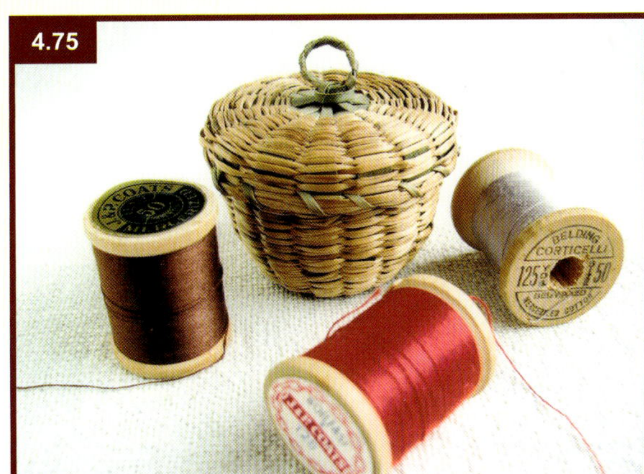

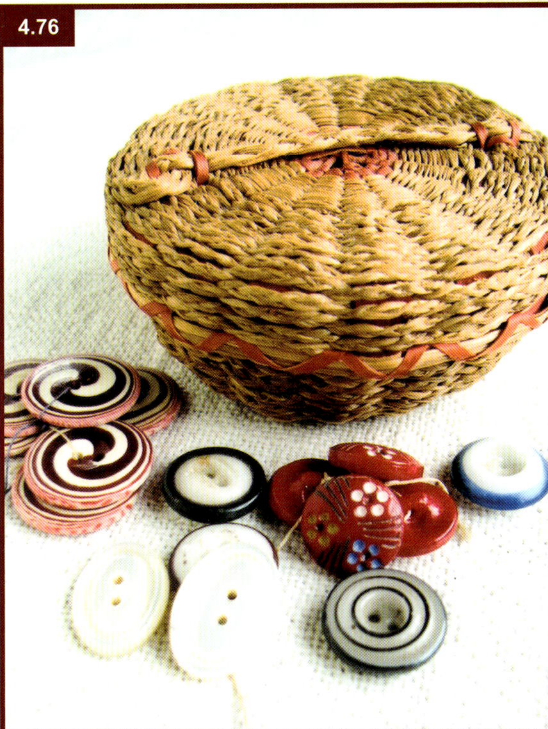

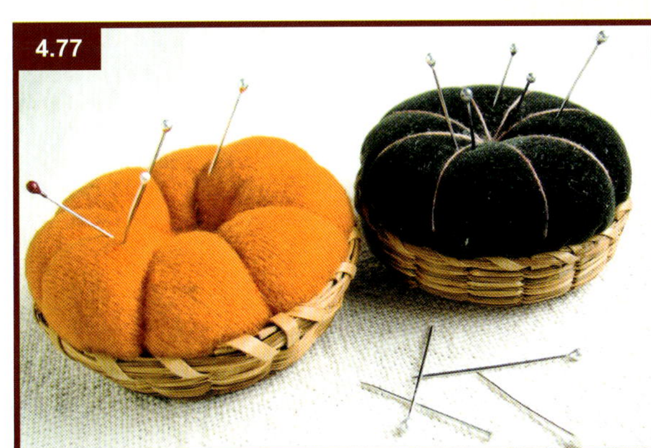

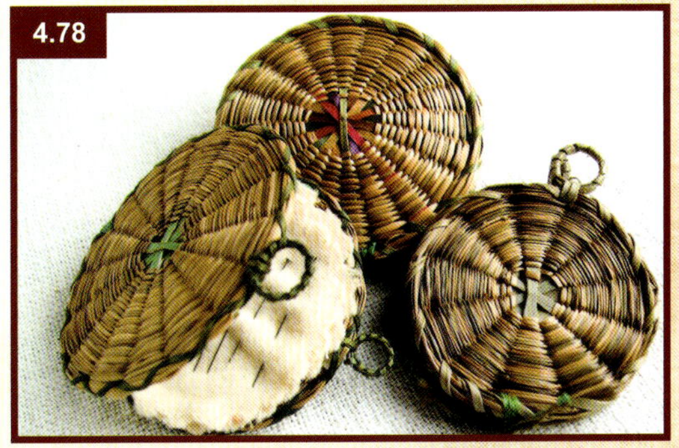

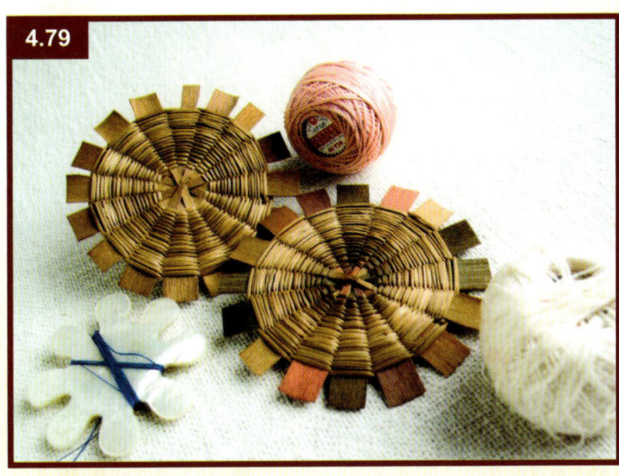

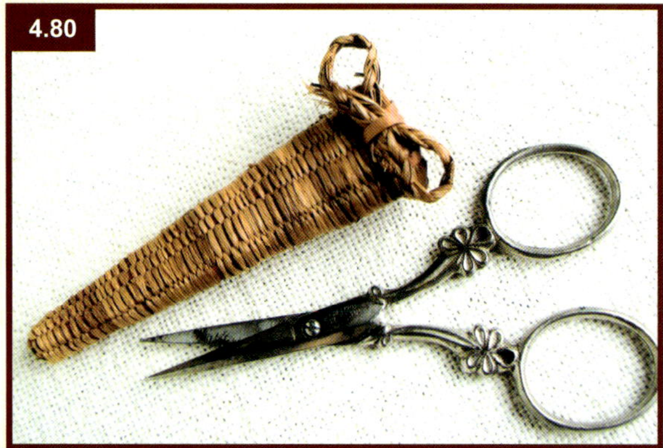

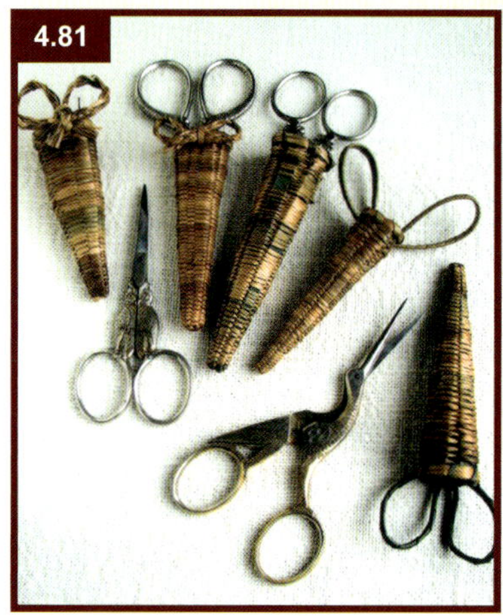

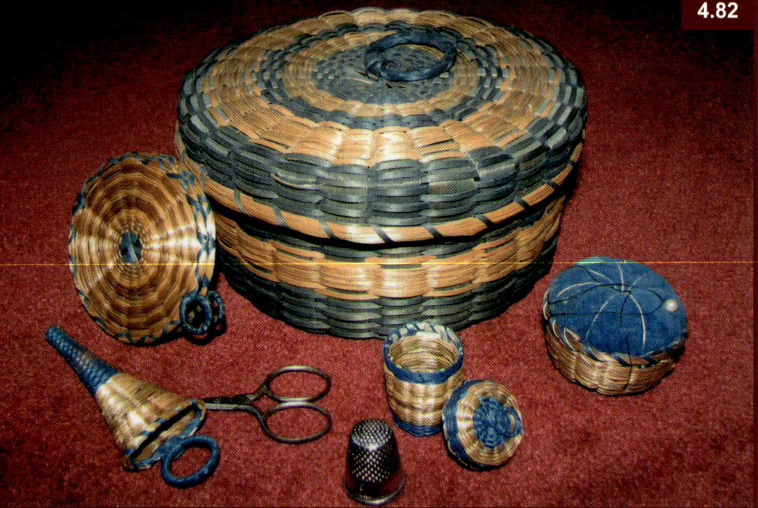

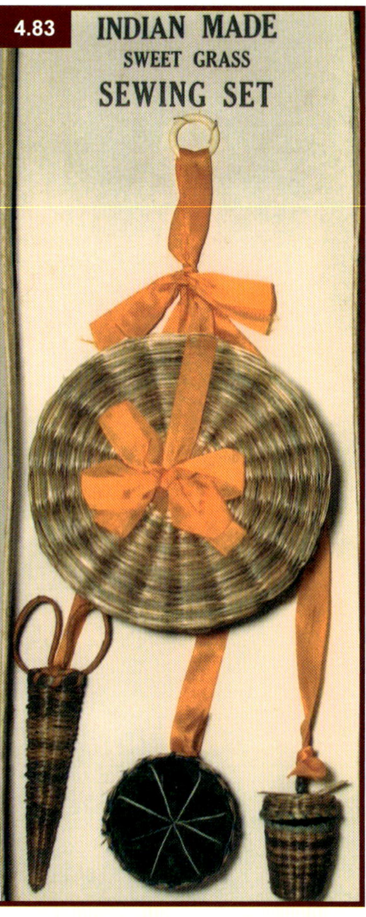

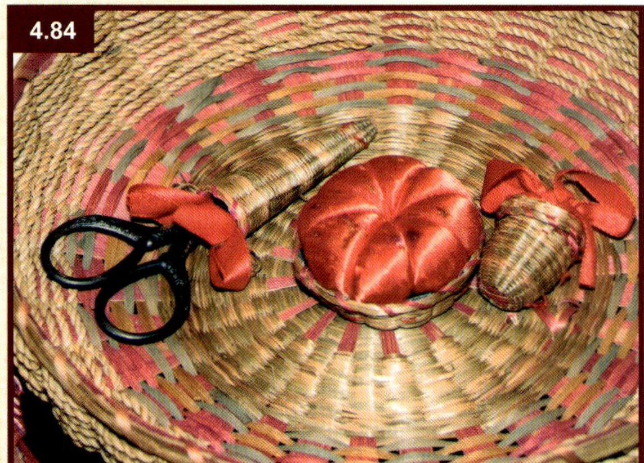

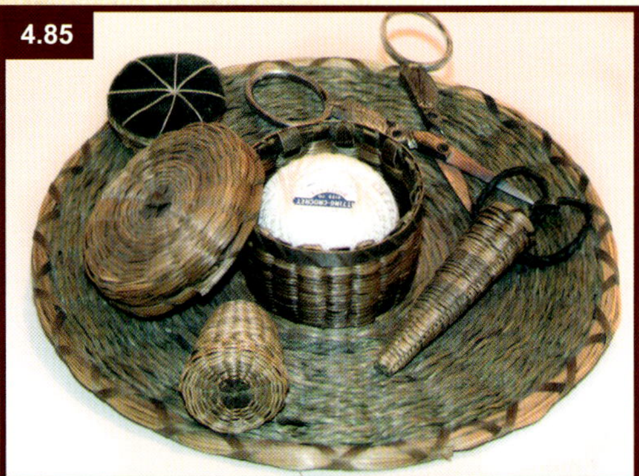

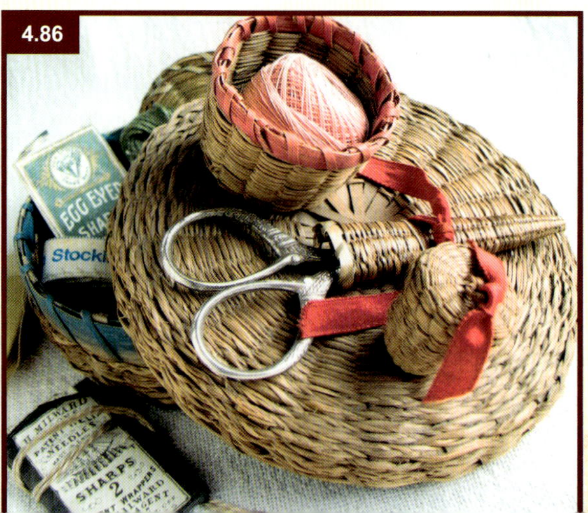

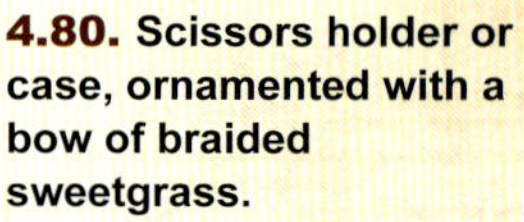

4.80. Scissors holder or case, ornamented with a bow of braided sweetgrass.

4.81. Scissors cases were fairly uniform, though their lengths varied somewhat, early 1900s, about 2.5" to 3" long.

4.82. Some seamstresses housed matching sets of small basketry cases for sewing items in their covered sewing baskets, like these accessory baskets by Camilla Lyon Sockalexis, Penobscot, 1930s, needle case (left, against basket) is 2.5" diameter.

4.83. Abenaki (Québec) boxed "chatelaine" or set of small sewing accessory baskets held together on silk ribbons, could be purchased separately and custom-fitted to one's favorite sewing basket, early to mid-1900s, 11.5" long.

4.84. Small accessory baskets stitched onto the inner surface of the cover to a sewing basket, c. 1920s–1930s.

4.85. Small accessory baskets stitched onto a flat basketry mat could be loosely placed in the base of a covered sewing basket or kept separately, early 1900s, 7" diameter.

4.86. Small sewing basket with scissors, spool, and thimble cases attached to the outer cover, early 1900s, 5" diameter.

FOCUS:

Rings 'n' Things

Pull handles adorning lids and sides of many Northeastern woodsplint baskets are often embellished, sometimes exuberantly. Styles vary widely and are frequently shaped by the personal preferences of individual basketmakers. Woodsplint baskets may be finished off with pulls of rings or ribbons, bows or braids, loops or tendrils, or appliquéd petals or leaves. Plus, some knobs may even be created by using a miniature basket.

4.87–4.92. **Rings as handles and pulls.**

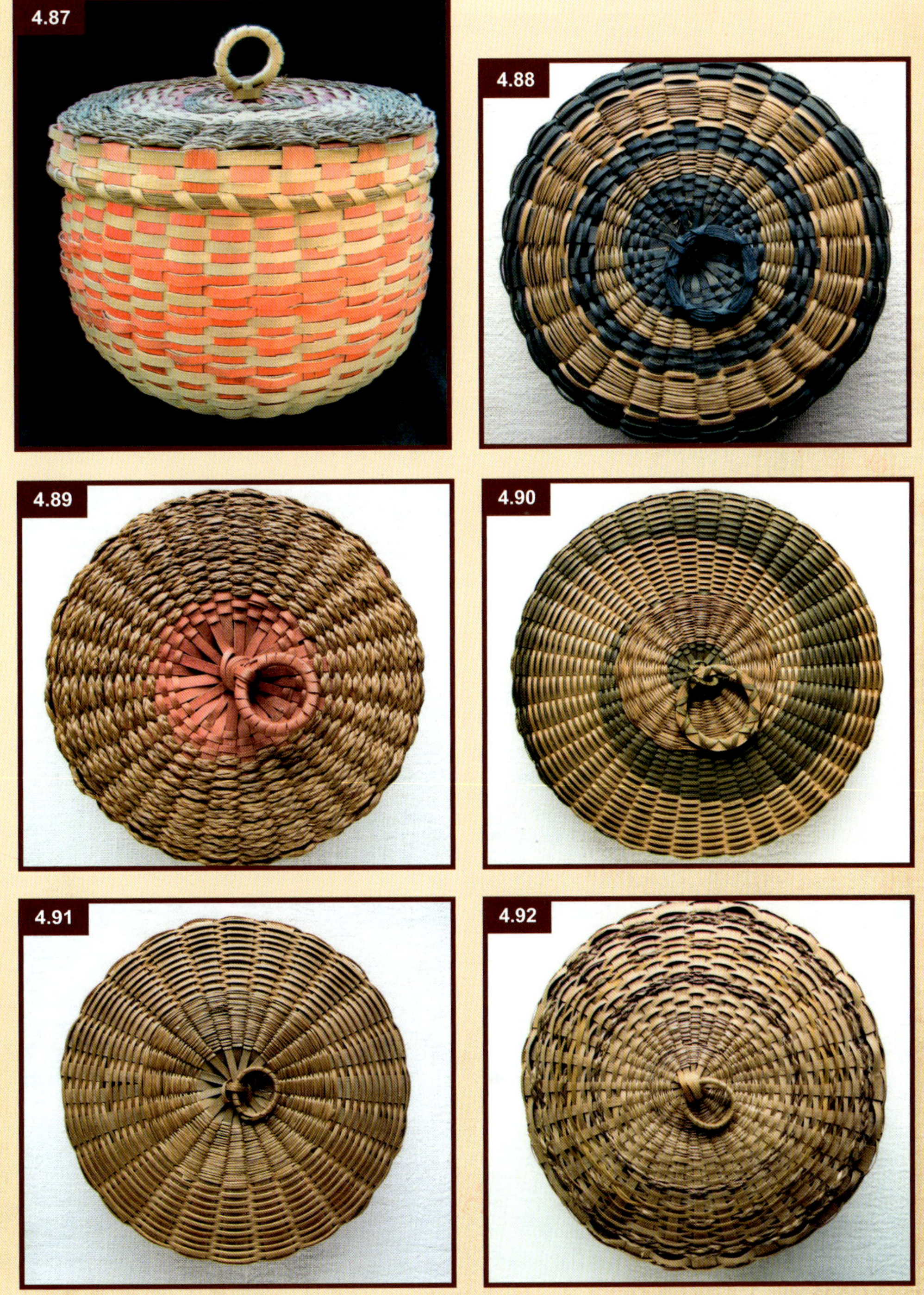

FOCUS:

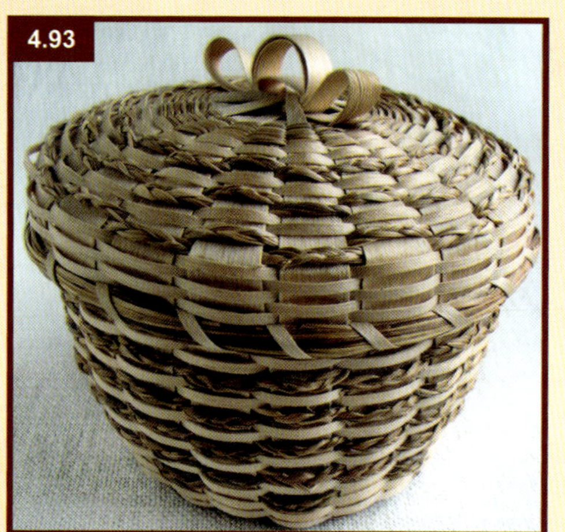

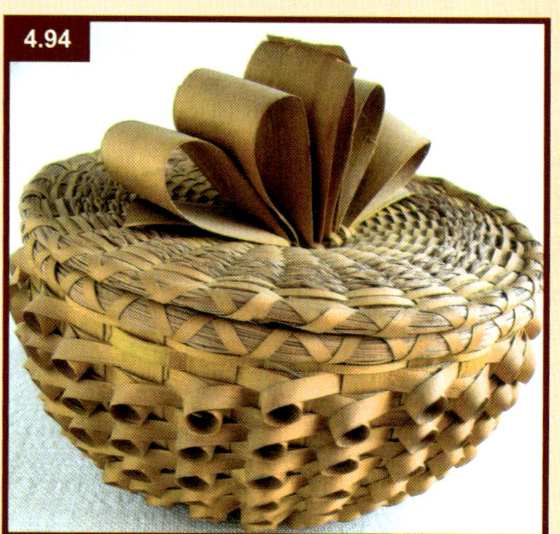

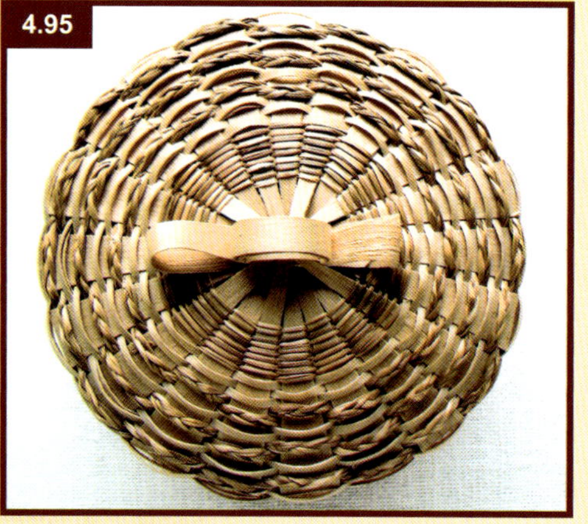

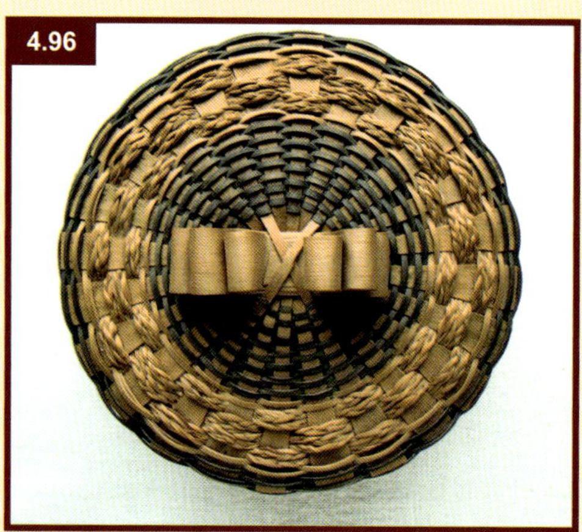

4.93–4.96. Varieties of ash splint ribbons and bows.

4.97–4.100. Varieties of braids looped into rings and pulls.

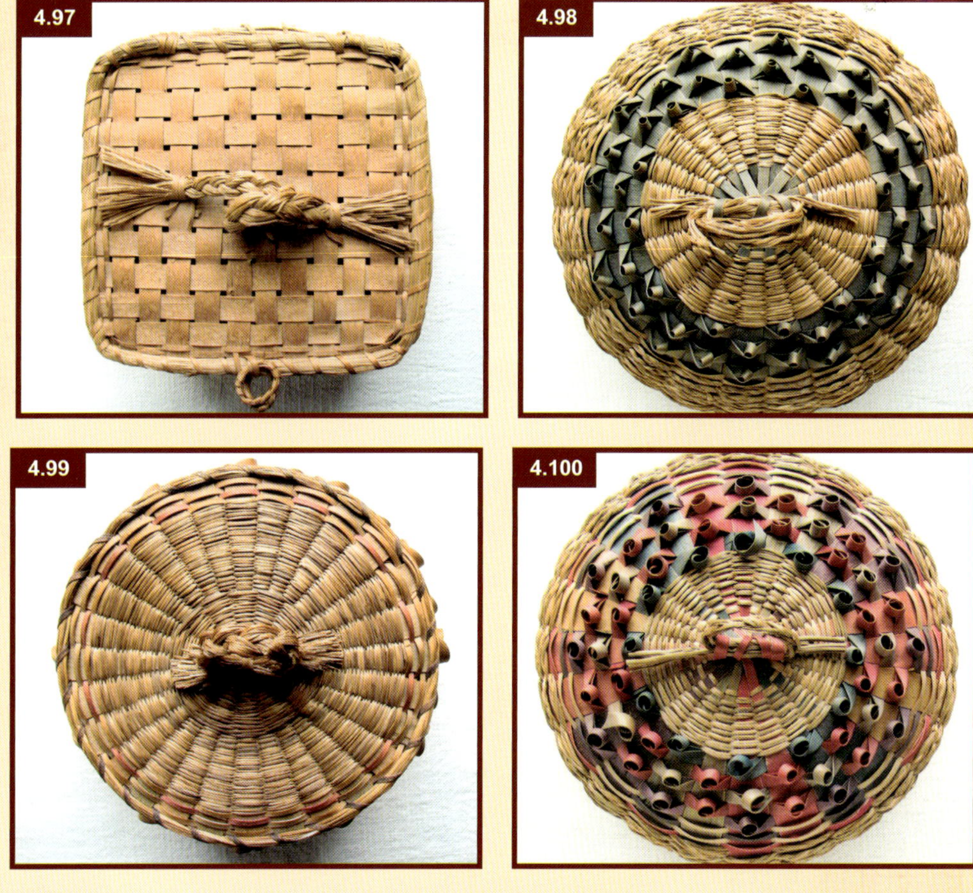

4.101. A miniature basket doubles as a knob.

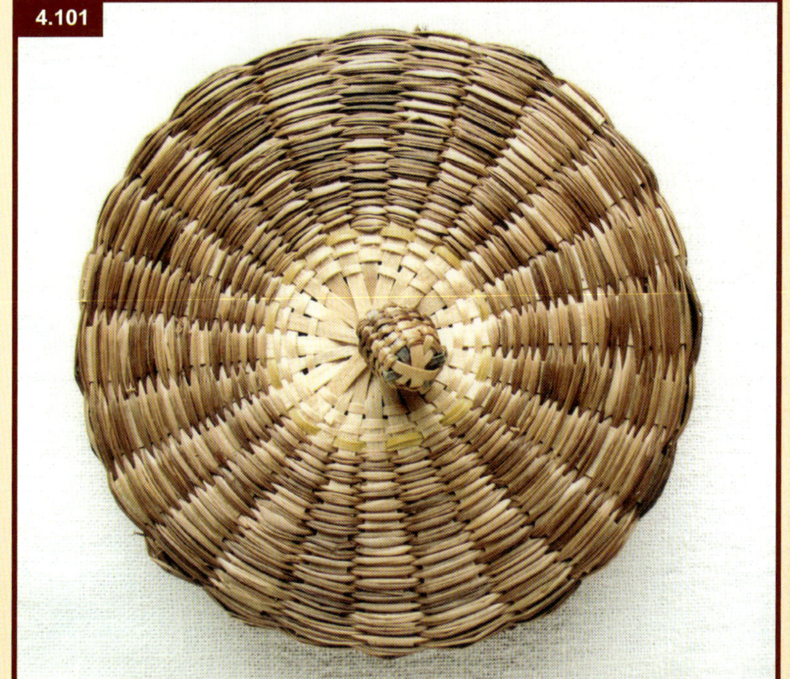

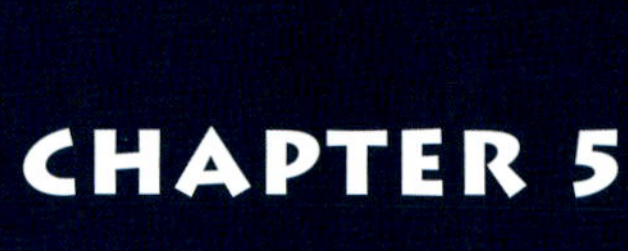

CHAPTER 5

FUN & FANCY BASKETS

Extravagantly ornamented Victorian households were lavishly decorated with layers of elaborate curtains and draperies, intricately embellished table and bed linens, doilies, and antimacassars for chair backs. This environment encouraged late 19th-century Native basketmakers to exercise their skills to create ever more colorful, more elaborate, and more whimsical forms. Basketry trends paralleled the handiwork products of talented homemakers who were using other materials—often held or stored in Native-made woodsplint handiwork baskets—to fabricate complex embroidery, satin-ribbon work, tatting, crochet, and cut and drawn lacework, as well as highly patterned hooked rugs.

During this era, form was definitely not restricted by function. The more overdone, the more excessive, and the more frilly a woodsplint basket was, the more highly valued it was, and the more likely it was to sell. Whimsical but still-useful baskets filled Northeastern bazaars and county fairs and cavorted across the pages of popular women's periodicals. Farmers' wives and city homemakers quickly adopted them. Some of these baskets were intended for particular household roles. Others were created for specific personal uses. A few, though functional, were made especially for display. These novelties include miniatures that today still testify to the superlative basketmaking skills of Native virtuosos.

5.1

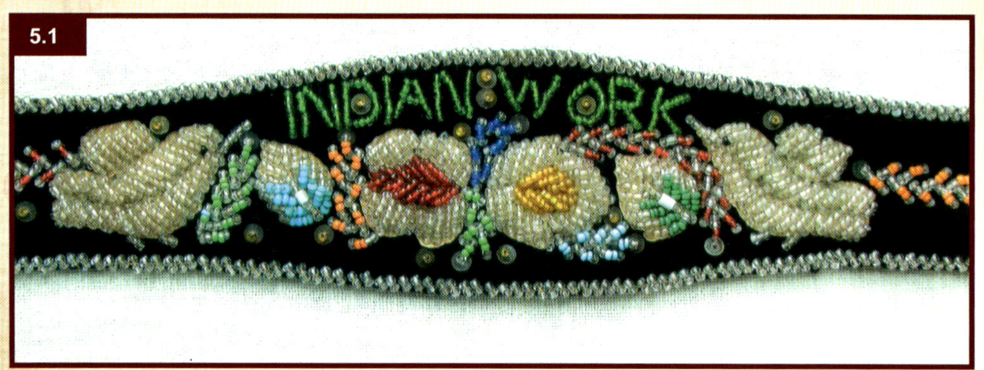

5.1. **"Indian Work" described a number of specialized crafts that were marketed to visitors and vacationers. In addition to basketry, Native artisans were supplying impressive amounts of beadwork souvenirs as early as the 1840s. Tuscarora women sold much of the beadwork, like this Iroquois belt, at Niagara Falls. Additionally, small birchbark items like canoes and model wigwams found their way into Native basket vendors' roadside stands and gift shops throughout the Northeast and Great Lakes area. Beaded velvet belt, Iroquois (possibly Tuscarora), c. 1880s–1910, 34.5" long.**

5.2. Passamaquoddy master basketmaker Molly Neptune Parker, a 2012 NEA National Heritage Fellow, unpacks her coveted baskets as she sets up for a MIBA basketmakers' festival.

5.3. Clara (Mitchell) Neptune of Indian Island making baskets, Penobscot, early 1900s. A "sea urchin" basket (right) balances atop a stack of her finished baskets.

5.4. Named for a small echinoderm that lives along the Maine seashore, the squat, globular "sea urchin" basket style is challenging to make. This Penobscot or Passamaquoddy example was plaited using splints in natural and "Roman-colored" dyed hues plus sweetgrass, c. 1900-1920, 8.5" diameter.

5.2

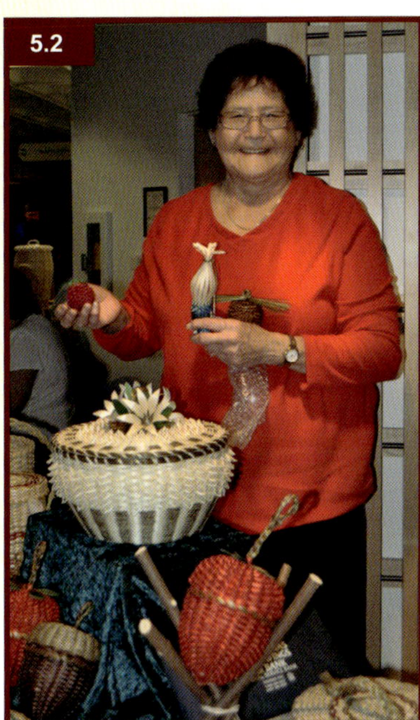

5.3

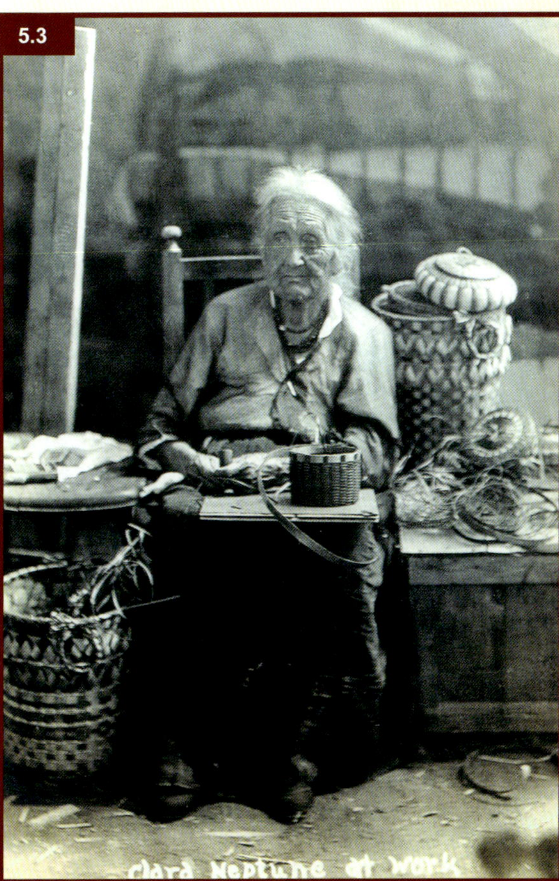

5.4

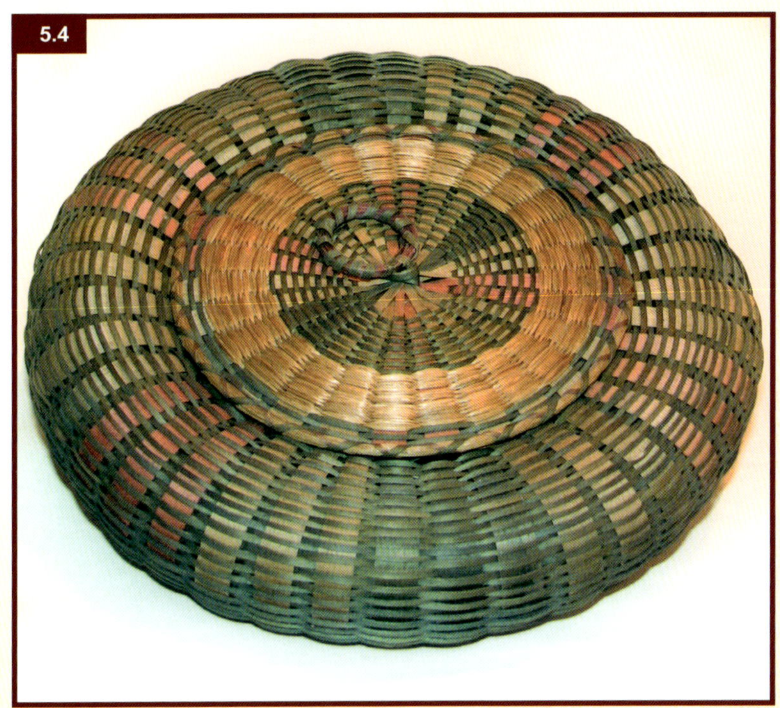

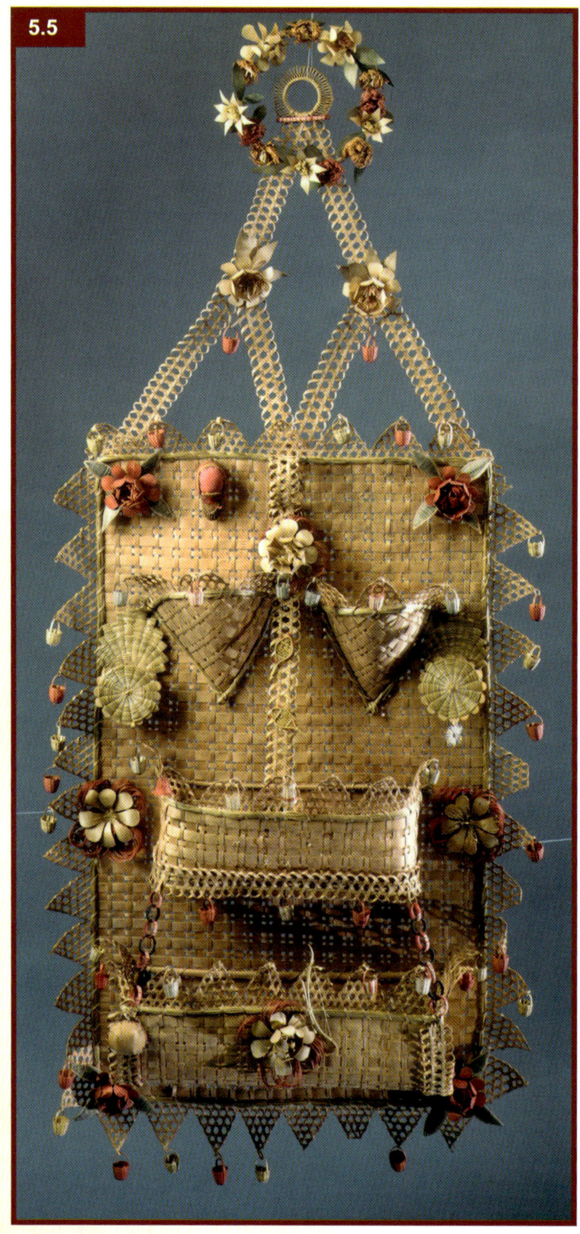

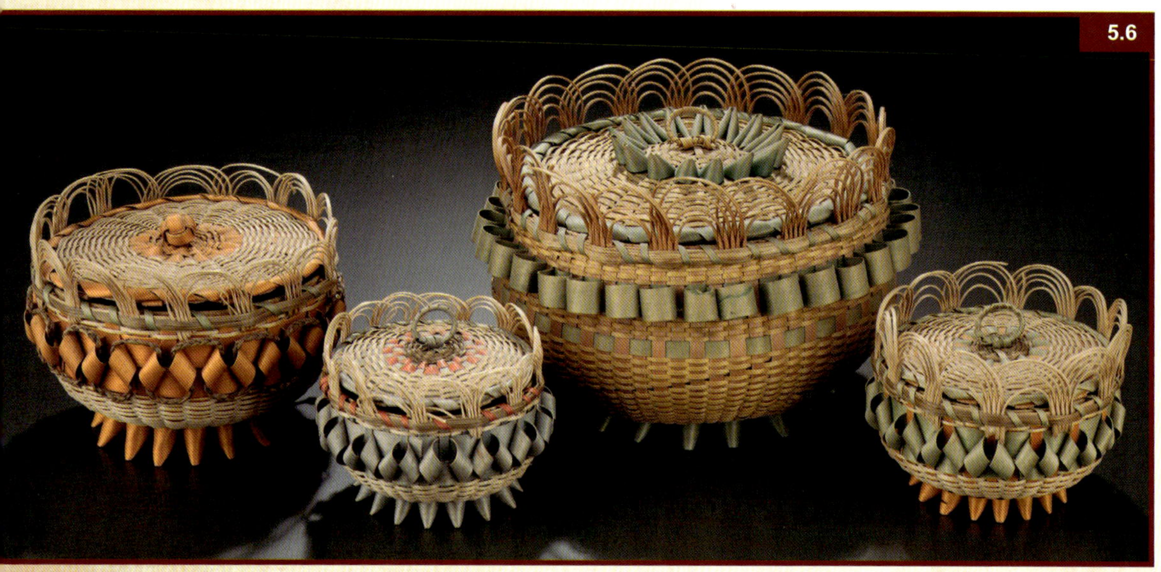

5.5. Agathe Athanase (Maliseet) of Rivière-du-Loup, eastern Québec, fashioned this elaborate basketry sampler of plaited woodsplint techniques for the 1893 Columbian Exposition in Chicago. Forty-five miniature baskets dangle from hex-weave lacework edging the five pockets and the border of this wall pocket or hanging "what-not." More than twenty wooden splint flowers, a tiny birchbark bowl, a pair of miniature snowshoes, a moccasin, and bow and arrow remain attached. Porcupine quills spell out the words "FORGET ME NOT" in the bar centered in the upper circlet of wooden flowers, and "WITH FOND LOVE TO THEE, REMENBER [sic] RIV DU LOUP, CANADA, INDIAN WORK" along the chain linking the lower two pockets. The opulence of this wall pocket resembles that of a Victorian valentine. Even its size is impressive at 42.5" high and 18.5" wide, late 1800s.

5.6. Attractive group of covered fancy baskets, embellished with brightly dyed splints, varieties of curly splintwork, and lacework edging. The largest basket is decorated with a green-dyed course of U-shaped "loop weave" curly splintwork below its rim. A diagonal "Abenaki spiral" is visible also on the body wall of the largest basket. The spiral occurs during plaiting when an even (not odd) number of warp strands, or standards, in spoke-like radial starts are used for plaiting a round form. The "Abenaki spiral" often appears in baskets made by Northern New England and Canadian Maritimes basketmakers, c. late 1800s-early 1900s.

New Twists on an Old Craft

Creative Northeastern Native basketmakers have devised numerous decorative innovations. Working with strips of hardwood did not deter craftpersons from pushing the limits of the medium. At least by the mid-19th century, basketmakers were introducing an extra twist as they passed a splint weaver horizontally between standards. This manipulation resulted in a decorative cone-like curly weave, sometimes called *cow-wiss*, that became increasingly popular. In time, many variations of the basic twisted "curly splintwork" were developed, along with other techniques like "lacework" edging. Some especially appealing methods included various curly splintwork techniques that bore different names in individual Native communities. Plain or diamond twists; shell, periwinkle, or wart curls; and sharp thistle, point, or porcupine-twist weaves are most frequently encountered.

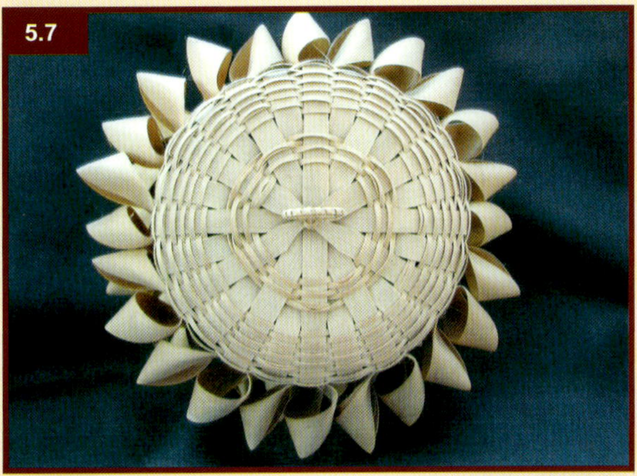

5.7. Decorative curly splintwork, sometimes called *cow-wiss.*

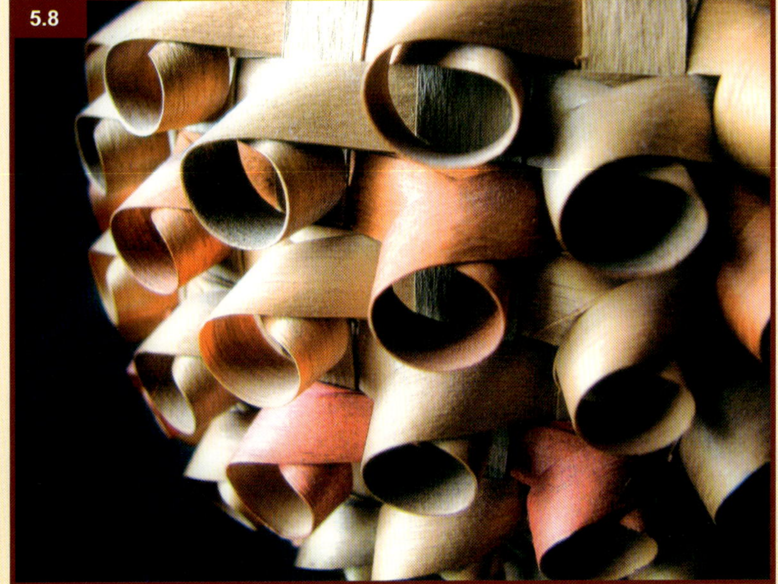

5.8. Curls called "shell," "periwinkle," or "wart" weave.

FOCUS:

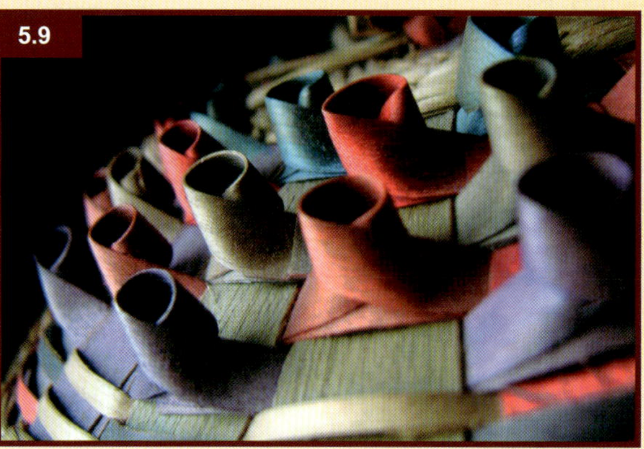

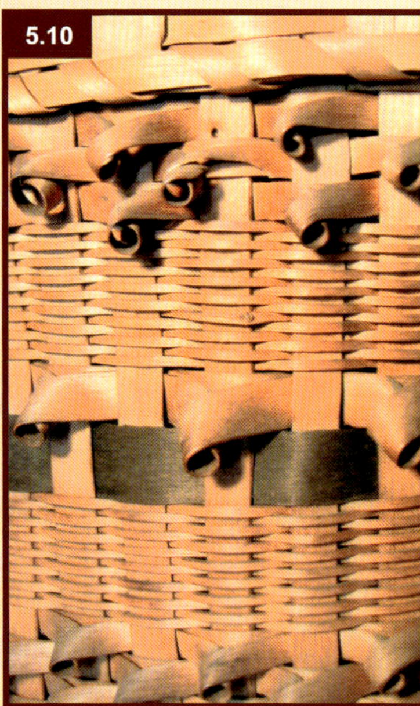

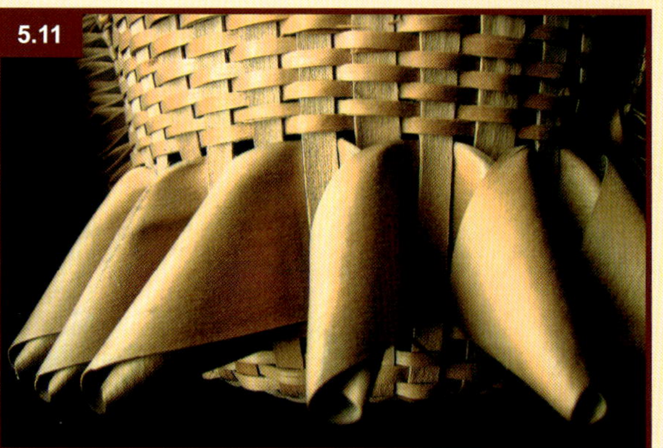

5.9–5.11. More "shell," "periwinkle," or "wart" weave curls.

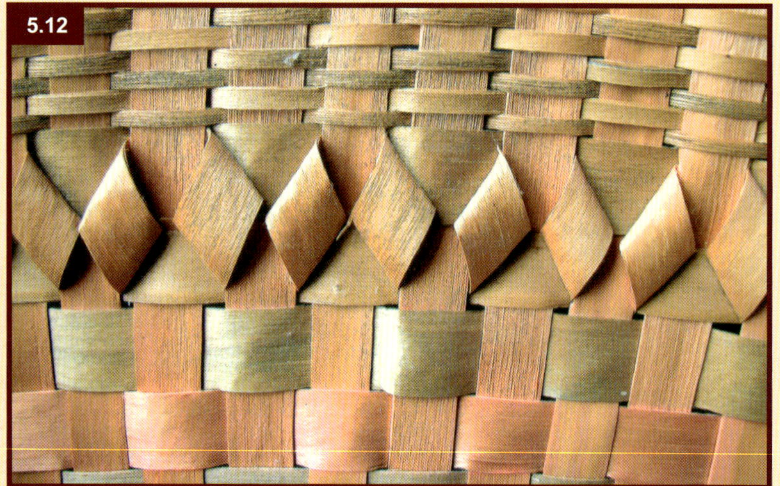

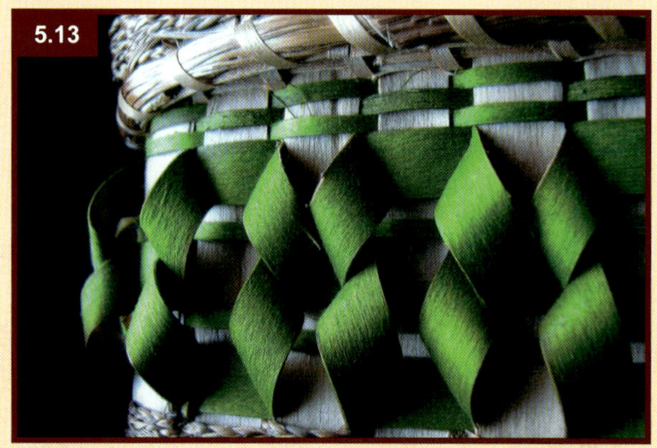

5.12–5.15. Twists called "plain" or "diamond" weave.

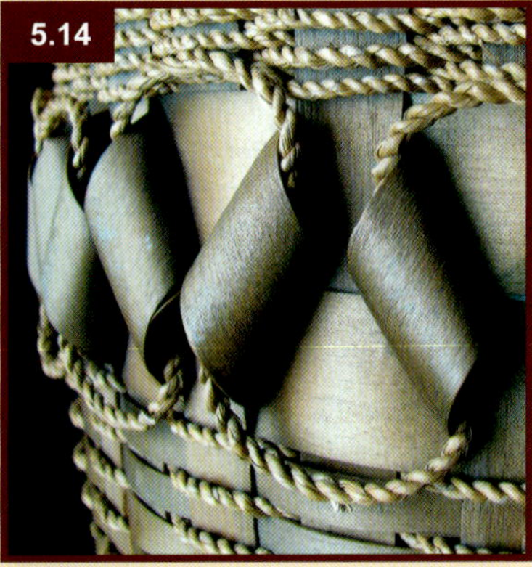

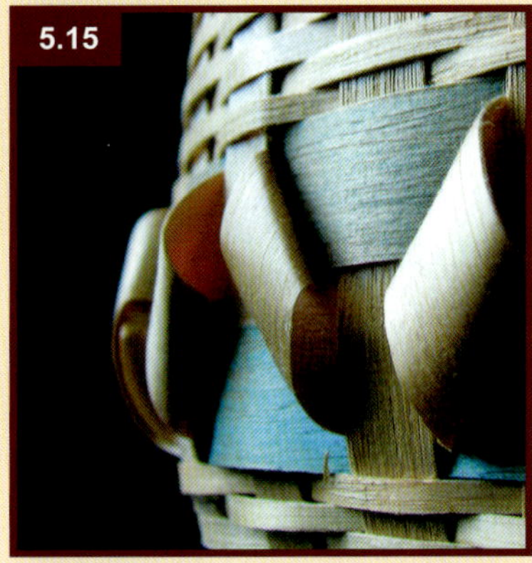

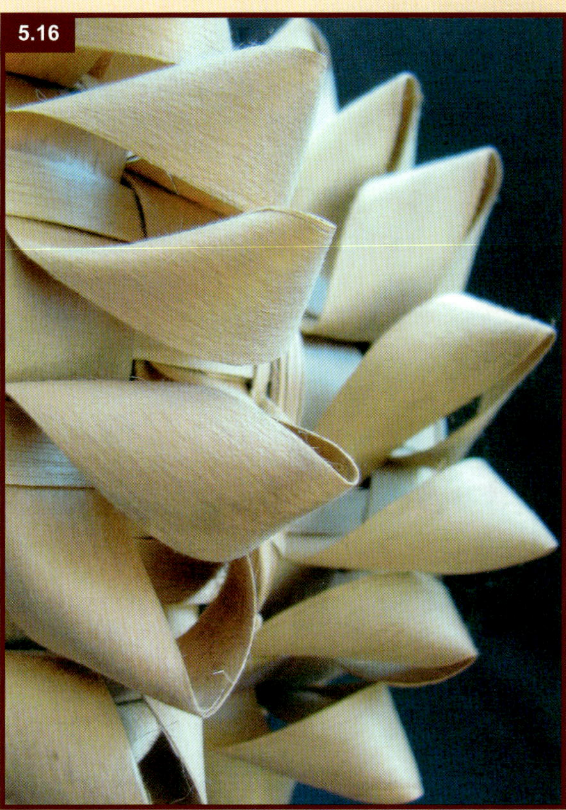

5.16. Sideways variation that Passamaquoddy call "seashell" weave.

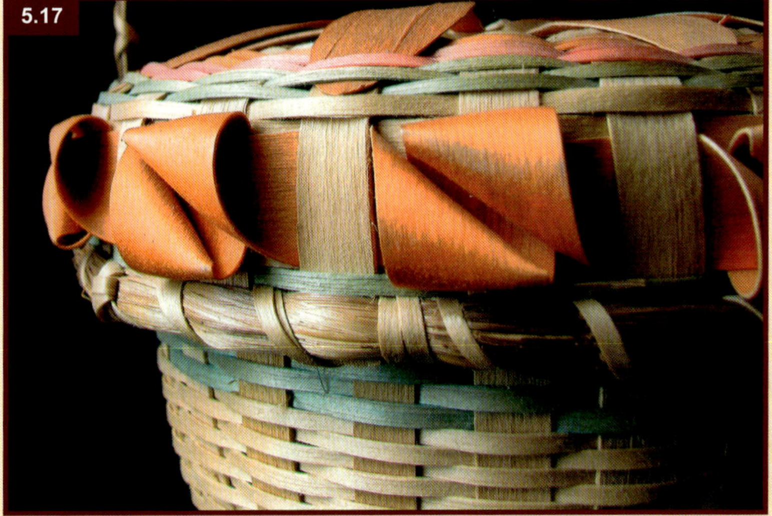

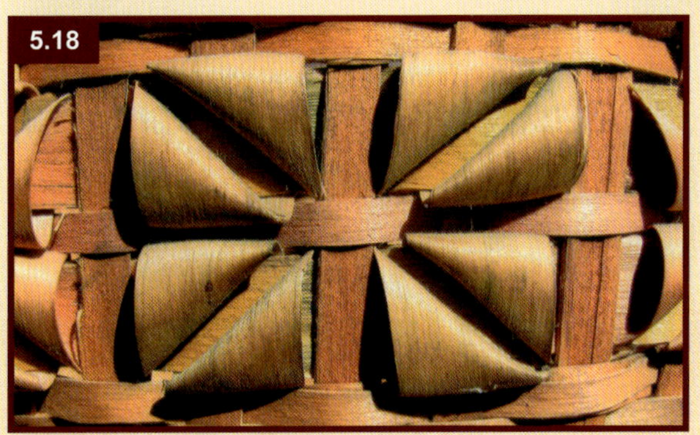

5.17, 5.18. More variations on the theme.

FOCUS:

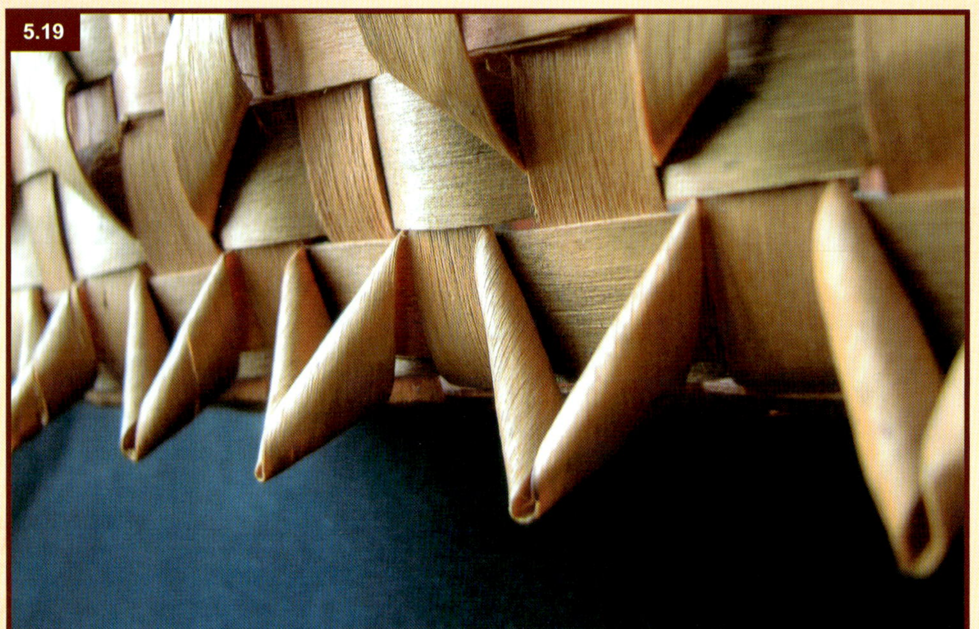
5.19

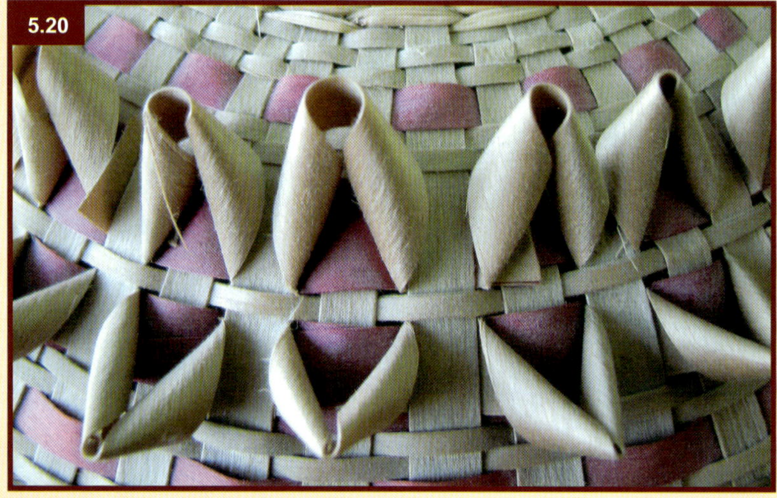
5.20

5.19, 5.20. Sharp double-twists called "point," "thistle," or "porcupine twist."

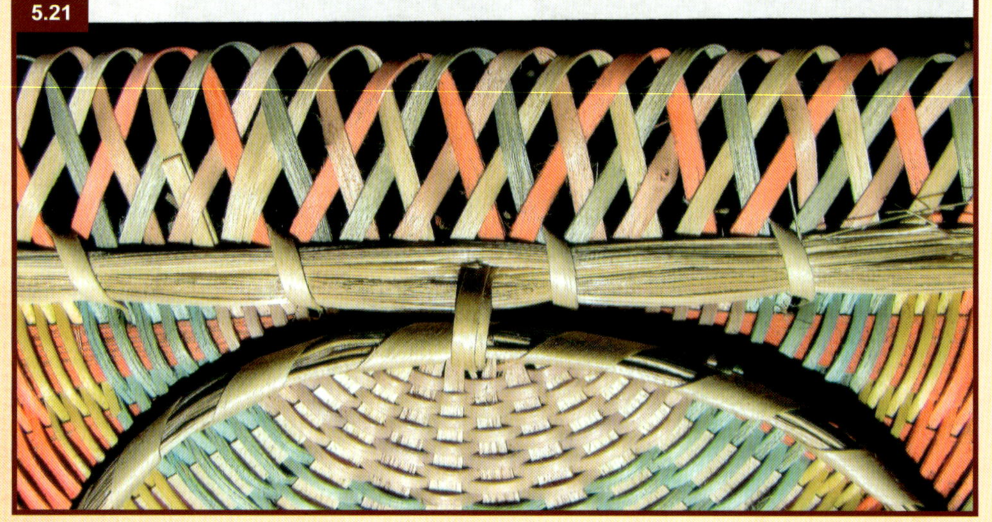
5.21

5.21. "Lacework" edging.

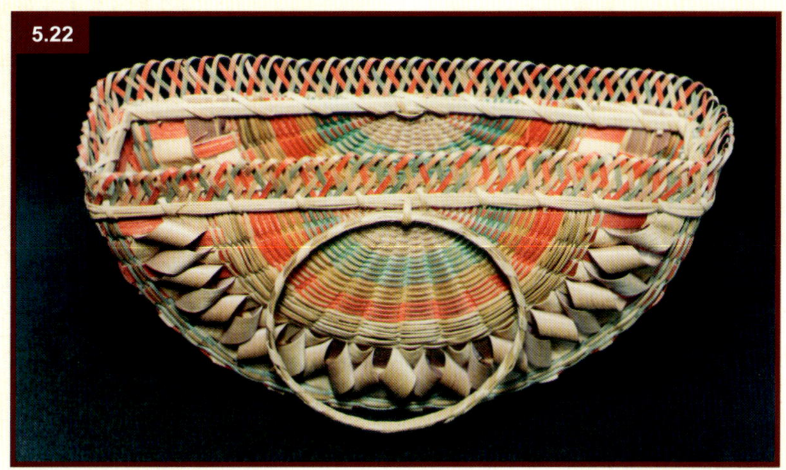

5.22. Sales agent C. N. Saba of Toronto illustrated half-moon-shaped "lunch baskets" for $12.00 per dozen in his wholesale Indian goods mail-order catalog, early 1900s. This frilly example is typical for its era, c. 1900, 8" long.

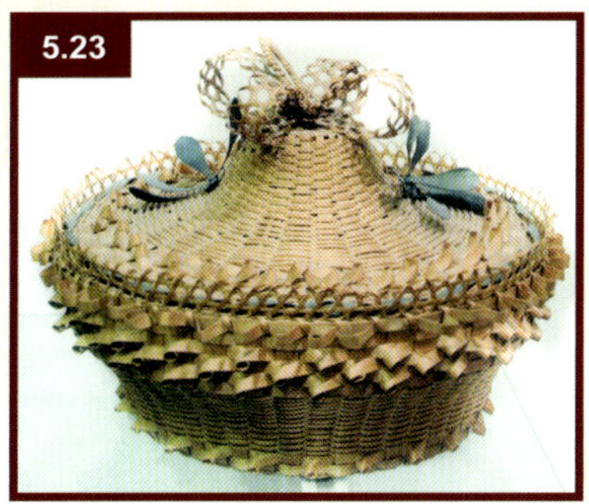

5.23. Handiwork baskets made in Northern New England and the Canadian Maritimes include this especially ornate example.

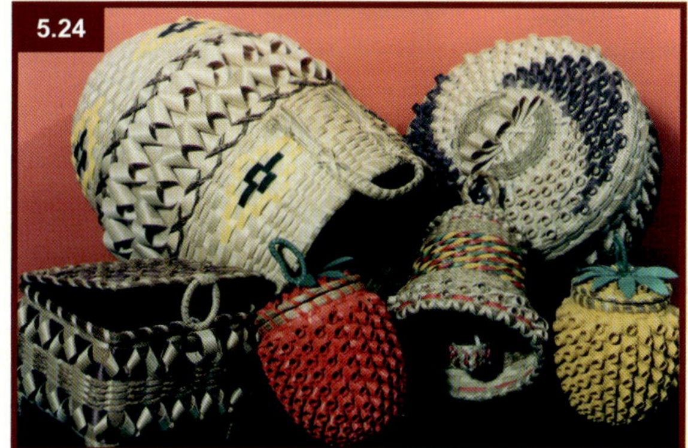

5.24. Curly splintwork examples (clockwise, from lower left): Covered jewelry box with feet, likely by Penobscot Leslie Ranco; Passamaquoddy ash splint and sweetgrass baskets include a wastepaper basket, covered deep sewing basket, and a yellow strawberry basket, bell with clapper, and red strawberry basket by Clara Neptune Keezer, 1980s; yellow strawberry is 7" high.

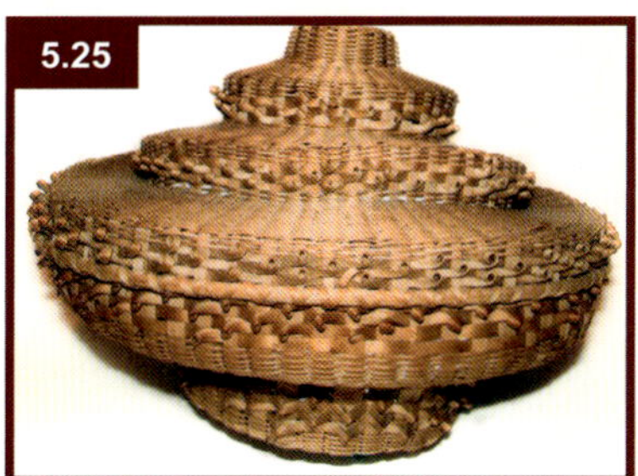

5.25. This elaborate multi-tiered basket resembles a wedding cake with fancy frosting, early 1900s, 11.5" diameter.

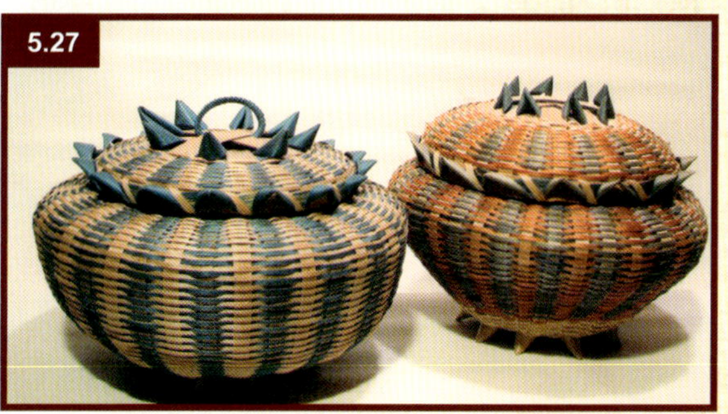

5.26. Covered hamper plaited with extensive curly splintwork, ribbon-like looped-weave handles and rings, and a single wide weft splint accenting its unusually large size, early 1900s, 26" high.

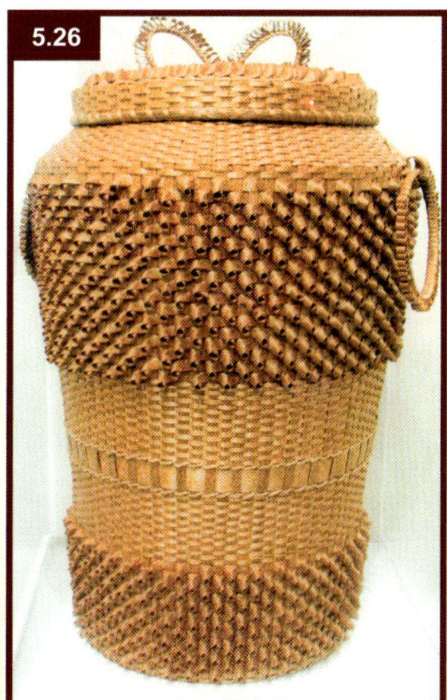

5.27. Ho-Chunk (Winnebago) covered baskets plaited with gauge-cut splints on a compound block and edged with pointed "porcupine twist" splintwork, signed by maker "Velma Marie Lewis," late 1900s, (left) 11.5" diameter.

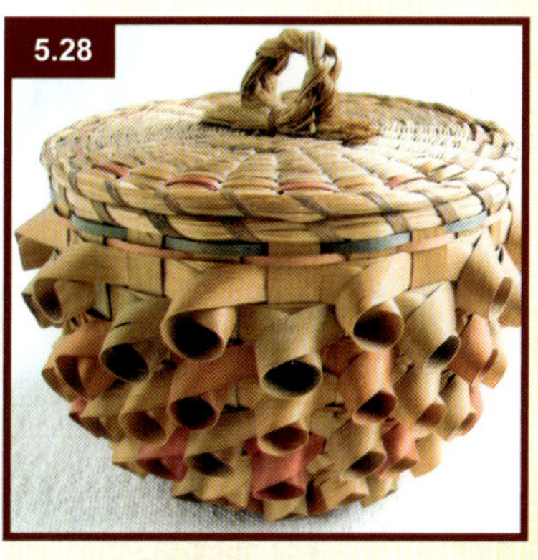

5.28. Covered basket with "shell" weave in the style of Camilla Lyon Sockalexis, Penobscot, c. 1930–1940, 5" diameter.

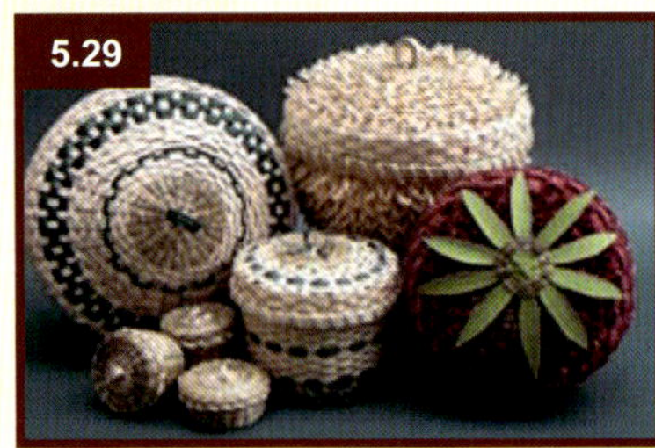

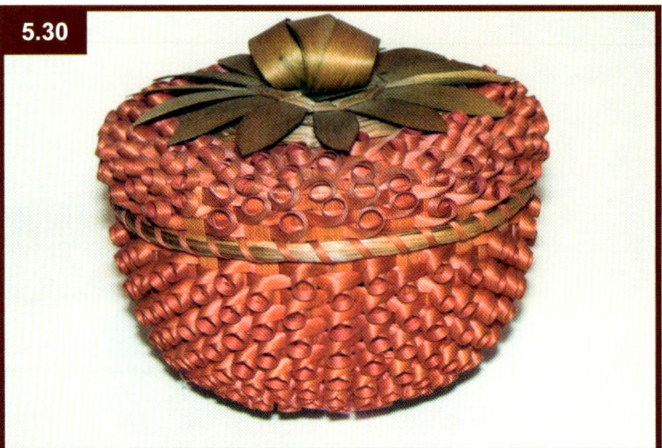

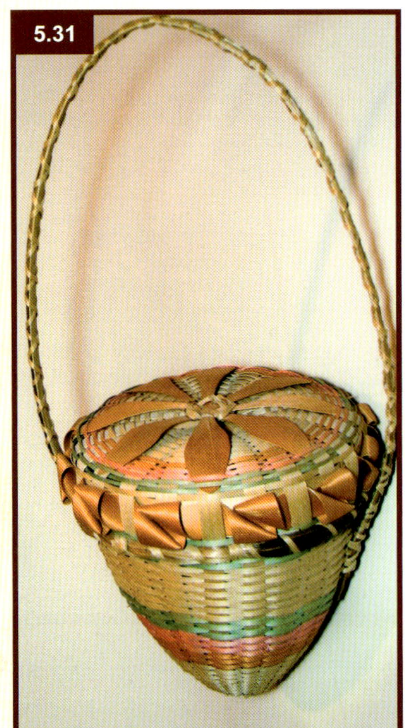

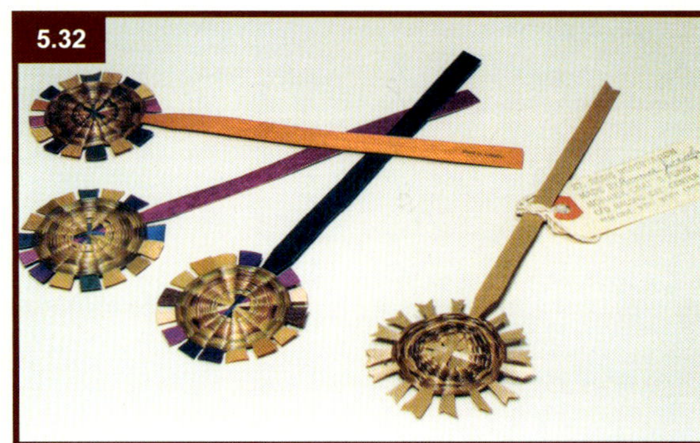

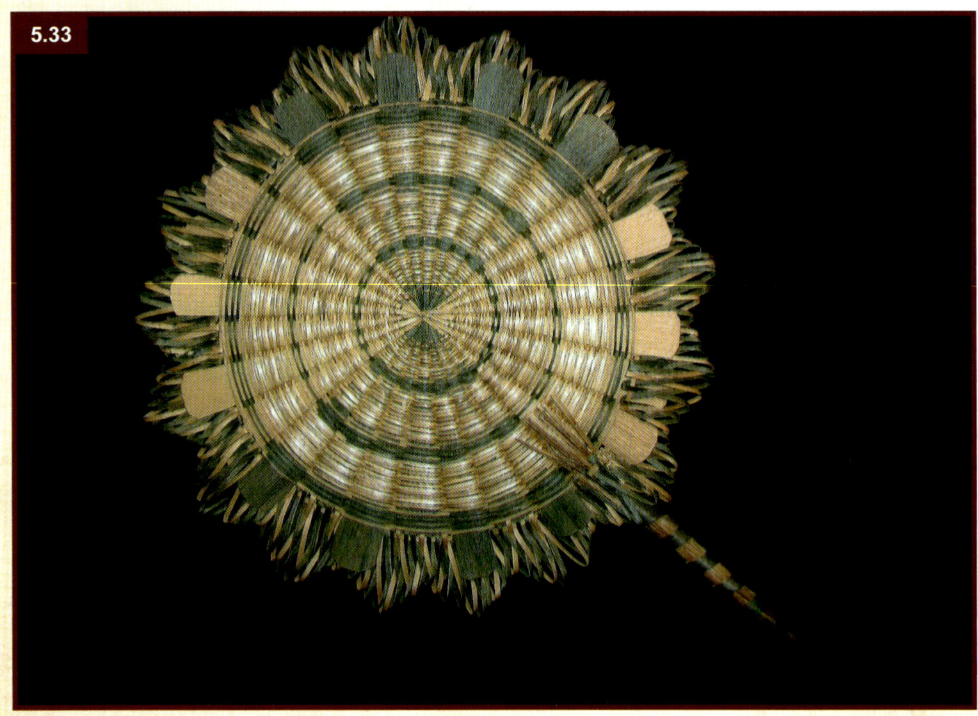

5.29. Group of fancy baskets made by Robin Lazore, Mohawk, 2000–2005.

5.30. Strawberry basket with dyed splints and curly splintwork, Akwesasne (St. Regis Mohawk), 1970s, 5.5" diameter.

5.31. Eight splint petal appliqués, curly splintwork, natural and brightly dyed ash splints, and an impressive handle distinguish this covered acorn basket; possibly Great Lakes, 1970s, 12" long with handle.

5.32. Ash splint and sweetgrass bookmarks include three Abenaki (Québec) examples (left) plaited with multi-hued "Roman-colored" splints, early 1900s, and one Akwesasne bookmark with pinked splint ends labeled as the work of Annie Jacobs, mid-1900s, 8.5" long.

5.33. Fan with lacework edging, Northern New England and Canadian Maritimes, c. 1890, 13.5" long.

5.34. A colorful and useful souvenir of visits to coastal and lakeside summer resorts, early to mid-1900s, 13" long.

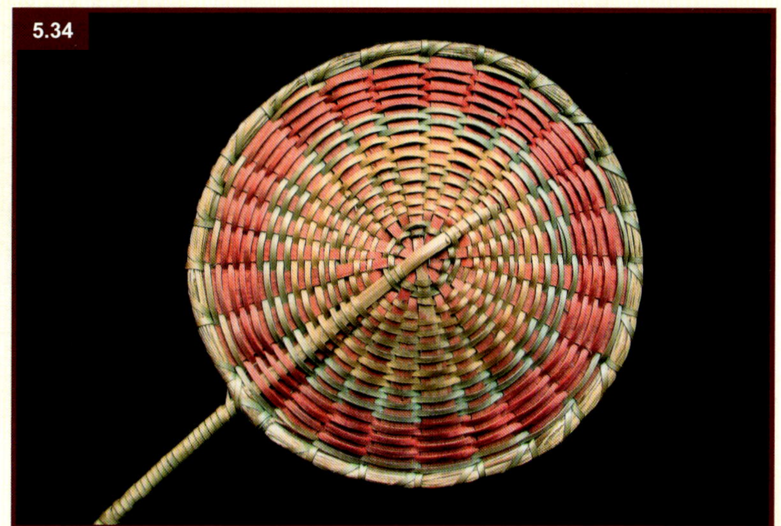

5.35, 5.36. Covered basket of white oak splints with yellow-dyed (faded) curly work, a wrapped ring pull on the cover, and sweetgrass edging, northern New England, 1986, 6.5" diameter.

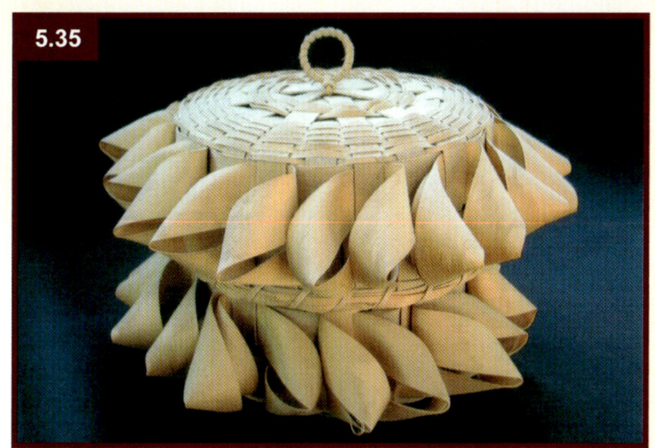

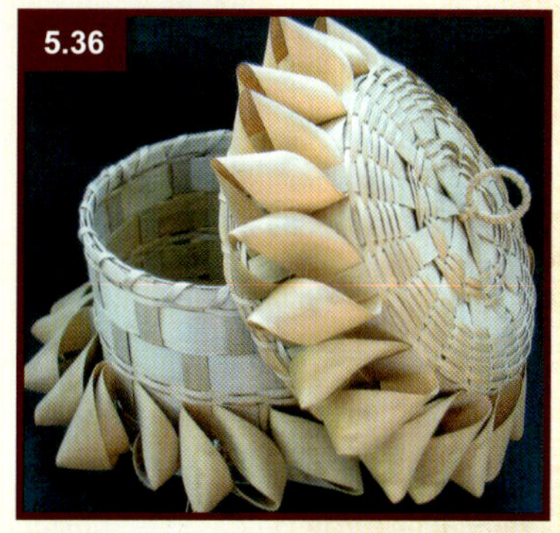

5.37. An impressive covered handiwork basket, early 1900s, 10" diameter.

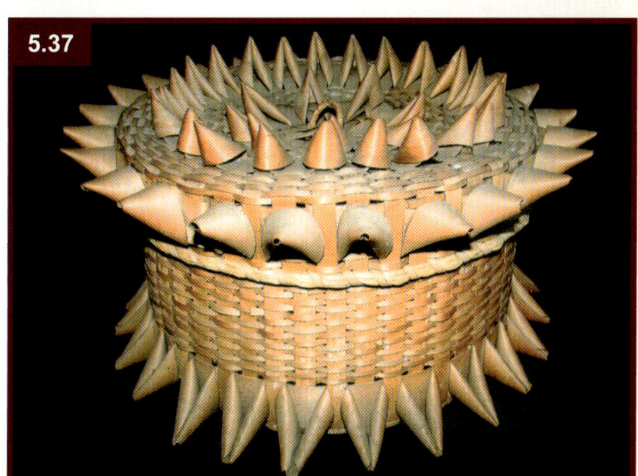

5.38. Fancy basketwork helped Natives throughout the Northeast region meet economic needs. Basketry novelties appealed to tourists and were readily carried home from lakeside and seashore resorts. This elaborate, now faded, loving cup has delicate ribbon-like looped-weave splint handles and curly work, 1930s, 8.5" high.

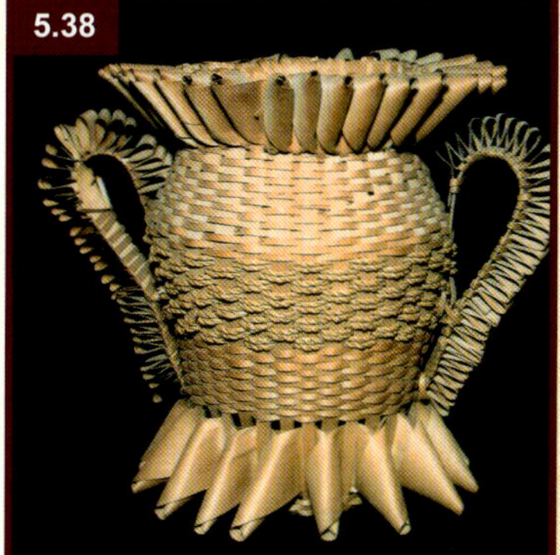

5.39. Decorative doll cradle with splint runners, Passamaquoddy style, mid-1900s, 8" long.

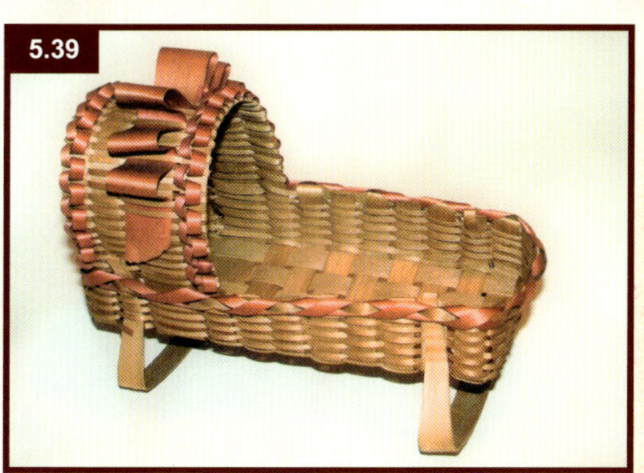

SETTING:

A Great Lakes Indian Trading Post

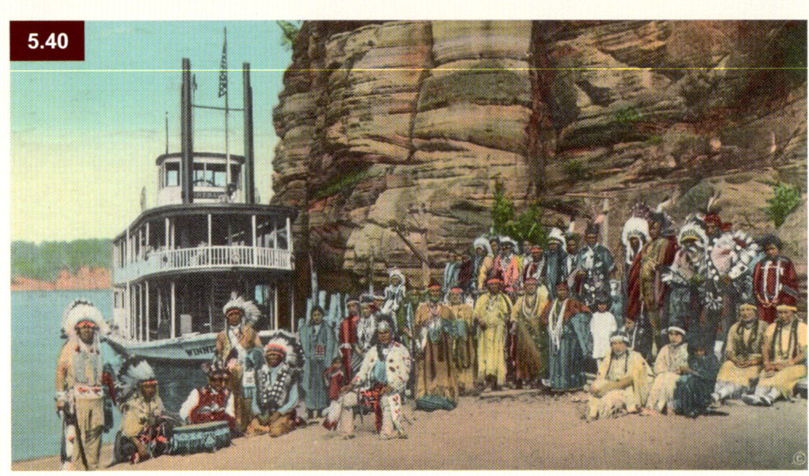

5.40. Early postcard view of the steamboat *Winnebago* and Indians at the Palisades near Stand Rock, on an Upper Dells trip along the scenic Wisconsin River, 1930s.

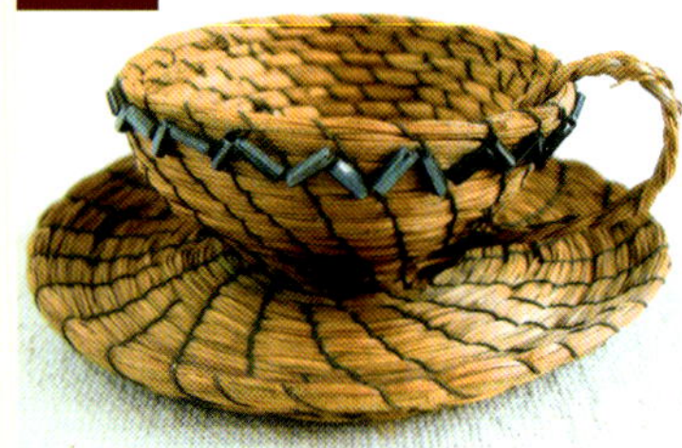

5.41. Whimsical teacup and saucer embellished with black glass beads, 4" diameter.

The steamer's loudspeaker blared as the riverboat rounded the bend. The breathy whistle echoed up and down high sandstone cliffs along the Wisconsin River, heralding the boat's arrival. The riverboat, filled with sight-seeing tourists curious about Winnebago Indian history and lore, would dock near the Wisconsin Dells trading post shortly. Most of its passengers would attend the Stand Rock Indian Ceremonial. For the past several years, the nightly performance of Winnebago dances and skits was becoming more popular than ever.

Many Winnebago men and women had set up wigwams near the trading post in "Indian Village." They would be selling their Native arts and crafts here throughout the summer. Judging from the capacity crowds already visiting the Village, this summer promised to yield another good season.

As the steamer docked, the trading post manager pulled her long braid forward over the shoulder of her beaded buckskin dress. She carefully adjusted a beaded headband across her forehead and pinned on a tag bearing the name "Mrs. Indian Jim." If the tourists assumed her costume and nickname were more traditional than they actually were, she thought, what was the harm in it? She was both popular and memorable with visitors. Her image, preserved in their instant Polaroid snapshots, helped to keep them coming back, year after year.

The woman remembered all too well how her Winnebago family had barely eked out a living wage working in the local cranberry bogs. But over the years, her job at this trading post, with its modest profits, had enabled "Mrs. Indian Jim" to buy a nice little home in town. She had even built up a small savings account for herself.

"Mrs. Indian Jim" quickly glanced around the trading post. She scooped up a couple of wayward Polaroid instant negatives that had been discarded under an Indian drum and tossed them into an oversized woodsplint wastebasket just inside the door. As she checked the inventory on display one last time before the first tourists entered, she felt pleased. A variety of souvenirs and Indian-made arts and crafts filled the shelves this summer, including some new Chippewa coiled sweetgrass whimseys stitched with black cotton thread.

"Mrs. Indian Jim" had priced the sweetgrass teacups and pendants reasonably, confident they were going to sell well.

5.42. Basketry novelties include teacups with attached saucers (clockwise, from upper left): plaited ash splint and sweetgrass with one yellow-dyed wide weft splint, likely Iroquois; two Chippewa or Ojibwe versions of coiled sweetgrass stitched with commercial black thread, all c. 1940-1980, 4" to 4.5" diameter.

5.43. Bundle-coiled sweetgrass hat made by Paul St. John, Mohawk/ Maliseet/ Passamaquoddy, c. 2000, 10" brim diameter.

5.44. Unusual plaited hat with curly splintwork and hex-weave edging, Northern New England or Canadian Maritimes, 1930s, 10" brim diameter.

5.45. Small covered powder-puff box in the shape of a hat, plaited with fragrant braided sweetgrass and green-dyed ash splints, sports Clara Neptune Keezer's signature splint-bow ribbonwork, Passamaquoddy, 1970s, 5" brim diameter.

5.46. Two dyed splint flowers by Madeleine Joe Knockwood, Micmac, c. 1940, blossom 4.5" diameter.

5.47. Remarkable example of a Victorian lady's fancy woodsplint bonnet with twill plaiting, curly splintwork, lacework edging, appliqué flowers, and more; Northern New England and Canadian Maritimes, 12" brim diameter.

5.42

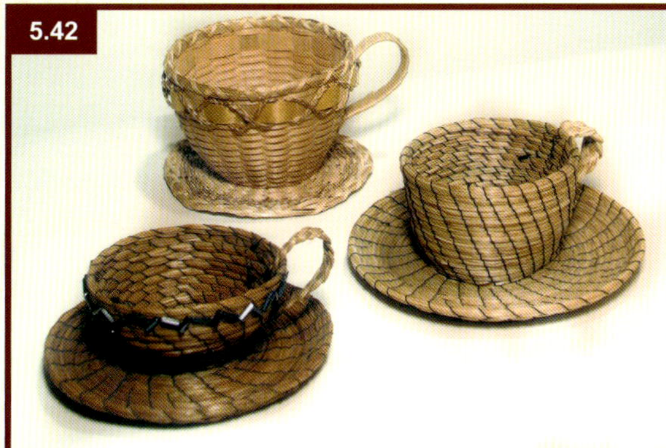

5.43

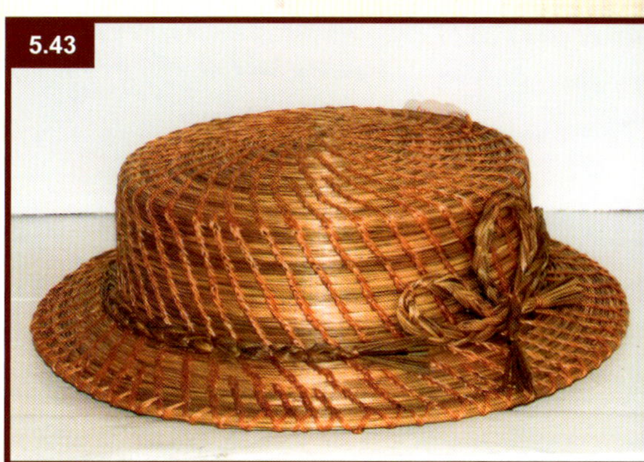

5.44

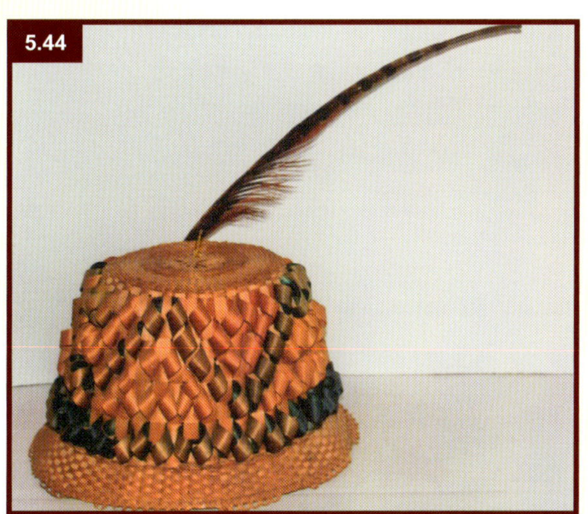

5.45

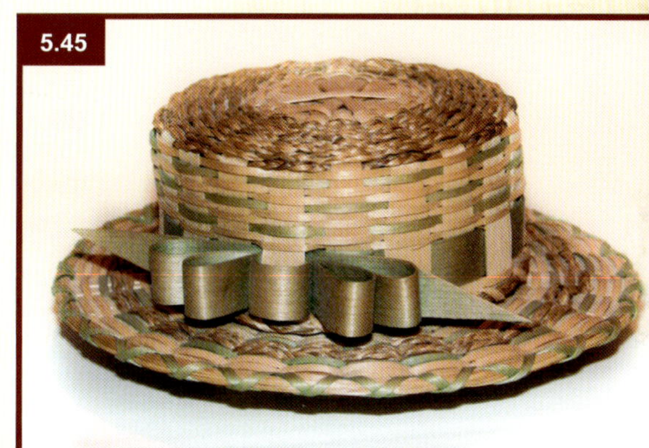

5.46

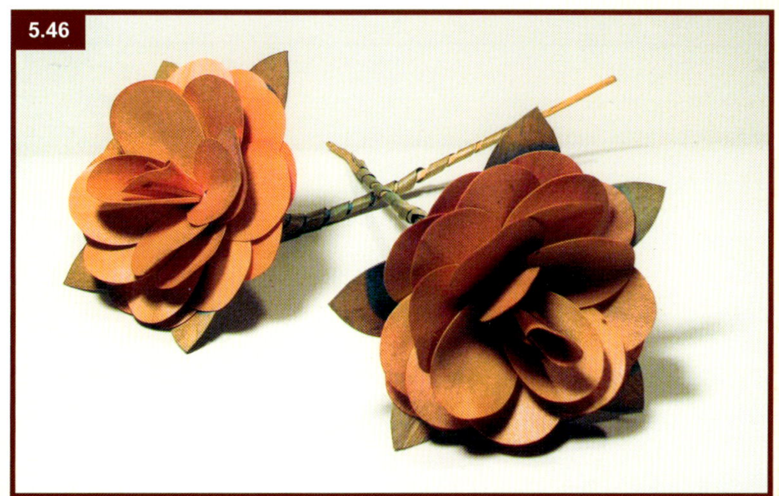

5.47

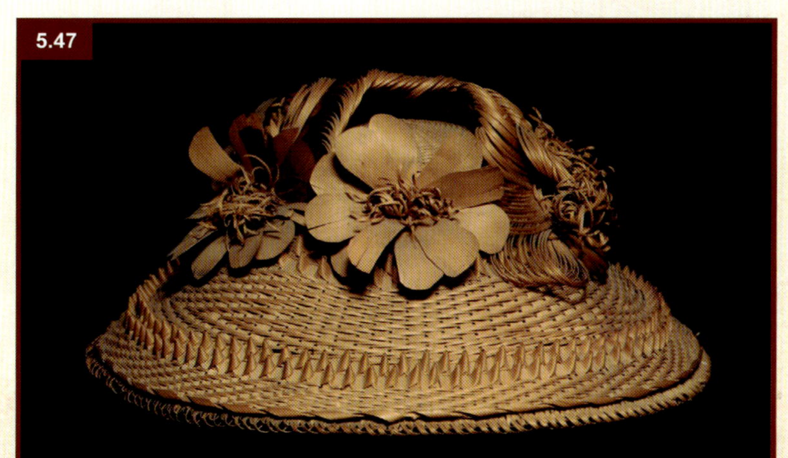

FOCUS:

Tiny Treasures

The unique appeal of miniaturized versions of ordinary objects may be universal. Ancient Egyptians furnished Pharaoh's tomb with scaled models of his earthly possessions. In more recent times, the concept continued to charm Victorian-period Europeans and Americans, whose fascination motivated a desire for elaborately furnished doll houses and armies of diminutive lead soldiers. Native basketmakers took up the challenging art of the miniature in earnest by the late 19th century as they exploited commercial opportunities. Requiring careful preparation of the highest quality materials and an investment of time far exceeding their scale, tiny woodsplint and sweetgrass baskets of varied forms, some smaller than a fingertip, testify to the skill of basketmaking artisans. These miniatures still excite many collectors today.

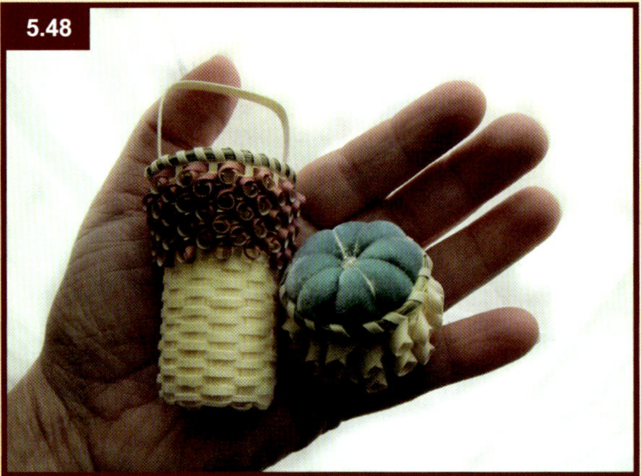

5.48. Miniature ash splint and sweetgrass baskets by Jennifer Sapiel Neptune, Penobscot, early 2000s.

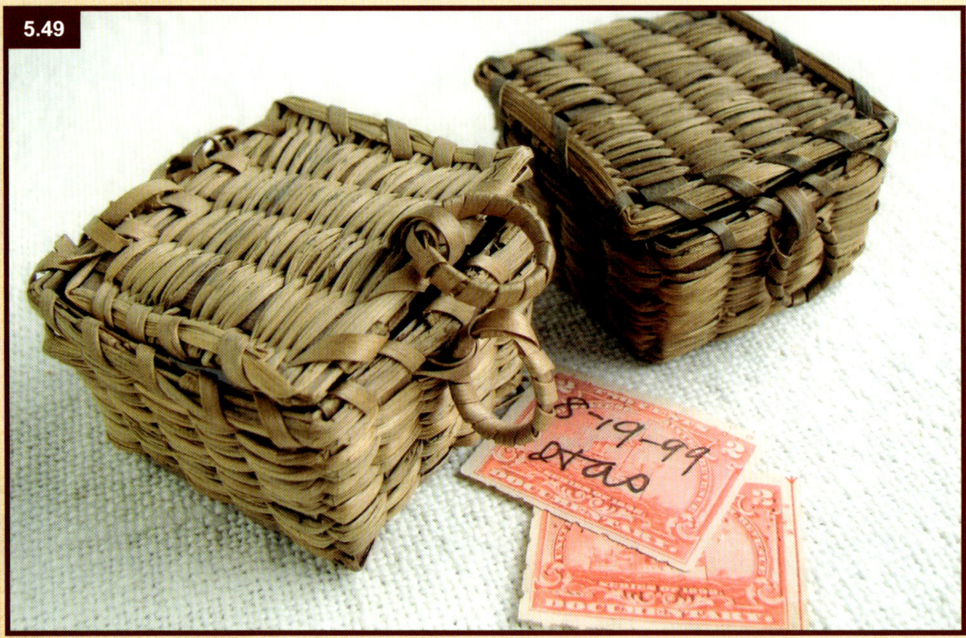

5.49. Small covered boxes, early to mid-1900s.

5.50. Blueberry basket, late 1900s, 1.5" diameter.

5.51. Tiny acorn basket by Jennifer Sapiel Neptune, Penobscot, early 2000s.

5.52. Small covered cases for watches, accessories, and other sundries, early to mid-1900s, 2" to 3" diameter.

5.53. Mini market basket, signed "W R," mid- to late 1900s.

5.54. Small "beaver" baskets or melon-shaped baskets with "God's-eye" handle finishes are a testament to their maker's skill, likely Micmac or Maliseet, mid-1900s, 1.5" long.

5.55. Unusual commercially-dyed straw baskets made by Wampanoag family members Zerviah Gould Mitchell or her daughters Melinda and Charlotte living at Betty's Neck, Lakeville, Massachusetts, or their sister Emma (Mitchell) Safford of Ipswich, Massachusetts, c.1880s–1910s, (left) 2.75" long.

5.56. Small "beaver" or melon-shaped half-basket with "God's-eye" handle finish, made for hanging on a wall, late 1900s, 3" long.

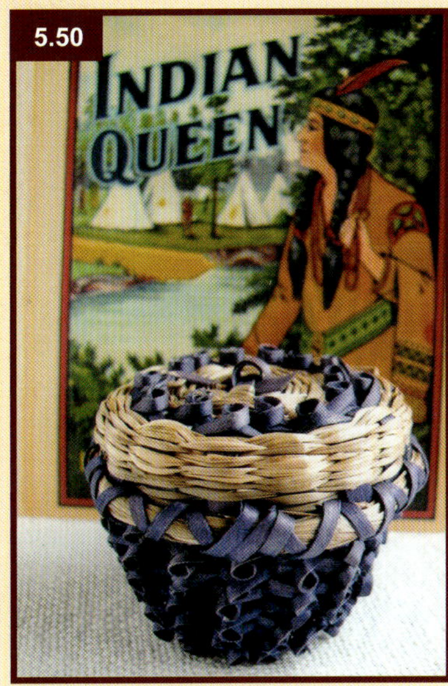

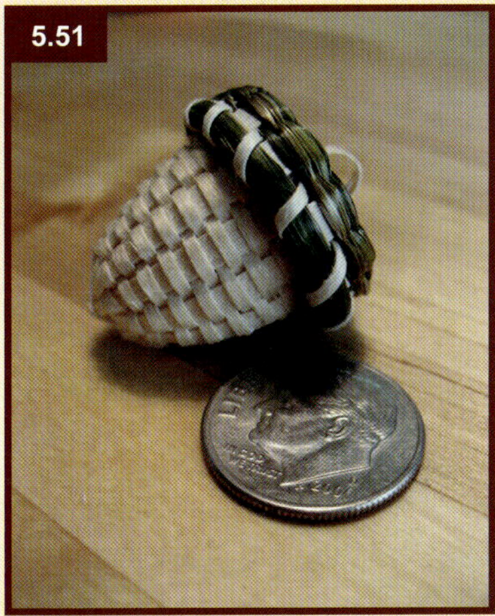

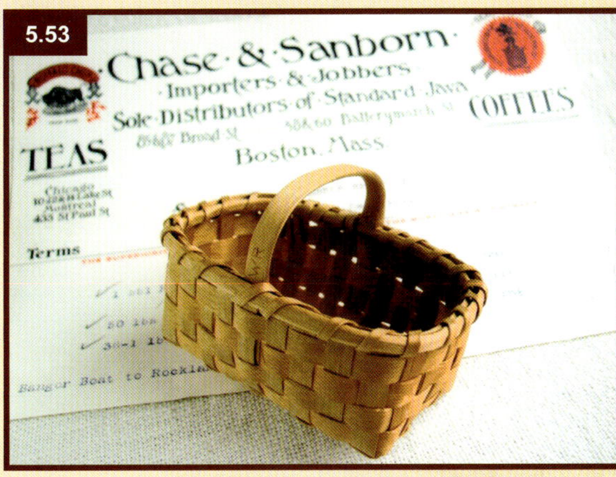

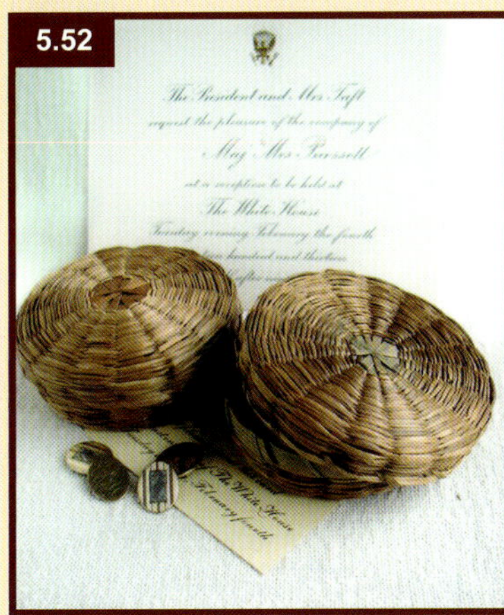

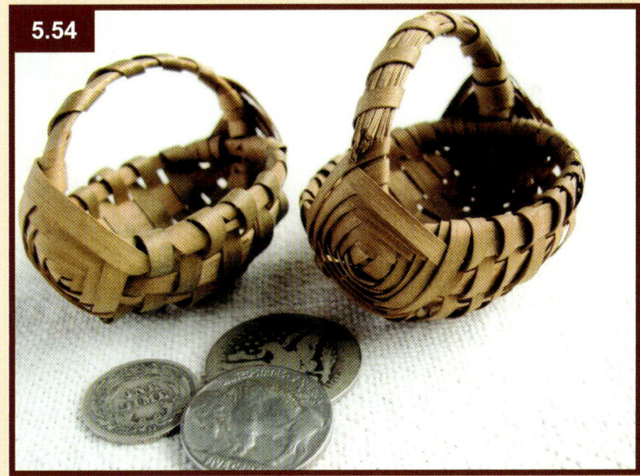

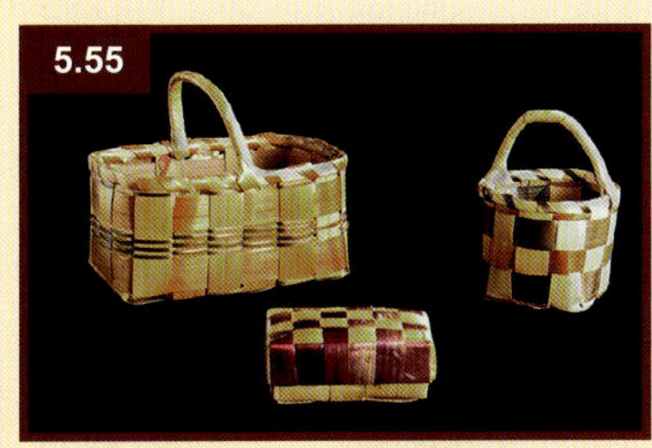

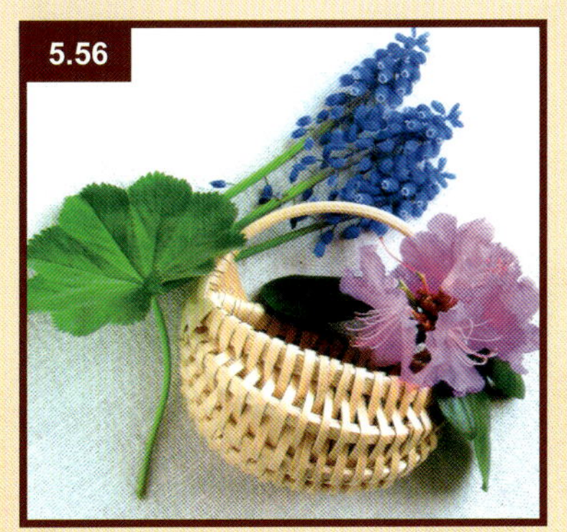

FOCUS:

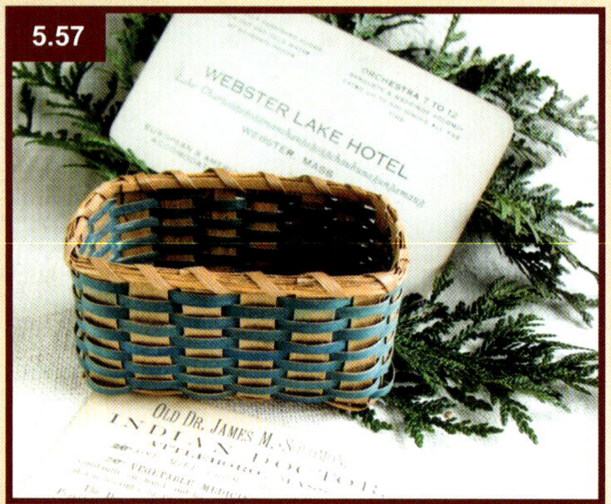

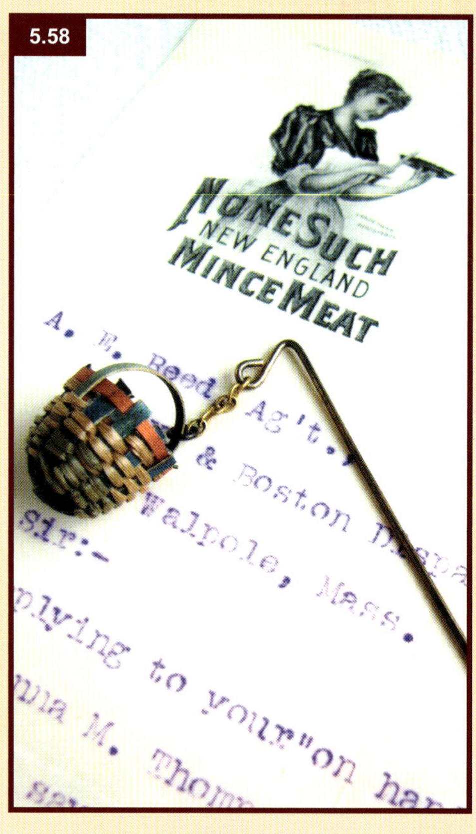

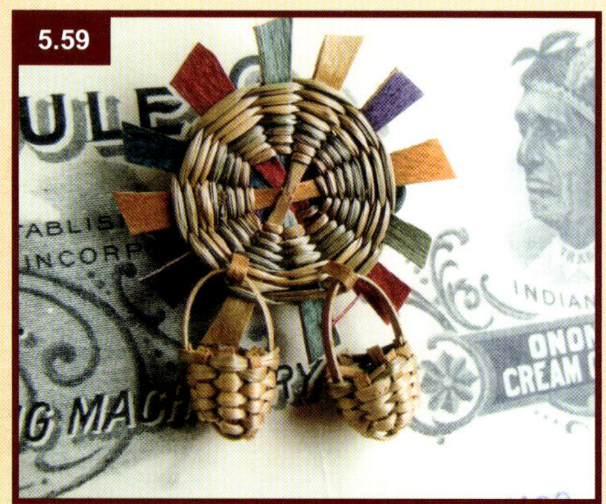

5.57. Small brightly-dyed insert for a larger basket, early to mid-1900s, 4" long.

5.58. Stickpin with tiny ash splint basket, early 1900s.

5.59. Pin with tinier baskets, early 1900s.

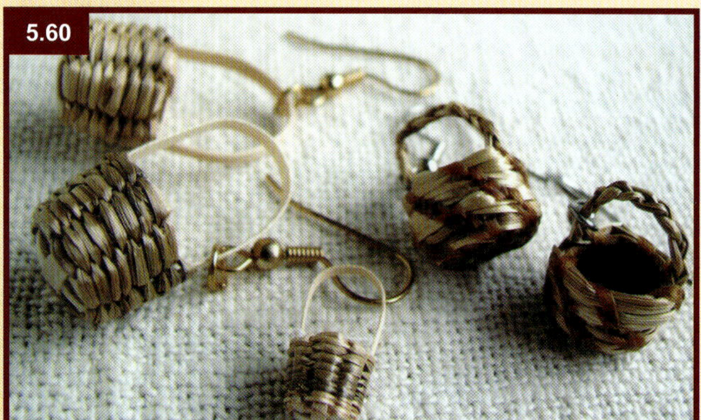

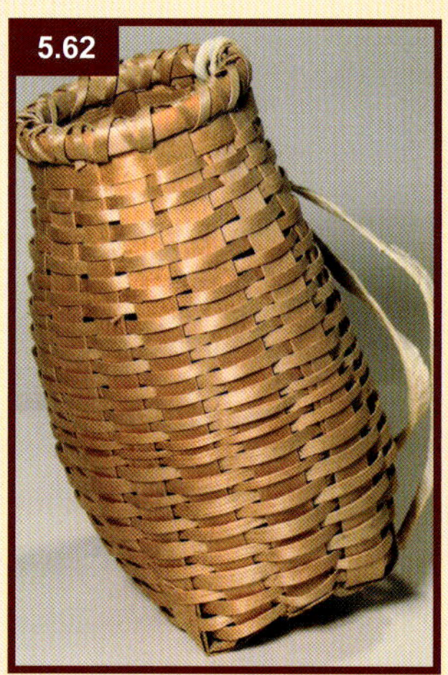

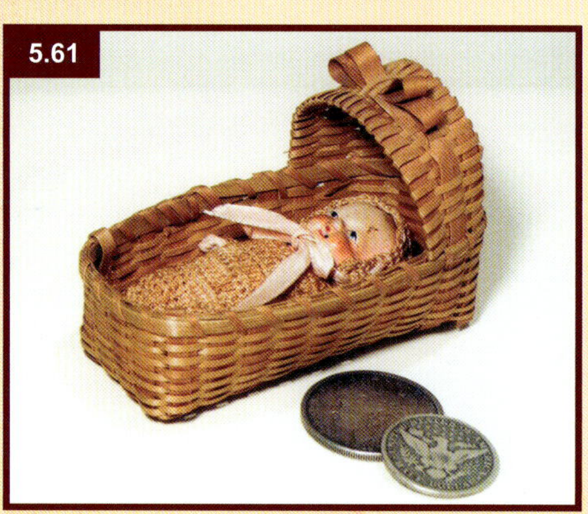

5.60. More basketry jewelry: Earrings and pendant (left) by Frances Smith, Passamaquoddy, c. 2000; earrings stitched with sinew (right) by Hilde Barnes, Mohawk/Akwesasne, c. 2010; all are 0.25" to 0.5" high plus handles.

5.61. Little woodsplint bed for a doll, Passamaquoddy, mid-1900s, 4.5" long.

5.62. Miniature pack basket, signed "M. P. Dennis, Abenaki from Odanak," 6" high.

5.63. Small sweetgrass turtle started on an oval birchbark disk and stitched with commercial black thread, Great Lakes region, mid- to late 1900s, 2.75" long.

5.64. Miniature ash splint and sweetgrass turtles by Gerald Barnes, Passamaquoddy, c. 1990.

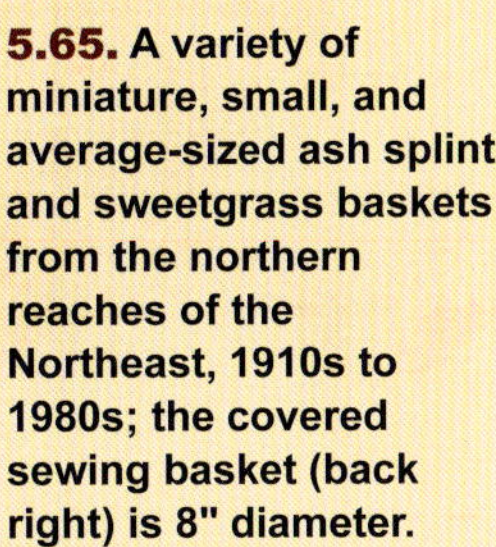

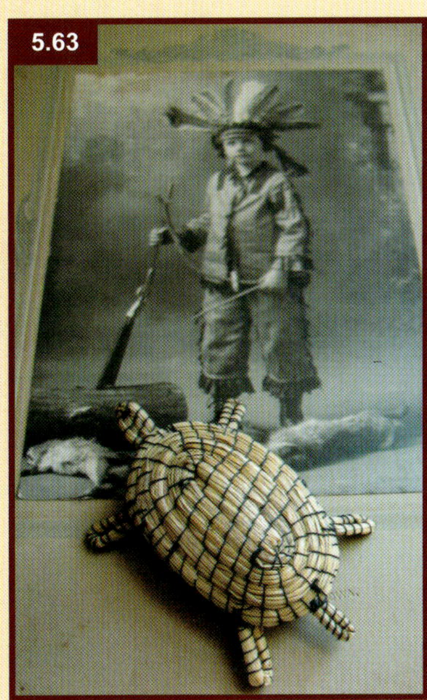

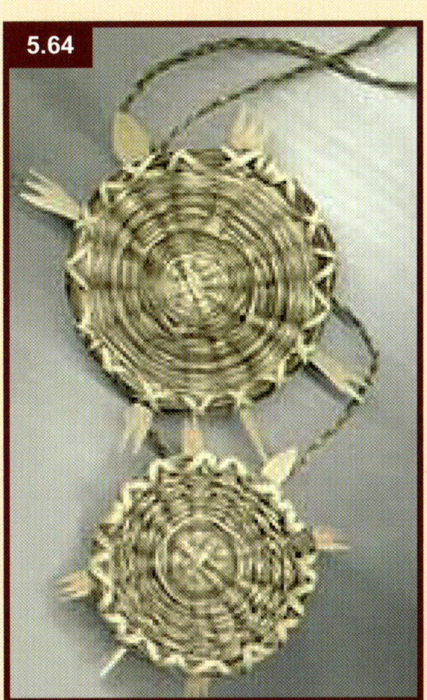

5.65. A variety of miniature, small, and average-sized ash splint and sweetgrass baskets from the northern reaches of the Northeast, 1910s to 1980s; the covered sewing basket (back right) is 8" diameter.

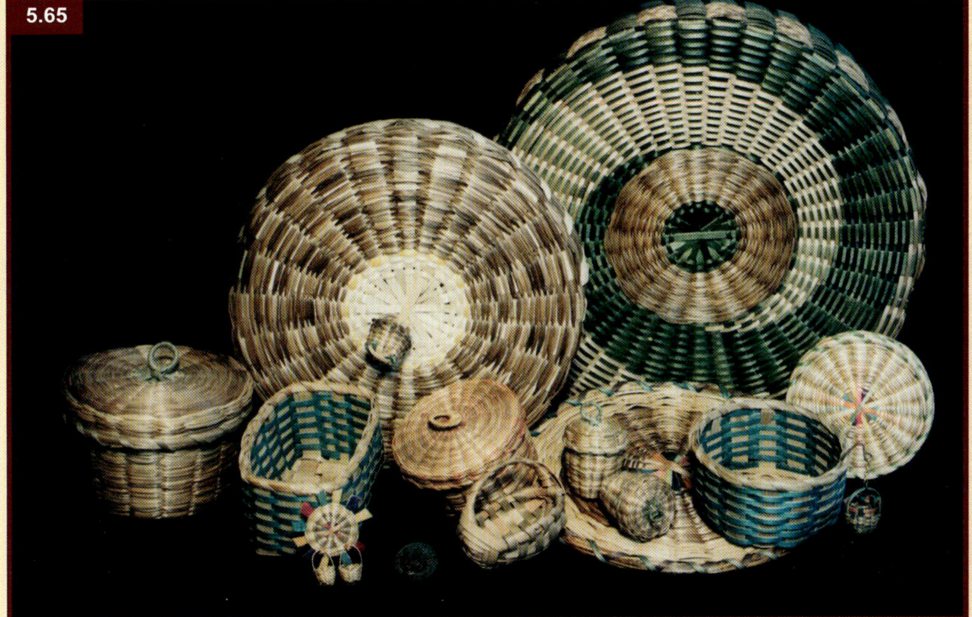

CHAPTER 6

A HUMBLE CRAFT BECOMES AN ART

Native Northeastern basketmakers working at the close of the 20th and the beginning of the 21st century continue to draw from the deep well of tradition. At the same time, a growing number of individual crafters are also finding inspiration beyond the conventional sources. Incorporating elements from an expanded universe of Native and non-Native traditions, their baskets combine new forms, techniques, decorative approaches, and materials. By drawing on these resources, contemporary basketmakers are charting a new course for their ever-evolving craft as an art form. These trends have set Northeastern Indian basketry on an exciting new trajectory as it clears customary boundaries and moves further into the first century of a new millennium.

6.1. A basketmaking workshop on Indian Island, Maine, offered through the Maine Indian Basketmakers Alliance (MIBA).

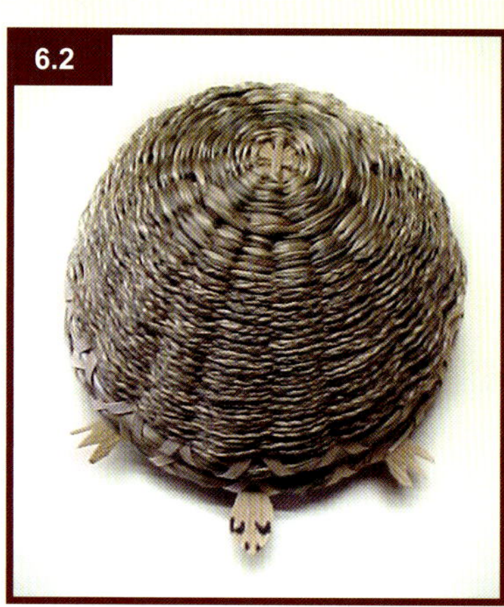

6.2. Ash splint and sweetgrass turtle, symbolizing longevity, by Gerald Barnes (Passamaquoddy), sold through the Indian Craft Shop, Indian Arts and Crafts Board, U.S. Department of the Interior, Washington, D.C., which promotes contemporary Native artisans and their work, 2003.

6.3. Inspired by 17th-century twined bags (see **2.44**) of southern New England, Julia Marden (Gay Head or Aquinnah Wampanoag) is one of a few Native weavers reviving the art, 2010.

6.4. Indian corn basket by master basketmaker Theresa Secord, Penobscot, founding executive director of MIBA.

6.5. Indian corn ears by Kelly Church, Grand Traverse band, Ottawa/Ojibwe, who adds non-traditional materials like copper, 2013.

6.6, 6.7. A work in progress becomes a completed gem of a pineapple basket, by Jennifer Sapiel Neptune, Penobscot.

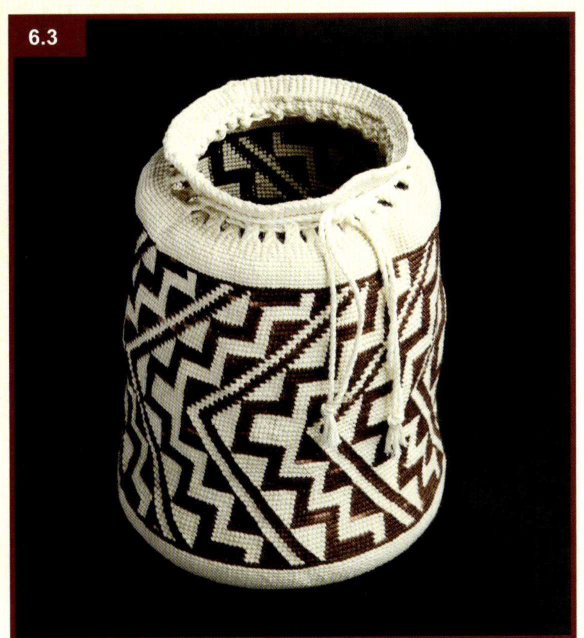

6.3

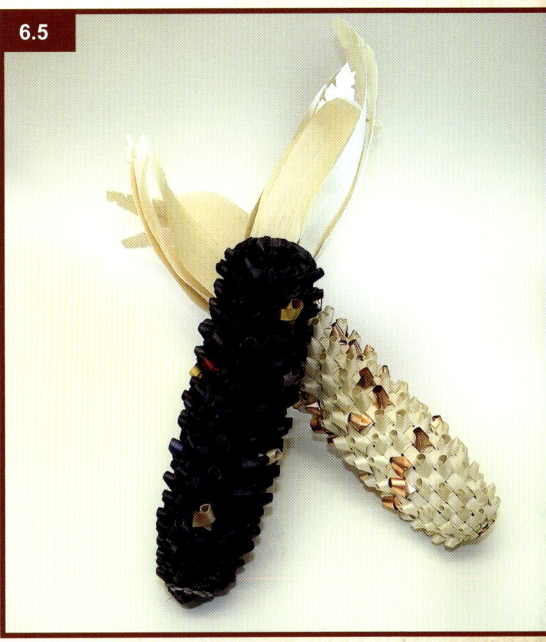

6.5

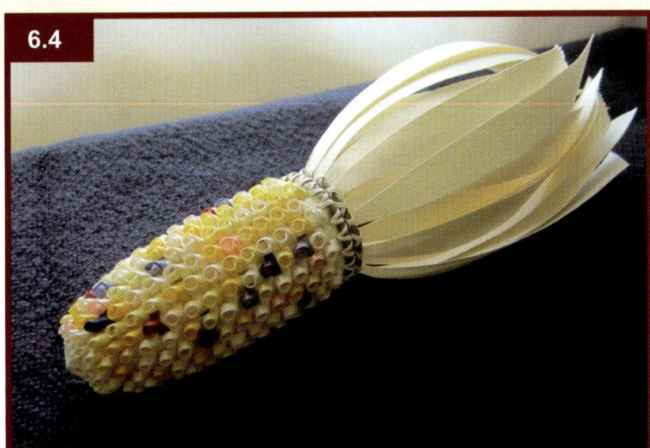

6.4

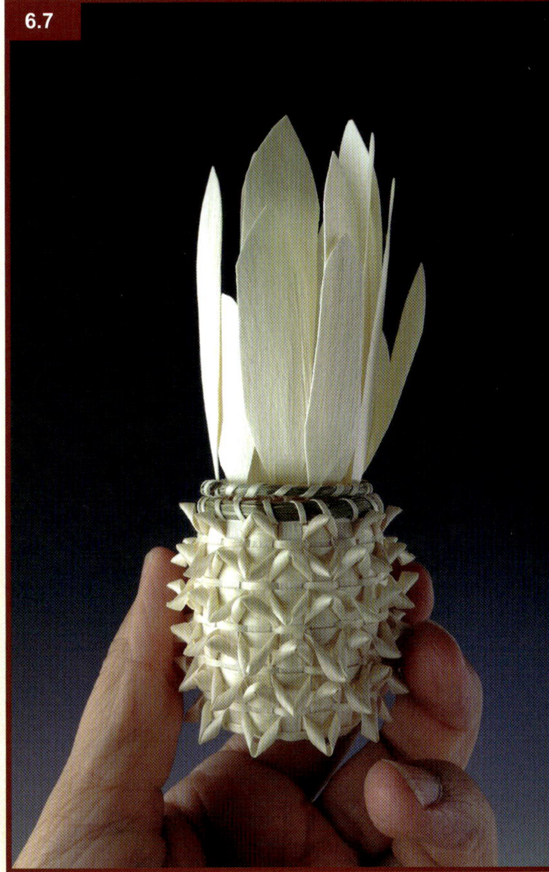

6.7

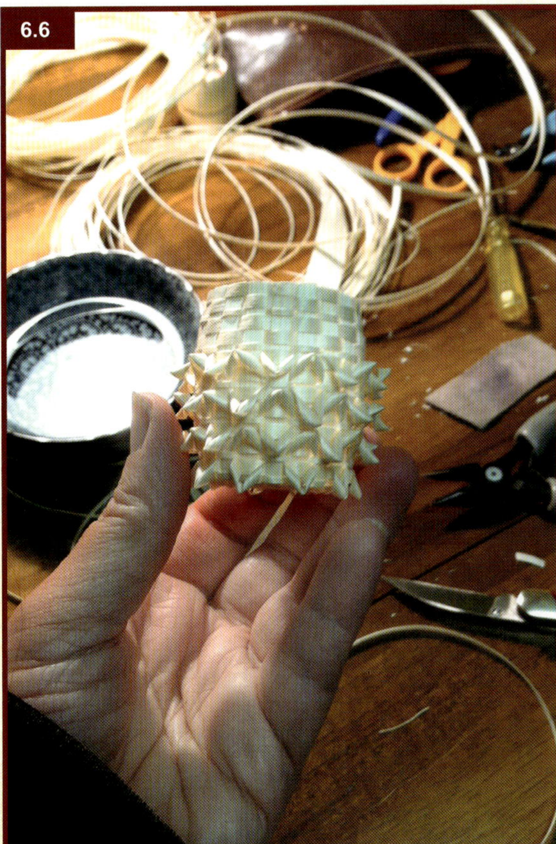

6.6

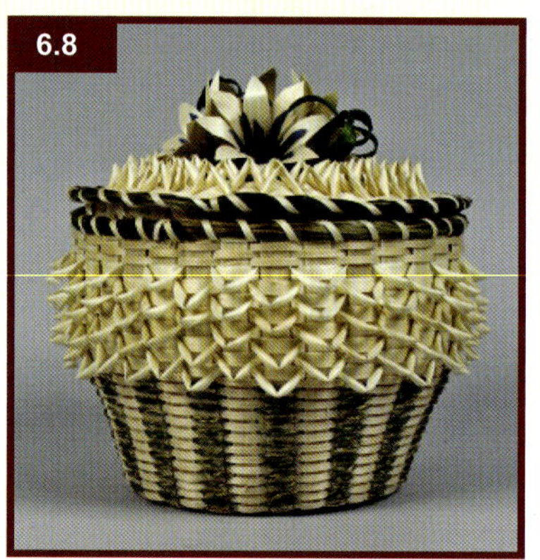
6.8

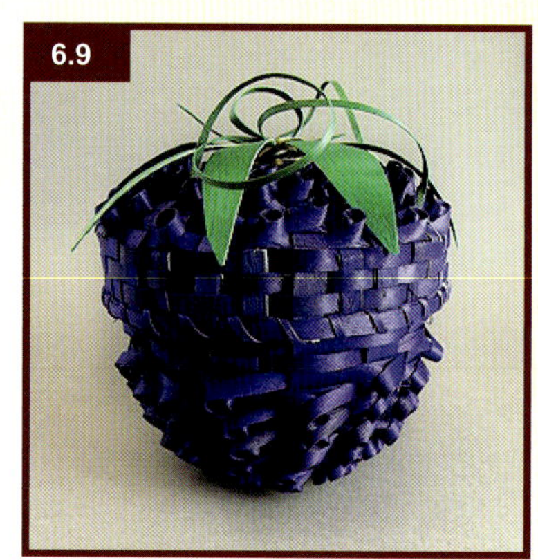
6.9

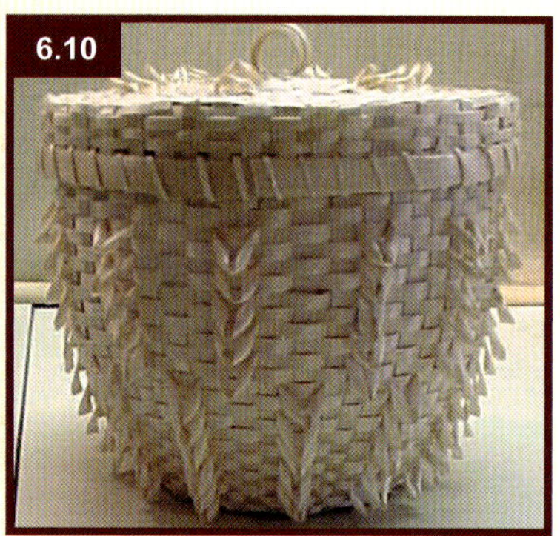
6.10

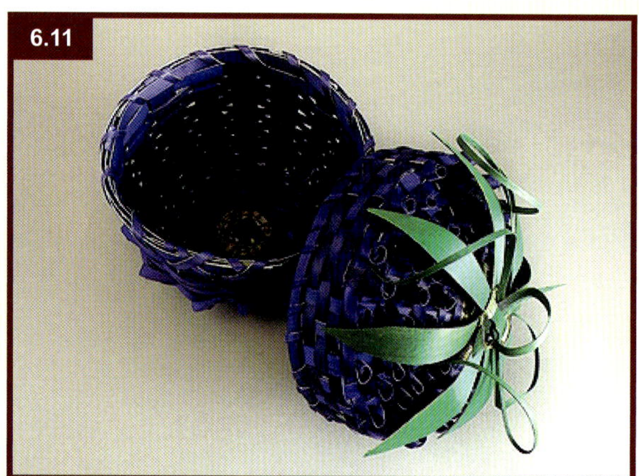
6.11

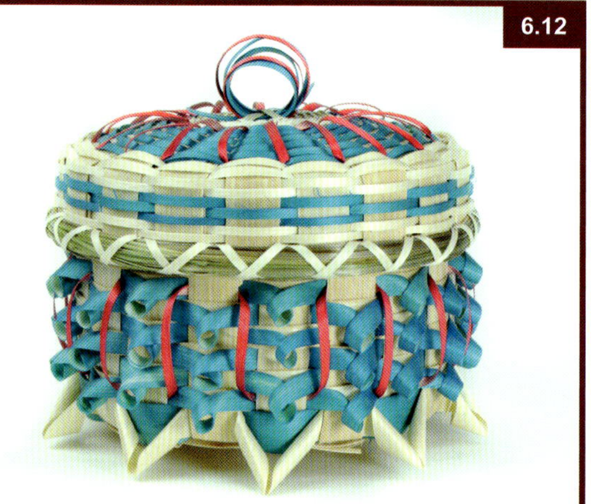
6.12

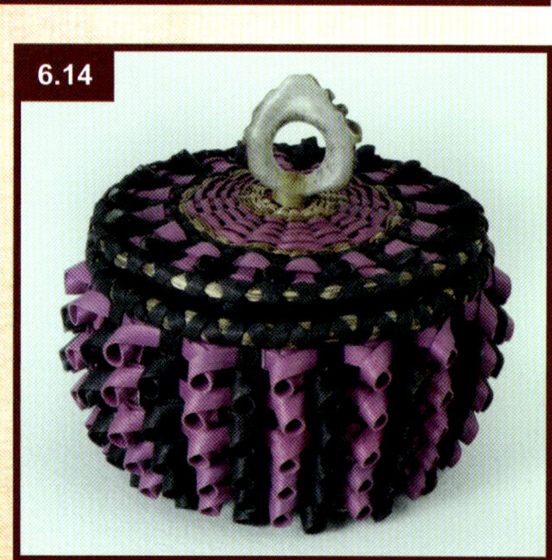
6.14

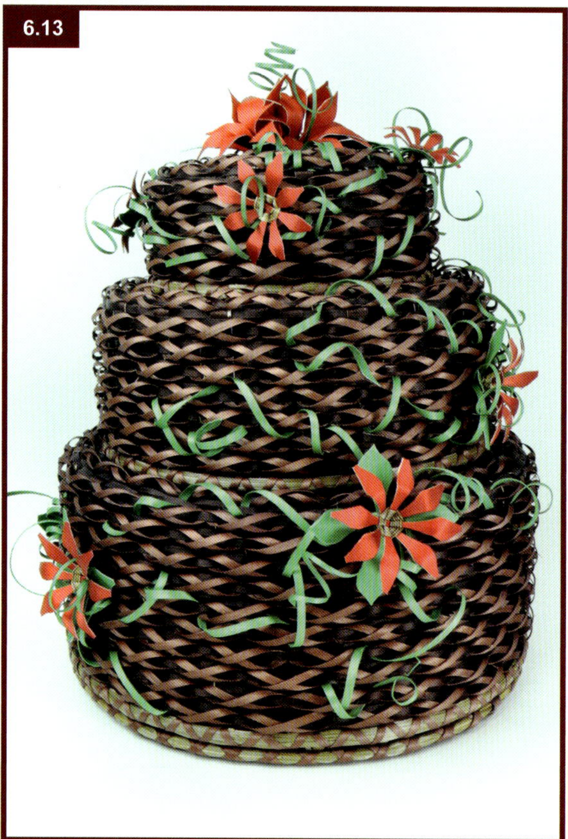
6.13

6.8. Molly Neptune Parker, Passamaquoddy, a 2012 NEA National Heritage Fellow, is the third generation of her family to weave their signature flower-top basket, 2012, 8" high.

6.9. The blueberry basket, like this example by Robin Lazore, Mohawk, is a favorite form made in several Northeastern regions.

6.10. Morning Star basket by Robin Lazore, Mohawk, 2013.

6.11. An inner view of **6.9** reveals its ash splint and sweetgrass start.

6.12. This basket by Gerald Jacobs, Passamaquoddy, combines an unusually eclectic range of decorative approaches.

6.13. Multi-tiered basket by George Neptune, Passamaquoddy.

6.14. Covered purple and gray urchin basket with carved deer antler pull by Sarah Sockbeson, Penobscot.

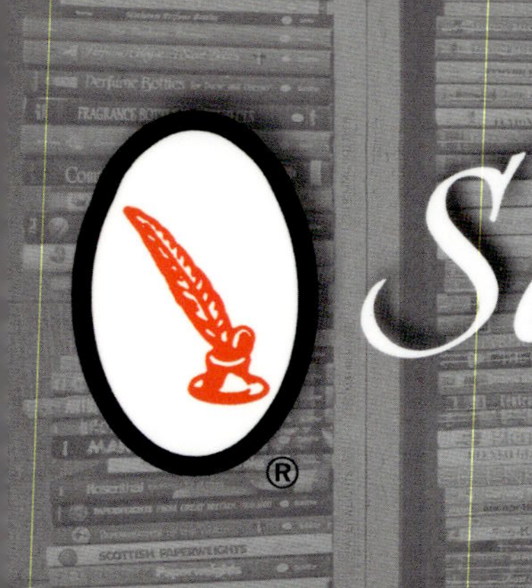
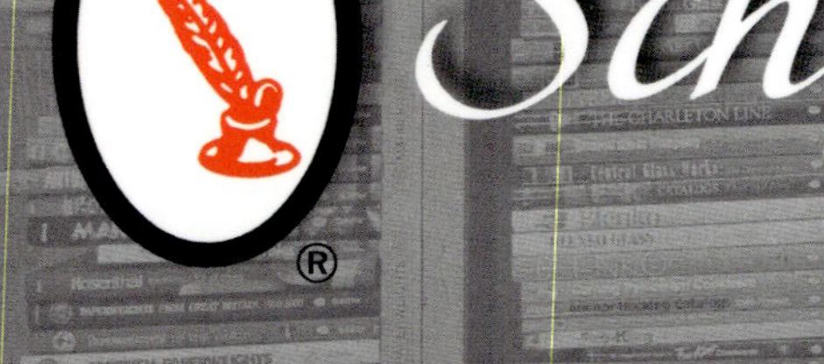
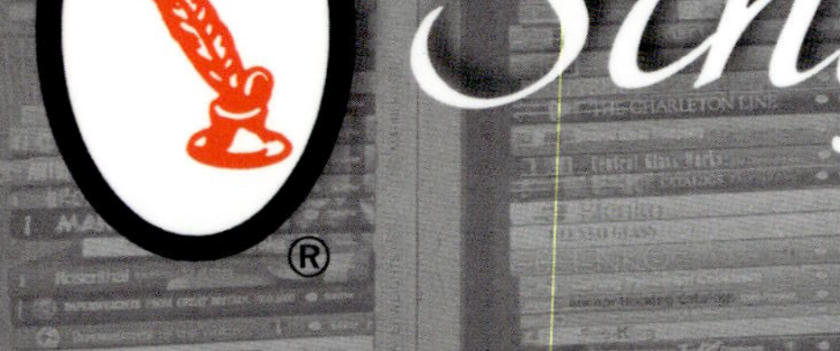
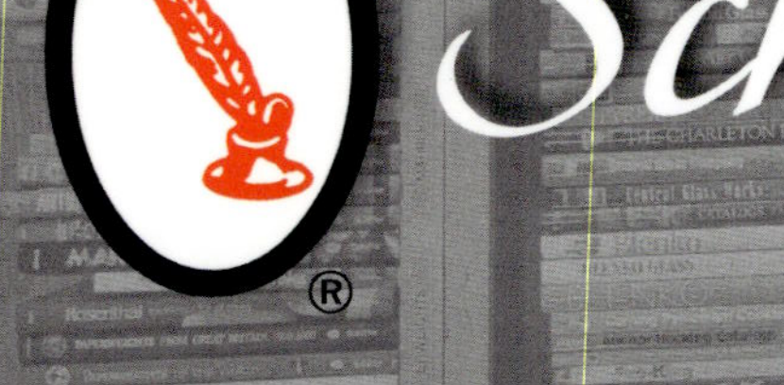
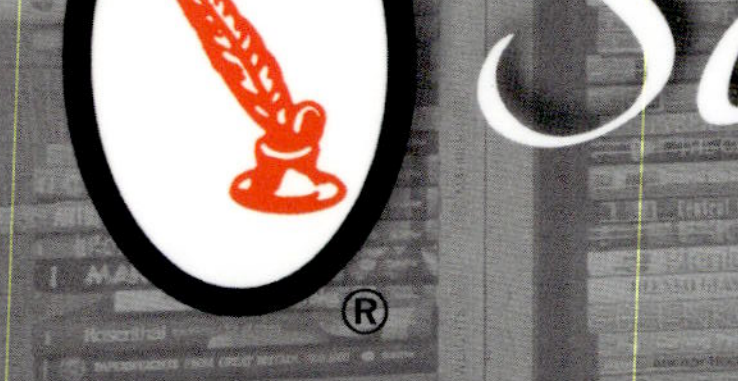
Schiffer Publishing

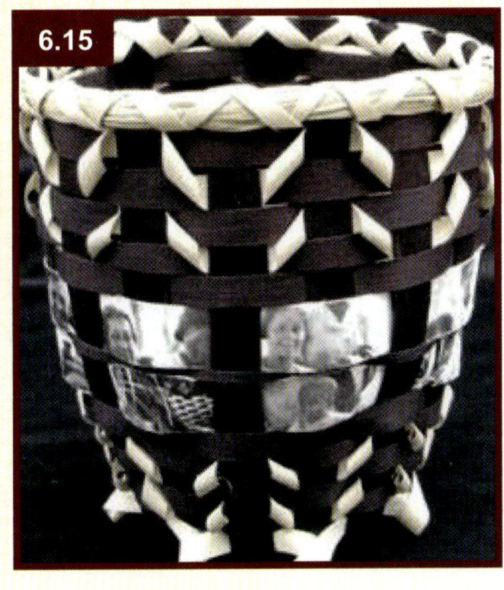

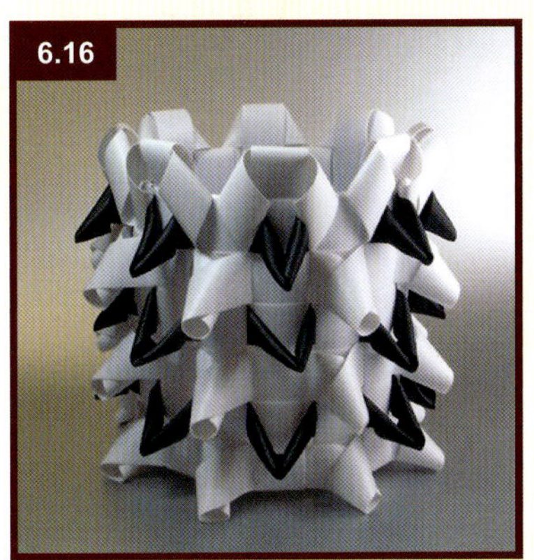

6.15. Woodsplint basket with photographs by Kelly Church, Grand Traverse band, Ottawa/Ojibwe.

6.16. Black satin ribbon and white vinyl blinds replace the usual woodsplints, by Kelly Church, Grand Traverse band, Ottawa/Ojibwe.

SETTING:

A Native Crafts Fair

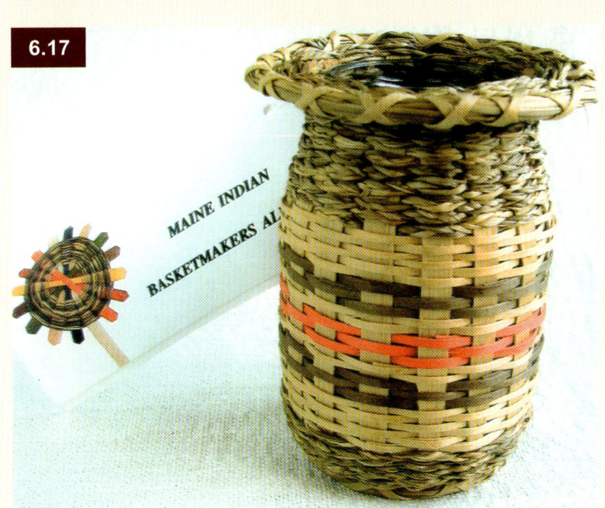

6.17. Basketry vase, signed "Jill Shibles, Penobscot 1998," sold in a MIBA show, 4" high.

The wall clock in the family room chimed twelve times for midnight, but Lily, lying in her narrow little bed, was wide awake. She was so excited that she could not sleep. Her parents, her young brother Henry, and she had attended a powwow and basket gathering earlier that day. Three dozen Native Wabanaki basketmakers had exhibited their brown ash splint and sweetgrass baskets at a nearby museum. The baskets made by a Passamaquoddy man had particularly inspired the young girl. The man's colorful woodsplint globes were innovative yet still traditional looking, and they were selling quickly for very high prices.

Lily and her mother had spoken briefly with the nice lady who ran the basketmakers' group sponsoring the show. The organization had partnered with the museum that was providing gallery space for the event. The helpful woman explained that the talented man had been making baskets for only ten years. He already was very famous. He had won national awards and "Best of Show" ribbons for his baskets, even way out West in Arizona and California.

Suddenly, Lily wanted to learn how to make baskets more than anything else. She wished she could make baskets that were as splendid as his. The lady cautioned her that she would have to start by learning the basics. Then she would have to practice, practice, practice to get good at it. The patient woman added that the basketmakers' alliance offered community classes and apprenticeships for motivated Wabanaki persons like Lily who wanted to learn to make baskets. She had encouraged the young girl to apply for their program. Lily's mother had responded that she and Lily's father would have to talk it over.

In the car on the way home, Lily's father told his children that their Penobscot great-grandmother had been a master basketmaker in Indian Township. But neither Lily's grandfather nor he, Lily's father, had learned the skill. The young girl became even more enthused. She wanted to find out more about her Penobscot great-grandmother and the baskets she had made. Most of all, though, the young girl wished to learn how to make baskets herself.

Lily dreamed of making beautiful baskets like those she had seen at the show; fancy baskets like her great-grandmother's; brown ash splint and sweetgrass baskets that would make her family proud.

Today, Native Northeastern basketmaking is moving in more directions than in previous decades. Some artisans are achieving national and international recognition both in and out of the mainstream of Native art. While many work independently, others blossom and excel with guidance, encouragement, and sponsorship provided by Native basketmaking classes, apprenticeships, and scholarships.

In northern New England, support is offered through the Maine Indian Basketmakers Alliance (MIBA) in cooperation with the Maine Arts Commission and organizations like the Abbe Museum and the Hudson Museum. Similarly, Native groups and museums in the upper New York State and Great Lakes regions also mentor participants to develop technical proficiency while exploring individualistic ways of expressing their heritage through their creations.

6.18. Since MIBA's inception in 1993, the average age of Native Maine basketmakers has dropped from 63 to 40. Native weavers have increased in number from 55 to 200. Here, master basketmakers and apprentices pose at a MIBA apprenticeship awards program.

6.19

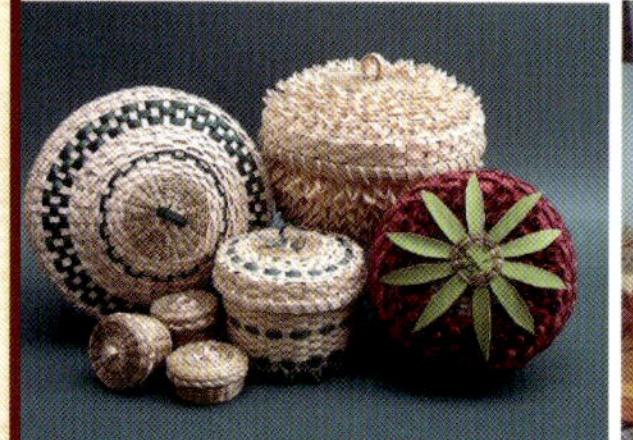

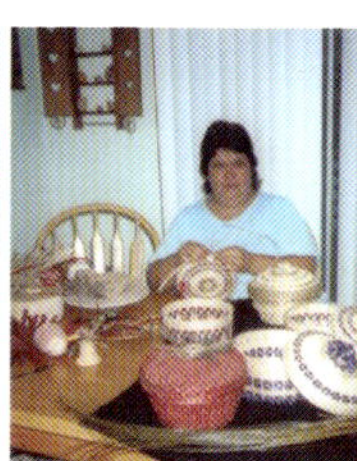

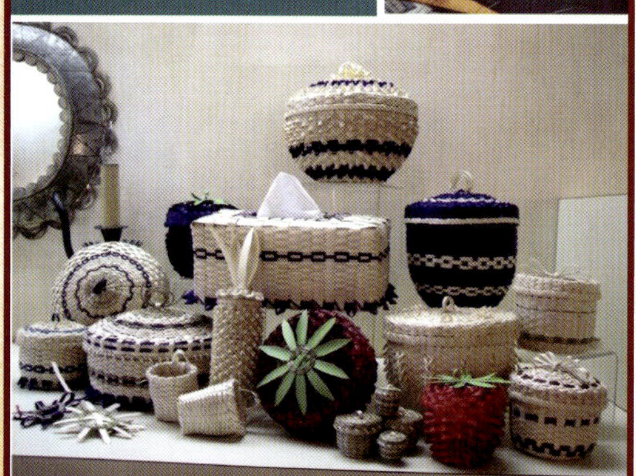

6.20

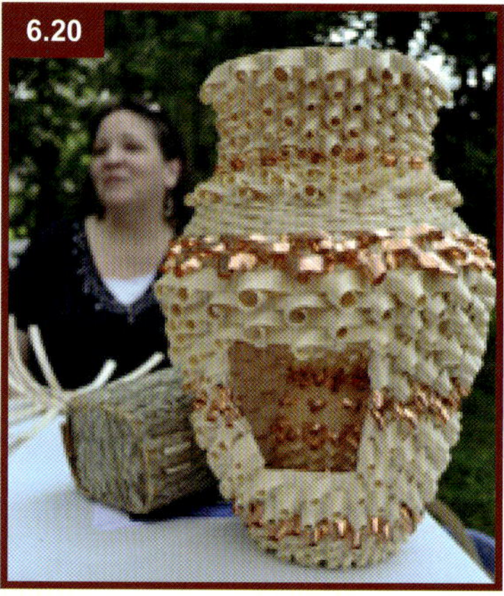

6.19, 6.20. Programs for assisting and promoting apprentices and artists from throughout the northeastern region, like master basketmakers (**6.19**) Robin Lazore, Mohawk, and (**6.20**) Kelly Church, Grand Traverse band, Ottawa/Ojibwe, are offered today through state universities, museums, and national organizations.

6.21

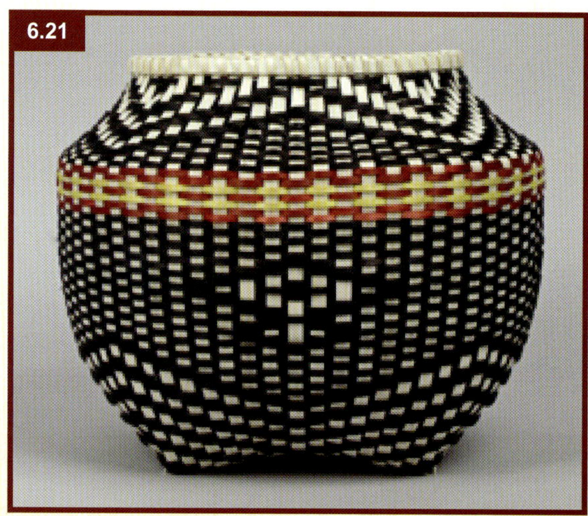

6.21. Drawing from traditional roots and contemporary inspiration, Fred Tomah, Houlton band, Maliseet, twill plaited this ash splint basket (*Medicine Series #1*) freehand, without the aid of a basketmaking mold, 2013, 8" high.

FOCUS:

Millennial Baskets

In 2012, the Hudson Museum and MIBA collaborated on a project and exhibition, *Transcending Traditions*, with support from the National Museum of the American Indian's Indigenous Contemporary Art Program. The work of five young contemporary Maine Indian basketmakers—Ganessa Bryant, George Neptune, Sarah Sockbeson, Jeremy Frey, and Eric "Otter" Bacon—drives their ancient ash splint and sweetgrass basketry tradition beyond the bounds set by customary convention.

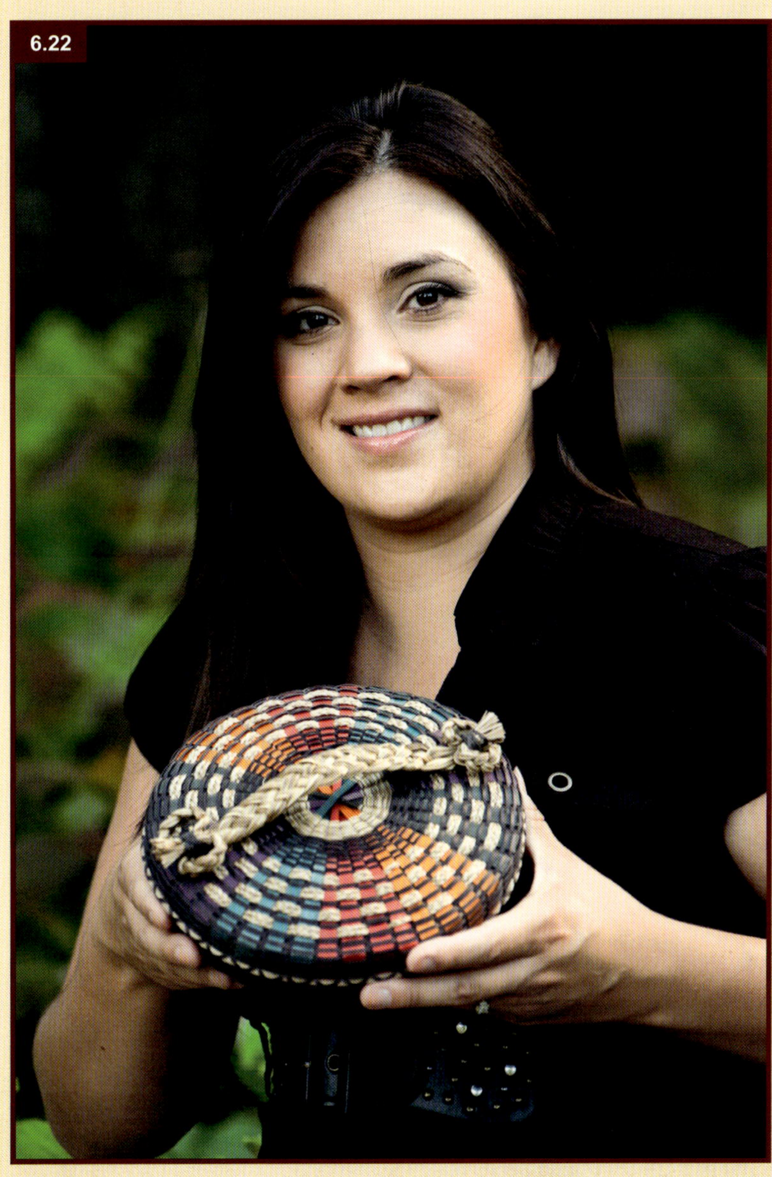

6.22. Ganessa Bryant, Penobscot, 2012.

Focus:

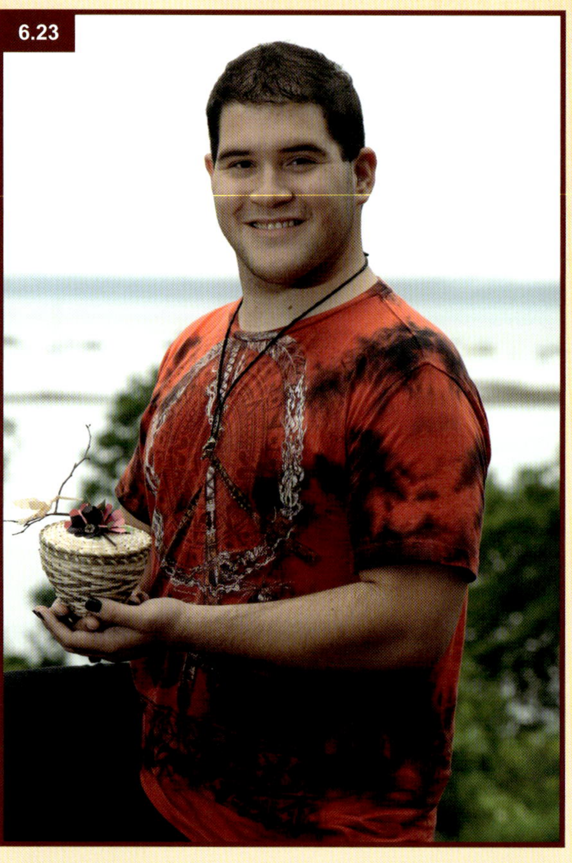

6.23. George Neptune, Passamaquoddy, 2012.

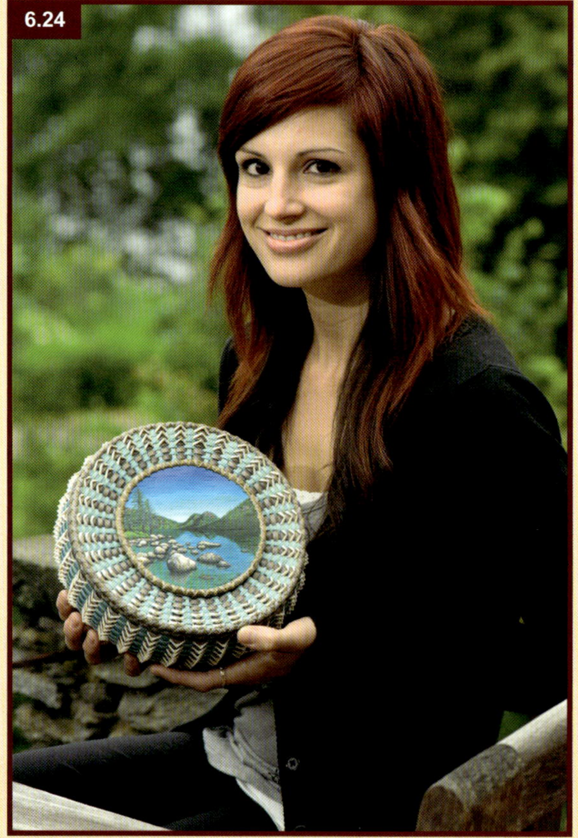

6.24. Sarah Sockbeson, Penobscot, 2012.

6.25. Eric "Otter" Bacon, Passamaquoddy, 2012.

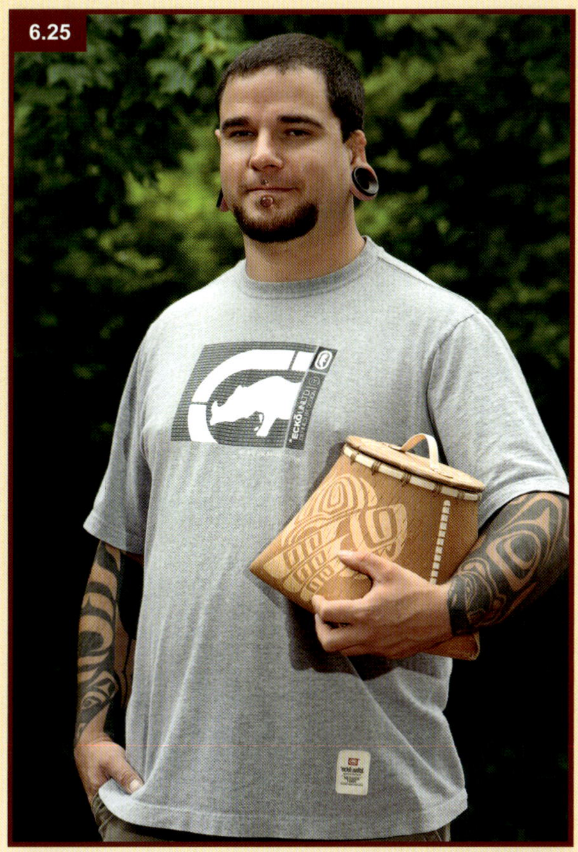

6.26. Jeremy Frey, Passamaquoddy, 2012.

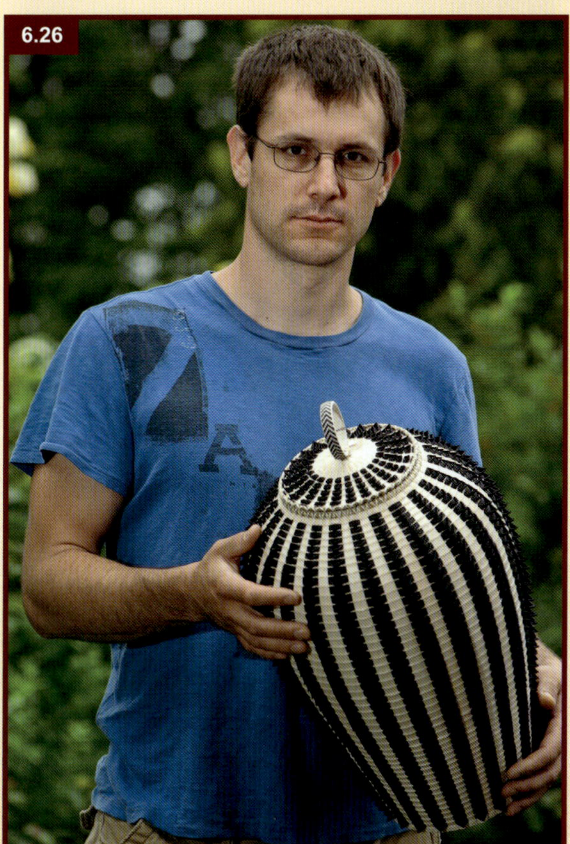

Native Northeastern basketry is evolving. As today's basketmakers venture beyond the boundaries of yesteryear's established limits, they are taking their craft to new levels. While building upon the past and expressing, interpreting, and honoring their cultural heritage, their current work has become art. Examples of several masterful "millennial baskets" are featured here.

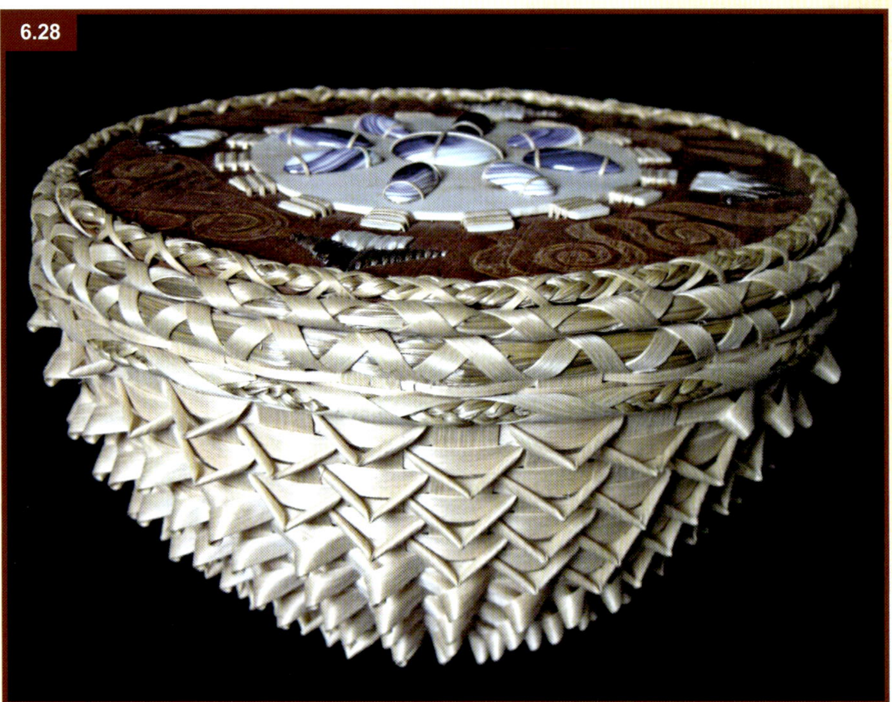

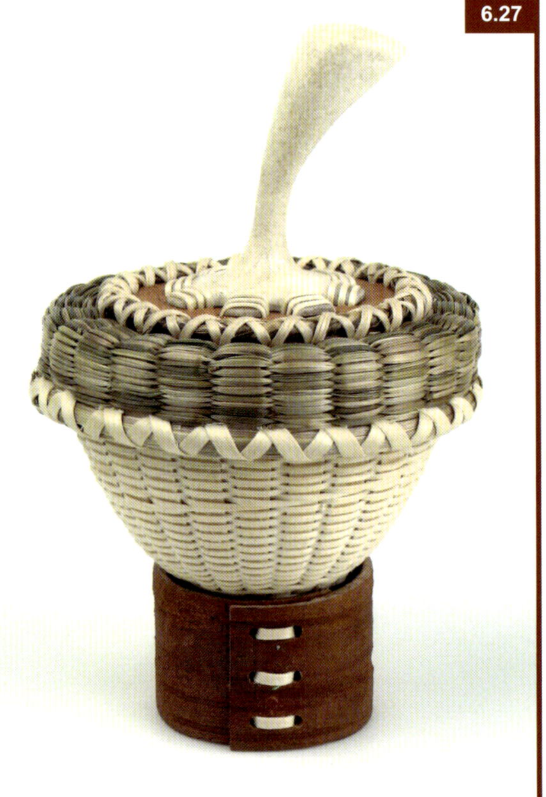

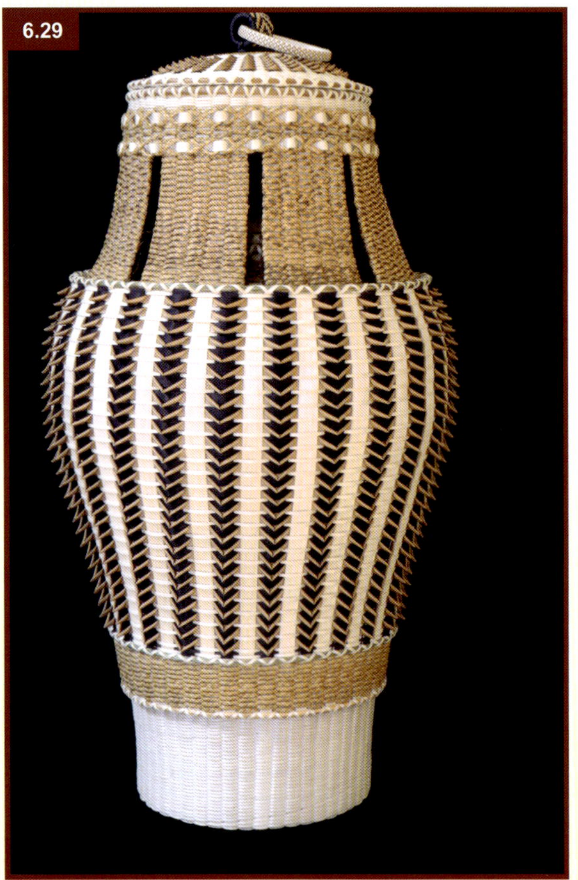

6.27. Acorn basket of ash splints, sweetgrass, birchbark, and carved moose antler by Eric "Otter" Bacon, Passamaquoddy, 3" high plus handle.

6.28. Ash splint and sweetgrass masterpiece with an inset medallion of etched birchbark and porcupine quillwork arrows pointing in the sacred four directions, plus a carved moose antler disk with attached wampum (quahog shell) cabochons, by Eric "Otter" Bacon, Passamaquoddy, 2012, 4" high.

6.29. Masterpiece of majestic scale by Jeremy Frey, Passamaquoddy, 2012.

SECTION THREE

RESOURCES

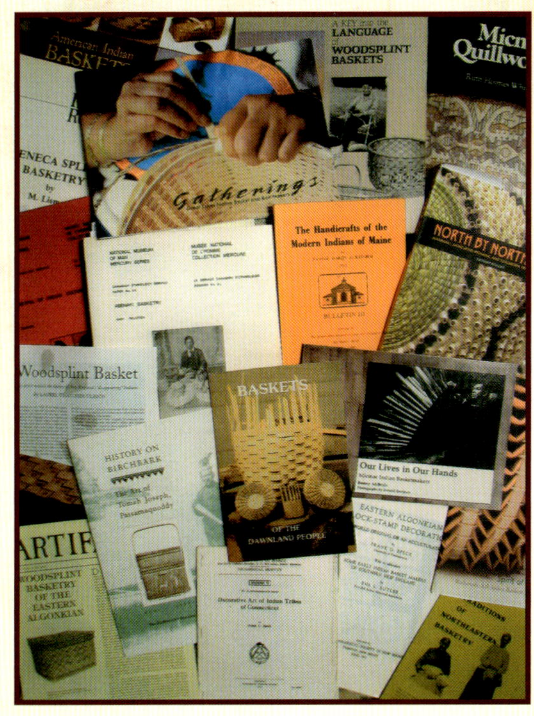

Selected Bibliography and Further Reading

Adovasio, James M. 2010. *Basketry Technology: A Guide to Identification and Analysis.* Revised and expanded from 1977 edition. Chicago, IL: Aldine Publishing.

Artifacts. 1985. Northeast Basketry Issue, 12(3). Washington, CT: American Indian Archaeological Institute.

Bardwell, Kathryn. 1986. "The Case for an Aboriginal Origin of Northeast Indian Woodsplint Basketry." *Man in the Northeast* 31, pp. 49-67. Rindge, NH.

Benedict, Salli. 1983. "Mohawk Basketmakers of Akwesasne." *American Indian Basketry Magazine* 3(1):10-16. Portland, OR.

Biron, Gerry. 2013. "Teweelema, Betty's Neck and Wampanoag Rye-straw Basketry." In, *Historic Iroquois and Wabanaki Beadwork*, archived blogspot, August 4, 2013. <http://iroquoisbeadwork.blogspot.com>.

Brasser, Ted J. 1975. "A Basketful of Indian Culture Change." *National Museum of Man Mercury Series, Canadian Ethnology Service Paper* 22. Ottawa, ON: National Museums of Canada.

Butler, Eva L. 1947. "Some Early Indian Basket Makers of Southern New England." Addendum to Frank G. Speck, *Eastern Algonkian Block-Stamp Decoration: A New World Original or an Acculturated Art*, pp. 35-54. Trenton, NJ: The Archaeological Society of New Jersey.

———, and Wendell S. Hadlock. 1957. *Uses of Birch-bark in the Northeast.* Bar Harbor, ME: Robert Abbe Museum.

Chancey, Jill R. (ed.). 2005. *By Native Hands: Woven Treasures from the Lauren Rogers Museum of Art.* Laurel, MS: Lauren Rogers Museum of Art.

Cole-Will, Rebecca. 2006. "'Delicate Sweet Dishes Too They Make': Birchbark Art in the Abbe Museum's Collections." *American Indian Art Magazine* 31(3):58-65. Scottsdale, AZ.

Cook, Stephen W. 2005. "Baskets of the Northeastern Woodlands." In, Jill R. Chancey (ed.), *By Native Hands: Woven Treasures from the Lauren Rogers Museum of Art*, pp. 218-237. Laurel, MS: Lauren Rogers Museum of Art.

Curtis, William Conway. 1904. "The Basketry of the Pautatucks and Scaticooks." *The Southern Workman* 33:385-390. Hampton, VA: Hampton Institute.

Dow, Sue Ellen. 1998. "Native Baskets of the Northeast." *Indian Artist* 4(3):42-47. Santa Fe, NM.

Drooker, Penelope B., and George B. Hamell. 2004. "Susannah Swan's 'Wampum Bag.'" In, Penelope Ballard Drooker (ed.), Perishable Material Culture in the Northeast. *New York State Museum Bulletin* 500, pp. 197-215. Albany, NY: New York State Education Department.

Eckstorm, Fannie Hardy. 1980. *The Handicrafts of the Modern Indians of Maine.* Reprint of 1932 edition. Bar Harbor, ME: Robert Abbe Museum.

Faulkner, Gretchen Fearon. 2010. "Tree and Tradition: Maine Indian Brown Ash Basketry." *American Indian Art Magazine* 35(2):36-45. Scottsdale, AZ.

———, and Theresa Secord Hoffman. 1998. "Introducing the Art of Basket Making: The Basketry of Maine." *Indian Artist* 4(2):44-49. Santa Fe, NM.

Gogol, John M. 1985. "Potawatomi Indian Basketry." *American Indian Basketry Magazine* 5(1):4-5. Portland, OR.

Gordon, Joleen. 1990. "Micmac Indian Basketry." In, Frank W. Porter III (ed.), *The Art of Native American Basketry: A Living Legacy*, pp. 17-43. Westport, CT: Greenwood Press.

Green, Adriana Greci. 2012. "'Many Gifted Workers': Odawa Quill Artists Participating in the Works Progress Administration." *American Indian Art Magazine* 37(3):48-59. Scottsdale, AZ.

Handsman, Russell G., and Ann McMullen. 1987. "An Introduction to Woodsplint Basketry and Its Interpretation." In, Ann McMullen and Russell G. Handsman (eds.), *A Key into the Language of Woodsplint Baskets*, pp. 16-35. Washington, CT: American Indian Archaeological Institute.

Holmes, William Henry. 1896. "Prehistoric Textile Art of Eastern United States." *Annual Report of the Bureau of American Ethnology* 13(1), pp. 9-46. Washington, D.C.: Government Printing Office.

Irwin, John Rice. 1982. *Baskets and Basket Makers in Southern Appalachia.* Atglen, PA: Schiffer Publishing.

James, George Wharton. 1901. *Indian Basketry.* Pasadena, CA: Privately printed.

———. 1904. *How to Make Indian and Other Baskets.* Second edition. Pasadena, CA: George Wharton James.

Kline, Jonathan. 2011. *Black Ash Baskets: Tips, Tools, and Techniques for Learning the Craft.* Mechanicsburg, PA: Stackpole Books.

Lauersons, Judith. 1996. *Basketmakers of Akwesasne: Teionkwahontasen (Sweetgrass Is Around Us).* Hogansburg, NY: Akwesasne Museum.

Lester, Joan. 1987. "'We Didn't Make Fancy Baskets Until We Were Discovered': Fancy-Basket Making in Maine." In, Ann McMullen and Russell G. Handsman (eds.), *A Key into the Language of Woodsplint Baskets*, pp. 38-59. Washington, CT: American Indian Archaeological Institute.

———. 1993. *History on Birchbark: The Art of Tomah Joseph, Passamaquoddy.* Bristol, RI: Haffenreffer Museum of Anthropology.

———. 1994. "Art for Sale: Cultural and Economic Survival." In, Laurie Weinstein (ed.), *Enduring Traditions: The Native Peoples of New England*, pp. 151-167. Westport, CT: Bergin & Garvey.

Lismer, Marjorie. 1982. *Seneca Splint Basketry.* Reprint of 1941 edition. Ohsweken, ON: Iroqrafts.

Lyford, Carrie A. 1990. *Iroquois Crafts*. Reprint of 1945 edition. Ohsweken, ON: Iroqrafts.

———. 1982. *Ojibwa Crafts*. Reprint of 1943 edition. Stevens Point, WI: R. Schneider.

MacDowell, Marsha (ed.). 1999. *Gatherings: Great Lakes Native Basket and Box Makers*. East Lansing, MI: Michigan State University Museum.

McBride, Bunny. 1990. *Our Lives in Our Hands: Micmac Indian Basketmakers*. Gardiner, ME: Tilbury House.

McFeat, Tom. 1987. "Space and Work in Maliseet Basket-Making." In, Ann McMullen and Russell G. Handsman (eds.), *A Key into the Language of Woodsplint Baskets*, pp. 61-73. Washington, CT: American Indian Archaeological Institute.

McMullen, Ann. 1982. "Woodsplint Basketry of the Eastern Algonkian." *Artifacts* 10(5):1-9. Washington, CT: American Indian Archaeological Institute.

———. 1983. "Tribal Style in Woodsplint Basketry: Early Paugusset Influence." *Artifacts* 11(4):1-4. Washington, CT: American Indian Archaeological Institute.

———. 1987. "Looking for People in Woodsplint Basketry Decoration." In, Ann McMullen and Russell G. Handsman (eds.), *A Key into the Language of Woodsplint Baskets*, pp. 102-123. Washington, CT: American Indian Archaeological Institute.

———. 1990. "Many Motives: Change in Northeastern Native Basket Making." In, Frank W. Porter III (ed.), *The Art of Native American Basketry: A Living Legacy*, pp. 45-78. Westport, CT: Greenwood Press.

———. 1992. "Talking through Baskets: Meaning, Production and Identity in the Northeast Woodlands." In, Linda Mowat, et al. (eds.), *Basketmakers: Meaning and Form in Native American Baskets*, pp. 19-35. Hertford, England: Pitt Rivers Museum.

———. 2001. "Eastern Woodlands." In, Lydia L. Wyckoff (ed.), *Woven Worlds: Basketry from the Clark Field Collection at the Philbrook Museum of Art*, pp. 149-171. Tulsa, OK: The Philbrook Museum of Art.

McMullen, Ann, and Russell G. Handsman (eds.). 1987. *A Key into the Language of Woodsplint Baskets*. Washington, CT: American Indian Archaeological Institute.

Mason, Otis Tufton. 1904. "Aboriginal American Basketry: Studies in a Textile Art without Machinery." *Report of the U.S. National Museum under the Direction of the Smithsonian Institution, for the Year Ending June 30, 1902*, pp. 171-548. Washington, D.C.: U.S. National Museum.

———. 1984. *Aboriginal American Basketry: Studies in a Textile Art without Machinery*. Reprint of 1904 edition. Glorieta, NM: Rio Grande Press.

Mundell, Kathleen. 2008. *North by Northeast: Wabanaki, Akwesasne Mohawk, and Tuscarora Traditional Arts*. Gardiner, ME: Tilbury House.

Neiro, Michaela. 2006. "Caring for Your Basket Collection." *Historic New England Magazine* 7(2):8-9. Boston, MA: Historic New England.

Neptune, Jennifer Sapiel. 2008. "Spirit of the Basket Tree: Ash Splint Baskets of the Wabanaki." In, Hood Museum of Art, *Spirit of the Basket Tree: Wabanaki Ash Splint Baskets from Maine*, pp. 2-14. Hanover, NH: Dartmouth College.

Newman, Lisa K. 2010. "Basketry as Economic Enterprise and Cultural Revitalization: The Case of the Wabanaki Tribes of Maine." *Wicazo Sa Review* 25(2):89-106. Minneapolis, MN: University of Minnesota Press.

Nicholas, Joseph A. (ed.). 1980. *Baskets of the Dawnland People*. Calais, ME: Project Indian PRIDE.

Odegaard, Nancy. 1999. "Basketry: An Introduction to Materials, Techniques and Conservation." *American Indian Art Magazine* 24(3):36-43. Scottsdale, AZ.

Paxson, Barbara. 1985. "Potawatomi Indian Black Ash Basketry." *American Indian Basketry Magazine* 5(1):6-11. Portland, OR.

Pelletier, Gaby. 1982. "Abenaki Basketry." *National Museum of Man Mercury Series, Canadian Ethnology Service Paper* 85. Ottawa, ON: National Museums of Canada.

Petersen, James B., and Nathan D. Hamilton. 1984. "Early Woodland Ceramic and Perishable Fiber Industries from the Northeast: A Summary and Interpretation." *Annals of Carnegie Museum* 53:413-445. Pittsburgh, PA: Carnegie Museum of Natural History.

Petersen, James B., Tonya Largy, and Robert W. Carlson. 1987. "An Aboriginal Basketry Fragment from Lake Cochituate, Natick, Massachusetts." *Bulletin of the Massachusetts Archaeological Society* 48(1):2-8.

Phillips, Ruth B. 1998. *Trading Identities: The Souvenir in Native North American Art from the Northeast, 1700-1900*. Seattle, WA: University of Washington Press.

———. 2001. "Quilled Bark from the Central Great Lakes: A Transcultural Art History." In, Christian F. Feest (ed.), *Studies in American Indian Art: A Memorial Tribute to Norman Feder*, pp. 118-131. Seattle, WA: University of Washington Press.

Porter, Frank W. III (ed.). 1984. *The Art of Native American Basketry: A Living Legacy*. Westport, CT: Greenwood Press.

——— (compiler). 1988. *Native American Basketry: An Annotated Bibliography*. Westport, CT: Greenwood Press.

Prins, Harald E. L., and Bunny McBride. 1989. "A Social History of Maine Indian Basketry." In, Carolyn Herter (ed.), *Maine Basketry Past to Present* (exhibit catalog), pp. 5-14. Waterville, ME: Colby College Museum of Art.

Richmond, Trudie Lamb. 1987. "Spirituality and Survival in Schaghticoke Basket-Making." In, Ann McMullen and Russell G. Handsman (eds.), *A Key into the Language of Woodsplint Baskets*, pp. 126-143. Washington, CT: American Indian Archaeological Institute.

Sentance, Bryan. 2001. *Art of the Basket: Traditional Basketry from around the World*. London: Thames & Hudson.

Shaw, Robert. 2000. *American Baskets*. New York: Clarkson Potter.

Speck, Frank G. 1915. "Decorative Art of Indian Tribes of Connecticut." *Canadian Geological Survey, Memoir 75, Anthropological Series* 10. Ottawa, ON: Government Printing Bureau.

———. 1947. *Eastern Algonkian Block-Stamp Decoration: A New World Original or an Acculturated Art*. Trenton, NJ: The Archaeological Society of New Jersey.

Swain, Margaret. 1975. "Moose-Hair Embroidery on Birch Bark." *The Magazine Antiques* 107(4):726-729. New York, NY.

Tantaquidgeon, Gladys. 1930. "Newly Discovered Straw Basketry of the Wampanoag Indians." *Indian Notes* 7:475-484. New York, NY: Museum of the American Indian, Heye Foundation.

———, and Jayne G. Fawcett. 1987. "Symbolic Motifs on Painted Baskets of the Mohegan-Pequot." In, Ann McMullen and Russell G. Handsman (eds.), *A Key into the Language of Woodsplint Baskets*, pp. 94-101. Washington, CT: American Indian Archaeological Institute.

Trigger, Bruce G. (vol. ed.). 1978. *Handbook of North American Indians*, Vol. 15: *Northeast*. Washington, D.C.: Smithsonian Institution.

Turnbaugh, Sarah Peabody. 1992. *Native American Basketry*. Cambridge, MA: Hurst Gallery.

———. 1996. "Native New England Baskets." *Tidings* 14(4): 4-9. Westerly, RI.

——— and William A. Turnbaugh. 1987. "Weaving the Woods: Tradition and Response in Southern New England Splint Basketry." In, Ann McMullen and Russell G. Handsman (eds.), *A Key into the Language of Woodsplint Baskets*, pp. 76-93. Washington, CT: American Indian Archaeological Institute.

———. 2004. *Indian Baskets*. Revised 1986 edition. Atglen, PA: Schiffer Publishing.

Turnbaugh, William A., and Sarah Peabody Turnbaugh. 1999. *Basket Tales of the Grandmothers: American Indian Baskets in Myth and Legend*. Peace Dale, RI: Thornbrook Publishing.

———. 2013. *American Indian Baskets: Building and Caring for a Collection*. Atglen, PA: Schiffer Publishing.

Ulrich, Laurel Thatcher. 2001. "An Indian Basket, Providence, Rhode Island, 1676." In, *The Age of Homespun: Objects and Stories in the Creation of an American Myth*, Chapter 1, pp. 41-74. New York: Alfred A. Knopf.

———. "A Woodsplint Basket, Rutland, Vermont, after 1821." In, *The Age of Homespun: Objects and Stories in the Creation of an American Myth*, Chapter 10, pp. 340-373. New York: Alfred A. Knopf.

Webber, Alika. 1978. "Wigwamatew: Old Birch Bark Containers." *American Indian Art Magazine* 4(1):56-61. Scottsdale, AZ.

Whiteford, Andrew Hunter. 1977. "Fiber Bags of the Great Lakes Indians." *American Indian Art Magazine* 2(3):52-64. Scottsdale, AZ.

———. 1977. "Fiber Bags of the Great Lakes Indians, Part II." *American Indian Art Magazine* 3(1):40-47, 90. Scottsdale, AZ.

———. 1978. "Tapestry-Twined Bags, Osage Bags and Others." *American Indian Art Magazine* 3(2):32-39. Scottsdale, AZ.

———, and Nora Rogers. 1994. "Woven Mats of the Western Great Lakes." *American Indian Art Magazine* 19(4):58-65. Scottsdale, AZ.

Whitehead, Ruth Holmes. 1982. *Micmac Quillwork*. Halifax, NS: The Nova Scotia Museum.

———. 1991. *Elitekey: Micmac Material Culture from 1600 A.D. to the Present*. Halifax, NS: Nimbus.

Willoughby, Charles C. 1905. "Textile Fabrics of the New England Indians." *American Anthropologist* (new series) 7:85-93. Lancaster, PA: American Anthropological Association.

Wolverton, Nan. 2004. "American Indian Baskets Made in New England." *The Magazine Antiques* 165(1):184-191. New York, NY.

Wyckoff, Lydia L. (ed.). 2001. *Woven Worlds: Basketry from the Clark Field Collection at the Philbrook Museum of Art*. Tulsa, OK: The Philbrook Museum of Art.

Videos

Gabriel Women: Passamaquoddy Basketmakers. 1999. Gorham, ME: University of Southern Maine Center for the Study of Lives. (28 min.)

Mohawk Basketmaking: A Cultural Profile. 1980. University Park, PA: Pennsylvania State University. (28 min.)

Our Lives in Our Hands. 1986. Watertown, MA: Documentary Educational Resources. (50 min.)

Penobscot Basketmaker—Barbara Francis. 2003. Brunswick, ME: www.folkfilms.com. (52 min.)

Websites

ABBE MUSEUM

www.abbemuseum.org

The website reinforces the museum's mission of inspiring new learning about the Wabanaki Nations (Maliseet, Micmac, Penobscot, and Passamaquoddy) of Maine. Check for current information on the annual Native American Festival and Basketmakers Market, held each July at the College of the Atlantic in Bar Harbor, Maine.

BASKETMAKERS

www.basketmakers.com

A website created by basketmaker Susi Nuss as "a comprehensive informational site for basketmakers, basket artists, vendors of basketmaking materials and all others interested in the art of basket weaving."

HUDSON MUSEUM

www.umaine.edu/hudsonmuseum

Explore the museum's extensive on-line collection of Northeastern basketry examples, check out current exhibits, and keep up with basketry-related events, including the annual Maine Indian Basketmakers Sale and Demonstration, held each December at the Collins Center for the Arts, University of Maine.

MAINE INDIAN BASKETMAKERS ALLIANCE (MIBA)

www.maineindianbaskets.org

A Native non-profit organization "to preserve the ancient tradition of ash and sweetgrass basketmaking among the Maliseet, Micmac, Passamaquoddy and Penobscot tribes." The website accesses video interviews with prominent Maine Indian basketmakers (including Clara Keezer, Molly Neptune Parker, Theresa Secord, Mary Sanipass, and Jeremy Frey), produced by MIBA and the University of Maine's Hudson Museum.

NATIONAL BASKETRY ORGANIZATION

www.nationalbasketry.org

Founded by and for basketmakers and collectors, the NBO promotes "the art, skill, heritage, and education of traditional and contemporary basketry" through its website and a high-quality quarterly publication and on-line newsletter. The group supports and sponsors workshops, conferences, and exhibitions.

American Museums with Northeastern Indian Basketry Collections

This guide lists a selection of U.S. and Canadian public museums that house Northeastern American Indian basket collections. Bear in mind that collection size and representativeness are not always the best gauge of significance. Some museums hold a relatively modest group of baskets, but those examples may be carefully selected, or they may document a defined cultural area or even an individual tribe.

Larger museums generally exhibit only a fraction of their total Native basket collection at any given time. Duplicates and more ordinary baskets, as well as imperfect examples, may remain forever in storage, available for study but unlikely to be viewed by the general public.

Today, though, many museums are opening their entire holdings through on-line access. Visit the institution's homepage, locate the appropriate tool bar heading (usually something like "Collections," "Exhibits and Collections," or "Research"), and then follow instructions. Often, one can take a virtual tour of the collection or even research individual items of special interest with just a few clicks of the mouse. You save on gas and no appointment or white gloves are required!

In addition to their basket exhibits and permanent collections, some museums host periodic basketry demonstrations or workshops. A number of them have museum shops that offer Indian baskets for purchase. Consult individual websites for further information.

The alphabetical list below includes the street address of each museum's physical (GPS) location, its mailing address (post office box if separate from the street address), and the primary website location. A summary of the museum's Northeastern American Indian basketry holdings follows.

ABBE MUSEUM

26 Mount Desert Street
Bar Harbor, Maine 04609
www.abbemuseum.org

Featuring Maine's rich Indian culture, history and art, the Abbe maintains one of the largest collections of Wabanaki ash splint baskets anywhere, with almost 1,000 specimens, nearly half of them donated by children's author Anne Molloy Howells.

AKWESASNE CULTURAL CENTER

321 State Route 37
Hogansburg, New York 13655
www.akwesasneculturalcenter.org/museum

The Akwesasne Museum collection includes over 700 ethnographic objects, including a great variety of baskets made by the Mohawk community of Akwesasne for their own use and for sale.

AMERICAN MUSEUM OF NATURAL HISTORY

Central Park West at 79th Street
New York, New York 10024
www.amnh.org

The museum's North American ethnographic collection is exceptional for its size, scope, and age, and for its extensive documentation in museum publications. The American Indian basket holdings represent all cultural regions, including the Northeast U.S.

BOSTON CHILDREN'S MUSEUM

308 Congress Street
Boston, Massachusetts 02210
www.bostonchildrensmuseum.org

Counted among the museum's more than 4,000 objects in the Northeast Native American Collection are typical examples of woodsplint basketry as well as a selection of etched birchbark items made by the famous Passamaquoddy artist Tomah Joseph.

Canadian Museum of History (formerly Canadian Museum of Civilization)

100 Laurier Street
Gatineau, Québec K1A 0M8
www.historymuseum.ca

The museum's comprehensive Northeastern American Indian/First Peoples ethnographic collection numbers more than 2,000 basketry specimens, including hundreds of birchbark examples as well as woodsplint and sweetgrass baskets and the tools (splint gauges, knives, and wooden molds) used in making them.

Hood Museum of Art

Dartmouth College
Hanover, New Hampshire 03755
www.hoodmuseum.dartmouth.edu

Among the holdings of this teaching museum are outstanding examples of contemporary Northeastern Indian baskets, including acquisitions selected from the museum's 2009 exhibition, "Spirit of the Basket Tree: Wabanaki Ash Splint Baskets from Maine."

Hudson Museum

The University of Maine
Collins Center for the Arts
Orono, Maine 04469
www.umaine.edu/hudsonmuseum

The Maine Indian collection houses more than 180 Maliseet, Micmac, Passamaquoddy, and Penobscot baskets from 1870 to the present, plus dozens of basketmaking tools—basket molds, splint gauges, crooked knives, awls—and samples of basketmaking material including ash splints, Hong Kong cord, and sweetgrass braids.

Institute for American Indian Studies

38 Curtis Road
P.O. Box 1260
Washington, Connecticut 06793
www.iaismuseum.org

Although the museum has a broad range of objects representing indigenous peoples of the entire Western Hemisphere, the collections and programming emphasize Eastern Woodlands Indians, including their basketry.

Iroquois Indian Museum

324 Caverns Road
P.O. Box 7
Howes Cave, New York 12092
www.iroquoismuseum.org

The museum recognizes the significant role Iroquoian peoples have had in producing varied tourist items from the mid-1800s through the turn of the 20th century, including the well-known Akwesasne basket whimseys. Today the tourist market remains important to Iroquois craftspeople.

Lauren Rogers Museum of Art

565 North Fifth Avenue
P.O. Box 1108
Laurel, Mississippi 39440
www.lrma.org

Displayed in a modern gallery within a gracious southern mansion, Catherine Marshall Gardiner's turn-of-the-20th-century collection of 500 North American Indian baskets has been expanded to represent all regions, including typical baskets from the Northeast.

Leelanau Historical Society Museum

203 East Cedar Street
P.O. Box 246
Leland, Michigan 49654
www.leelanauhistory.org

The museum's Traditional Anishnabek Arts Room features a key collection of black ash baskets and quillwork on birchbark, primarily the work of Leelanau Peninsula's Ottawa artists.

Logan Museum of Anthropology

Beloit College
700 College Street
Beloit, Wisconsin 53511
www.beloit.edu/logan

The museum's substantial collection of Indian baskets includes many examples from Great Lakes tribes such as Ho-Chunk and Potawatomi, as well as Seneca and other Iroquoians and the Micmac and Penobscot peoples of the Northeast.

MASHANTUCKET PEQUOT MUSEUM & RESEARCH CENTER

110 Pequot Trail
P.O. Box 3180
Mashantucket, Connecticut 06338
www.pequotmuseum.org

Northeastern regional basketry in the collections at "the world's largest Native American museum" includes examples from southern and northern New England and adjacent Canadian provinces that date from the early 19th century to the present day.

MILLE LACS INDIAN MUSEUM

43411 Oodena Drive
Onamia, Minnesota 56359
www.sites.mnhs.org/historic-sites/mille-lacs-indian-museum

Ojibwa woven bags and basketry, as well as birchbark containers and souvenir items, are among the many categories of Native craft collected by the proprietors of the historic Mille Lacs Indian Trading Post and now preserved in the museum's Harry and Jeanette Ayer Collection.

MILWAUKEE PUBLIC MUSEUM

800 West Wells Street
Milwaukee, Wisconsin 53233
www.mpm.edu

Well-represented in the museum's basketry collection are Great Lakes, Southwest, California, and Northwest Coast groups. Woodlands basketry and textiles are especially notable.

MITCHELL MUSEUM OF THE AMERICAN INDIAN

3001 Central Street
Evanston, Illinois 60201
www.mitchellmuseum.org

The museum's exhibition galleries showcase the Native cultures of North America, with many fine objects from the Eastern Woodlands. The collections house additional outstanding examples of porcupine quillwork boxes and splint basketry, among many other items.

MONTCLAIR ART MUSEUM

3 South Mountain Avenue
Montclair, New Jersey 07042
www.montclair-art.com

The Native American collection of more than 4,000 objects has particular strengths in basketry and other crafts from seven major regions, including the Eastern Woodlands.

MT. KEARSARGE INDIAN MUSEUM

18 Highlawn Road
Warner, New Hampshire 03278
www.indianmuseum.org

A wide range of basketry is included within exhibits that survey the primary Native North American cultural areas. Northeastern woodsplint and sweetgrass basketry is particularly well-represented.

MUSEUM OF OJIBWA CULTURE

500 North State Street
St. Ignace, Michigan 49781
www.museumofojibwaculture.net

The city-operated museum in Father Marquette Mission Park displays the culture and traditions of the 1670s when the Ojibwa, Huron, and French met in Saint Ignace. The nearby Native Expressions Ojibwa Museum Store, at 566 North State Street, claims to have the Upper Peninsula's best selection of locally made Native American art and craft, representing Ojibwa, Huron, Ottawa, and other Eastern Woodlands Indians.

MUSEUM OF PRIMITIVE ART AND CULTURE

1058 Kingstown Road, Suite 5
Peace Dale, Rhode Island 02879
www.primitiveartmuseum.org

Located in the heart of a historic New England mill village, the museum's period gallery exhibits some especially fine North American Indian baskets from California, the Southwest, and Northeast among other regions.

National Museum of the American Indian

Smithsonian Institution
Fourth Street & Independence Avenue, S.W.
Washington, D.C. 20560
www.nmai.si.edu

Baskets are legion among the museum's 88,000 objects of North American ethnology. The U.S. National Museum's basket collection (so closely associated with longtime curator of ethnology Otis T. Mason) includes, among many others, a variety of New England splint baskets.

New Brunswick Museum

Market Square
Saint John, New Brunswick E2L 4Z6
www.nbm-mnb.ca

The museum's large collection of local Indian-made basketry fully documents the great variety of fancy woodsplint products that were made primarily for tourists during the 19th and early 20th centuries. The museum also preserves examples of the basketmakers' wooden blocks or basket molds.

Nowetah's American Indian Museum

2 Colegrove Road (Route 27)
New Portland, Maine 04961
www.nowetahs.webs.com

This Indian-owned and -operated museum has a separate room devoted to over 600 historic Maine Indian baskets and bark containers, as well as baskets from other areas of the Northeast.

Old Sturbridge Village

1 Old Sturbridge Village Road
Sturbridge, Massachusetts 01566
www.osv.org

This outdoor "living-history" museum recreates life in a New England village from 1790 to 1840. Included is a defined collection of early 19th-century painted and stamp-decorated woodsplint baskets that mostly represent the nearby Nipmuc and Mohegan tribes.

Peabody Essex Museum

East India Square
161 Essex Street
Salem, Massachusetts 01970
www.pem.org

Begun in 1799 by Salem sea captains as the East India Marine Society, the museum's current historical and contemporary Native American art collection covers a range of time periods, cultures, and object categories. Some rare Northeastern Indian baskets date to the first half of the 19th century.

Peabody Museum of Archaeology and Ethnology

Harvard University
11 Divinity Avenue
Cambridge, Massachusetts 02138
www.peabody.harvard.edu

One of the nation's oldest and largest museums, with some 6 million ethnographic items, the Peabody holds representative Native American baskets from New England and every other cultural region.

Penobscot Nation Museum

12 Down Street
Indian Island, Maine 04468
www.penobscotnation.org/museum

This small museum provides a repository for contemporary Wabanaki art, such as paintings, woodcarvings, and basketry.

Philbrook Museum of Art

2727 South Rockford Road
P.O. Box 52510
Tulsa, Oklahoma 74152
www.philbrook.org

Over 1,100 basketry examples within the museum's Native American art holdings represent many tribes, including a few Northeastern basketmaking groups.

PHOEBE A. HEARST MUSEUM OF ANTHROPOLOGY

103 Kroeber Hall
Bancroft Way at College Avenue
University of California
Berkeley, California 94720
www.hearstmuseum.berkeley.edu

The museum's comprehensive research inventory of more than 12,000 Native North American baskets includes 200 examples from the Northeast U.S.

ROCHESTER MUSEUM & SCIENCE CENTER

657 East Avenue
Rochester, New York 14607
www.rmsc.org

The museum collection has some 100 Iroquois/Seneca splint baskets.

SMITHSONIAN INSTITUTION

see **National Museum of the American Indian**

TANTAQUIDGEON INDIAN MUSEUM

1819 Route 32
(Norwich-New London Turnpike)
Uncasville, Connecticut 06382
www.mohegan.nsn.us

Built by Harold and Gladys Tantaquidgeon with their father John in 1931, this museum of Mohegan culture claims to be "the oldest Indian owned and operated museum in America." It reopened by appointment on a seasonal basis in 2008, several years after Gladys Tantaquidgeon's death at age 106. Check locally for the museum's current status.

TIDES INSTITUTE & MUSEUM OF ART

43 Water Street
P.O. Box 161
Eastport, Maine 04631
www.tidesinstitute.org

The museum's wide-ranging cultural collection includes several dozen historical and contemporary Passamaquoddy and Micmac baskets, as well as examples of the tools used in creating them.

TOMAQUAG INDIAN MEMORIAL MUSEUM

390 A Summit Road
Exeter, Rhode Island 02822
www.tomaquagmuseum.com

Operated by Native people, the museum has exhibits that include local ash splint baskets from southern New England as well as woodsplint and birchbark containers from other areas of the Northeastern Woodlands.

Acknowledgments

The authors thank our many friends, family members, and colleagues who through their generosity and helpfulness toward us over the decades have benefitted this volume. In particular, we acknowledge the Museum of Primitive Art and Culture, Peace Dale, RI, and its staff members and trustees; David Maslyn, Dean of University Libraries, and Margaret "Mimi" Keefe, reference librarian, University of Rhode Island; faculty and staff of the University of Rhode Island anthropology and textiles programs; and Douglas Congdon-Martin and the team at Schiffer Publishing, as well as several individuals: Carolyn and Richard Curtis, Lisa Fiore, Dr. Russ Handsman, Mark Humpal, Susan and Richard Kutzleb, Dr. Ann McMullen, Gay and Kent Morris, Patt and Lynn Murphy, Dr. Harald Prins, and Susan Taylor.

We likewise appreciate the following institutions and individuals who assisted in locating and providing images for this book: Abbe Museum, Bar Harbor, ME: Julia Clark, Collections Manager; Art Gallery of Ontario (AGO), Toronto, ON, Canada: Felicia Cukier, Image Resources; Heritage Auctions, Houston, TX: Noah Fleisher, PR Director; Hudson Museum, University of Maine, Orono, ME: Gretchen Faulkner, Director; The Indian Craft Shop, U.S. Department of the Interior, Washington, DC: Susan Pourian, Director; Library and Archives Canada, Ottawa, ON, Canada: Helen Gillespie, Rights and Licensing Specialist; Maine Indian Basketmakers Alliance (MIBA), Old Town, ME: Theresa Secord, Founding Director, and Jennifer Sapiel Neptune, Executive Director; Nancy McClelland Historical American Wallpapers, New York, NY: Connie Athas; Milton Historical Society, Milton, MA: Judith Arlene Bookbinder, Curator, and Edith G. Clifford, President; Mt. Kearsarge Indian Museum, Warner, NH: Lynn Clark, Director, and Nancy Jo Chabot, Curator; Nantucket Atheneum, Nantucket, MA: Lincoln Thurber III, Head Reference Librarian, Laura Freedman, Technical Services, and Nancy Tyrer, Program Coordinator; New Brunswick Museum, Saint John, NB, Canada: Jennifer Longon, Archives and Research Librarian; Nova Scotia Archives, Halifax, NS, Canada: Philip Hartling, Senior Archivist; Nowetah's American Indian Museum, New Portland, ME: Nowetah and Tom Cyr, Wahleyah (Cyr) Black; Old Sturbridge Village, Sturbridge, MA: Jeannette Robichaud, Visual Resources Librarian; Peabody Museum of Archaeology and Ethnology, Harvard University, Cambridge, MA: Genevieve Fisher, Registrar, and Jessica Desany Ganong, Imaging Services Coordinator; *Pennsylvania Gazette*, University of Pennsylvania, Philadelphia, PA: Catherine L. Gontarek, Art Director, and Linda Ciazzo, Administrative Coordinator; Pennsylvania Historical and Museum Commission, Harrisburg, PA: Dr. Kurt Carr, State Archaeologist, and Janet Johnson, Curator of the Section of Archaeology, The State Museum of Pennsylvania; *The Providence Journal*, Providence, RI: Robert Selby, former staff artist, and Michael Delaney, Managing Editor/Visuals; Rhode Island Historical Society, Providence, RI: J. D. Kay, Imaging Specialist & Rights and Reproductions Manager; Skinner, Boston and Marlborough, MA: Douglas Deihl, Director of American Indian & Ethnographic Art, and S.K. de Bethune, Marketing Director, and Kathryn Gargolinski, Web Market Specialist; and Trotta-Bono Ltd., Shrub Oak, NY: James Trotta-Bono, Anna Bono, and Ted Trotta.

Illustration Credits

The authors prepared the photographs in this book except for those credited below. We gratefully acknowledge the following institutions and individuals for permission to use their provided photographs. Historic images and ephemera included in the illustrations but not listed below are held in private collections.

Courtesy of Abbe Museum Collections, Bar Harbor, ME: 6.8, 6.21

Courtesy of Art Gallery of Ontario (AGO), Toronto, ON, Canada: 1.17 (*The Basket Seller*, c. 1850/ oil on board/ 24.8 x 18.9 cm/ by Cornelius Krieghoff, Canadian, 1815-1872 / Gift from the Fund of the T. Eaton Co. Ltd. for Canadian Works of Art, 1951, 50/71)

Courtesy of Fred Bauer: 2.99, 2.100

Courtesy of Gerry Biron: 1.29, 1.32, 1.35, 1.44, 1.48, 1.49, 1.51

Courtesy of Susie and Bob Clendenen (photos by W.A.T.): 1.58, 3.105, 3.106, 4.25, 4.51, 4.52, 5.7, 5.16, 5.35, 5.36

Courtesy of Connecticut Historical Society: 2.43

Courtesy of Peter L. Corey (photo by Gerry Biron): 5.55

Courtesy of Charles and Blanche Derby: 1.75, 3.51, 3.53, 3.77

Courtesy of Heritage Auctions, Houston, TX: 5.6

Courtesy of Hudson Museum, University of Maine, Orono, ME: 6.22, 6.23, 6.24, 6.25, 6.26, 6.28

Courtesy of The Indian Craft Shop, U.S. Department of the Interior, Washington, DC: 1.59, 3.82, 5.29, 5.64, 6.2, 6.5, 6.9, 6.10, 6.11, 6.15, 6.16, 6.19

Courtesy of Nancy Kline: 2.92

Courtesy of Library and Archives Canada, Ottawa, ON, Canada: 1.40 (credit: Department of Supply and Services fonds/Canadian Government Expositions Centre/RG 72, Vol. 37, C-14195); 1.45, 1.46 (credit: Department of Supply and Services fonds/St. Francis Agency, Request of the Tanner Basket Co. of New York, items 4 and 5 of 14/Indian Affairs/RG 10, vol. 2964, file 206,868); 1.60 (credit: artist Mary R. McKie/ Peter Winkworth Collection of Canadiana, 2002 Acquisition/C-151329)

Courtesy of Maine Indian Basketmakers Alliance (MIBA), Old Town, ME: 1.50, 2.15, 3.7, 5.2, 6.1, 6.4, 6.12, 6.13, 6.14, 6.18, 6.29

From Otis T. Mason 1904, plate 121: 2.86

Courtesy of Robert Matterson III: 2.12

Courtesy of Nancy McClelland Historical American Wallpapers: 2.28

Courtesy of Milton Historical Society, Milton, MA, and Judith Arlene Bookbinder (photos by Margaret Sutermeister, 1894-1909): 1.26, 1.27

Courtesy of Gay and Kent Morris: 6.3

Courtesy of Mt. Kearsarge Indian Museum, Warner, NH (photos by W.A.T.): 1.9, 2.39, 2.73, 2.84, 5.23, 5.26

Courtesy of Museum of Primitive Art and Culture, Peace Dale, RI (photos by W.A.T./S.P.T.): 1.63, 1.77, 2.76, 3.8, 3.18, 3.22, 3.30, 3.41, 3.49, 4.64, 5.37

Courtesy of Nantucket Atheneum, Nantucket, MA (photo by Laura Freedman): 2.42

Courtesy of Jennifer Sapiel Neptune (Penobscot): 1.36, 5.48, 5.51, 6.6, 6.7

Courtesy of New Brunswick Museum, Saint John, NB, Canada: 1.16 (*Indians in New Brunswick Making Baskets*, c. 1845, watercolour over red chalk on wove paper, by John Thomas Stanton, Acc. #5179.2), 2.3 (*Going to Market*, c. 1845, watercolour over red chalk on wove paper, by John Thomas Stanton, Acc. #5179.1)

Courtesy of Nova Scotia Archives, Halifax, NS, Canada: 2.62 (NSARM 48-2/neg #6154)

Courtesy of Nowetah Cyr and Nowetah's American Indian Museum, New Portland, ME (photos by Wahleyah Black): 2.8, 2.13, 3.3, 3.11, 3.27, 3.33, 3.36, 3.72, 3.108, 3.109, 3.110, 3.116, 4.13, 4.53, 4.60, 4.61, 4.62, 4.63, 5.43, 5.44

Courtesy of Old Sturbridge Village Collections, Sturbridge, MA (photo by Henry Peach): 1.19 (Acc. #24.2.232)

Courtesy of President and Fellows of Harvard College, Peabody Museum of Archaeology and Ethnology, Harvard University, Cambridge, MA: 1.1 (ID #986-17-10/60032); 2.44 (ID #32-79-10/K156, 19-12-10/87357, 03-28-10/62807//digital file #60742707); 2.45 (ID #90-17-50/49302//digital file #47150009); 2.87 (ID #05-19-10/64736// digital file #26350420); 3.2 (ID #17-16-10/87069//digital file #60740317); 5.5 (ID #94-38-10/52510// digital file #60742539)

Courtesy of The Pennsylvania State Museum, Pennsylvania Historical and Museum Commission, Harrisburg, PA: 1.4

Courtesy of *The Providence Journal*, Providence, RI, and artist Robert Selby: end papers, 2.46 (*Sunday Journal Magazine* 5/18/1986:12-13)

Courtesy of the Rhode Island Historical Society, Providence, RI: 1.8 (1842.2.1; RHi X17 1685)

Courtesy of Skinner, Boston and Marlborough, MA, www.skinnerinc.com: 1.66, 1.73

Courtesy of Gladys Tantaquidgeon and the *Norwich* (CT) *Gazette*: 0.6

Courtesy of James Trotta-Bono Photography (photos by James Trotta-Bono): 1.15, 2.22, 2.24, 2.29, 2.47, 2.57, 3.16, 3.17, 3.25, 3.29, 3.69, 3.70, 5.47

Courtesy of Charles F. Wray: 1.12

Index

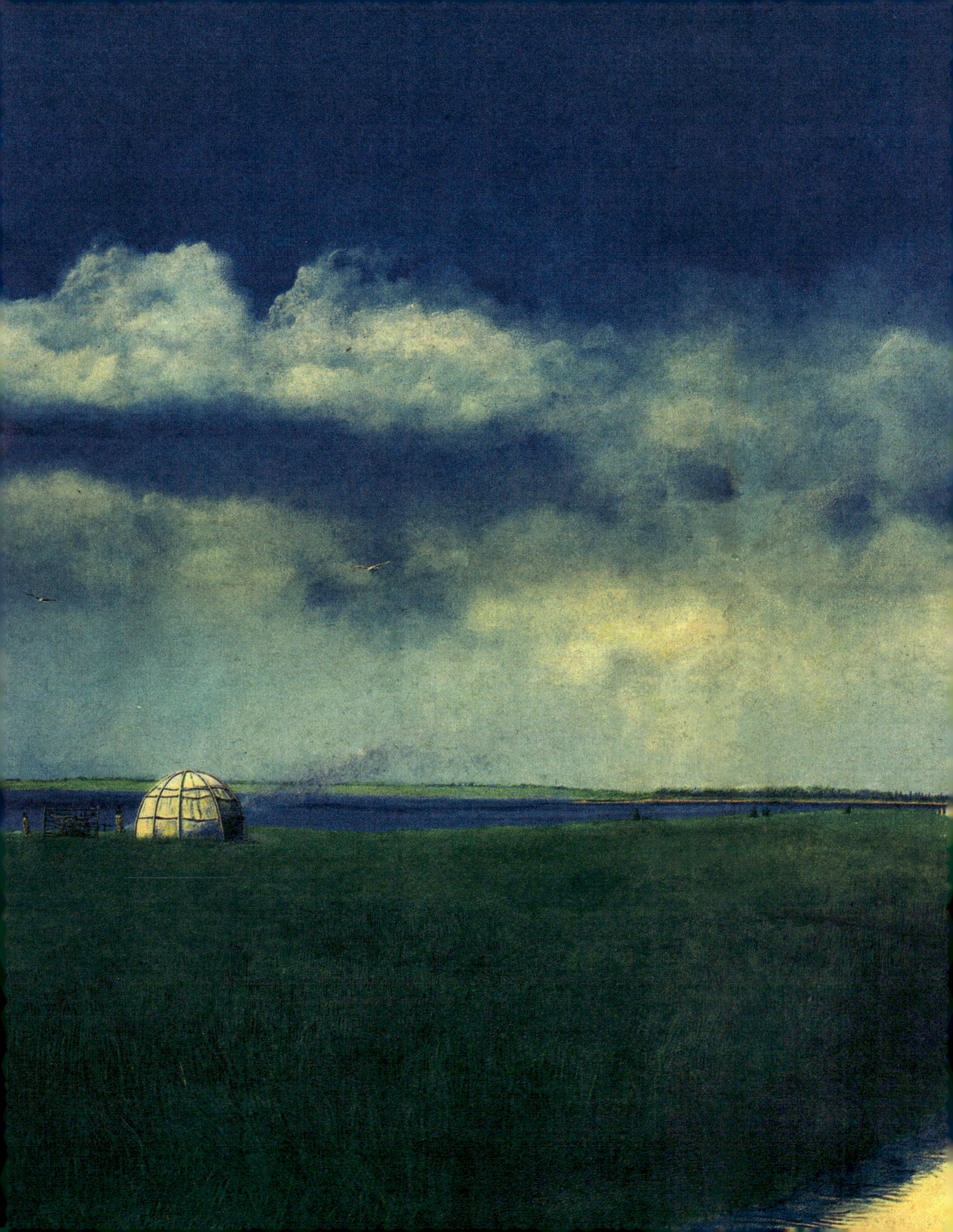